PROGRAMMING

PRIMER

PROGRAMMING

PRIMER

A Graphic Introduction to Computer Programming, with BASIC and Pascal

Robert P. Taylor
Teachers College, Columbia University

ADDISON-WESLEY
PUBLISHING COMPANY
Reading, Massachusetts
Menlo Park, California
London • Amsterdam
Don Mills, Ontario • Sydney

Library of Congress Cataloging in Publication Data
Taylor, Robert P.
  Programming primer.

  Includes index.
  1. Electronic digital computers—Programming.
I. Title.
QA76.6.T393   001.64′2   81-2209
ISBN 0-201-07400-1   AACR2

ISBN 0-201-07400-1
ABCDEFGHIJ-AL-898765432

GENERAL COMMENTS

This book is designed to introduce the process of computer programming to those with no previous knowledge of the subject. The text assumes no math background beyond the introductory secondary school level. Solved examples introduce the major facets of programming and focus on how to develop a problem solution suitable for computerization. A major area of concentration is the student's development of an appropriate approach to formulating problem solutions by means of FPL (First Programming Language), a well-structured programming language designed specifically for this purpose at Teachers College, Columbia University. Complete mastery of FPL requires no access to computers of any sort. Yet because FPL was designed to embody the best of current thinking on programming by computer professionals, mastery of FPL leads naturally to the successful use of many well-known computer languages. The book starts the student on the path to learning two such languages: the text demonstrates how solutions formulated in FPL may be translated directly and mechanically into well-structured programs in BASIC and Pascal.

WHO CAN USE THIS BOOK?

This book can be used successfully as a first text in programming at any of a number of levels. Though originally developed for educators, it is equally suited for others as well. Those who find the more mathematical approach adopted by most other programming texts to be a formidable barrier to getting started in programming may find this book a welcome alternative. At the same time, though it does not presuppose a mathematics background nor use much mathematics, it is a thorough introduction to the basic logic structures involved in all programming. It therefore can also serve admirably as an introduction to structured programming for students in engineering, the hard sciences, and computing. Because programming is primarily well-organized thought translated into instructions for a computer, all computing requires the same first achievement of the novice—learning to conceptualize a problem in a form suitable for computer solutions.

All kinds of students have used this material successfully, both as a class text and as an independent-study guide. Students using it have ranged in age from 12 to 60, in experience from none to extensive, and in occupation from housewife to computing professionals. They have come from developing as well as developed countries around the world.

The material has been used both as a review text and as a "first look" text. Whenever students are being introduced to computing with minimal help from instructional staff, this is a reasonable text to start with—whether the students are working completely on their own or loosely attached to a class. The text is designed to forestall their learning a lot of bad habits of structuring when they pursue programming on their own. Attention focuses on the organization of programming rather than on myriad details of hardware, languages, monitors, or operating systems. Study of this book profited a number of students who already knew considerable programming but who had learned eclectically and lacked a sense of good programming structure.

HOW LONG SHOULD IT TAKE
TO COVER THE MATERIAL IN THIS BOOK?

Though this text should prove equally suitable as an introduction to programming for all beginners regardless of their backgrounds or eventual objectives, though the principles presented must be mastered by anyone who would learn to program adequately, the speed with which the beginner can progress will depend on the particular background and objectives of the learner. Thus the text may be covered in the initial few weeks of courses designed for engineering and science students or in a few weeks of independent study by learners with considerable experience in logic and in organized thinking. Or it may be the basis for a full term or even a full year's work for those without much background in formal problem solving. Testing the material of the book with a wide range of learners has indicated that the type of previous educational experience, not educational level, is the best predictor of how fast the material will be mastered.

A NOVEL PRIMER

This text is novel in four respects. First, it relies heavily upon graphics to present the fundamental ideas of programming. Second, it goes into considerable detail and is therefore quite long for an introduction or "primer." Third, it requires no access to hardware to study and master most of the principal ideas. Fourth, it embodies a multilingual approach.

The Graphic Presentation of Programming

The reason for using a graphic presentation in FPL is pedagogical. Human beings use graphic representation constantly, are familiar with symbols of all kinds, and use them constantly to organize ideas of every sort. Till now, with the possible exception of von Neumann flowcharting, little use has been made of graphical approaches to teaching programming. Instead, texts and manuals have emphasized the use of written character languages exclusively and have emphasized exactly how these written languages look, in the form *computers* find it convenient to display. Everything is thus reduced to sequential listings of "statements" from the particular language. However, human thinking is seldom actually purely sequential. Human beings often think in terms of hierarchies and parallel structures. Therefore the natural organization of thinking is *not* solely in the form of a sequential listing of ideas, the form a computer finds most convenient. FPL as used in this text departs from this traditional approach to teaching programming and deliberately takes advantage of not being bound to sequential display. Parallel thoughts are represented side by side. Alternatives are shown in appostion. Hierarchical thinking is encouraged immediately.

The rough thinking essential to solving any but the simplest problem is encouraged by including a formal representation of rough ideas, the EPISODE, as one of the primary FPL constructs. The graphic approach makes this inclusion simple and natural, and students are consistently encouraged to represent rough ideas in successive drafts of each program. Through both the model program solutions and the exercises, students are thus encouraged to see problem solving as the processs it is, rather than to think mistakenly that it is an inspired, instantaneously realized event.

The Length of Detail of This Primer

This primer is long because it assumes that few things are self-evident to the novice, that the "QED" or "clearly, it follows from here" approach that produces short texts and that leaves to the imagination much of the detailed logic of a program or a problem solution is not a fruitful approach for teaching new material to the uninitiated. Many explanations are therefore presented in great detail, with illustrations of intermediate stages. The approach assumes it's better to present explanations long enough to help those who need them than to omit such detail. If present, the detail can always be skipped over by those who don't need it; if omitted, it is not available to those who do need it. The extensive presentation of examples is also based on the idea that learning occurs by modeling; thus every chapter concludes with a complete program embodying the major idea of the chapter.

The Hardwareless Aspect of This Approach

The material in this book depends on access to hardware only for the BASIC and Pascal interpretations—the primary presentation in FPL requires no computer. This approach has been taken for several reasons. Because there is considerable general educational benefit involved in learning how to program and because computing hardware is not always directly available to many who might profit from this learning experience, one major motivation for developing FPL was to develop a sound way to teach programming even in the absence of access to hardware. At the same time, even where hardware is readily accessible, there are strong advantages to mastering basic structural concepts before using that hardware extensively. The overall and most important thing to learn is *not* a collection of eccentric details about a given language or piece of computer hardware but how to move from a problem to a well-organized solution for that problem. Trying to learn how to solve problems by organizing things while simultaneously trying to learn all the transitory eccentricities of a language designed to "fit" a particular piece of hardware is at best pedagogically questionable. Such simultaneous approaches have often contributed directly to the unfortunate situation now prevalent in computing generally: great quantities of programmer time are spent trying to fix up and change programs that were poorly conceived and badly written in the first place.

The Multilanguage Approach

While some courses using this material have taught only the FPL and ignored the BASIC and Pascal interpretations altogether, it is more usual to have the students learn one or both of the other languages along with FPL. Whether the material on BASIC or Pascal should be introduced gradually, in parallel with the FPL (as the text presents it), or presented in some more concentrated fashion (e.g., after all FPL has been learned) is a matter of choice for the learner and the teacher.

The two sets of interpretations are designed to provide a simple, mechanical technique for translating FPL solutions. Neither set is intended to be a complete text suitable for fully mastering that language; each set is only a carefully designed springboard into its appropriate use. Teachers can be of immense help in guiding the student into these languages, but the student can also make the transition alone, provided appropriate reference manuals and documentation on how to use each particular language in the local environment are available.

SUMMARY

The major objectives of this book are to teach students how to generate problem solutions suitable for computerizations, to give them a strong sense that programs are written to be intelligible to other people, and to convince them that good program structure is an essential characteristic of any intelligible program. To achieve these objectives, the programming *process* is presented in considerable detail, using FPL, a language specially designed for just this purpose. That language distills the essence of programming into a minimum of graphically represented components the student can easily remember and mechanically translate into other computer languages. The translation languages included are BASIC and Pascal.

January 1982   R.P.T.
New York City

contents

Chapter 3
A Package of Data Items—
The RECORD

Chapter 4
Forcing the Computer to Repeat—
The WHILE

Chapter 11
Simplifying Program Creation
—The Parametric Block

Chapter 12
Dividing the Labor—
Independent Parametric Blocks

Fundamentals

INTRODUCTION

Computer programming is the process of instructing computers to carry out specific tasks. The instructions are called *programs* and the "language" in which the set of instructions is cast is called a *computer language.*

Most computers perform only a limited number of specific electrical actions. A computer language puts the computer's electrical activity at the command of the programmer. The programmer instructs the machine by linking a set of instructions together so that the computer produces the actions desired by the programmer when it reads the instructions. This means, of course, that the computer program must be put into a machine-readable form so that the computer, via one of the external devices attached to it, can read the program. By feeling or seeing the patterns of holes punched into a series of computer cards or by sensing the electrical signals generated by keys on a typewriter-like terminal, the computer can translate a program into electrical actions. The actual transformation of the instructions into electrical actions is called running or executing the program.

There are many different languages and many different computers. Some languages run on many different sizes, makes, and types of computers; and some run on only one. Some languages are relatively old and include "fossil" components representing computer hardware requirements that no longer exist; some languages are so new that only a few programmers have yet learned them. *All* languages have their eccentricities and *none* is implementable on all computers or known to all programmers.

This book is based on FPL or *First Programming Language.* It is given this title because it is designed to be used as the first programming language taught to a beginner. Although FPL incorporates features common to various languages, it does not actually run on any computer.

The design of FPL is based on the assumption that a general approach to programming should be independent of the details of particular languages. It is better to learn programming without worrying about the inevitable eccentricities and exceptions of a particular machine and a particular language. Once this approach has been mastered, the student should have no trouble moving from FPL to other languages.

The components of FPL will be introduced gradually. In this chapter we will introduce several, beginning with one component crucial to all program development. It exemplifies the idea that the creation of any computer program is an extended process.

EPISODES

Programs do not spring suddenly into the programmer's head in completed form; instead they are developed gradually through the refinement of a number of rough ideas. The episode is the FPL construct for representing such rough thoughts on paper.

Figure 1.1 shows some typical episodes. Each symbolizes the programmer's wishes in rough form; it is given an appropriate descriptive title and a rough, cloudy shape. This rough thinking may start with only a general idea of what must be accomplished and no clear conception whatever of details. As the program develops and its major shape becomes definite, the programmer may gradually replace the broader ideas with specific FPL statements and use episodes only to represent smaller collections of yet-to-be-worked-out details. This process of expressing details in a programming language is called program coding, and what it produces, code. Finally, in considering the details, the programmer may go back and revise the original rough, main ideas.

Fig. 1.1 Episodes.

We consider two simple programming problems to see exactly how this process of program development begins.

Title reading: Read the title of this book, and print it out.

Score averaging: Take four scores and average them.

An FPL program to solve the first problem can be started by two episodes (Fig. 1.2). From there we go on to fashion the finished program. It may or may not have another major episode, but that can come with second and further stages if appropriate.

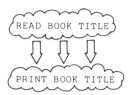

Fig. 1.2 First, rough solution
to the title-reading problem.

THE NEXT

We place PRINT BOOK TITLE *under* READ BOOK TITLE because we want the printing to be done after the reading. In most programs there is so much of this sort of sequencing of steps that we have a special construct, the *NEXT,* to make these sequential relationships absolutely definite. In Fig. 1.3 the same program is shown with the two episodes appropriately connected by a NEXT. The NEXT is a straight, vertical line connecting any two FPL components; execution of the program *always* proceeds *downwards.*

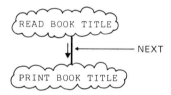

Fig. 1.3 The NEXT.

Even this very simple program illustrates a crucial point: any program must guide the computer *exactly.* What may be obvious to human beings must be explicitly stated for computers. The beginning and the end of a program, for example, must be clearly indicated to the computer, particularly if a program has several sections or parts—the computer must be told which part is the main argument. Every program in FPL must have one main argument, which begins with an initial NEXT and ends with a final NEXT. START and STOP circles must show where the program begins and ends. Figure 1.4 shows our title-reading program with an appropriate start and stop added.

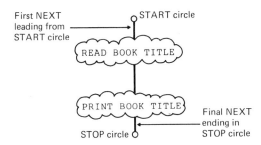

Fig. 1.4 The START and STOP circles.

A FIRST LOOK AT REFINEMENT:
THE PROCESS OF PROGRAMMING

A program is created by a process of refinement of the episodes. For example, a first-stage program to meet the requirements of the score-averaging problem might begin as a single episode as shown in Fig. 1.5(a); almost immediately this is developed into a two-episode program as shown in Fig. 1.5(b), and then into the three-episode version shown in Fig. 1.5(c). Instructions such as AVERAGE 4 NUMBERS are often adequate when human beings rather than computers are being programmed. We *assume* that we will be told *which 4 numbers* in due course and we *assume* that someone will ask us *what answer* we got and that we'll tell them—either through speech or in writing. In creating a set of instructions for a computer, though, one must be far more explicit.

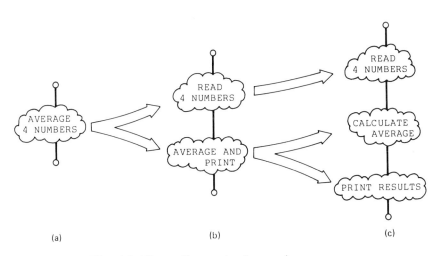

(a)   (b)   (c)

Fig. 1.5 First refinements of averaging program.

The computer usually has a set of basic instructions; anything it does must be directed by some combination of such instructions. Hence in a program we must put together the specific set of instructions required to accomplish whatever task it is we are trying to program. Though it is true that hardware and software companies have developed useful prefabricated job or task handlers, there remain many tasks for which handlers cannot be prefabricated. To create programs to handle such tasks, the programmer must learn to assemble programs from the most basic building blocks.

So although Fig. 1.5a may be a good starting point, it's not at the basic building-block level yet. For example, suppose you want to get four numbers into the computer and then to average them (Fig. 1.5b). We still need to express the result, say, by printing or displaying it. (Fig. 1.5c). This process must go on until everything is specified in terms of the basic building-block instructions of the computer language we are using. Figure 1.6 presents our next version, expanding our initial READ 4 NUMBERS episode into four episodes.

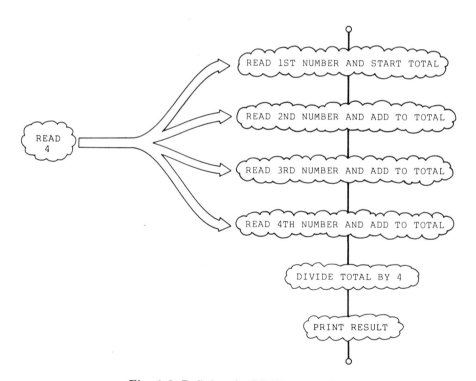

Fig. 1.6 Refining the READ 4 episode.

ASSIGNMENTS, DATA NAMES, AND STORAGE

We introduce *assignments,* the most basic of all building blocks for programs, and *storage,* the place where data is kept inside the computer, by returning to the title-reading program. The code we had developed so far is shown again in Fig. 1.7.

Fig. 1.7 Title-reading code.

In this program, the computer must be given the title before it can print it. In FPL, we represent this by the truncated rectangle shown in Fig. 1.8. An inward pointing arrow must pierce the truncated end to indicate that the information is coming in. However, this representation alone is incomplete.

Fig. 1.8 Indication of incoming information.

Returning to our analogy with human reading and writing, we recognize immediately that reading involves not simply seeing but storing the words that are read. The computer must also store what it reads. In FPL, the programmer gives the computer a name for a piece of data; throughout the program the computer associates that name with the place in which it stores that data. Whenever that name is mentioned in the program, the computer *knows* where to find that piece of information.

Datanames

We call these names "datanames" or "data names" and require that they be formed according to the following simple rules: (1) datanames must begin with a letter; (2) they can include any combination of letters and digits; (3) they can include the underscore (_) as a word separator. Here are some representative datanames.

AVERAGE

BOOK_TITLE

COUNT_SCORES

DAYS_IN_TAX_PERIOD

HIGHEST_PAY_RATE

N

R3

SALARY

SCALE

SPEED

TOTAL_CNT

X_COORD

Good datanames clearly suggest the type of data to be stored. Programs using cryptic datanames like X, PA2, and Q3, or cute ones like JOKER and BILLS _GOOF are much more difficult to follow than are programs that use suggestive datanames like CITY_SALES_TAX, LIGHT_YRS_TRAVELED, and NMBR_OF_SCORES_READ. Though it may take longer to write a program using meaningful datanames, the result will be much easier to read and modify—and that turns out to be a *mighty* consideration.

External Assignments

If we use BOOK_TITLE as the dataname under which the computer stores whatever title it reads, we can execute one basic FPL instruction, the *external assignment*. It is represented in Fig. 1.9 and is called an "assignment" because data is *assigned* to a particular location. It is labeled "external" because the data (in this case, a book title) is coming from outside the computer.

Fig. 1.9 The external assignment.

We can immediately replace the READ BOOK TITLE episode of our title-reading program with this exact instruction, and thus bring the program one step nearer to completion as shown in Fig. 1.10. Having done so, we can turn to the "write" episode.

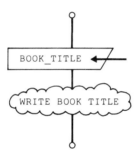

Fig. 1.10 External assignment to read data.

Before *we* can write something, we need to retrieve a copy of it from memory. The computer must do something similar. To write the book's title, the computer must retrieve a copy of the title from the location in which it has been stored. Once retrieved, that copy must be sent to a printer, terminal, or another computer. Because in many respects the process of writing the title is the reverse of reading it, the FPL symbol for writing reflects this reversal. As with reading, we place the appropriate dataname inside the external assignment box. To indicate writing though, we reverse the direction of the piercing arrow, making it point outward as shown in Fig. 1.11 to suggest what happens: the computer retrieves a copy of the title from the location associated with the dataname BOOK_TITLE, and then assigns this copy to an appropriate external device.

Fig. 1.11 External assignment to transmit data.

We now refine our first complete FPL program, arriving at the code shown in Fig. 1.12.

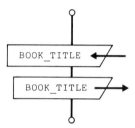

Fig. 1.12 Completed title-reading program.

Private Practice

P1.1   Create an episodic program to do the following.

a. Read through a collection of 300 employee ID numbers and associated names, locate number 6731, and print out that employee's name.

b. Read through a payroll file, locate all females who have worked for the company more than seven years, and list them.

c. Read in a collection of 2,000 periodical titles, sort them into alphabetical order, and print them out.

P1.2   Create descriptive datanames for each of the following.

a. The rating given a political candidate (1 to 10);

b. The age of any fourth grader in a class;

c. The name of each country in Africa in 1962;

d. The rate of population growth in Kenya in 1973;

e. The names of tribes in Kigezi province.

P1.3   Modify the program shown in Fig. 1.12 so that it reads and writes a second book title after finishing the first. Assume that your program is used to handle the titles *Slaughterhouse Five* and *August 1914.* Act as computer and see if your program works.

P1.4   Create a program with appropriate datanames to read and write the age of each of two boys.

An Intuitive Picture of Storage

A simple visual model of computer memory (storage) will help our discussion of assignments. Let's represent a single storage area in the computer as a jar with a name, and represent the value stored there (its contents) by an entry on a piece of paper in the jar. Figures 1.13 and 1.14 depict the relationship between datanames and storage locations in the context of the title-reading program. Figure 1.13 shows how data is initially read into a storage location, and Figure 1.14 shows how a copy of the value stored in a location is transmitted (printed out).

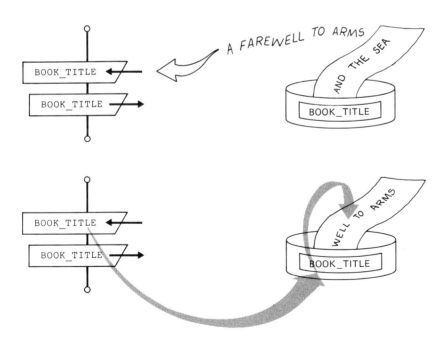

Fig. 1.13 Reading data into the computer.

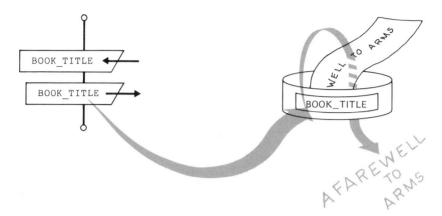

Fig. 1.14 Transmitting data from the computer.

Note that executing an external assignment to read new data *replaces* the old value stored in the location; executing an assignment to transmit the data *does not change it*. The process is analogous to using a simple tape recorder: reading is a form of recording; transmitting, a form of playing back.

We must stress that the computer may contain far *more* jars than a program needs, or it may contain far *fewer. In FPL we always assume that it contains more.* Now when the computer puts something into a jar, whatever was in there before is removed. At the same time, once something has been put into the jar, it stays there *even if the jar is not used for several successive programs.* At the start of any program, the programmer should assume that every jar contains leftovers from previous programs. Programmers use the word "garbage" to describe such contents; so in FPL we symbolize such contents with a miniature garbage can.

Internal Assignments

In contrast to external assignments, internal assignments deal exclusively with information *inside* the computer and they always cause the contents of some location (jar) to be changed (rewritten). As shown in Fig. 1.15, the internal assignment is represented graphically by a simple rectangle. It is always connected to other portions of the program by a NEXT.

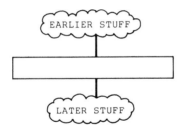

Fig. 1.15 The internal assignment.

Three variations   Three variations on the internal assignment are represented in Fig. 1.16: (a) assigns a value of zero to the location named COUNT; (b) assigns the value of OLD_PAY's contents to the location named NEW_PAY; and (c) assigns the resulting value of an expression to the location named COUNT. To be certain you understand each, consider one at a time. They are represented with appropriate storage locations in Figs. 1.17, 1.18, and 1.19.

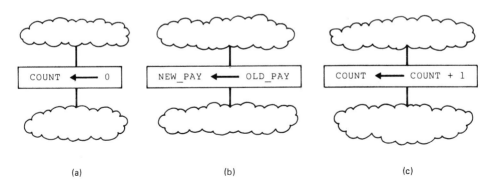

Fig. 1.16 Common variants of internal assignments.

In Fig. 1.17, the process of executing an internal assignment is represented in two steps: finding the storage location named as the target of the assignment, and rewriting the stored value so that the new value agrees with that cited in the assignment. The value assigned to COUNT by this assignment will always be the same every time the assignment is executed—zero. For that reason, a fixed value like zero in a program is referred to as a "constant." For the opposite reason—because its value varies completely with assignments made to it—a storage location like COUNT is referred to as a "variable."

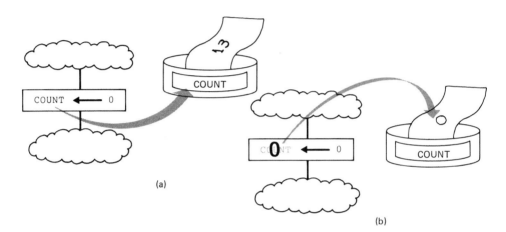

Fig. 1.17 Assigning a constant value to a variable.

In Fig. 1.18 the execution of a different assignment is illustrated in four steps: locating the storage location (OLD_PAY) containing the value to be assigned, using the value from that location in the assignment, finding the storage location named as the target of the assignment, and rewriting the stored value there. In the assignment illustrated, the value of the contents of NEW-_PAY *may* differ each time the assignment is executed, depending on the value of the variable OLD_PAY. Note how different this is from the case of a constant assignment. Note, too, that this assignment *does not* alter the value of OLD_PAY; only the value of the target location is changed in an internal assignment.

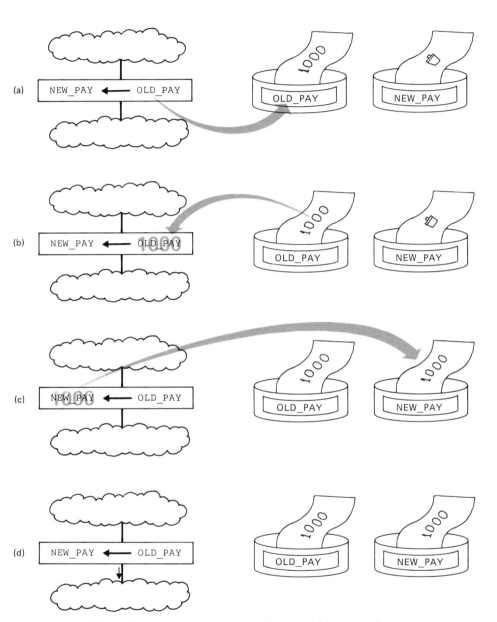

Fig. 1.18 Assigning the value of one variable to another.

Figure 1.19 depicts the five-step execution of the remaining assignment from Fig. 1.15: finding the storage location (COUNT) containing the value to be used in the expression (COUNT + 1); using the value (37) from that

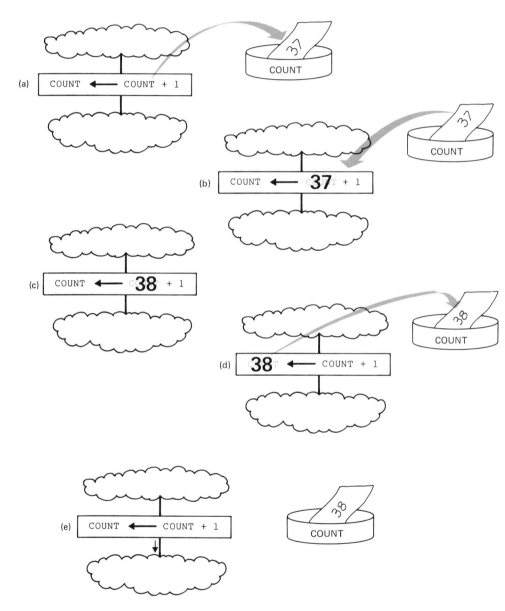

Fig. 1.19 Assigning an expression's value to a variable.

location in the expression (37 + 1); computing the value of the expression (38); finding the storage location (COUNT) named as the target of the assignment; and rewriting over the old value (37) stored there so that its new value (38) agrees with that computed for the expression.

Operators   In assignments involving expressions, the expression must be evaluated before any value can be assigned to the target location. To simplify the programmer's task, expressions such as COUNT + 1 or RATE * .3 use operation symbols to indicate the desired evaluation. Figure 1.20 gives a complete list of FPL operation symbols and illustrates their use.

SYMBOL	OPERATION	EXAMPLE	SAMPLE VALUES	RESULT
:	join	(A : B)	A is "O", B is "K"	"OK"
+	add	(A + B)	A is 3, B is 7	10
−	subtract	(A − B)	A is 6, B is 2	4
*	multiply	(A * B)	A is 5, B is 8	40
/	divide	(A / B)	A is 8, B is 4	2
**	exponentiate	(A ** B)	A is 5, B is 2	25

Fig. 1.20 Operation symbols used in FPL.

Note two things. (1) The symbol *must* appear or the operation won't be done—AB is not the same as A * B; and (2) parentheses should be used to indicate order and grouping in the expression—(A + B) * PAY is not the same as A + (B * PAY).

The colon (:) in the table is used only in connection with data formed from strings of characters. Quotes (" ") are used to set off string data to distinguish a string from a dataname. For example, NAME ⟵ "IQL" assigns the string of three characters *IQL* to the location NAME; NAME ⟵ IQL assigns whatever value is in the variable IQL to be the new value in NAME. For purposes of readability, we always represent the position of each blank within a string by the caret (∧) when we display strings in this text. Thus "United∧ States" is 13 characters long and includes the character blank between the d in United and the S in States. Although in actually talking to the computer, we must use the character blank wherever we want a space to occur in a string, our textual use of the caret in place of the invisible blank will make all our string examples clearer.

The colon comes into play when we wish to concatenate or join strings together to form new strings or when we wish to affix labels to our answers when printing them out. Thus PHRASE ⟵ "See∧" : "Dick" assigns the string value "See∧Dick" to the variable PHRASE. Our use of strings as labels for answers will appear later in this chapter.

Private Practice

P1.5   Assume that, before the execution of *each* assignment shown below, the value of RESULT is set to 132, of PAY to 34, of CUT to 10, and of COUNT to 2. Illustrate each execution through a series of drawings similar to those in Figs. 1.17, 1.18 or 1.19.

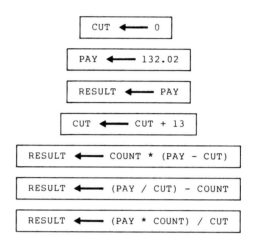

P1.6   Write the value assigned to MESSAGE by each assignment below. Each execution begins with the same values: FRONT_END is set to "PUPPY"; REAR_END to "∧LOVE∧". Use quotes to delimit your string answer and carets to show the location of blanks.

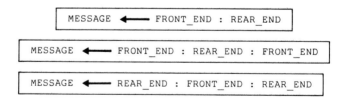

P1.7   Assume that, prior to execution of the following assignment, the value of ABC is 45, of DAYS is 5, of NMBR_OF_EMPLOYEES is 3, and of INDUCEMENT is 30.

```
ANSWER  ◀─── ABC / DAYS * NMBR_OF_EMPLOYEES + INDUCEMENT
```

Copy the expression to the right of the assignment arrow, showing where parentheses should be inserted to ensure that the value of the contents assigned to ANSWER will be 33. Copy the expression two more times; by inserting the parentheses in still other places, develop expressions that would produce a second and third result to be assigned to ANSWER.

CREATING A COMPLETE PROGRAM

Let us return to the score-averaging program. Review the program shown in Fig. 1.6. Now, using assignments, we can finish this program.

First, we note that the last two episodes may be directly refined into assignments. We need only provide datanames for the average and for the total used in computing the average. Let's call the average AVERAGE and the total TOTAL. Because of assignments in the first portion of the program, we assume that TOTAL contains the total of the four numbers. Then the last two episodes translate directly into the assignments shown in Fig. 1.21.

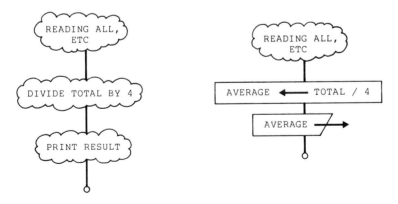

Fig. 1.21 The last two episodes refined.

Second, we note that all the earlier episodes involve reading a number and adding it to the amount stored in TOTAL. We thus need a dataname for the number; call it NUMBER. We see immediately that the reading and the adding represented in the first episodes separate naturally into an external assignment and an internal assignment, as shown in Fig. 1.22.

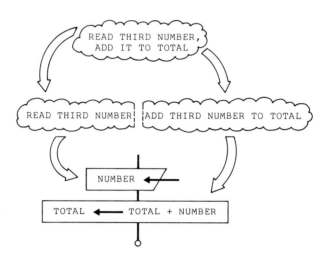

Fig. 1.22 Refining the read and add episode.

Note in particular the last assignment. In effect, it tells the computer to add together the values in the locations TOTAL and NUMBER, and to store the new result of this addition in the location called TOTAL. This is a common type of internal assignment, useful for accumulating values. In this type of assignment, the dataname of the location where the cumulative total is being kept must appear on *both* sides of the assignment arrow, not merely on the left (target) side.

Third, we note that by merely repeating the code shown in Fig. 1.22 we can refine our program to the stage shown in Fig. 1.23. (We do not try to replace the very first episode that way because the total must be started there.)

Finally, we turn our attention to refining READ FIRST NUMBER AND START TOTAL, the only remaining unrefined episode.

The first episode must not only read the first number but also "start the total." Again we'll need an external and an internal assignment, but the

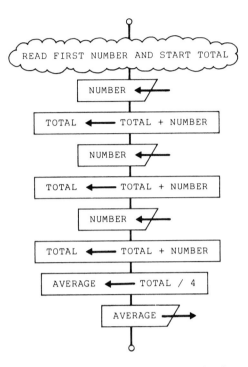

Fig. 1.23 Program with all but the first
episode refined.

internal assignment will merely assign the value of the first number read to
TOTAL without adding to what was previously in that location. After such a
rewrite, TOTAL will be assigned the value of the first number read. The refinement of this first episode is shown in Fig. 1.24.

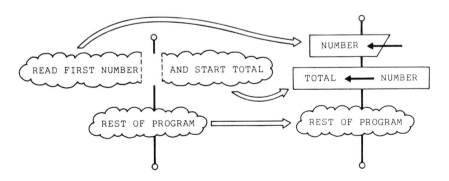

Fig. 1.24 Refinement of first episode.

As with most programming refinements, however, there is an alternative. As Fig. 1.25 shows, this alternative includes the code common to the other read/accumulate refinements realized in Fig. 1.23. Such inclusion often makes the refinement more useful although longer, and we will adopt it for our final version.

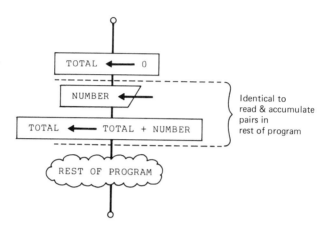

Fig. 1.25 An alternative refinement of our first episode.

The final version of the score-averaging program is shown in Fig. 1.26. Compare it with the versions refined from Figs. 1.5 to 1.6 and then successively through 1.21, 1.22, 1.23, and 1.25. This succession of versions teaches an essential lesson: *programs are developed by refining rough thinking.*

Note the label affixed to the result by the colon in the final external assignment. Programs should always be designed to label the answers so that the user of the program knows what is being displayed. Nothing is more confusing than one or more numbers displayed with no explanation whatever as to what each represents!

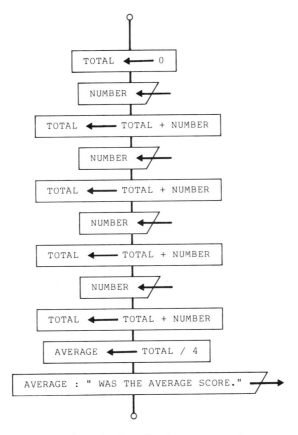

Fig. 1.26 Completely refined score-averaging program.

TESTING THE PROGRAM—TEST DATA AND TRACE TABLES

We now wish to test our program by running it against some sample data. As execution proceeds downwards, we need to record changes in the contents of three locations: (1) TOTAL, (2) NUMBER, and (3) AVERAGE. We identify a series of points on the code so that we can refer to them in recording the contents. Finally, because jars are time-consuming to draw, we will use a table to record contents rather than a series of jars. We call such a table an "execution trace table," or just a "trace table."

The series of points at which we will examine storage location contents are labeled in Fig. 1.27 and are called "execution reference points." Running this program requires beginning at the top and working downwards, one assignment at a time. We examine the contents of storage locations TOTAL, NUMBER, and AVERAGE at each of execution reference point to see how the execution affects their values, and record our findings in the next line of the trace table.

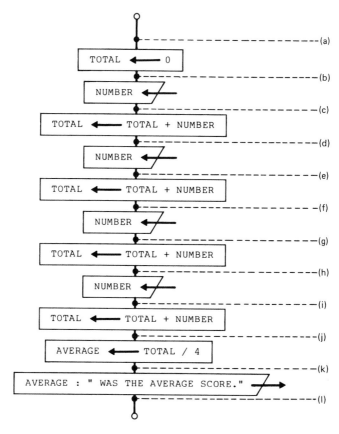

Fig. 1.27 Program with execution reference points.

The data that we will run the program upon is shown in Fig. 1.28. It consists of four numbers (data items or pieces of data). We assume that the order in which our program reads them is the order shown, from left to right (leftmost data item is read first, etc.).

ORDER	first	second	third	fourth
DATA ITEM	100	50	60	30

Fig. 1.28 Test data for score-averaging program.

The process of completing the first four lines of the trace table is illustrated in Fig. 1.29. The table reflects changes in the contents of TOTAL, NUMBER, and AVERAGE as execution proceeds through points (a), (b), (c), and (d) successively. (Only the relevant portion of the program itself is shown.) At program startup, all storage contents are garbage (a). The first assignment

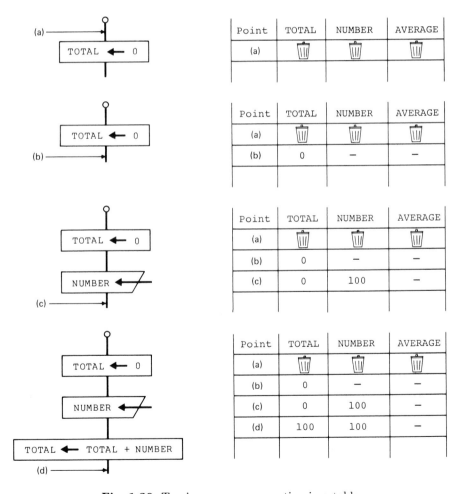

Fig. 1.29 Tracing program execution in a table.

alters only TOTAL, assigning that variable a value of 0 (b). The second assignment reads in a value and assigns it to NUMBER (c). The next assignment
computes a new total value and assigns it to TOTAL (d).

The trace table for the entire run is shown in Fig. 1.30.

Point	TOTAL	NUMBER	AVERAGE
(a)	🗑	🗑	🗑
(b)	0	–	–
(c)	0	100	–
(d)	100	100	–
(e)	100	50	–
(f)	150	50	–
(g)	150	60	–
(h)	210	60	–
(i)	210	30	–
(j)	240	30	–
(k)	240	30	60
(l)	240	30	60

Fig. 1.30 The completed trace table.

Note several things. First, because AVERAGE is not used until after
point (j), its contents remain undefined (garbage) until late in the execution.
Second, TOTAL has undefined contents until assigned a zero between points
(a) and (b); and NUMBER has undefined contents until assigned the first data
item by the assignment between points (b) and (c). Third, the execution of each
accumulation assignment affects the contents of TOTAL, but not the contents
of NUMBER. Fourth, computation of the average, and assignment of the result
to AVERAGE, affects the contents of AVERAGE but not the contents of TO-
TAL (the assignment between (j) and (k)). And fifth, the contents of AVER-
AGE are not changed by the final assignment of the program, which prints the
average.

Private Practice

P1.8   Complete a trace table similar to that in Fig. 1.30, but based on the following data values.

ORDER	first	second	third	fourth
DATA ITEM	30	60	90	20

P1.9   Modify the program shown in Fig. 1.27 so that it can handle five numbers instead of only four.

P1.10   Complete a trace table for this modified program, based on the following data values.

ORDER	first	second	third	fourth	fifth
DATA ITEM	40	70	35	55	100

P1.11   Create a program that can count to five. Begin your work with episodes and end it by doing a test run. Show by means of a table how the contents of all appropriate storage locations are changed during the execution of the counting program.

P1.12   Create a program that counts to five and prints the sum of all numbers counted, up to and including the count point, as it counts. For example, when your program reaches the number 5, it should print out the number 15 because 15 is the sum of 1 and 2 and 3 and 4 and 5. Test your program by completing a trace table.

P1.13   Write a program that will read in four words (data strings) and concatenate (join) them together into a sentence (bigger data string). For test data, use the following.

(1) "The∧",   (2) "world∧",   (3) "ends∧", and   (4) "tonight∧".

Test your program by completing a trace table.

A Closer Look at Data- Declarations

INTRODUCTION

In Chapter One we introduced datanames and their correspondence with storage locations. To avoid drowning you in new and confusing detail, we did not discuss the form data takes during its transmission or storage. Now we must consider this form carefully.

THE FORM IN WHICH DATA IS TRANSMITTED

As Fig. 2.1 suggests, data is transmitted to and from the computer as a stream of electrical signals. Like a light switch, a signal may be either on (1) or off (0). The signals are interpreted in packets, each of which includes the same number of signals. Using a standard coding scheme, the computer is able to interpret each packet as a letter, a number, a punctuation mark, or some other character. The example portrays data coded in a scheme called EBCDIC that requires eight signals (bits) to represent each character.

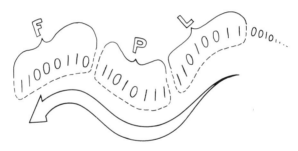

Fig. 2.1 Data transmitted as a coded stream of electrical signals.

In receiving data, the computer must decide how many packets grouped together correspond to the item named in the external assignment. The computer must extract enough data to fill the data storage location corresponding to the dataname referenced in the assignment (Fig. 2.2).

Sending data out of the computer reverses the process of getting it in. Thus stored data must be collected from its storage location, transformed into a string of pulses, and transmitted in a stream to a device such as a terminal, printer, or cardpunch in a stream.

For either sending or receiving data, the computer must have accurate information about the data. Only then can it extract from the stream enough signal packets to fit the cited storage location; only then can it copy and trans-

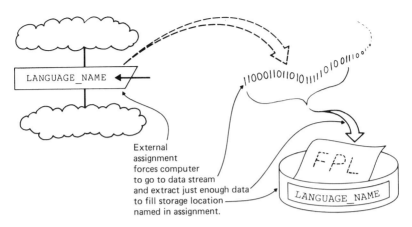

Fig. 2.2 External assignments, data stream, and storage.

mit data from its memory and transmit it back to the external world. Now let's consider how the computer stores data internally. That, too, requires coded representation and leads directly to what the programmer must specify about data.

THE FORM DATA ASSUMES INSIDE THE COMPUTER

Digital computers store information as coded packets of signals or bits and represent data values through standard coding schemes. However, different representations may be used to store the same piece of data, depending upon how that piece is to be used. For example, Fig. 2.3 shows how a number like 123 might be represented in one way in storage if it is to be used arithmetically during the program, and in quite a different way if it is not. For the computer, one representation serves arithmetic purposes much better than another. This should not seem strange. We do much the same thing. In English, for example, we might write "One hundred twenty-three" in an essay but "123" on an arithmetic exercise.

Arithmetic	Character		
01111011	11110001	11110010	11110011
123	1	2	3

Fig. 2.3 Alternative coded representations.

The problem with having alternative representations for a stored piece of data lies in using the correct representation for a given programming situation. Numbers represented in a nonarithmetic form cannot be used by a program in calculation, and letters mistakenly represented as numbers can sometimes be used by the computer to produce bizarre results! It is the programmer's job to make sure such problems do not arise by specifying at the start of each program exactly what representation is to be used for every data value in the program. This is done through the DECLARATION. In FPL, four different data types can be declared to force appropriate representation: (1) STRING, (2) INTEGER, (3) FIXED, and (4) FLOAT.

String Data

String data are composed of contiguous strings of characters, like "FPL", "123 Oak Street", or "M T". (The quotation marks used here and whenever strings appear as constant terms in assignments are *not* part of the strings. They are necessary to make reading easier and to enable the computer to distinguish between a string data constant such as "GEOGRAPHY" and a dataname such as GEOGRAPHY.) A string is usually coded into a form that makes movement and comparison of items fast but makes arithmetic impossible or unpredictable. To guarantee that the computer codes such data correctly, the dataname of each variable (storage location) that will hold string data must be declared (as in Fig. 2.4) at the beginning of the program. Each data item declaration must include the dataname, the type of data to be stored in that location, and the length or size of that data item. The declarations are housed in the special declaration symbol shown.

As the figure suggests, declarations force the computer to reserve storage for each item declared. For the three data variables shown, it sets aside a ten character-sized location for LANGUAGE_NAME, a twenty character-sized location for STREET_ADDRESS, and a three character-sized location for ID.

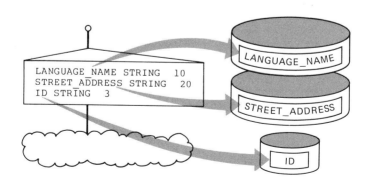

Fig. 2.4 Declarations for string data storage.

Fixed-length strings   Figure 2.5 illustrates how fixed-length strings are handled. The length declared is *exactly* the length that will be retrieved, stored, and transmitted. When the string "FPL" is assigned to LANGUAGE_NAME, the computer adds seven blanks to the right-hand end of the data string to make it ten characters long, and stores "FPL∧∧∧∧∧∧∧". (The caret (∧) appears in place of a blank, merely to aid the reader.) On the other hand, when "AZ63Q" is assigned to ID, the computer chops off the last two characters on the right ("3Q") to get the declared length of three characters, and stores "AZ6" only. Subsequent retrieval and transmission of the two stored values yields the padded "FPL∧∧∧∧∧∧∧" and the shortened "AZ6".

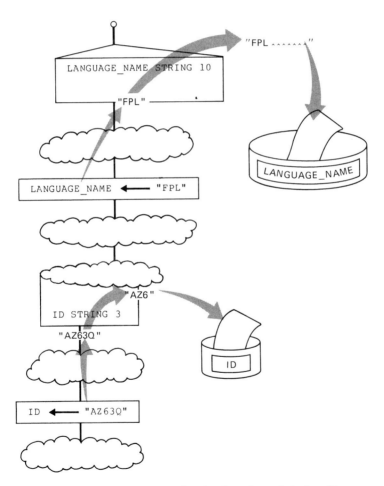

Fig. 2.5 Effect of declared string length on data handling.

Private Practice

P2.1   Assume each pair of string examples shown below is representative of a whole set of similar strings. Complete the declaration of a suitable storage location for each set. (The caret ∧ represents a blank.)

string pair	dataname	TYPE	SIZE
"ABC", "MNO"	ALPHABET	STRING	_____
"13dh2", "72AX2"	ID	STRING	_____
"123∧Oak∧AVENUE∧∧∧∧∧"			
"106∧MORNINGSIDE∧∧∧∧"	_____	STRING	_____
"HARRIET∧∧∧∧∧∧∧",			
"JAMES∧∧∧∧∧∧∧∧∧"	_____	STRING	_____

P2.2   Use the code below to complete the accompanying trace table. Make the stored contents of NAME fit its declared length, even if you must chop or pad the string value being stored. Use a caret ∧ to stand for each blank.

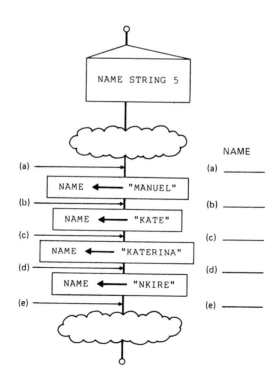

Variable-length strings   In addition to strings of fixed length, strings of variable length are also quite common in programming languages. Unlike the fixed storage reserved for fixed-length string data, the storage reserved for variable-length strings changes to match the length of the string most recently assigned to it. We do not therefore declare a specific SIZE for such areas. Instead, we specify the SIZE as VARYING. Figure 2.6 illustrates a declaration for a variable-length string and shows that the length of what is stored actually varies with the length of what is assigned.

Figure 2.7 presents a portion of code and its trace table, involving assignments to a variable-length item named KEY. The three assignments produce a longer and longer string, yet storage in the VARYING location presents no problem.

Private Practice

P2.3   Complete the trace table for the code shown. *Remember:* The string stored in TITLE can vary in length!

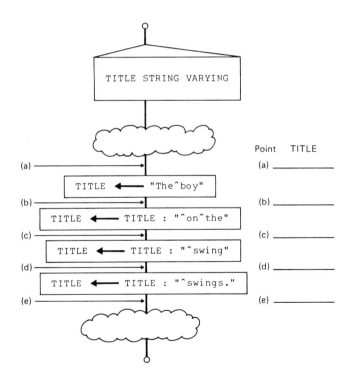

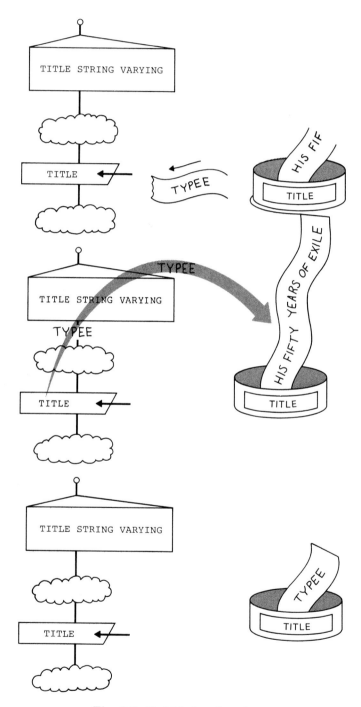

Fig. 2.6 Variable-length strings.

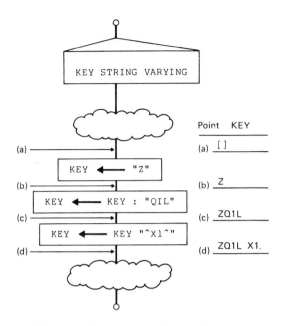

Fig. 2.7 Tracing variable-length strings.

Numeric Data

There are three common types of numeric data; integer, fixed, and floating point. They differ somewhat in the way they are coded and in the results gained from manipulating them arithmetically. Most computers have at least two types and many have all three. In each case there are arithmetic operations tailored to each data type.

Integers   Integers are whole numbers without any fractional or decimal portion, e.g., 3, 67, 987450, and 450. (Integers can be negative as well as positive so −8, −98765, and −73 are also integers.) On the other hand, 1/9, 5.66, and 3¼ are not integers.

With integers we need merely declare the number of digits we want the data item to have. Some typical integer declarations might be those shown in Fig. 2.8. As tracing the four assignments to CASE_COUNT suggests, the length declared is observed exactly. If the value assigned requires fewer positions than declared, the value assigned is padded *on the left* to fill the declared size. If the value assigned requires more positions than declared, digits are chopped from the left of the number till the remainder fits the declared size.

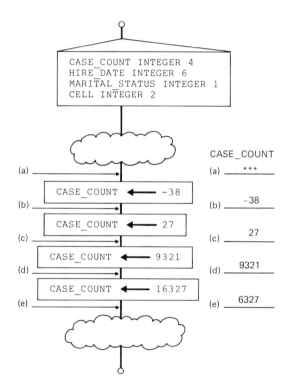

Fig. 2.8 Integer declaration and assignment.

When the computer performs arithmetic upon integers, the result is also an integer. For example, in Fig. 2.9, the result of dividing the integer 1 by the integer 4 will not itself be an integer, but the portion of the result stored in SLOPE *must* be because of SLOPE's declaration. Hence even though the "real" answer is something like 0.25, only the integer portion, 0, is stored in SLOPE.

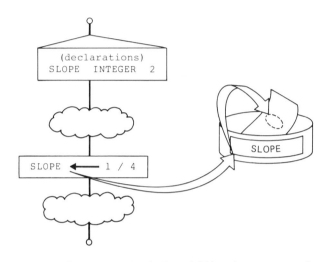

Fig. 2.9 Integer manipulation yielding the unexpected.

A very common use of integer data (as we shall see in later chapters) is their use as subscripts in vectors, matrices, and arrays. Such subscripts must be integers because there is no cell *8.3* or *7 and ½!*

Private Practice

P2.4   Assume each pair of integers below is representative of a whole set of similar integers. Complete the declaration of a suitable storage location for each.

integer pair	dataname	TYPE	SIZE
10, 27	COUNT	INTEGER	_____
10326, 10092	_____	INTEGER	_____
−28, 31	_____	INTEGER	_____

P2.5   Use the code below to complete the accompanying trace table. Make the stored contents of TOTAL and AVERAGE fit the size declared. Indicate the glaring inadequacy in the code and suggest how to fix it.

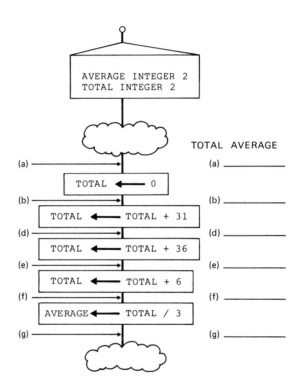

Fixed (decimal) data   Fixed numeric data has a specified length but, unlike INTEGER data, a certain portion of that length is "fixed" as the decimal portion. For example, 456.9, 378.2, and 056.9 are all fixed data of the same size and precision: each is four digits long and has one digit to the right of its decimal point. In many languages the decimal point need not be present in the data so long as the programmer indicates where it is to fall. The computer then preserves the point's location, no matter what arithmetic it puts the data item through.

Figure 2.10 shows several declarations for fixed numeric data items. With fixed data we need to declare both the total number of digits and the number of digits to the right of the decimal point. We use a pair of integers to do this, separated by a comma, as in (3, 1) or (6, 2) or (5, 4). The integer to the left of the comma indicates how many digits the data is to have altogether. The integer to the right of the comma indicates how many digits are to the right of the decimal point. The *difference* between the two, of course, indicates the number of digits to the left of the point. For example, (4, 2) means that the number will only have four digits in all, and two of them will be to the right of the decimal.

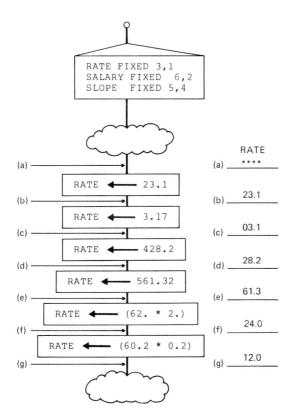

Fig. 2.10 Fixed numeric declaration and assignment.

As the trace table in Fig. 2.10 shows, assignments to FIXED variables tailor the data to fit the SIZE declared. If the value being stored does not fit the declared size, it will be chopped or padded to fit; the adjustments may be made to both ends of the number, depending on its size. Thus both ends of 561.32 are chopped off to make it fit its declared size, which is (3,1).

Another interesting example of computer arithmetic is provided by the set of assignments in Fig. 2.11. The variable SLOPE is an imaginary one that might be used by a builder or architect in a program to analyse drainage. Its use here is strictly illustrative. Together, the set of three assignments performs an overall operation equivalent to dividing one by three and multiplying the result by three. We would expect the result to be 1.0000. It may not be. The contents of HOLD may end as 0.9999! Some computers and some languages protect you from some problems like these, but none will protect you from all of them.

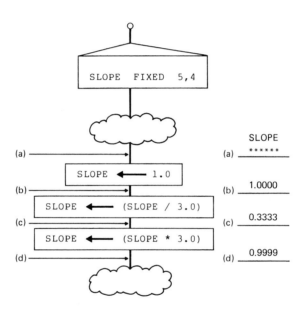

Fig. 2.11 Fixed numeric manipulation yields an unexpected result.

Private Practice

P2.6   Assume each triplet of fixed values below is representative of a whole set of similar values. Complete the declaration of a suitable storage location for each.

sample triplet	dataname	TYPE	SIZE
3.2, 6.1, 0.9	RATE	FIXED	_____
100.33, 99.62, 138.20	AVERAGE_SCORE	FIXED	_____
−27.3, −38.6, 29.5	TEMPERATURE	FIXED	_____
.00132, .00091, .00613	MICRONS	FIXED	_____

P2.7   Use the code below to complete the accompanying trace table. Make the stored contents of TEST_VALUE fit its declared size, even if you must chop both ends off the assigned value.

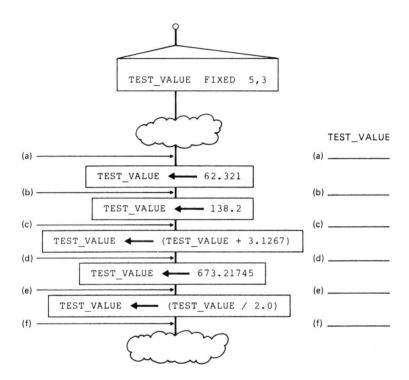

Floating point data   When numeric data is designated as *floating point,* the coding scheme used to store it is one that floats the decimal point to the most significant portion of the number, while always remembering where that point belongs. Figure 2.12 presents declarations for three floating point items. The TYPE is FLOAT and the SIZE is the number of significant digits.

Figure 2.12 depicts a two-chamber jar for each item, thus stressing the fact that two pieces of information must be kept for any data item declared as floating point: (1) the significant digits and (2) their location with respect to the decimal point. For example, the information stored in SPEED_OF_LIGHT includes the significant digits 2.99 and the decimal point location 8. There are three digits because SPEED_OF_LIGHT is declared as FLOAT 3; the *positive* 8 indicates that the decimal point belongs eight positions *to the right* of its location in the stored significant digits. Thus the value represented is equivalent to 299,000,000. The values stored for NUCLEUS_DIAMETER are by contrast those of a small number: 0.000000000000013. There, a *negative* 14 indicates that the decimal point actually belongs *far to the left* of its position in the stored 1.3.

FLOAT type data is extremely important for handling very large or very small numeric values and some sort of floating point data type appears in every language used for scientific programming. Floating arithmetic delivers floating results.

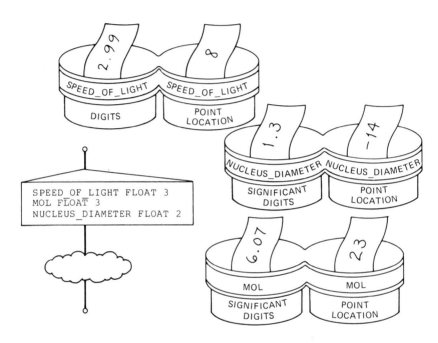

Fig. 2.12 Floating point numeric data.

Private Practice

P2.8   What number is represented by the information stored in the two chambers of MOL in Fig. 2.12?

P2.9   Name and complete declarations for five data items that would require floating point storage.

	dataname	TYPE	SIZE
(1)	_____	FLOAT	____
(2)	_____	FLOAT	____
(3)	_____	FLOAT	____
(4)	_____	FLOAT	____
(5)	_____	FLOAT	____

Mixed arithmetic   In doing arithmetic on an expression that contains more than one type of numeric data, the computer decides which kind of arithmetic to perform—integer, fixed, or float. As you work with various hardware and language combinations, you may find that this creates problems. To minimize problems, consult the appropriate manuals and do some experimentation.

A SECOND LOOK AT GETTING
DATA IN AND OUT OF THE COMPUTER

Declarations must be quite specific about data type and size if the computer is to handle the data. Figure 2.13 suggests how the declaration is used at one end of the process.

Although all data is stored in coded form, this example simply shows it in everyday form: MARY. In reality, no letters such as those making up the word MARY could be stored *as letters*—they would be stored in the location as coded magnetic or electrical patterns, probably in a code still different from that used for transmission. We show the stored data in readable form merely to make clearer the illustration of transmission. In fact, however data is stored, it must be translated into a coded form appropriate to its declaration.

The process for handling incoming data is just the reverse. As Fig. 2.14 suggests, the basic declaration information is used to determine how much data must be extracted from the data stream for each item; the extracted data is then coded and assigned to storage as declared. We assume that information in the data stream is transmitted character by character. Hence, in the illustration, the declaration of KEY tells the computer to extract the next three packets from the stream to form a three-digit integer, and then store the recoded result in KEY.

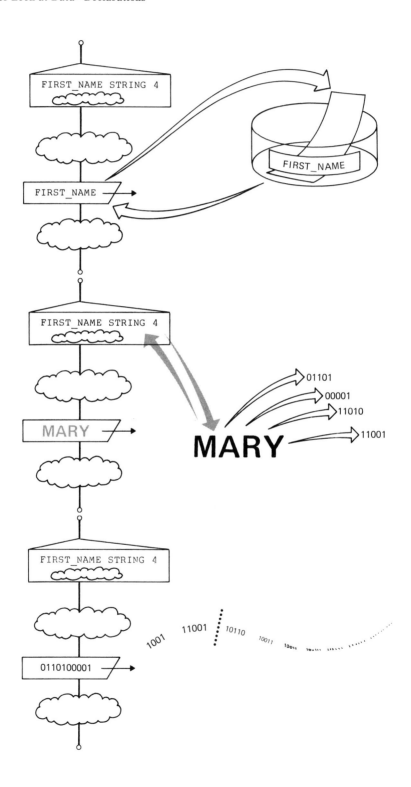

Fig. 2.13 Use of declaration information in data transmission. (a) Retrieve a copy of data stored in location whose dataname appears in the external assignment. (b) Use the declaration information that indicates the current code in which the data is stored, and translate the value into coded form for transmission outside. (c) Add the pulse packets so created to the stream of outgoing data.

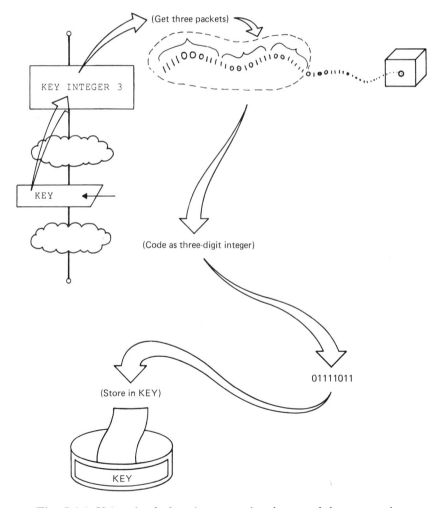

Fig. 2.14 Using the declaration to receive the stored data correctly.

Private Practice

P2.10   For each data item listed below, complete an appropriate declaration entry to its right.

item	data item	dataname	TYPE	SIZE
(1)	"ABCD"			
(2)	173			
(3)	42.20			
(4)	"The∧Jazz∧Age"			
(5)	0.0000000000000045			
(6)	6			
(7)	1200.00			

P2.11   Declare a dataname, type, and size for each of the following, and place them all together in a single declaration symbol.

a. A counter that will not have to hold a count higher than 3756;
b. A street name that will be no longer than "Workington Drive";
c. A town name that will be no longer than "Entebbe";
d. A tax that can hold a dollars-and-cents amount up to one hundred dollars;
e. An account number that is always 15 digits long.

P2.12   For each item declared in Fig. 2.4, 2.8, 2.10, and 2.12, cite *two* data values—one that suits the item's declared type and size, and one that suits only its type.

P2.13   Produce a three-step figure analogous to Fig. 2.14. Assume that the data being received is a single score of three digits.

P2.14   For each school in Clearwater District, three pieces of information have been assembled for a report.

	school name	enrollment	average family income
(1)	FOXMEADOW	300	$19,500.00
(2)	BROOKVIEW	450	$18,700.00
(3)	CROSSTRACKS	500	$15,675.00

Write a program that will report the facts on each school and produce a clearly labeled average enrollment and average family income for the district as a whole. Declare all variables used, and test your program.

A PROGRAM ILLUSTRATING DECLARATIONS

Figure 2.15 presents a short program that incorporates declaration of all four types of data. When given appropriate input, it produces a single-line report

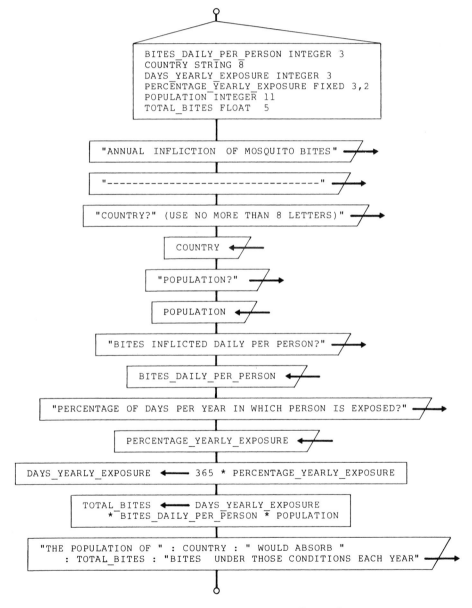

Fig. 2.15 BITES—a declaration illustration.

estimating the total number of mosquito bites annually inflicted on a country's population. This program is written to be run interactively, as the data is entered. Many messages are transmitted to guide the program's user in entering the data.

Private Practice

P2.15   Assume that in a major city there are 5000 pigeons per square mile and that each pigeon drops 13 feathers on the streets per day. Write FEATHERS, a program structured like BITES, to report on the total number of feathers dropped per year in any city for which data is entered.

P2.16   Modify FEATHERS so that the number of pigeons per square mile and the number of feathers dropped per pigeon are both entered as data by the program's user.

BASIC Interpretation of Chapter 1

INTRODUCTION

The following is the first of a series of sections on interpreting FPL in a particular, commonly available language, BASIC. One such section will follow every chapter or two of FPL. The sections and figures are keyed to corresponding FPL material. Most figures are translations of FPL programs and cite the original program by figure number. The figure identifiers in these BASIC sections are themselves unique because each includes the letter B for BASIC. For example, the very first figure bears the legend Fig. B1.1: BASIC for Figure 1.26. Labeling it (B1.1) suggests it is a BASIC (B) figure for Chapter one (1) and the first figure in the section (.1).

Because BASIC is an old language, many versions do not recognize lowercase letters except in data or within quotation marks. Examples in this text follow this convention. Note that most terminals do not allow a curvature distinction between open (") and closed (") quotes, using (") for both.

FUNDAMENTALS IN BASIC

Translating FPL into BASIC is simple and direct, as shown in Fig. B1.1. However, since BASIC for one computer tends to differ slightly from BASIC for the next computer, you should anticipate the need to adjust the BASIC material here slightly for use on your particular computer. In general, you should try

```
00010 REM---TRANSLATION OF FIG. 1.26-------------
00020 REM     NORMA KAISER     11/11/80
00030 REM A : AVERAGE
00040 REM N : NUMBER
00050 REM T : TOTAL
00060 REM---------------------------------------
00100 T = 0
00200 INPUT N
00300 T = T + N
00400 INPUT N
00500 T = T + N
00600 INPUT N
00700 T = T + N
00800 INPUT N
00900 T = T + N
01000 A = T / 4
01100 PRINT "The average score was "; A
01200 END
```

Fig. B1.1 BASIC for Fig. 1.26.

what is suggested here, and if it doesn't work, consult an expert (experienced user) or the manufacturer's documentation for your computer's BASIC.

Compare the BASIC translation to the original and note the following.

1. Details take the form of uniquely numbered *lines* in BASIC.

2. The REM (short for REMARK) statements are not interpreted by the computer as an instruction to do anything; a REM is merely listed and ignored. REMs should be used to identify the program and programmer.

10 REM—TRANSLATION OF FIGURE 1.26
12 REM BY: NORMA KAISER 11/11/80

They can also be used to clarify other details (see (6)).

3. The NEXT connection is established in BASIC by the sequential order of the line numbers—thus line 700 will be executed after line 600, line 1100 after line 1000. The increment between successive line numbers is arbitrary but should leave room for the insertion of additional lines when the inevitable modification becomes necessary.

4. In internal assignments, = replaces ←——— . Thus

100 T = 0

replaces

TOTAL ◄— 0

5. In external assignments, the key word INPUT replaces ←——— ; the key word PRINT replaces ——→ . Thus

200 INPUT N

replaces the first

NUMBER ◄—

and

    1100 PRINT "AVERAGE WAS:"; A

replaces

    "THE AVERAGE SCORE WAS": AVERAGE $\longrightarrow$

6. Datanames are so short that comments (REM statements) explaining them are required.

    20 REM N : NUMBER

(Some BASICs allow longer datanames. Use them if your version has them.)

7. To label outgoing values in external assignments, ; replaces : . (See the assignments involving AVERAGE in (5).)

8. The key word END replaces the STOP circle.

RUNNING YOUR PROGRAM ON YOUR COMPUTER

To enter a BASIC program, you must first inform your computer that you are going to work in BASIC. You should either ask someone familiar with your machine or consult the manufacturer's documentation as to how to do this. Once you have found out (usually a fairly simple process), begin typing in your program. At any point, you can list what you have typed in so far by typing

    LIST

and pressing (RETURN) (the RETURN key).

To help correct errors and make changes, your computer will provide some sort of editing facilities. To find out how to use them, consult an experienced user or the manufacturer's documentation. The simplest facilities may work as follows.

1. To delete a line: type the line's number and press [RETURN]

2. To change a line: type the line's number, retype the line, press [RETURN].

3. To add or insert a line: type a previously unused number followed by the desired text in BASIC, press [RETURN]. (To insert between two existing lines, choose a number whose value lies *between* those of the two lines.)

Try these steps out, consulting your computer's documentation if surprising results occur.

Warning: Try all these things out on a little program until you are confident about how they work on your machine. It is better to learn before you start manipulating any large programs whose size alone would make retyping a chore.

While you are working on your program, it is in the computer's memory; when you sign off, logout, or quit, it will be erased. To preserve your program for use later, you must name it and tell the computer to save it under that name by storing it on disk, tape cassette, or other external medium. For example, suppose we call the program above ADDER. On most systems, it could be saved merely by typing

SAVE ADDER [RETURN]

To retrieve a program previously saved, you cite the program name in a different command. For example, most systems retrieve ADDER if one of the following is entered.

OLD ADDER [RETURN]

or

LOAD ADDER [RETURN]

To run a program currently in memory, simply type

RUN [RETURN]

For variations on this command and on the others already mentioned, see an experienced user or the documentation for your system.

Private Practice BASIC

BP1.1   Find out how to type the program in Fig. B1.1 into your particular computer and do so. Run the program. (The INPUT lines will probably prompt you with a ? for input: Respond by typing in a value for NUMBER.)

BP1.2   Translate your solution to (P1.4) into BASIC and run it on your computer. Use ages 13 and 10.

BP1.3   Using your FPL solution to (P1.9) as a guide, modify your BASIC for (BP1.1) to handle five numbers instead of only four.

MAKING THE COMPUTER CREATE THE TRACE TABLE

Having the computer create a trace table for a BASIC program is also simple and direct. Figure B1.2 shows the temporary additions (extra PRINT lines) inserted in the averaging program to produce a trace of the execution. Each extra PRINT line forces the computer to print one line of the trace table.

PRINT "T: ";T; "N: ";N; "A: ";A

```
00010 REM---TRANSLATION OF FIG. 1.27-------------
00020 REM      NORMA KAISER     11/11/80
00030 REM A : AVERAGE
00040 REM N : NUMBER
00050 REM T : TOTAL
00060 REM-----------------------------------------
00075     PRINT "T: "; T; "    N:"; N; "    A:"; A
00100 T = 0
00150     PRINT "T: "; T; "    N:"; N; "    A:"; A
00200 INPUT N
00250     PRINT "T: "; T; "    N:"; N; "    A:"; A
00300 T = T + N
00350     PRINT "T: "; T; "    N:"; N; "    A:"; A
00400 INPUT N
00450     PRINT "T: "; T; "    N:"; N; "    A:"; A
00500 T = T + N
00550     PRINT "T: "; T; "    N:"; N; "    A:"; A
00600 INPUT N
00650     PRINT "T: "; T; "    N:"; N; "    A:"; A
00700 T = T + N
00750     PRINT "T: "; T; "    N:"; N; "    A:"; A
00800 INPUT N
00850     PRINT "T: "; T; "    N:"; N; "    A:"; A
00900 T = T + N
00950     PRINT "T: "; T; "    N:"; N; "    A:"; A
01000 A = T / 4
01050     PRINT "T: "; T; "    N:"; N; "    A:"; A
01100 PRINT "The average score was "; A
01150     PRINT "T: "; T; "    N:"; N; "    A:"; A
01200 END
```

Fig. B1.2 Using extra PRINT lines to trace.

Here the labels printed are the datanames used in the BASIC program. It may sometimes be more helpful to print more descriptive labels such as

PRINT "TOTAL: ";T, "NUMBER: ";N, "AVERAGE: ";A

The choice is the programmer's.

Remember: To enter such trace lines in a program already in memory, simply type the additional lines, one at a time, with the appropriate line numbers thus.

150 PRINT "T: ";T; "N: ";N; "A: ";A `RETURN`

The computer will insert each into the program according to its line number.

Private Practice BASIC

BP 1.4   Enter the trace lines in your program and rerun it. (Don't be surprised because the trace table is interrupted regularly by your inputting of the values for NUMBER!)

BP 1.5   Rerun the trace version (BP1.4) using the data in (P1.8) and compare the results with the table you generated by hand for (P1.8).

BP 1.6   Add a PRINT statement before each INPUT statement in your (BP1.1) program so that the user of the program will be prompted with an appropriate word (rather than just a ?) to solicit input of the number.

BASIC Interpretation of Chapter 2

DECLARATIONS IN BASIC

Declarations are minimal in BASIC as suggested by the BASIC translation shown in Fig. B2.1.

```
00100    REM-----TRANSLATION OF FIG. 2.15----------------------
00200    REM        BOB GANNON        9/21/79
00300    REM C1$ : COUNTRY, 8 LETTERS
00400    REM P1% : P%, 11 DIGITS
00500    REM B1% : BITES_DAILY_PER_PERSON, 3 DIGITS
00600    REM E1  : PERCENTAGE_YEARLY_EXPOSURE, FIXED 3,2
00700    REM E2 : DAYS_YEARLY_EXPOSURE, 3 DIGITS
00800    REM T1  : TOTAL_BITES, 5 SIGNIFICANT DIGITS (FLOAT)
00900    REM --------------------------------------------------
01000    PRINT "Annual Infliction of Mosquito Bites"
01100    PRINT "----------------------------------"
01200    PRINT "Country (use no more than 8 letters)"
01300    INPUT C1$
01400    PRINT "Population"
01500    INPUT P1%
01600    PRINT "Bites inflicted daily per person"
01700    INPUT B1%
01800    PRINT "Percentage of days per year in which person is exposed"
01900    PRINT "     (Enter as decimal, eg, for 73%, enter .73)"
02000    INPUT E1
02100    E2 = 365 * E1
02200    T1 = E2 * B1% * P1%
02300    PRINT "The population of ";C1$; " would absorb ";T1; " bites";
02400    PRINT " annually under those conditions."
02500    END
```

Fig. B2.1 BASIC translation of Fig. 2.15.

Compare this program to the FPL original and note the following about declarations.

1. Declaration in BASIC is limited to TYPE. *TYPE is assumed by default to be FLOAT.* To force the computer to treat a variable as other than FLOAT, that variable's dataname must end in a special character: $ for STRING, % for INTEGER. For example, in this program C1$ (COUNTRY) is STRING and P1% (POPULATION) is INTEGER. *There is no FIXED type in BASIC.*

2. SIZE cannot be declared or otherwise set by the programmer; it is handled by default assumptions built into the particular BASIC implementation. If the program is designed to expect a particular size integer or fixed value, the user entering the value should be instructed accordingly.

1800 PRINT "Percentage of days per year in which person is exposed"

1900 PRINT "(Enter as decimal, e.g., for 73%, enter .73)"

It is the programmer's job to warn about limits on the size of any particular value where the size of the value a user might naturally choose would exceed the limit allowed by the BASIC implementation. In this program for example, if the implementation determined integer size limit were six digits, the programmer could change P1% to P1 and advise the user that populations greater than 999,999 must be entered in FLOAT format.

3. The SIZE of all string data is VARYING, within a maximum length (the maximum is set by the implementation and might be anything from one to several hundred characters, depending on the implementation). If the program expects a string of a particular length, the program should so inform the user.

1200 PRINT "Country (use no more than 8 letters)"

4. A numeric item not declared to be integer (%) will be printed in decimal notation unless it is too large or too small. If it is too large or too small, it will be printed in FLOAT format. (You will illustrate this for yourself in (BP2.1) and (BP2.5).)

5. Since declaration is done indirectly in BASIC and relies heavily on defaults, the descriptive REMs with which the program begins should include exact data characteristics for each variable.

300 REM C1% : COUNTRY STRING 8

6. Variable types may have to be adjusted to avoid size limitation problems. For example, in this program T1 must be FLOAT to avoid the assignment of too large an integer value in

2200 T1 = E2 * B1% * P1%

Because so many implementation details vary slightly from one version of BASIC to another, you should experiment with yours to identify exactly how it works.

Private Practice BASIC

BP2.1   Enter the program in Fig. B2.1 into your computer and run it. By feeding it very small values on one run and very large on another, try to discover how it handles numeric data (e.g., what size forces it to use floating point notation upon output? How large an integer will it accept as input?).

BP2.2   Omitting episodes and including appropriate REMs, translate each of the following into BASIC: (P2.2), (P2.3), (P2.5), and (P2.7).

BP2.3   Translate your program for (P2.14) into BASIC and run it.

BP2.4   Translate your second FEATHERS program (P2.16) into BASIC and run it.

BP2.5   Implementers of BASIC often include a facility called *immediate mode* in their implementation. In immediate mode, a line of BASIC not preceded by a line number is executed as soon as RETURN is pressed. If your implementation of BASIC includes an immediate mode, experiment with it to learn more about how BASIC handles very large numbers, long and short strings, and decimals. For example, to see how large an integer your BASIC will print in integer form, enter the following four statements in immediate mode, one after another.

        A = 123
        B = 12345678
        C = 1234567890123
        PRINT A, B, C

From the result, experiment further to find out how to enter a floating point value through an INPUT statement. Experiment with inputting, concatenating, and printing various strings as well.

A Package of Data Items– The RECORD

INTRODUCTION

So far, we have discussed individual data items. Frequently, we also treat a *collection* of individual data items and their storage locations as though the whole comprised a single data item with its own dataname. In such cases, a program can reference, by name, the collection or any constituent item. FPL calls such collections *data structures*. We deal with two, the record and the array.

WHAT IS A RECORD?—A SIMPLE EXAMPLE

A *record* is a collection of distinct data items that belong together. For example, suppose we wished to collect test scores on each of a number of participants in a program to improve reading abilities. For each such student, we need his or her (1) name, (2) age in years, (3) year in school, and (4) test score. For each student this information forms a record of the form suggested by Fig. 3.1. Though items such as *name* and *test score* differ sharply in type (string versus numeric type), they are nonetheless collected into a single record. Every student, after all, has both a name *and* a test score.

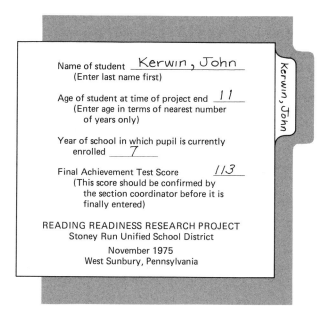

Fig. 3.1 Typical record of a student in a reading project.

Since each item forming a part of the record has a distinct identity, it is common to refer to each by its own name.

Thus, as Fig. 3.2 suggests, not only does the record (collection) as a whole have a dataname but each field (item) within the record also has its own individual dataname. This combination of group and individual datanames gives the programmer a great deal of flexibility in addressing and manipulating the data constituting the record. He or she has access to the record as a whole through the record's dataname, and to any of the record's fields through the individual datanames of the separate fields.

Record or record component	Appropriate dataname
The student's reading record	STUDENT_REC
The student's name	NAME
The student's age in years	AGE
The student's year in school	YEAR_IN_SCHOOL
The student's final score on reading achievement test	TEST_SCORE

Fig. 3.2 Listing the components of a record.

Since a record is a collection of data items, the computer must be informed of its collective nature at the start of any program in which a particular record is used. For example, the record shown above is officially declared in Fig. 3.3. As shown, the declaration sets aside storage areas that can be addressed either individually or as a collection.

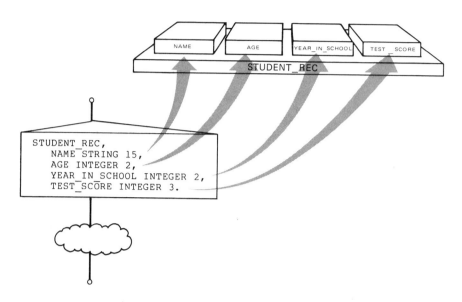

```
STUDENT_REC,
    NAME STRING 15,
    AGE INTEGER 2,
    YEAR_IN_SCHOOL INTEGER 2,
    TEST_SCORE INTEGER 3.
```

Fig. 3.3 Record declaration and storage.

The dataname of the record is listed first, on the top line; the data-name of each field is then listed beneath, one field per line. Field datanames are indented to show their subordinate character within the hierarchy of the collection. Each field must carry its own declaration. Each line of the record declaration must end with a comma, except the last, which ends with a period. Note that no type or size is specified for the dataname of the record as a whole. Such a specification would be meaningless because the collection itself has no single type or size.

RECORD DECLARATION AND USE

Though the exact way in which records are manipulated depends on the hardware particulars of the computer, the general process does not and *must* be understood by any competent programmer.

Figures 3.4–3.7 illustrate how records and their fields can be manipulated. The particular record (PUPIL_RECORD) used has three parts (NAME, STREAM, and AGE), and the corresponding memory locations are presented as boxes, resting on a common record frame. An additional data variable (TO-TAL) is also shown, along with its corresponding memory box. The illustrations include a pair of assignments to manipulate the data variables: the first is external, the second internal.

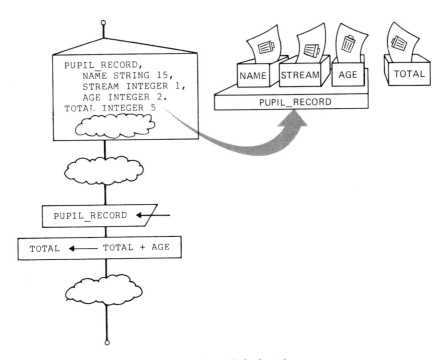

Fig. 3.4 Record declaration.

First, as suggested by Fig. 3.4, the computer must be forced to set aside appropriate storage for the record. This requires that distinct locations be set aside and datanamed for each field in the record (NAME, STREAM, and AGE in the example), and that the collection of fields be given its own, overall dataname (PUPIL_RECORD in the example). This is essential so that separate fields (NAME, STREAM, and AGE), as well as the record as a whole (PUPIL_RECORD), can be addressed in the subsequent program.

Figure 3.5 presents a set of stored data values resulting from the execution of all code prior to point (t). It includes values for TOTAL, NAME, STREAM, and AGE.

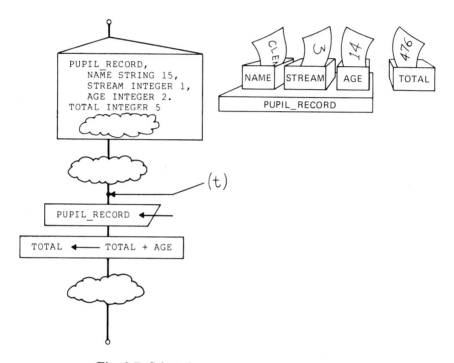

Fig. 3.5 Selected memory contents, at point (t).

By citing the record dataname in an assignment, the programmer can force the computer to manipulate all the fields in the record. In Fig. 3.6, the illustrated external assignment forces the computer to read enough data to fill each field in the record. Thus the value ARISTOTLE replaces CLEMENCEAU in the location datanamed NAME; the value 2 replaces 3 in the location datanamed STREAM; and the value 13 replaces 14 in the location datanamed AGE—all as the result of citing one dataname in one external assignment. (Though not shown in the example, an external assignment designed to write out the contents of PUPIL_RECORD would work in the reverse fashion.) Figure 3.7 illustrates in four stages how access to items within the record is also retained. By citing the dataname of a specific field within a record, the programmer can force the computer to deal *only* with that field, just as though it

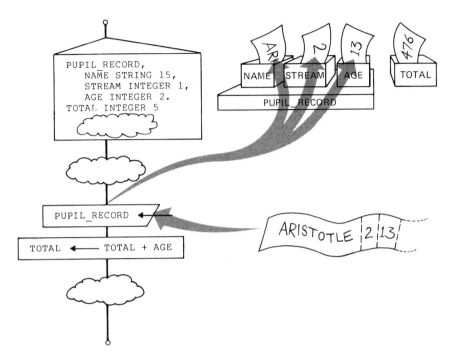

Fig. 3.6 Executing a record-citing assignment.

were any individual dataname and not part of a structure. This sequence illustrates (1) how values are looked up and retrieved from their datanamed memory locations (Stages I and II), (2) how the result of the specified computation
involving these values effectively replaces the expression leading to the computation (Stage III), and (3) how that resulting value is used to rewrite the contents of the memory location named as the target of the assignment (Stage IV).
(Thus the value 13 from AGE and the value 476 from TOTAL are added and
the result, 489, is stored as the new contents of the specified location, TOTAL.)
Though our example deals only with AGE in PUPIL_RECORD, other fields of
the record could be similarly cited and manipulated. Whether used in external
or internal assignments, datanames of fields within records can be used freely—
the computer will correctly locate and manipulate the value stored in the appropriate storage location just as if the field were an individual data item.

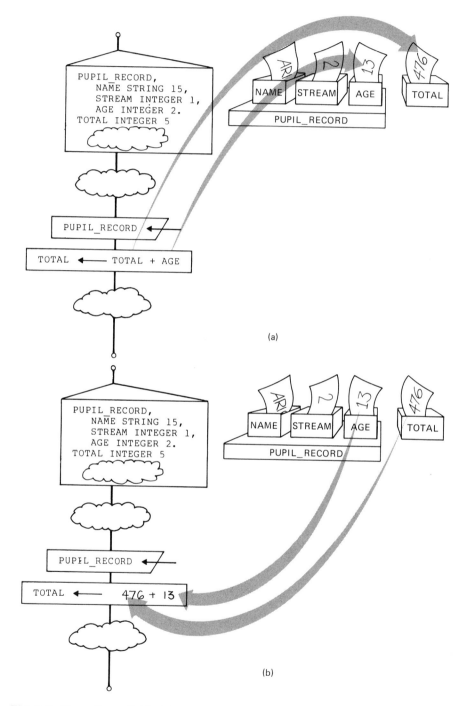

Fig. 3.7 Executing a field-citing assignment (a) Stage I; (b) Stage II; (c) Stage III; and (d) Stage IV.

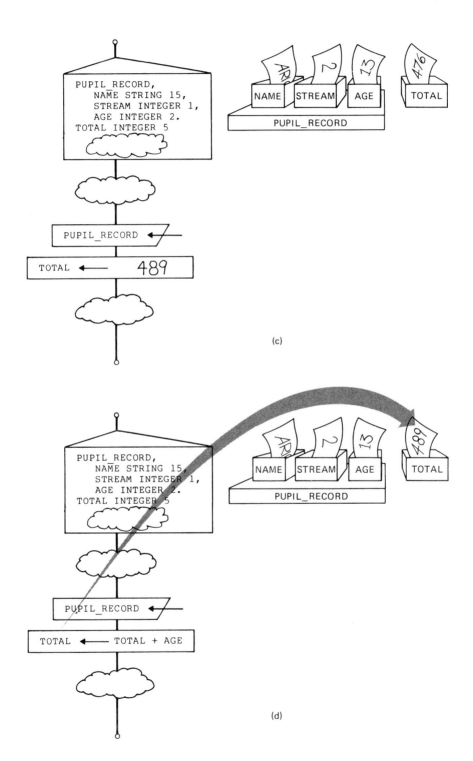

(c)

(d)

READING RECORDS OF DATA FROM THE DATA STREAM

Let's illustrate how records are used to read from the data stream with a short example. In the process, we will further illustrate trace table usage. Figure 3.8(a) presents a brief segment of FPL in which a record is used to read data into the computer from the data stream. Appropriate execution reference points are labeled on the code. At the bottom of the illustration is a length of data stream, encoded for easy reading. Each time the external assignment is executed, a complete record's worth of data is extracted from the stream, as suggested in the illustration. Figure 3.8(b) presents a trace table completed when the program was run against the data stream.

Private Practice

P3.1   Design a record to handle the following information on each of a number of books: (1) title, (2) author, (3) publisher, (4) publication date, and (5) cost. Illustrate your design with storage locations for your record, representing them with jars or boxes.

P3.2   Assume that the external assignment involving PUPIL_RECORD in Fig. 3.6 was incorrectly written and should have shown the arrow pointing outward. Completely redraw the figure, so that it shows the transmission of data *from* a record. (Assume the data values shown in PUPIL_RECORD in Fig. 3.5.)

P3.3   Suppose that in the series of drawings making up Fig. 3.7, the external assignment should read

Using the same incoming data (ARISTOTLE, etc.), what changes (if any) should be made in the series of drawings to illustrate the effect of this new, alternative assignment? How would the execution of this new assignment differ from that of the original?

P3.4   Revise the code shown in Fig. 3.7(d) so that instead of adding the age to some total, the stream value for the pupil is changed to one more than whatever was found in the record. Then cause this new value of STREAM to be printed out, along with the pupil's name, without printing his or her age.

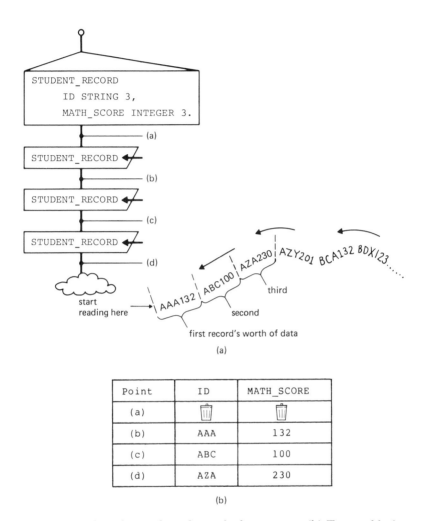

Fig. 3.8 (a) Record-reading code and sample data stream. (b) Trace table for record-reading code.

P3.5   The following program reads three student records and averages their scores, printing each record after reading it and printing the computed average at the end. Use the test data of the three records shown after the program to run it. Create a table, setting up appropriate column headings for the various datanames, and fill in the table as you run the program on the test data. If you detect any errors, specify what they are.

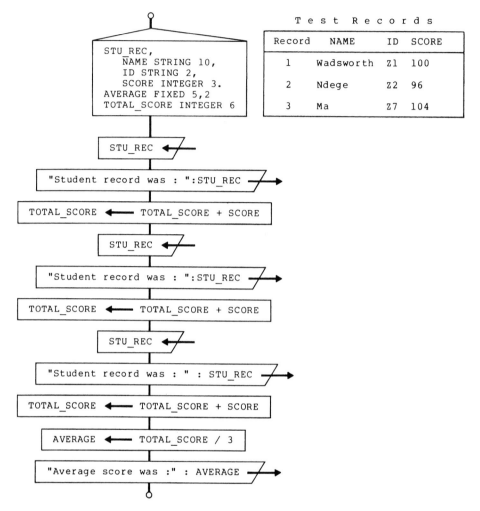

MORE ABOUT DATA STREAMS—FILES

Most programs use at least two different streams of data—one or more incoming, and one or more outgoing. Just as it is necessary to provide names (datanames) by which the computer can identify each data item and record it, so is it necessary to provide names by which the computer can identify each data stream it must use.

Data streams are referred to as *data files* probably because of the association with manual record keeping and filing systems. In such systems, a collection of paper records is often referred to as a *file,* whether it is a collection of personnel records, of student records, or of machine part records.

Files are given names primarily so that they can be distinguished from each other within a single program. If a program, like many of the programs presented in this book, uses only two files (one input and one output), it is unnecessary to name the files. For such programs, we assume the computer can identify the file merely by the direction of the arrow in each external assignment. In a sense, the computer tracks files by *default naming,* and we say any file not explicitly named by the programmer must be one of the two default files. In FPL, we do not concern ourselves with the specific devices (printer, card reader, terminal, other computer or TV-like screen) reading or writing default files, though when you begin to use other languages, you will need to know such details. In most problems and illustrations in this book, we will continue to primarily use the two default files. Occasionally, however, problems will require multiple files that must be named. They will be named as suggested below.

Naming and Declaring Files

Of course some programs use more than two files. For example, a program designed to produce grade reports for students might require both a course-results file and a student-address file, so that it can prepare a mailable record for each student. Such a program must indicate to the computer which file is to be read by each external assignment, so that data can be extracted from the correct file.

We handle this in FPL by displaying a specific *filename* immediately to the right of the arrow piercing the external assignment. The filename appears inside a file symbol. Figure 3.9 illustrates that records are read from both ADR_MASTER and GRADE_MASTER and that they are transmitted into GRADE_MAILERS.

Each named file must be declared. The declaration must indicate whether the file is for input or for output. It must be declared as INPUT if the program is to receive data from that file, as OUTPUT if the program is to transmit data into that file. Figure 3.10 presents reasonable declarations for the files discussed above. Above the file declarations are those of the three records respectively associated with them by assignments such as in Fig. 3.9.

ADR_MASTER is a file of student addresses, each in the form ADDRESS_REC. Similarly, GRADE_MASTER is a file of grades for the students. The data for one student has the form GRADE_REC. Both ADR_MASTER and GRADE_MASTER are files from which the program will read or receive records. On the other hand, the file called GRADE_MAILERS is created by this program as an outgoing stream of data formatted into records matching STU_GRADE_RPT.

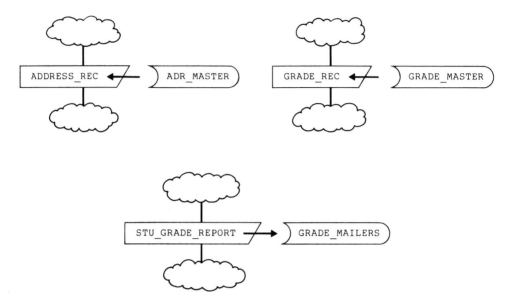

Fig. 3.9 External assignments using named files.

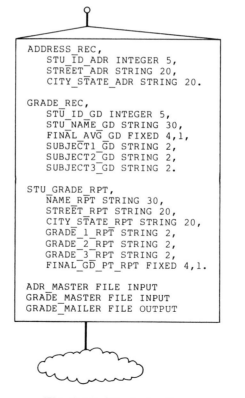

```
ADDRESS_REC,
    STU_ID_ADR INTEGER 5,
    STREET_ADR STRING 20,
    CITY_STATE_ADR STRING 20.

GRADE_REC,
    STU_ID_GD INTEGER 5,
    STU_NAME_GD STRING 30,
    FINAL_AVG_GD FIXED 4,1,
    SUBJECT1_GD STRING 2,
    SUBJECT2_GD STRING 2,
    SUBJECT3_GD STRING 2.

STU_GRADE_RPT,
    NAME_RPT STRING 30,
    STREET_RPT STRING 20,
    CITY_STATE_RPT STRING 20,
    GRADE_1_RPT STRING 2,
    GRADE_2_RPT STRING 2,
    GRADE_3_RPT STRING 2,
    FINAL_GD_PT_RPT FIXED 4,1.

ADR_MASTER FILE INPUT
GRADE_MASTER FILE INPUT
GRADE_MAILER FILE OUTPUT
```

Fig. 3.10 File declaration.

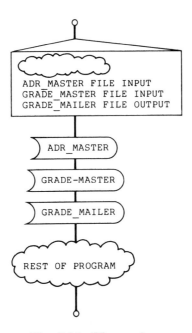

Fig. 3.11 File opening.

Finally, each file cited by name must be opened before it can be used by external assignment. As shown in Fig. 3.11, a file is opened by inserting its name box between NEXTs, immediately following the declarations. Opening sets the reading or writing to begin at a particular place in the file, usually (in this book *always*) at the beginning. For example, following the file opening in Fig. 3.11, the first execution of

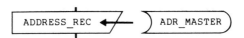

will place a copy of the first record in ADR_MASTER in ADDRESS_REC.

A Program to Create a File of Records

A program to create a file of records is shown in Fig. 3.12, along with sample data. It puts record data for exactly two students into a file that is called STU-DENTS. The input is coming from an unnamed file but output is going to the declared STUDENTS. Note that STUDENTS must be opened.

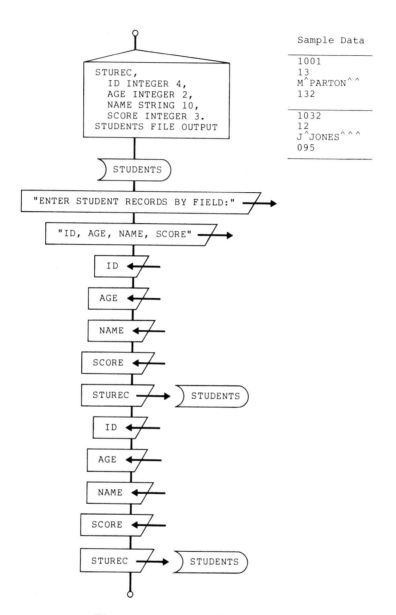

Fig. 3.12 Creating a file of records.

A Program to Read Records from a File

A program to read records from STUDENTS appears in Fig. 3.13. (The three execution reference points are included for later use.) It reads the records, averages the scores in them, and reports the average. This time the input comes from the named file STUDENTS and the output goes to the default output file. Again, the named file must be opened.

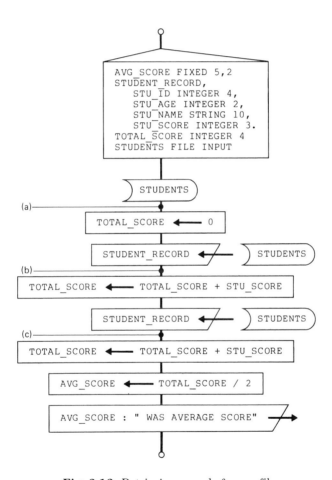

Fig. 3.13 Retrieving records from a file.

Note that each of the two programs uses a differently named record to work with the file STUDENTS. However, for corresponding fields, the types and sizes agree exactly.

Tracing the Process of Reading Records

Besides the usual trace table completion, it is often useful to trace the execution of a program through the contents of each of its data files. To do this, we arrange the contents in a row and use a vertical arrow to indicate the point to which the reading or writing has advanced.

For example, from the sample data shown, the program in Fig. 3.12 would produce a version of STUDENTS which we would arrange as

100113M∧PARTON∧∧132103212J∧jones∧∧∧095

We can trace execution through the file in terms of points (a), (b), and (c) (Fig. 3.13), as the program is executed. Immediately after opening the file, execution point (a) would have been reached, and the file reader would be set to the start of the file

100113M∧PARTON∧∧132103212J∧jones∧∧∧095
|

(a)

After reading one record (b), the file reader would be set at the start of the next record

100113M∧PARTON∧∧132103212J∧jones∧∧∧095
                    |

(b)

After reading the next record (c), the file reader would be set at the start of the following record (in this particular case, the end of the file).

100113M∧PARTON∧∧132103212J∧jones∧∧∧095
                                     |

(c)

A complete trace of the program's reading of this file would be

100113M∧PARTON∧∧132103212J∧jones∧∧∧095
| | |

(a)   (b)   (c)

A Final Note: Different Types of Files

The type of file discussed so far is referred to as *sequential* because the items or records are organized in a given sequence within the file. Figure 3.14 illustrates a sequence of student records stored on magnetic tape. Sequential file organization is the simplest and the most commonly used of all schemes of file organization. Its simplicity has a price, however, that makes it unsuitable for some applications. To read any particular record on the file, *all* preceding records on the file must be read first. Thus in the tape file shown, record 3 could not be read until records 1 and 2 had first been read. In situations involving thousands of records, where only selected records deep within the file are of interest, sequential organization results in thousands of unnecessary records being read.

The alternative involves going directly to a particular record within a file. That scheme of file organization is called *direct access* because it allows the program to go directly to the record desired, without reading any other records. Direct access schemes of organization require that, as a record is entered in the file originally, a unique key to that record be entered as well.

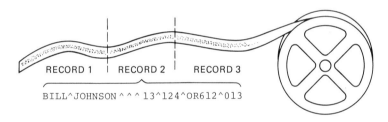

Fig. 3.14 Sequential file.

The computer stores the record on some device controlled by, but outside of, the computer, and in an index stores the key and the exact address where it stored that particular record. At any subsequent time, given the key, the computer is able, by the index, to retrieve the exact record wanted, without reading any of the other records in the file.

Private Practice

P3.6   The following data is in STUDENTS

122014JOHNSTONE∧126123613SMITH∧∧∧∧∧115129114BALDWIN . . .

Execute the reading program (Fig. 3.13) on this file and trace execution through this file by using a vertical arrow to mark the spot within the file to which reading has advanced by the time execution has reached each of the points (a), (b), and (c).

P3.7   Modify the data reading program (Fig. 3.13) so that it reports on the average age rather than score and so that it writes this average into a sequential file called AGE.

P3.8   Modify the programs in Figs. 3.12 and 3.13 so that they deal with teacher salary rather than student scores. Assume a record format identical to

STAFF_REC,

ID	INTEGER 6,
CODE	INTEGER 2,
SALARY	FIXED 7,2

Assume data on ten teachers is in that sequential file TEACHER, and that your report is to be written into a file called STFRPT. That report should list the code and salary of each staff member and end with the average salary of them all. To write the data on one teacher, transmit CODE, SALARY into STFRPT.

BASIC Interpretation of Chapter 3

RECORDS AND FILES IN BASIC

Transmitting records into a file is illustrated by the BASIC in Fig. B3.1; reading records from a file, in Fig. B3.2.

Note the following.

1. There is no record structure in BASIC. Handling a collection of two or more items as a record can be accomplished by citing all the items in the record, in order, in any external assignment involving the record. For example, in Fig. B3.1, a "record" is written by

01750 PRINT #1, I1% ; "," ; A1% ; "," ; N1$; "," ; S1%

and in Fig. B3.2, a "record" is read by

02000 INPUT #5, I2%, A2%, N2$, S2%

(The #5 and #1 are file identifiers explained in (4).)

2. Because there is no record structure, a record cannot be declared to the computer. However, if two or more items are to be treated as a record conceptually, the program should declare this to the reader through appropriate REMs.

00400	REM STUDENT_RECORD,
00500	REM I2% : STU_ID INTEGER 4
00600	REM A2% : STU_AGE INTEGER 2
00700	REM N2$: STU_NAME STRING 20
00800	REM S2% : STU_SCORE INTEGER 3

3. A file's name, use (INPUT or OUTPUT), and identity number must be declared in an OPEN statement at the start of the program.

1100 OPEN "STUBAS.DAT" FOR OUTPUT AS FILE #1 is an example from the program in Fig. B3.1. The file's name is STUBAS.DAT, its use is for output (data will be transmitted into it), and its identity number is #1. A second example is provided by the OPEN in Fig. B3.2 (line 1600). Other uses besides INPUT and OUTPUT exist and can be explored in terms of your version of BASIC if appropriate. For example, some BASICs have a MODIFY that allows data to be added to the end of a previously created file. We will not explore such uses in this book.

```
00100    REM----TRANSLATION OF FIG. 3.12--------------------
00200    REM          BILL GORMAN      9/80
00300    REM
00400    REM STUREC,
00500    REM     Il% : ID, 4 DIGITS
00600    REM     Al% : AGE, 2 DIGITS
00700    REM     N1$ : NAME, 20 CHARACTERS
00800    REM     S1% : SCORE, 3 DIGITS
00900    REM STUBAS.DAT : STUDENTS, OUTPUT FILE
01000    REM-------------------------------------------------
01100    OPEN "STUBAS.DAT" FOR OUTPUT AS FILE #1
01200    PRINT "Enter student record by fields"
01300    PRINT "ID, AGE, NAME, SCORE"
01400    INPUT Il%
01500    INPUT Al%
01600    INPUT N1$
01700    INPUT S1%
01750    PRINT #1, Il%; ","; Al%; ","; N1$; ","; S1%
01800    PRINT "Enter student record by fields"
01900    PRINT "ID, AGE, NAME, SCORE"
02000    INPUT Il%
02100    INPUT Al%
02200    INPUT N1$
02300    INPUT S1%
02350    PRINT #1, Il%; ","; Al%; ","; N1$; ","; S1%
02400    CLOSE #1
02500    END
```

Fig. B3.1 BASIC translation of file-creating program in Fig. 3.12.

```
00100    REM---TRANSLATION OF FIG. 3.13 ---------------------
00200    REM          BILL GORMAN      9/80
00300    REM
00400    REM STUDENT_RECORD,
00500    REM     I2% : STU_ID, 4 DIGITS
00600    REM     A2% : STU_AGE, 2 DIGITS
00700    REM     N2$ : STU_NAME, 20 CHARACTERS
00800    REM     S2% : STU_SCORE, 3 DIGITS
00900    REM T1% : TOTAL_SCORE, 5 DIGITS
01000    REM A4 : AVG_SCORE, FIXED 5,3
01400    REM STUBAS.DAT : STUDENTS, INPUT FILE
01500    REM-------------------------------------------------
01600    OPEN "STUBAS.DAT" FOR INPUT AS FILE #5
01700    PRINT "This program reads file of student records"
01800    PRINT " and calculates the average score."
01900    T1% = 0
02000    INPUT #5, I2%, A2%, N2$, S2%
02100    T1% = T1% + S2%
02200    INPUT #5, I2%, A2%, N2$, S2%
02300    T1% = T1% + S2%
02400    A4 = T1%/2
02500    PRINT A4; " was average score."
02600    CLOSE #5
02700    END
```

Fig. B3.2 BASIC translation of file-reading program in Fig. 3.13.

4. The file is identified outside the OPEN by number, not name. For example, once STUBAS.DAT has been opened as FILE #1 in Fig. B3.1, it is thereafter cited by number only: lines 1750, 2350, and 2400. Similarly, once opened as FILE #5 in Fig. B3.2, STUBAS.DAT is thereafter cited only as #5: lines 2000, 2200, and 2600. Thus with the file identified by number and record elements all cited individually, the BASIC

01750 PRINT #1, I1%; ","; A1%, ","; N1$; ","; S1%

replaces the FPL

and in Fig. B3.2,

02000   INPUT #5, I2%, A2%, N2$, S2%

replaces the FPL

5. The computer must be told to close the file at the end of its use of that file. This is done through the CLOSE as illustrated in Fig. B3.1.

2400 CLOSE #1

Figure B3.2 provides a second example in line 2600.

The conventions for naming files vary from one version of BASIC to another and hence the examples here will not work for every BASIC, nor will the OPENs themselves. (Some BASICs do not include significant file-handling capabilities at all!) You should consult the documentation for your BASIC to discover the acceptable form for file names.

You have noticed by this point that PRINT and INPUT statements are used to access files and that they look like regular PRINT and INPUT statements except for the presence of the file number between the key word and the dataname(s). This parallel format allows the computer to assume a default file of the terminal if no file number is specified. Thus

01750   PRINT #1, I1%; ","; A1%; ","; N1$; ","; S1%

sends the data to the file identified by 1, while

01800   PRINT "Enter student record by fields"

sends the data to the default file, the user's screen or printer.

Private Practice BASIC

BP3.1   Enter the program in Fig. B3.1 into your computer and run it, creating a file containing two records. Make up your own data.

BP3.2   Enter the program in Fig. B3.2 into your computer and run it, using as data the file created by (BP3.1).

BP3.3   Modify your versions of both programs (BP3.1 and BP3.2) so that four records instead of two are created and retrieved.

BP3.4   Modify your versions of both again, this time so that the record includes an additional, final field declared in FPL as

SCHOOL_FEES FIXED 7,2

BP3.5   Translate your solution to (P3.8) into BASIC, create a file TEACHER with data on ten teachers, and run your program on that file.

Pascal Interpretation of Chapters 1, 2, and 3

INTRODUCTION

The following is the first of a series of sections on interpreting FPL programming concepts in a particular, commonly available language, Pascal. One such section will follow every chapter or two of FPL. The sections and the figures in them are keyed to FPL material, as figure identifiers suggest. For example, in the identifier

Fig. P1.3

P signifies Pascal, 1 signifies a tie to Chapter One FPL, and .3 signifies the third figure in this section.

Because Pascal is a textual language and cannot represent constructs graphically the way FPL does, it must represent them by key words. Though Pascal makes no distinction between uppercase and lowercase letters, in the examples that follow, key words appear in uppercase letters. Note that most terminals do not make a curvature distinction between open (") and closed (") quotes, using (") for both.

A PROGRAM ILLUSTRATING FUNDAMENTALS

Translating FPL into Pascal is simple and direct, as shown in Fig. P1.1.

```
PROGRAM clf26 (input,output);
     (* Translation of Fig. 1.26 *)
     (* Jim Gorman      10/80 *)
     VAR
         number, total : INTEGER;
         average : REAL;
     BEGIN
         total := 0;
         READ (number);
         total := total + number;
         READ (number);
         total := total + number;
         READ (number);
         total := total + number;
         READ (number);
         total := total + number;
         average := (total / 4);
         WRITELN ('The average score was ', average:6:2)
     END. (* clf28*)
```

Fig. P1.1 Pascal translation of Fig. 1.26.

Compare this translation to the original FPL and note the following.

1. The program line (first line) is analogous to the FPL START circle. It must include the program name (clf18), the files to be used by the program (input, output), and a terminal semicolon. (The only files used by this
program are the default ones but they must be cited in the program line.)

2. Declarations are required and are recorded in a separate section,
much as in FPL. They begin on the line following the key word VAR and follow
on uniformly indented successive lines until all variables used in the program
have been declared. Thus

        VAR
                number, to tal : INTEGER;
                average   :
        REAL;

replaces the FPL

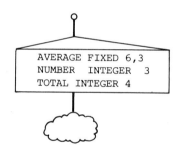

Note that size is not specified and that two or more items of the same type can
be declared together. Items are separated from each other by commas and from
the type specification by a colon. A type specification is followed by a semicolon. The standard TYPEs provided by Pascal include *integer, real,* and *char*
plus some types we will not deal with in this book. The program in Fig. P1.1
illustrates only integer and real. The next program (Fig. P2.1) illustrates
CHAR.

```
PROGRAM c2f15 (input,output);
     (* Translation of Fig. 2.15 *)
     (*  Nancy Smith      2/20/81   *)
   VAR
     country : ARRAY[1..8] OF CHAR;
     population : INTEGER;
     bitesdailyperperson : INTEGER;
     percentageyearlyexposure : REAL;
     daysyearlyexposure : REAL;
     totalbites : REAL;
   BEGIN
     WRITELN('Annual infliction of mosquito bites');
     WRITELN('---------------------------');
     WRITELN('Country?  (exactly 8 letters -- if too long, abbreviate');
     WRITELN('      if too short, add blanks)');
     READLN;
     READ(country[1]);
     READ(country[2]);
     READ(country[3]);
     READ(country[4]);
     READ(country[5]);
     READ(country[6]);
     READ(country[7]);
     READ(country[8]);
     WRITELN('Population?');
     READ(population);
     WRITELN('Bites inflicted daily per person (estimate)?');
     READ(bitesdailyperperson);
     WRITELN('Percentage of days per year in which person is exposed ');
     WRITELN('      to mosquitoes? (Use decimal, eg, .73 for 73%, etc)');
     READ(percentageyearlyexposure);
     daysyearlyexposure := 365.0 * percentageyearlyexposure;
     totalbites := daysyearlyexposure * bitesdailyperperson * population;
     WRITELN('The population of ',country, ' would absorb ',totalbites:4,
             ' bites under such conditions.');
   END. (* c2f15 *)
```

Fig. P2.1 Pascal translation of Fig. 2.15.

3. The main body of the program starts with the key word BEGIN and terminates with the key word END. The latter is analogous to a STOP circle.

4. Indentation is used to set off details from key heading words such as VAR and BEGIN.

5. An assignment ends in a semicolon or the key word END.

6. An internal assignment uses := in place of ⟵ as the following comparison suggests.

total := total + number | TOTAL ⟵ TOTAL + NUMBER |

7. An external assignment to bring data into the computer uses the key word READ in place of ← as the following suggests.

READ(number);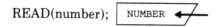

8. An external assignment to transmit data out of the computer uses the key word WRITE or WRITELN (see below for a brief discussion of the difference) in place of ⟶ as the following comparison suggests.

WRITE(average:6:2,' was average'); | AVERAGE:" WAS AVERAGE" ⟶

(The :6:2 controls the size of the value printed and is explained in a later section entitled Further Notes on Datanames, Declarations, and Assignments.) A label may be concatenated to an outgoing variable value by a comma and the text of a label (or any other textual literal) must be enclosed between single quotes.

9. The NEXT connection is established solely by the physical order of the lines. For example, the Pascal at the right is equivalent to the FPL at the left in this program translation.

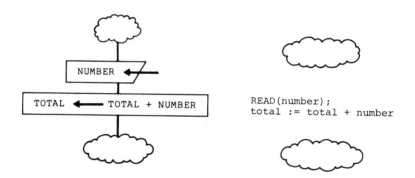

```
READ(number);
total := total + number
```

10. A comment about the program or any of its details can be embedded directly in a program line by bracketing the comment text between comment indicators. All versions of Pascal include such indicators. This text uses parentheses and asterisks as shown in the program's second line.

(∗ Translation of Fig. 1.26 ∗)

Read, Readln, Write, and Writeln

READ gets the next value or, if more than one variable is cited, values from the data stream. An alternative not shown here, READLN, does that and more. READLN sees the data stream as divided into pieces of a given length called lines. READ extracts what it needs to match the variable names cited, period. READLN does the same, but then sets the computer to the beginning of the next line, regardless of whether there may be additional values on the current line or not.

For transmitting data there is an analogous pair, WRITE and WRITELN, though only WRITELN is shown here. WRITELN sees the outgoing data stream as divided into pieces called lines; WRITE simply sees it as a stream. As a general rule, successive WRITELN use successive lines; successive WRITE (unless the line is full) deposit successive values in the same line.

READ, READLN, WRITE, and WRITELN may be implemented differently in different versions of Pascal. You should experiment with using them until you feel comfortable about how they work on your computer's implementation of Pascal.

FURTHER NOTES ON DATANAMES, DECLARATIONS, AND ASSIGNMENTS

Here are some things you ought to know that are not necessarily evident from this example.

1. A dataname must be composed exclusively of letters and digits (no underscores or other special characters allowed). However, a dataname may contain either the uppercase or the lowercase form of any letter. In this text, datanames are shown in lowercase only; key words in uppercase only, thus making it easier for readers to distinguish between the two.

Though datanames may be any length, some versions of Pascal actually use only a leftmost portion (e.g., ten characters). If your version only uses the first ten characters, then you must not expect

allbeenread

to be recognized as a different variable from

allbeenreadyontime

Both will be identified as the same dataname because the computer uses only

allbeenrea

2. Declarations may involve other sections, prior to the VAR section. (An example will be presented in Fig. P3.1.)

3. There is no FIXED numeric type in Pascal; only integer and real. A real number will be printed in floating point notation unless formatting values are provided by the programmer, in the external assignment. For example,

WRITELN(average, ' was average');

would print a value for average in the form

1.00312E02

whereas

WRITELN(average:6:2, ' was average');

would print

100.31

as if it had been declared in FPL: FIXED 6,2.

4. Though no size can be declared for integers, the size for printing can be controlled. For example,

WRITE(total:7, ' was total.');

would print total as if it had been declared in FPL: INTEGER 7.

5. *NOTE:* The acceptable form for external assignments may vary slightly from version to version of Pascal. Study your version's documentation and examples, particularly if a program presented in this book does not execute on your system.

6. Operators +, /, −, and * are used as in FPL. Pascal has neither an exponentiation nor a concatenation operator.

RUNNING YOUR PROGRAM ON YOUR COMPUTER.

The Pascal programs in this book will run on your computer if it has a Pascal language system. You may have to modify them slightly in response to messages generated by your system when you try to run the programs. To get started, use your system's Pascal documentation and any expert help available. You will have to enter each program into the computer either directly through a keyboard connected to the computer, or indirectly by keypunching it onto cards. The nature of your system will dictate which method to use.

To enter a program directly, find out (1) how to enter a Pascal program; (2) how to get the Pascal system in your computer to examine your program; and (3) how to get that Pascal system to run your program. You may find two of these steps combined but probably (1) will take place through some sort of "editor" program. In step (3), be prepared to supply additional information about files, in a dialogue with your system. It may need such information before it will actually begin to execute your program.

If you have to keypunch your program onto cards to get it into your computer, find out before beginning to keypunch if your system places any restrictions on what card columns you may use. After you have keypunched the program into a deck of cards, find out what additional cards you must submit with that deck to identify your program and its files to the computer.

Private Practice Pascal

PP1.1   Enter the program in Fig. P1.1 into your computer and run it.

PP1.2   Alter the format specified for printing average and rerun it. For example, try *average:8:3* or *average:7:1*.

PP1.3   Insert trace printing lines in the program at the points suggested by Fig. 1.27. Use

(WRITELN(number:5, ' ', total:7, ' ', average:6:2, ' ');

to print individual lines of the trace table. Run the program again and compare the trace with the one you generated earlier by hand.

PP1.4   Translate the program you created for (P1.10) into Pascal and run it.

PP1.5   Modify the program so that it issues the prompt NUMBER ? to elicit each value from the user.

PP1.6   Modify the program (PP1.1) so that it begins by telling the user what it will do and what the user is supposed to do. For example, you might have it print the information

This program will average any four numbers you enter.

Enter each number at the prompt: NUMBER ?

Be sure your modification produces a neat result with spacing between your message and the user's interactivity.

A SECOND PROGRAM EXAMPLE

A second example of Pascal appears in Fig. P2.1. It includes further examples of real and integer variables and, for the first time, a string variable.

String handling is cumbersome in standard Pascal, particularly in reading in a string data value. A string must be declared as a row (ARRAY) of individual characters, specifying how many characters are in the row. For example,

country : ARRAY[1 .. 8] OF CHAR;

states that the data string in country will be eight characters long.

Establishing or changing letters in the string is done by position in the row. For example,

country[1] := 'U';

makes U the first letter in the string,

country[2] := 'G';

makes G the second, and

country[1] := 'e';

changes the first letter to lowercase e. A string data value must be read into such a variable one character at a time.

This makes the programming required to read string values into the computer tedious and has spurred some Pascal implementors to include a way around this process. Their implementations hide this character-by-character process from the programmer and allow input into a string to be accomplished in a single assignment merely by citing the name of the string. For example, in such an implementation

READ(country);

would function like its FPL counterpart

Examine the documentation for your version of Pascal. If it restricts you to the tedious way of string reading, you must use it. If it doesn't, use the way around provided.

Fortunately, standard Pascal allows you to *transmit* the characters in a string as a group. Thus

WRITELN('Country : ' , country);

would transmit all eight characters in country when executed.

Private Practice Pascal

PP2.1   Enter the program in Fig. P2.1 into your computer and run it.

PP2.2   Study the documentation for your version and, if it allows an entire string to be loaded in one assignment, alter your program accordingly. Rerun it.

PP2.3   Translate (P2.2), (P2.5), (P2.7), (P2.8), and (P2.10) into Pascal.

PP2.4   Translate your program for (P2.14) into Pascal and run it.

PP2.5   Translate FEATHERS (P2.16) into Pascal and run it.

TWO FINAL EXAMPLES:
CREATING AND RETRIEVING RECORDS IN FILES

Transmitting records into a file is illustrated by the Pascal in Fig. P3.1; reading records from a file, in Fig. P3.2.

Compare these programs to the originals and note the following.

(Unless otherwise indicated, illustrations are from first figure (P3.1).)

1. The record's structure or shape is declared in the TYPE section, separately from the record's name.

> TYPE
>   sturecshape =
>   RECORD
>   etc.
> END

This TYPE declaration does *not* set aside any storage for data; it merely indicates what the record will look like.

2. The record's structure is named (i.e., sturecshape) and associated by = with the fields listed between the key words RECORD and END.

```
PROGRAM c3f12 ( input, output, twostu);
    (* Translation of Fig. 3.12 *)
    (*     Marjorie Cochran     6/30/80    *)
    TYPE
      sturecshape =
            RECORD
              id : INTEGER;
              age : INTEGER;
              name : PACKED ARRAY [1 .. 10] OF CHAR;
              score : INTEGER
            END;
    VAR
        twostu : FILE OF sturecshape;
        sturec : sturecshape;
    BEGIN
        REWRITE(twostu);
        WRITELN('Enter student record, one field per line: ',
                ' ID, AGE, NAME, SCORE');
        READLN;  READ( sturec.id );
        READLN;  READ( sturec.age );
        READLN;  READ( sturec.name );
        READLN;  READ( sturec.score );
        twostu^ := sturec;
        PUT(twostu);
        WRITELN('Enter student record, one field per line: ',
                ' ID, AGE, NAME, SCORE');
        READLN;  READ( sturec.id );
        READLN;  READ( sturec.age );
        READLN;  READ( sturec.name );
        READLN;  READ( sturec.score );
        twostu^ := sturec;
        PUT(twostu);
    END. (* c3f12 *)
```

Fig. P3.1 Pascal translation of file-creating program in Fig. 3.12.

3. The record's storage location name (i.e., sturec) is declared in the VAR section, by associating it with the record's structure name

   sturec : sturecshape;

This automatically sets aside correspondingly named fields and storage for the record.

4. A file of such records must be named (i.e., twostu) in the PROGRAM line and declared in the VAR section as a FILE OF records having that record's structure.

   twostu : FILE OF sturecshape;

```
PROGRAM c3f13 ( output, twostu);
     (* Translation of Figure 3.13 *)
     (* Robert Mead        4/81 *)
     TYPE
       studentstructure =
            RECORD
              idnumber : INTEGER;
              age : INTEGER;
              name : PACKED ARRAY [1 .. 10] OF CHAR;
              score : INTEGER
            END;
     VAR
          twostu : FILE OF studentstructure;
          sturecord : studentstructure;
          totalscore : INTEGER;
          avgscore : REAL;
     BEGIN
          totalscore := 0;
          RESET(twostu);
          sturecord := twostu^;
          totalscore := totalscore + sturecord.score;
          GET(twostu);
          sturecord := twostu^;
          totalscore := totalscore + sturecord.score;
          avgscore := totalscore / 2;
          WRITELN(avgscore:6:2, ' was average score');
     END. (* c3f13*)
```

Fig. P3.2 Pascal translation of file-reading program in Fig. 3.13.

5. Each file must be opened and that opening indicate the use of the file (input or output). Thus in the first program (c3f12) the file is opened so that output can be sent to the file

REWRITE(twostu) ;

and in the second program (c3f13) the file is opened so that input can be read from it

RESET(twostu) ;

6. The record *as record* may only be cited in an external assignment associated with a file named and declared as in (4). In standard Pascal, such citation cannot occur in READ, READLN, WRITE, or WRITELN assignments; only in connection with assignment pairs involving ∧ (the up arrow) and GET or PUT, for example (second program), the pair

sturecord := twostu∧;
GET(twostu) ;

7. Such reading and writing involves two steps. To transmit a record (first program),

twostu∧:= sturec;

transfers data from the record into a temporary, intermediate storage location used only between the file and the record, and

PUT(twostu) ;

copies the data from the temporary area (twostu∧) to the actual file (twostu).

A reverse process takes place in reading from such a file (second program). To read in a record,

GET(twostu) ;

moves a record's worth of data from the actual file (twostu) to a temporary storage location (twostu∧) and

sturecord := twostu∧;

moves the data from the temporary storage to the location named as the record. In reading from a file, the RESET not only opens the file but it also performs a first GET.

You should study the sequence of these pairs as they occur in each program until the order is well established in your thinking.

8. An individual field of the record may be named by prefixing the record's name to the field's name (e.g., sturec.id or sturec.age). Such a field may be cited *anywhere* in the program, just as it might in FPL.

Further Notes on External
Assignments Involving Files and Records

Two quite different types of files are used by the alternative forms of external assignments available in Pascal—*binary* and *text*. Binary, using GET and PUT, transfers data to or from the file in a form suitable only for direct use by the machine (i.e., numbers are in a binary code) and not in a form immediately intelligible to human beings. In this type, the record can be cited as record and the whole collection of values making up the records is transferred as a collection.

By contrast, *text* files, using READ, READLN, WRITE, and WRITELN transfer the data to or from the file in character form, even for numeric data, converting to or from internal form as appropriate. READ, READLN, WRITE, and WRITELN do not handle an entire record as record, therefore. They work properly only upon *fields* of the record, cited individually as fields.

If Pascal implementation regards a terminal as by default a text file, only individual fields of records can be cited in assignments that direct output to or collect input from the terminal. Program c3f12 reads the information to build a record from a text file being created at a terminal, so it cites the fields individually while reading. It transmits the complete record to a binary file (twostu) though, so it uses PUT and cites the record name rather than individual fields in that process.

```
twostu∧ := sturec;
    PUT(twostu) ;
```

The reverse process is embodied in program c3f13. It reads the entire record from a binary file, using a GET and citing the record name, then displays the record by transmitting it to the text file represented by the terminal. To send it to the text file, it must cite the individual fields and revert to using WRITE or WRITELN.

Private Practice Pascal

PP3.1   Enter c3f12 into your computer and run it, creating a file containing two records. Make up your own data.

PP3.2   Enter c3f13 into your computer and run it, using as data the file created by (PP3.1).

PP3.3   Modify your versions of both c3f12 and c3f13 so that four records instead of two are created and retrieved.

PP3.4   Modify your versions of both again, this time so that the record includes an additional, final field declared in FPL as

SCHOOL_FEES FIXED 7,2

Forcing the Computer to Repeat –The WHILE

INTRODUCTION

So far we have studied assignment statements, the NEXT construct (which forces the computer to execute statements in the order in which they appear vertically on the paper), the episode, and concepts of data storage and movement. What we have learned so far is important. All programs are composed primarily of assignments; adherence to top-to-bottom execution order is essential to keeping programs intelligible; and the concept of the episode is a powerful tool for developing the programming solution to any given programming problem. But the material covered so far does not include everything we need.

REPEATING EPISODES:
TWO EXAMPLES—SEARCHING AND AVERAGING

Many programs require the repetition of particular episodes. The FPL programmer achieves such repetitions by using the WHILE.

Search problems typically involve repetitions. For example, suppose that several thousand student records have been prepared for computer analysis. Each corresponds to a single student who has been participating in a mathematics project and therefore includes a student's identification number, age, name, and final examination score. The director of the mathematics project has just learned that the score recorded for student 3453 may be wrong and wants to see what score actually has been recorded. Because the records are not in order by identification number, a program is required that can read through the records, locate the one belonging to student 3453, and print out the score in question.

Using only the FPL introduced so far, there is no way to create the required program. We have neither a way to repeat the reading nor a way to compare the number read with 3453. Because we don't know how many external assignments will have to be executed before the right record is found, we don't know how many such assignments we'll need. The best we can do at this point is shown in Fig. 4.1.

Averaging problems also involve repetition. In contrast to the search problem, the task of constructing a program that will read in 30,000 three-digit scores and compute their average could be solved using only the FPL introduced in Chapter One. But such a solution would require 60,003 statements. We need something that could force the repeated execution of a single external assignment, though this time (in contrast with the search problem), we know exactly how many times that assignment is to be repeated.

In both the search and the averaging problem, repetition can be handled by the same FPL construct—the WHILE. Before formally defining this construct, let's consider a situation that may suggest how this construct should work.

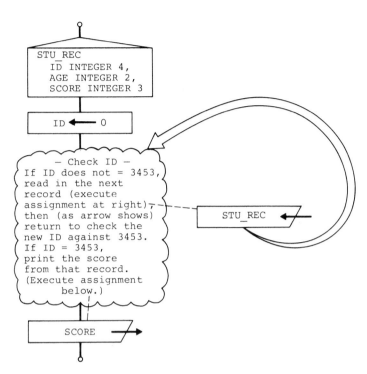

Fig. 4.1 Rough version of program to search for 3453.

One   A student is preparing to go to class. She collects her books. She puts on her sweater. She sharpens her three pencils. She picks up her reading glasses from her desk and slips them into her pocket. She is about to start for the door when she recalls that she must return a certain form to her instructor that day. She recalls that the form is in one of the many folders on her desk, but she does not recall which folder it is in.

Two   She stops her preparations and begins a search. She opens the top folder, sees that the paper she wants is not in it, and turns to the second folder. She opens the second folder, sees that the paper she wants is not in it, and turns to the third folder. This process is repeated over and over until the paper being sought is finally found in the fourteenth folder.

Three   The student then resumes her preparation for class. She places the form in her notebook. She closes the window by her bed. She switches off the electric lights in the room. She closes and locks the door and then departs.

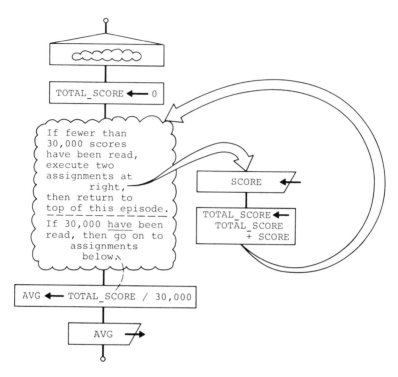

Fig. 4.2 Rough version of FPL program to average 30,000 scores.

The first and third paragraphs both describe a series of unique actions performed one after the other. By contrast, the second paragraph involves only a single repeated action. This looking-for-the-paper-in-the-next-folder is done as a sort of renewable aside or digression from the main activity of getting ready for class. If we consider the first and third paragraphs as FPL episodes, we might graphically represent the analogy in Fig. 4.3.

Private Practice

P4.1   A runner reports to the athletic field for her daily workout. She begins her warm-ups by doing 30 calf stretches. Create a graphical representation of this warm-up similar to the one we created for the search problem in Fig. 4.3.

P4.2   Develop your own analogy for the repetition construct, using some familiar activity. Create a graphical representation of your analogy.

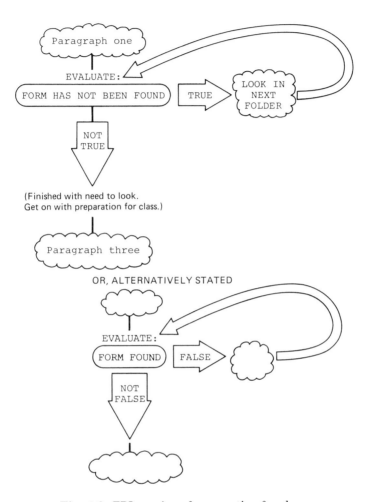

Fig. 4.3 FPL version of preparation for class.

THE WHILE—
THE FPL CONSTRUCT FOR ACCOMPLISHING REPETITION

Our three problems suggest what the WHILE must include (1) a way to establish the conditions under which repetition is to occur, and (2) the FPL to be executed when those conditions are met. In the WHILE, the *assertion* provides the programmer with a means to establish the conditions and the *digression* specifies the FPL to be executed when those conditions are met.

The general structure of both the assertion and the digression are shown in the upper portion of Fig. 4.4. Their conjunction as a WHILE appears beneath, tailored to suit our ID-search program.

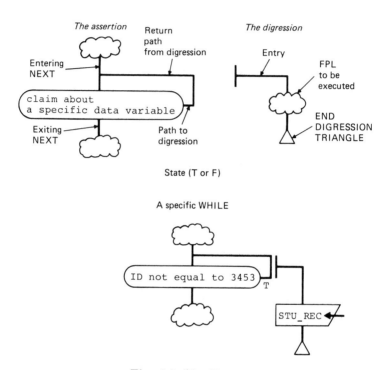

Fig. 4.4 The WHILE.

Together, the assertion and the T or F specified determine whether the digression is executed. The two possibilities are shown schematically in Fig. 4.5.

The computer evaluates the assertion to see if it matches the T or F specified, i.e., true matches T, false matches F. If they match, the digression is executed, the END DIGRESSION TRIANGLE is reached, and the computer returns to the top of the WHILE to evaluate the assertion all over again.

If there is no match, the digression is not executed. As soon as the computer determines that there is no match, the computer considers execution of the WHILE to be complete and passes on to the next portion of the program, through the exiting NEXT beneath the assertion.

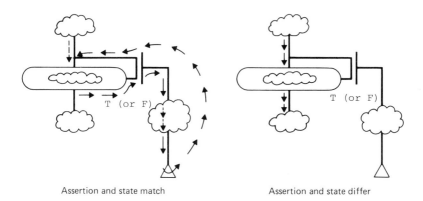

| Assertion and state match | Assertion and state differ |

Fig. 4.5 WHILE execution.

The match between assertion and state may or may not be destroyed by executing the FPL in the digression. If it is not, the execution of the WHILE will be repeated. From this situation comes its name—*while* the assertion and state match, repetition continues.

Understanding assertion evaluation is the key to understanding WHILE execution. The process is illustrated in Fig. 4.6, showing the two possibilities for a particular assertion text: ID = 101. The value of ID determines whether the assertion is true or not, which in turn determines whether the digression is executed. The sequence on the left illustrates an instance in which the evaluated assertion and the state specified do match, e.g., false with F; that on the right, an instance when they do not.

The WHILE in the Search Problem

To consolidate our understanding of the WHILE, let's trace execution of the fully refined search program. Our preliminary version (Fig. 4.1), refined to include an appropriate WHILE and labeled with execution reference points, appears in Fig. 4.7, along with a set of test data.

Before beginning the test run, let's summarize what we expect just from studying Fig. 4.7. The ID will be set to zero to guarantee that it does not initially equal 3453. At least one digression will therefore be executed along the path (c)–(d)–(e)–(f)–(b). This same circular path or loop will be repeated while ID continues to have values other than 3453. Thus we should see this pattern repeated in the trace table. If the computer reaches (b) when the value of ID is 3453, then it takes the downward path (b)–(c)–(g).

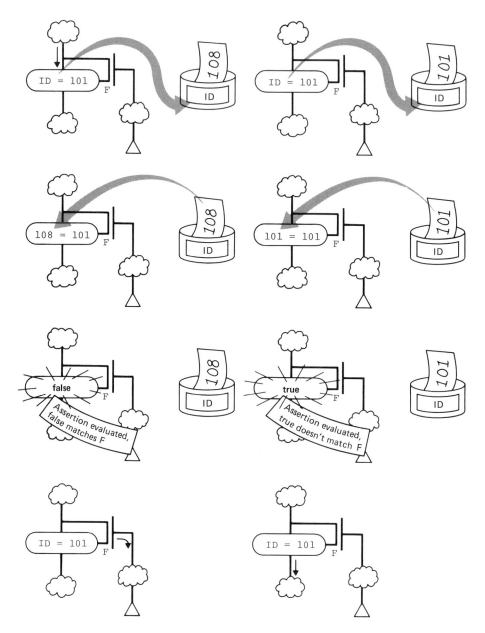

Fig. 4.6 Assertion evaluation process—two possibilities.

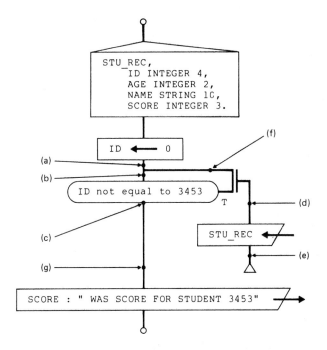

```
STU_REC,
    ID INTEGER 4,
    AGE INTEGER 2,
    NAME STRING 1C,
    SCORE INTEGER 3.
```

ID ◄——— 0

(a)
(b)

ID not equal to 3453   T

(f)

(d)

STU_REC ◄———

(e)

(c)

(g)

SCORE : " WAS SCORE FOR STUDENT 3453"

Test Data

Record	ID	AGE	NAME	SCORE
(1)	1234	12	JAWALRU	127
(2)	4321	13	SMANA	113
(3)	3145	11	MANITU	138
(4)	3453	12	JONES	110
(5)	3862	13	WELCH	122

Fig. 4.7 Search program with reference points and test data.

Figure 4.8 shows the trace table. In addition to indicating the value of ID at each point, the table indicates which test record was most recently read (1, 2, 3, 4, or 5), and whether the assertion was true when last evaluated. Only the ID field of STU_REC is included; the other fields have no direct bearing on whether repetition occurs or not. The anticipated pattern (c–d–e–f–b) of trace points is clearly evident.

Point	Record	ID value	Assertion state
(a)	none yet	0	—
(b)	none yet	0	—
(c)	none yet	0	true
(d)	none yet	0	true
(e)	(1)	1234	true
(f)	(1)	1234	true
(b)	(1)	1234	true
(c)	(1)	1234	true (again)
(d)	(1)	1234	true
(e)	(2)	4321	true
(f)	(2)	4321	true
(b)	(2)	4321	true
(c)	(2)	4321	true (again)
(d)	(2)	4321	true
(e)	(3)	3145	true
(f)	(3)	3145	true
(b)	(3)	3145	true
(c)	(3)	3145	true (again)
(d)	(3)	3145	true
(e)	(4)	3453	true
(f)	(4)	3453	true
(b)	(4)	3453	true
(c)	(4)	3453	false (finally)
(g)	(4)	3453	false

Fig. 4.8 Search program trace table.

Upon emphasizing this pattern in Fig. 4.9, we note that when the assertion evaluation result (true) agrees with the state specified (T), the pattern c–d–e–f–b recurs in the column of points traced. This suggests how the construct works and again suggests the source of its name.

Digressions executed	Point	Record	Assertion state
	a	—	—
	b	—	—
	c	—	true
	d	—	true
	e	1	true
1	f	1	true
	b	1	true
	c	1	true
	d	1	true
	e	2	true
2	f	2	true
	b	2	true
	c	2	true
	d	2	true
	e	3	true
3	f	3	true
	b	3	true
	c	3	true
	d	3	true
	e	3	true
4	f	4	true
	b	4	true
	c	4	false
	g	4	false

Fig. 4.9 Trace table with WHILE pattern highlighted.

Private Practice

P4.3   For each WHILE, draw a series of figures illustrating the process and result of assertion evaluation. Use Fig. 4.5 as a model. Use HUGUENOT as the value of NAME and 41 as the value of TOTAL.

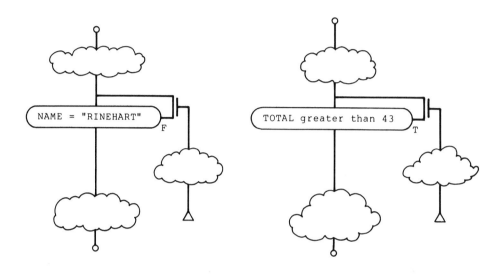

P4.4   Run the data below through the search program shown in Fig. 4.7. Record the run information in a display similar to that shown in Fig. 4.8.

Record	ID	AGE	SCORE	NAME
1	3214	11	113	ODOI
2	2314	11	112	JOHNSON
3	1324	11	115	SALVATORE
4	4321	12	118	KAMIZU
5	2345	12	122	LEE
6	3453	13	120	HAUSMANN

Arrange the data as it would appear in a file called PUPILS, modify the program so that it reads from PUPILS, and trace the execution through this file in the manner discussed in Chapter Three.

P4.5   The mathematics project coordinator wishes to know how many records must be read before ID 3453 is located. Modify the search program so that it can count the records read and print the figure wanted by the coordinator.

P4.6   The coordinator has just discovered a possible error in student 1234's score. Modify the program created in (P4.5) so that it locates 1234.

The WHILE in the Averaging Problem

We now apply the WHILE to our second problem. A rough program appeared in Fig. 4.2. To finish it, we need only refine the episode into an appropriate WHILE. To create the WHILE, we must (1) specify an assertion, (2) specify the state that the evaluated assertion must match to cause the execution of a digression, and (3) complete a digression.

Because the computer must repeat the digression until exactly 30,000 scores have been read and averaged, the assertion must say something about how many scores have been read. To create such an assertion, we need a data variable whose value is the number of scores read. Suppose we name it SCORE_COUNT. Because our program reads 30,000 scores, let's assume that our assertion should involve a comparison between SCORE_COUNT and 30,000. The first step toward our final WHILE is shown in Fig. 4.10.

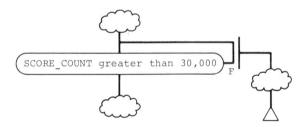

Fig. 4.10 A complete assertion for the score averaging WHILE.

This assertion causes the digression to be executed *if* the *count* in SCORE_COUNT *is less than or equal to 30,000*. Two things that accompany this particular assertion are missing in Fig. 4.10.

First, if SCORE_COUNT is to contain a count of scores read in, the digression must include an assignment to add 1 to this count after the score is read. The assignment for "incrementing" this count is shown in Fig. 4.11.

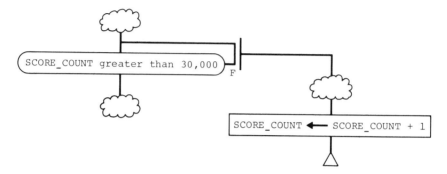

Fig. 4.11 Refinement to count scores.

Second, if SCORE_COUNT is to contain a correct count, it should contain a 1 after the first score has been read, a 2 after the second, and so on. Thus it must contain zero when the counting begins. This will occur only if some assignment above the WHILE sets the value of SCORE_COUNT to zero. The assignment for setting this value to zero (sometimes called "initializing to zero") is shown in Fig. 4.12.

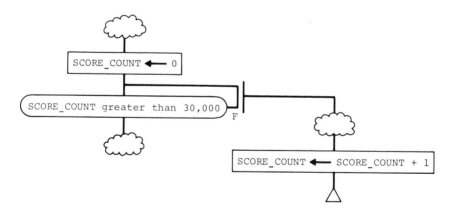

Fig. 4.12 Refinement to initialize the score counter.

The code in Fig. 4.12 is *almost* correct, but not quite. We must make it *exactly* correct! The error can be detected by asking what the value of SCORE_COUNT will be after the last score is read. SCORE_COUNT is zero when the first score is read in the digression. After the first is read, the count is incremented to 1; after the second, to 2; and so on; after the 30,000th, the count is incremented to 30,000 (not to 30,001). *We do not want the program to read and include in the average any scores after that,* yet when the assertion is evaluated next, the value in SCORE_COUNT is *not* greater than 30,000, the assertion is *false,* and *the digression will be executed one last time,* thus including an unwanted extra score in the total. The constant we really want in the assertion is thus 29,999, not 30,000. The final program appears in Fig. 4.13. It includes final assertion modification as well as complete refinement of the remaining episodes.

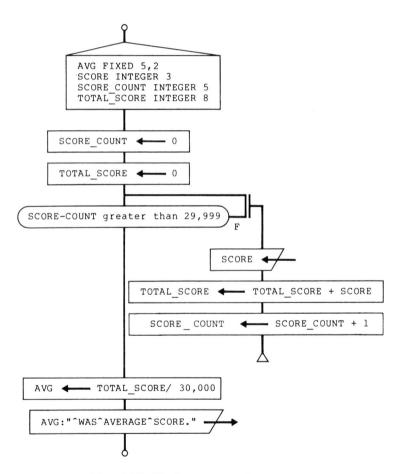

Fig. 4.13 Final score averaging program.

Before tracing this program's execution, it is worth noting two things about our correction.

First, using 30,000 is a legitimate way to begin working out the WHILE and illustrates problem solving by stages. Obviously 30,000 was approximately the value we wanted; we used this figure to work out the details, then refined this choice to 29,999.

Second, though this procedure is often useful in solving problems of all kinds, the programmer should *never* consider his or her work done until all the rough thinking and all the approximate values have been fully refined. A program that is basically right is not finished unless it does exactly what it is supposed to do. So, use rough thinking and approximate values freely in developing programs, but don't leave any traces of them in the finished product!

Closely Watching the WHILE in the Averaging Program

Now we will trace the execution of this program on some representative data. Figure 4.14 presents test data and the program labeled for testing. The assertion is modified to simplify testing; we can learn as much from handling three scores as 30,000.

Figures 4.15 and 4.16 illustrate one complete execution of the digression, reference point by reference point. Each individual drawing corresponds to one line in the shaded portion of Fig. 4.17, a complete trace table for the data in Fig. 4.14.

Before beginning the next Private Practice, study the drawings and table until you can see their correspondence clearly and can yourself plot the path of execution through such a digression. Note, too, that as in the table for the search program (Figs. 4.8 and 4.9), a *pattern* of points *recurs* (b–c–d–e–f).

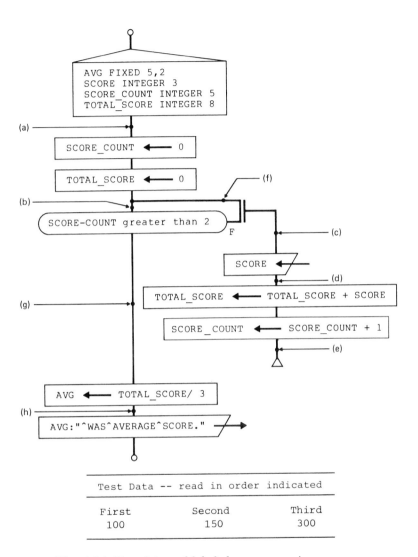

Fig. 4.14 Test data and labeled score-averaging program

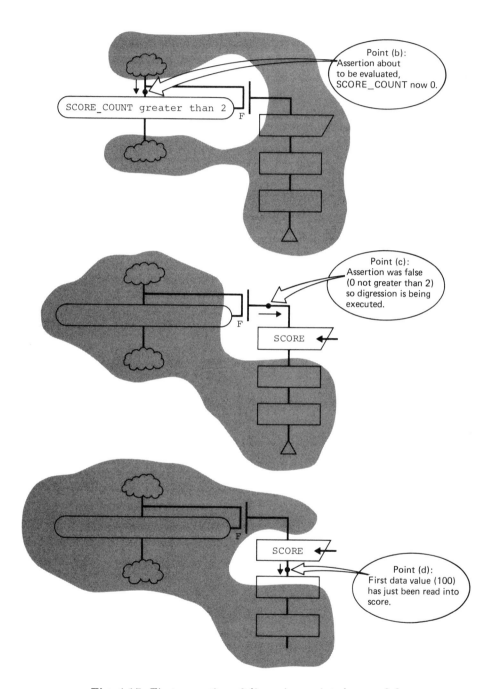

Fig. 4.15 First execution of digression, points b, c, and d.

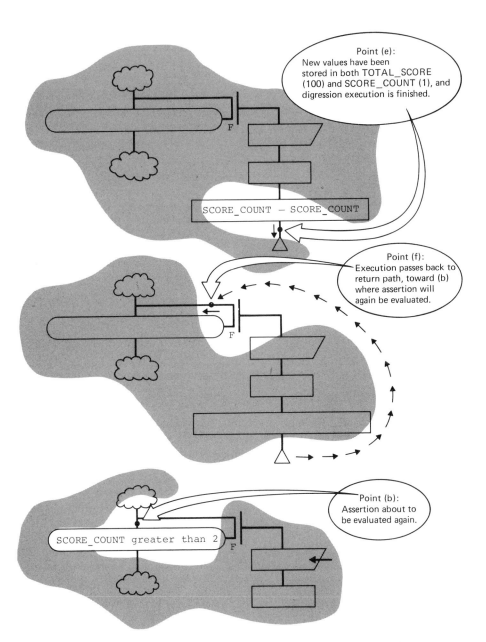

Fig. 4.16 First execution of the digression, points e, f, and b.

Reference point	Digression executed	Assertion evaluated	Assertion state	SCORE	SCORE COUNT	TOTAL SCORE	AVG
a	0	0	"	"	"	"	"
b	0	0	"	"	0	0	"
c	0	1	false	"	0	0	"
d	0	1	–	100	0	0	"
e	0	1	–	100	1	100	"
f	0	1	–	100	1	100	"
b	1	1	–	100	1	100	"
c	1	2	false	100	1	100	"
d	1	2	–	150	1	100	"
e	1	2	–	150	2	250	"
f	1	2	–	150	2	250	"
b	2	2	–	150	2	250	"
c	2	3	false	150	2	250	"
d	2	3	–	300	2	250	"
e	2	3	–	300	3	550	"
f	2	3	–	300	3	550	"
b	3	3	–	300	3	550	"
g	3	4	true	300	3	550	"
h	3	4	–	300	3	550	183.33

Fig. 4.17 Complete trace table for score averages.

Private Practice

P4.7   Test the program below by running the accompanying data through it. Create both a trace table and, to illustrate the first digression execution, a series of drawings similar to Figs. 4.15 and 4.16. The test data is read from the data stream in the order shown, from left to right.

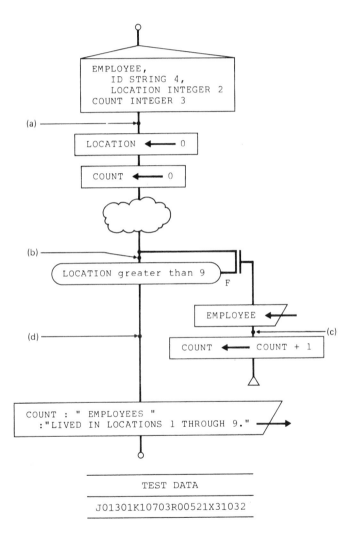

P4.8   In any program how do the number of digressions executed compare with the number of assertions evaluated? (Justify your answer.)

P4.9   Suppose SCORE_COUNT had been initialized to 1 rather than to 0 in the averaging problem. What modifications would have to be made to other parts of this program to ensure that all 30,000 scores would still be read and properly accounted? In the revised program, which of the following assignments should precede the other in the WHILE digression? Why?

P4.10   Assume the following values form a sequential file. Their order in the file corresponds to their order on the page with 0027 first and 5000 last.

        0027   0307   0212   3000   0570   3062   1372   5000

What value of NUMBER will be printed by the program below if run on this file? Verify your answer by creating an execution trace table.

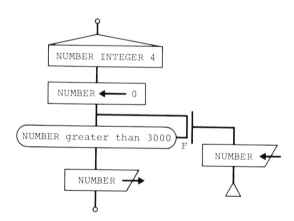

P4.11   Assume the same file and program as in (P4.10). If the assertion were changed to *NUMBER greater or equal to 3000,* which number would then be printed out?

P4.12   Assume the same data and program as in (P4.10). If the assertion remained the same but the state specified were changed to T, which number would be printed out?

P4.13   The file SOFTWARE contains a large number of records of the form

```
SEGMENT,
        S_ID         INTEGER 3,
        S_DATE       INTEGER 3,
        S_DESCRIPTION    STRING 30.
```

The last record in the file has an S_ID of 999 and is the only record with that ID value. Write a program that will read all the records in SOFTWARE and report exactly how many there were. (It should not include the last record in the count.)

P4.14   How many times will the message "I LOVE YOU" be written out by the code below? What value of WRITEs will be printed out at the end?

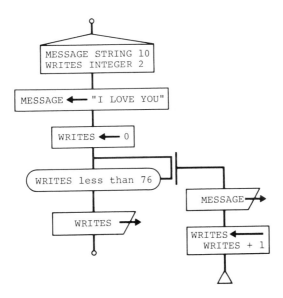

P4.15   Write a program that writes the message "I WILL ALWAYS DO MY WORK" 500 times and numbers the lines consecutively as follows.

    1 I WILL ALWAYS DO MY WORK
    2 I WILL ALWAYS DO MY WORK
    3 I WILL ALWAYS DO MY WORK
    4 I WI   . . . .
            etc. . . . .

P4.16   Write a program using a WHILE construct to add the counting numbers from 20 to 57 (that is, $20 + 21 + \cdots + 57$) and print out the result.

ABBREVIATING THE RELATION ASSERTED

Assertions are used so often in FPL and other computer languages that a shorthand way of asserting each relation is well worth learning. The complete set is shown in Fig. 4.18.

Symbol	Example	Explanation
$=$	$AZ = BO$	The value of AZ is equal to that of BO.
$<$	$AZ < BO$	The value of AZ is less than that of BO.
$\leq$	$AZ \leq BO$	The value of AZ is less than or is equal to *but is not greater than* that of BO.
$>$	$AZ > BO$	The value of AZ is greater than that of BO.
$\geq$	$AZ \geq BO$	The value of AZ is greater than or is equal to *but is not less than* that of BO.
$\neq$	$AZ \neq BO$	The value of AZ is greater than or is less than *but is not equal to* the value of BO.

Fig. 4.18 Assertion shorthand symbols.

Even if you have not used these symbols before, you will find them easy to learn and much quicker to write than the words that they replace. (If you are not familiar with them, note that the elbow or angle which denotes greater or lesser values ($<$ or $>$) has its bigger or open end on the side of the bigger value and points toward the smaller value.) Those symbols that combine other symbols ($\leq$ or $\geq$) may be the most confusing, but they also happen to be the most compact and timesaving. You can keep them straight by remembering that they are a sort of double shorthand as shown in Fig. 4.19.

Symbol	Example	Explanation
$\geq$	(AZ $\geq$ BO)	((AZ > BO) or (AZ = BO))
$\leq$	(AZ $\leq$ BO)	((AZ < BO) or (AZ = BO))
$\neq$	(AZ $\neq$ BO)	((AZ > BO) or (AZ < BO))

Fig. 4.19 Double-shorthand symbols.

Sample Evaluations of Assertions

Examining the use of such symbols is the best way to understand their meaning. Figure 4.20 is a table in which one data variable, YEAR, is compared with a particular (constant) string value. Figure 4.21 presents a table of such assertion evaluations involving two data variables IQ and SCORE. After studying these two figures carefully, do the Private Practice that follows.

YEAR	Assertion	State
1930	(YEAR < 1972)	true
1932	(YEAR $\neq$ 1972)	true
1984	(YEAR $\neq$ 1984)	false
1984	(YEAR > 1984)	false
1986	(YEAR > 1984)	true
1918	(YEAR $\leq$ 1935)	true
1935	(YEAR $\leq$ 1935)	true
1960	(YEAR $\geq$ 1970)	false
1970	(YEAR $\geq$ 1970)	true
1984	(YEAR $\geq$ 1984)	true

Fig. 4.20 Assertions comparing constants and variables.

IQ	Score	Assertion	State
113	146	(IQ = SCORE)	false
113	113	(IQ = SCORE)	true
113	111	(IQ = SCORE)	false
142	117	(IQ < SCORE)	false
142	161	(IQ < SCORE)	true
142	142	(IQ < SCORE)	false
151	118	(IQ ≤ SCORE)	false
151	151	(IQ ≤ SCORE)	true
151	170	(IQ ≤ SCORE)	true
108	111	(IQ > SCORE)	false
108	104	(IQ > SCORE)	true
108	108	(IQ > SCORE)	false
108	108	(IQ ≥ SCORE)	true
108	103	(IQ ≥ SCORE)	true
108	111	(IQ ≥ SCORE)	false
172	143	(IQ ≠ SCORE)	true
172	172	(IQ ≠ SCORE)	false
172	193	(IQ ≠ SCORE)	true

Fig. 4.21 Assertions comparing two data variables.

Private Practice

P4.17   Given the values shown for LENGTH and WIDTH, act as computer and evaluate each assertion.

Example	LENGTH (A)	WIDTH (B)	Assertion	State
(a)	27	6	$(A \neq B)$	true
(b)	27	13	$(A \leq B)$	_____
(c)	42	15	$(A \geq B)$	_____
(d)	17	17	$(A < B)$	_____
(e)	17	17	$(A \geq B)$	_____
(f)	17	17	$(A \leq B)$	_____
(g)	17	2	$(A > B)$	_____
(h)	17	2	$(A \geq B)$	_____
(i)	17	17	$(A \neq B)$	_____
(j)	17	20	$(A > B)$	_____

P4.18   In each case below, complete the assertion text, including the necessary assertion relationship symbol, so that the required evaluation specification is met.

Example	Incomplete assertion	Evaluation specificiation
(a)	COUNT	true while the value of COUNT is not greater than 1000
(b)	EOF	false whenever the value of EOF happens to be 1
(c)	NAME	false as long as NAME does not have the value "SAM"
(d)	BASE_REGENT	true if BASE_REGENT is at least 1.3 times as great as the value of PSEUDO_REGENT
(e)	RDG_SCORE	false if value of RDG_SCORE is not greater than the value of AVG
(f)	PASSES	true so long as the value of PASSES does not drop to zero or below zero

P4.19   A file of 300 records of the form

STAFF,
    NAME STRING 30,
    ID INTEGER 6,
    BUILDING INTEGER 2,
    RATE FIXED 4, 2.

has been created and on one of the records the ID may have been left as 000000, the value to which they all were initially set. Write a program that will report by count the position within the file of that record, if present. It is *not* the last record in the file.

P4.20   The square of a number is defined to be that number multiplied by itself; the cube, that number multiplied by itself twice. Thus the square of 3 is 3*3 or 9; the cube of 3 is 3*3*3 or 27. Write a program that lists numbers and their cubes, beginning with the number 1 and proceeding in order to include every number whose cube is less than 1327.

P4.21   Modify the BITES program from Chapter Two so that it works for four countries per run rather than just a single country.

BASIC Interpretation of Chapter 4

THE WHILE IN BASIC

Translating the WHILE into BASIC is direct, as shown in Figs. B4.1 and B4.2. Assertion symbols are identical to those used in FPL, with the exception of those shown in Fig. B4.3. The two WHILEs appear in context respectively in the translations of complete programs in Fig. B4.4 and B4.5.

The Search Program WHILE

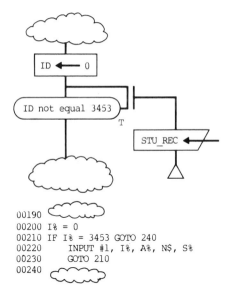

```
00190
00200 I% = 0
00210 IF I% = 3453 GOTO 240
00220     INPUT #1, I%, A%, N$, S%
00230     GOTO 210
00240
```

Fig. B4.1 BASIC translation of the WHILE from Fig. 4.7.

Compare the two interpretations and note the following.

1. The assertion is identifiable by the key word IF rather than a graphic symbol

00210 *IF* I% = 3453 . . . .

2. The NEXT exiting from the WHILE is replaced by a directive attached to the assertion, citing the line to be executed after the WHILE

00210 IF I% = 3453 *GOTO 240*

This exit will be taken only if the assertion is *true;* the digression will be executed otherwise. This restricts the programmer's freedom in wording the assertion somewhat but not seriously. The FPL assertion was designed to force execution of the degression if

(ID not equal 3453)

were true.

3. Except for their line numbers, all lines in the digression are consistently indented to highlight its presence.

00210 IF I% = 3453 GOTO 240
      00220 INPUT #1, I%, A%, N$, S%
      00230 GOTO 210
00230 PRIN . . . .

(Some BASICs do not preserve indentation. The rule should be: If you can indent, do!)

4. The END DIGRESSION TRIANGLE is replaced by a directive that sends the computer back to evaluate the assertion anew.

00230   GOTO 210

The Averaging Program WHILE

A second example of the WHILE translated into BASIC appears in Fig. B4.2.

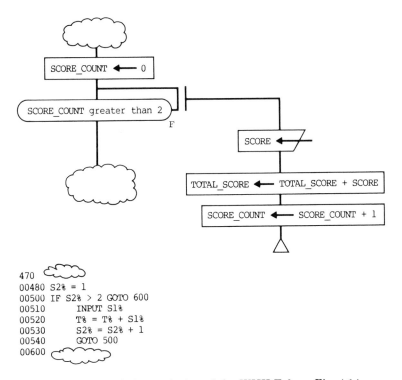

```
470
00480 S2% = 1
00500 IF S2% > 2 GOTO 600
00510     INPUT S1%
00520     T% = T% + S1%
00530     S2% = S2% + 1
00540     GOTO 500
00600
```

Fig. B4.2 BASIC translation of the WHILE from Fig. 4.14.

In comparing this program to the preceding one and the FPL original, note the following.

1. The assertion is again stated so that the exit from the WHILE will be taken when the assertion is true.

00500 IF S2% > 2 GOTO 600

The FPL uses the same assertion but in conjunction with an F state, requiring the computer to execute the digression if the assertion is true. The BASIC requires the computer to exit the WHILE if the assertion is true. The effect is identical.

2. The digression is again consistently indented and ends with a directive that sends the computer back to the assertion

```
00500 IF S2% > 2 GOTO 600
00510      INPUT S1%
00520      T% = T% + S1%
00530      S2% = S2% + 1
00540      GOTO 500
00600 A = T% ....
```

Assertion Relation Symbols

The assertion symbols that differ from FPL to BASIC are shown in Fig. B4.3.

BASIC Symbol	FPL Symbol
<= or =<	$\leq$
>= or =>	$\geq$
<>	$\neq$

Fig. B4.3 Assertion symbol differences.

THE COMPLETE SEARCHING
AND AVERAGING PROGRAMS IN BASIC

Complete translations of the FPL programs for searching and averaging are shown in Fig. B4.4 and B4.5, respectively. Before proceeding to the Private Practice, compare each program carefully with its original FPL counterpart.

```
00100 REM---TRANSLATION OF FIG. 4.7--------------------
00110 REM              DONALD YOUNG    5/30/81
00120 REM   STUDENT_REC,   : RECORD
00130 REM     I%   :  ID   INTEGER 4,
00140 REM     A%   :  AGE  INTEGER 2,
00150 REM     N$   :  NAME  STRING 10,
00160 REM     S%   :  SCORE  INTEGER 3.
00170 REM STUDENTS.DAT : FILE INPUT
00180 REM -----------------------------------------------------
00190 OPEN "STUDENTS.DAT" FOR INPUT AS FILE #1
00200 I% = 0
00210 IF I% = 3453 GOTO 240
00220    INPUT #1, I%, A%, N$, S%
00230    GOTO 210
00240 PRINT S%; " WAS THE SCORE FOR PERSON 3453."
00250 END
```

Fig. B4.4 BASIC translation of the search program in Fig. 4.7.

```
00100 REM---TRANSLATION OF FIG.4.14------------------------
00110 REM           JACK KERWIN    8/80
00120 REM
00130 REM A   : AVG   FIXED 5,2
00140 REM S1% : SCORE  INTEGER 3
00150 REM S2% : SCORE_COUNT INTEGER 5
00160 REM T%  : INTEGER 8
00190 REM
00200 REM -----------------------------------------------------------
00311 S2% = 0
00400 T% = 0
00440 PRINT "THIS PROGRAM TOTALS SCORES."
00445 PRINT "THE SCORES ENTERED SHOULD BE INTEGERS AND SHOULD BE ENTERED "
00450 PRINT "ONE PER LINE, IN RESPONSE TO THE PROMPTING   ? "
00455 PRINT "THIS TEST VERSION EXPECTS TO RECEIVE ONLY 3 SCORES."
00460 PRINT
00500 IF S2% > 2 GOTO 600
00510      INPUT S1%
00520      T% = T% + S1%
00530      S2% = S2% + 1
00540      GOTO 500
00600 A = T% / 3
00610 PRINT
00700 PRINT A; " WAS AVERAGE SCORE."
00900 END
```

Fig. B4.5 BASIC translation of the averaging program in Fig. 4.14.

Private Practice BASIC

BP4.1   Enter the serach program (B4.1) into your computer and run it on the data shown in Fig. 4.7.

BP4.2   Add seven PRINT statements to the program in the locations suggested by reference points (a) to (g) in Fig. 4.7 so that a pattern of points and ID values like that in Fig. 4.8 is produced when the program is executed. Except for the reference point named, the PRINT statements should be copies of

PRINT "(a)   ",   ID

BP4.3   Enter the averaging program (BP4.2) into your computer and run it on the data provided in Fig. 4.14.

BP4.4   Modify your solution to (BP4.3) to read scores from a file called SCORES. Write a program to create that file, then run it, creating the file for the first program. Run your modified solution to (BP4.3) on that new file.

BP4.5   Translate the program provided in (P4.10) into BASIC and run it on the data provided in that same problem.

BP4.6   Modify the program shown in Fig. B1.1 so that the repetitive part is handled by a WHILE. Manufacture ten values for NUMBER and test your program on those values.

BP4.7   Write a program to create a file matching the description provided in (P4.13), create a file of ten records, translate your solution to that problem into BASIC, and run it on the file created.

BP4.8   Translate your solution to (P4.15) into BASIC and run it.

BP4.9   Translate your solution to (P4.20) into BASIC and run it.

BP4.10   Translate your solution to (P4.21) into BASIC and run it. Modify the result so that it ends by displaying an appropriately labeled count of how many countries were analyzed.

Pascal Interpretation of Chapter 4

THE WHILE IN PASCAL

Translating the WHILE into Pascal is direct, as shown in Figs. P4.1 and P4.2. Assertion symbols are identical to those used in FPL, with the exception of those shown in Fig. P4.3. The two WHILEs appear in context respectively in the translations of complete programs in Figs. P4.4 and P4.5.

The Search Program WHILE

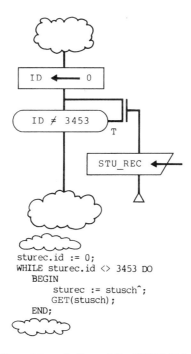

```
sturec.id := 0;
WHILE sturec.id <> 3453 DO
    BEGIN
        sturec := stusch^;
        GET(stusch);
    END;
```

Fig. P4.1 Pascal translation of the WHILE from Fig. 4.7.

The Averaging Program WHILE

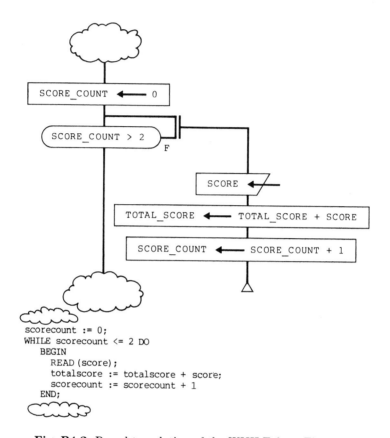

Fig. P4.2   Pascal translation of the WHILE from Fig. 4.14.

Note the following.

    1. In Fig. P4.1 the assertion is placed between the key words WHILE and DO rather than inside an oval-ended box.

    WHILE sturec.id <> 3453 DO

2. If initialization of variable used in the assertion is required, the initializing assignment is placed above the assertion, as in FPL.

scorecount := 0;

is placed above the assertion beginning the WHILE

WHILE scorecount <= 2 DO

3. The digression begins with the key word BEGIN, immediately below the assertion. The details are uniformly indented with respect to the assertion. The digression ends with the key word END, analogous to the FPL END DIGRESSION TRIANGLE. A typical example is

```
WHILE scorecount <= 2 DO
    BEGIN
        read (score);
        totalscore := totalscore + score;
        scorecount := scorecount + 1
    END;
```

4. The final assignment in the digression is terminated by the END of the digression and hence should not be terminated by a semicolon.

5. The "not equal" assertion symbol is <>, formed by joining the "less than" and the "greater than" symbols.

Assertion Relation Symbols

Most of the assertion symbols used in Pascal are identical to those used in FPL. The exceptions are shown in Fig. P4.3.

Pascal Symbol	FPL Symbol
<= or =<	$\leq$
>= or =>	$\geq$
<>	$\neq$

Fig. P4.3 Assertion symbol differences.

THE COMPLETE SEARCHING
AND AVERAGING PROGRAMS IN PASCAL

Complete translations of the FPL programs for searching and averaging are shown in Figs. P4.4 and P4.5, respectively. Before proceeding to the Private Practice, compare each program carefully with its original FPL counterpart.

```
PROGRAM c4f7 (stusch, output);
         (* Translation of  Fig. 4.7 *)
         (*  Alice Riddle     2/81 *)
      TYPE
        sturecshape =
            RECORD
              id : INTEGER;
              age : INTEGER;
              name : PACKED ARRAY [1 .. 10] OF CHAR;
              score : INTEGER
            END;
      VAR
         stusch : FILE OF sturecshape;
         sturec : sturecshape;
      BEGIN
        sturec.id := 0;
         RESET(stusch);
         WHILE sturec.id <> 3453 DO
            BEGIN
               sturec := stusch^;
               GET(stusch);
            END;
         WRITELN(sturec.score,' was score for student 3453.')
      END. (* c4f7 *)
```

Fig. P4.4 Pascal translation of the search program in Fig. 4.7.

```
PROGRAM c4f14(input,output);
       (* Translation of Fig. 4.14 *)
    VAR
      score, scorecount, totalscore : INTEGER;
      avg : REAL;
    BEGIN
      totalscore := 0;
      scorecount := 0;
      WHILE scorecount <= 2 DO
         BEGIN
            READ (score);
            totalscore := totalscore + score;
            scorecount := scorecount + 1
         END;
      avg := totalscore / 3;
      WRITELN(avg:5:2, ' was average score.')
    END. (* c4f14 *)
```

Fig. P4.5 Pascal translation of the score-averaging program in Fig. 4.14.

Pascal Private Practice

PP4.1   Enter the search program into your computer and run it, using the data provided in (P4.4).

PP4.2   Add seven WRITELNs to the program in the locations corresponding to reference points (a) to (g) in Fig. 4.7 so that a pattern of points and ID values like that in Fig. 4.8 is produced when the program is executed. Except for the reference point named, the seven statements should be copies of

WRITELN('(a) ',ID)

PP4.3   Enter the averaging program into your computer and run it, using the data provided in Fig. 4.14.

PP4.4   Modify your solution to (PP4.3) so that it reads scores from a file called SCORES. Write a program to create that file. Then run that program and create a file of 30 scores. Run your modified solution to (PP4.3) on that new file.

PP4.5   Translate the program shown in (P4.10) into Pascal. Run it, using the set of data values listed in (P4.10).

PP4.6   Modify the program in Fig. P1.1 so that the repetitive part is handled by a WHILE. Manufacture ten values for NUMBER and test your program on those values.

PP4.7   Write a program to create a file matching the description provided in (P4.13), use it to create a file of ten records, translate your FPL solution to (P4.13) into BASIC, and run it on the file created.

PP4.8   Translate your solution of (P4.15) into Pascal and run it.

PP4.9   Translate your solution of (P4.16) into Pascal and run it.

PP4.10   Translate your solution to (P4.21) into Pascal and run it. Modify the result so that it ends by displaying an appropriately labeled count of how many countries were analyzed.

A Row of Similar Data Items— The One-dimensional Array

INTRODUCTION

In Chapter Three, we studied the record, a structure for handling a collection of two or more data items. In a record, the constituent items are related by some common bond but need not be similar in either TYPE or SIZE. In this chapter, we introduce the array, a quite different sort of structure.

ARRAYS AND SUBSCRIPTED DATANAMES

Names that reflect parallel relations among data items are often useful to the programmer. In FPL and other programming languages, the array (also sometimes referred to as a matrix, table, or vector) is a structure that allows for such naming. Phone numbers, social security numbers, salary rates, and vocabulary words are collections that can be stored and manipulated in arrays. Within a given collection, each item requires the same TYPE and SIZE of storage location. This is symbolized by the way we dataname individual items within the array.

To arrive at a dataname for each item in an array, we first descriptively name the array (PHONE_NUMBER for phone numbers, VOC_WORDS for vocabulary words, etc.) and then number its items with a subscript (the lowest phone number might be subscripted "1," the next, "2," and so on). The dataname of any item is then defined as the name of the array followed by the item's subscript number, in square brackets (PHONE_NUMBER[1] refers to the first item in the array, PHONE_NUMBER[23] to the twenty-third, and PHONE_NUMBER[176] to the hundred seventy-sixth).

Figure 5.1 illustrates assignments involving items from three different arrays. It shows that, like any other data variable, an item from an array can be cited by dataname in an assignment. The first assignment assigns a string to cell number *1* of the vocabulary word array. The second assigns a copy of the contents of one cell of the phone number array to a different cell of that same array. The third assigns a copy of the contents of the *sixth* cell of the salary rate array to printer, terminal, or other such device.

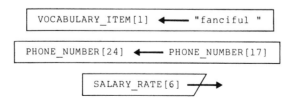

Fig. 5.1 Assignments involving array items.

Let us now examine how arrays work by considering a small collection of pupils' ages as the data we wish to store in our array. Each age will be an integer of no more than two digits. We simulate storage by a collection of desks. Each storage location is represented by its own desk and the contents of each location is written on a piece of paper lying on the desk. Figure 5.2 suggests how our desk memory will look and how nicely it can help us imagine the computer storage of an array of data.

Fig. 5.2 Desk memory.

The age of each pupil in the row is stored in the corresponding cell of the row of storage locations in the array. We associate the subscripted data name [1] with the leftmost desk in the row, [2] with the next desk, and AGE[3] with the rightmost desk. If we assume that the contents of each desk is initially garbage, our desk memory is shown in Fig. 5.2.

Some simple assignments involving two cells of the array AGE are shown in the FPL code in Fig. 5.3. The first assigns 8 to cell number 1, and the second, 9 to cell number 2. The results show up in Fig. 5.4. Note that the contents of the third desk have not been affected.

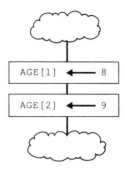

Fig. 5.3 Values assigned to two cells of AGE.

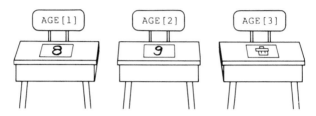

Fig. 5.4 Results of the assignments.

We can also use array references in external assignments. For example, the external assignment in Fig. 5.5 results in a printout of *9*, as shown.

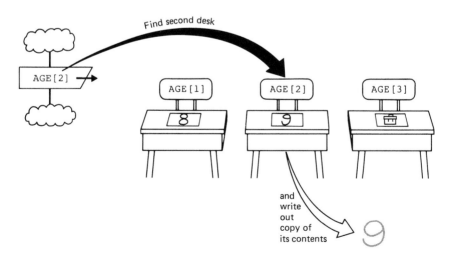

Fig. 5.5 Transmitting a cell's contents.

Note from examples that for a particular cell the value of its *contents* does not necessarily bear a relationship to its subscript (cell) number. Thus AGE[1] refers to the *first* desk memory location whether or not its contents happen to have the value 1. For example, in the case of the assignment in Fig. 5.5, the 2 in AGE [2] identifies the second desk as the desired storage location. We have to look and see what is in the location named by AGE [2] to see what will be written or printed out. As it happens, AGE[2] does not contain 2, but 9 instead.

Array Declarations

Figure 5.6 presents a declaration for the three-celled array AGE. Three memory locations suitable for storing a two-digit integer are required. Figure 5.7 presents the declaration of three different arrays. SCHOOL_NAME is a 20-celled array, each cell suitable for storing a ten-character string. SCORE is a 32-celled array, each cell suitable for storing a five-digit decimal. WORD_COUNT is a 150-celled array, each cell suitable for storing a three-digit integer.

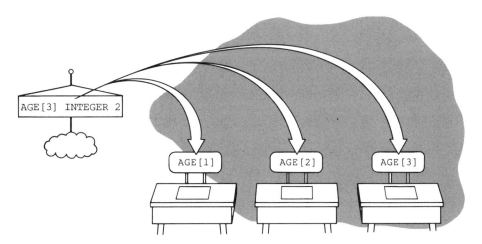

Fig. 5.6 Declaring an array.

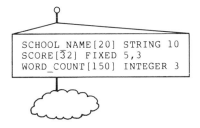

Fig. 5.7 Illustrative array declarations.

Private Practice

P5.1   Create declarations for (a) a collection of 100 butterfly names, none longer than 20 characters; (b) a collection of the 26 letters of the alphabet.

P5.2   Create declarations for (a) a collection of 3128 salaries, none bigger than $21,000.00; (b) a collection of 600 student identification numbers, each seven digits long.

P5.3   A collection of six key numbers is used repeatedly in examining the ID numbers of a large stock of textbooks. Assume that each key is between 1 and 772 and declare an array for storing the keys. Represent the storage locations for your array by a collection of desks or jars, in the fashion of Fig. 5.6.

P5.4   SCORES[10] is a ten-celled array used to store various test scores. Assume that the score values always fall between 0 and 323, create an appropriate declaration for the array, and then create the FPL code necessary to initialize the contents of every cell in the array to 0.

Data Variables as Subscripts

The subscript in an array reference need not be a constant. As Fig. 5.8 suggests, the subscript can instead be a variable, with a dataname and storage location of its own. In such circumstances, the current value of the subscript variable determines which cell is named by a particular reference. Thus AGE [CELL_NMBR] names the first cell of AGE while CELL_NMBR is 1; the second cell while CELL_NMBR is 2; and so on.

Figure 5.8 shows the process of evaluating a subscripted dataname: look up the current value of the subscript variable (CELL_NMBR); use it to determine which cell of the array is being named (AGE[2]); locate that cell in the array; and use the value found there (6), as required for executing the assignment.

Of course we can also assign a nonsensical value to subscript, as illustrated in Fig. 5.9. When NUMBER is 5, AGE[NUMBER] refers to AGE[5]. But there is no fifth cell in our desk memory: this value of NUMBER is garbage! Unfortunately, such out-of-bounds values can easily be assigned by a sloppy program. This is disastrous if the erroneous subscript prompts the computer to go to an unintended memory location.

Figure 5.10 presents a program segment in which the assignments cite array cells with variable and constant subscripts. It also presents a trace table created when the program is executed. Note that the value of GRADE absolutely identifies *which* cell of CLASS is referenced but *not* the *value* assigned to it. Note, too, that the last assignment cannot be executed because of an out-of-bounds subscript value.

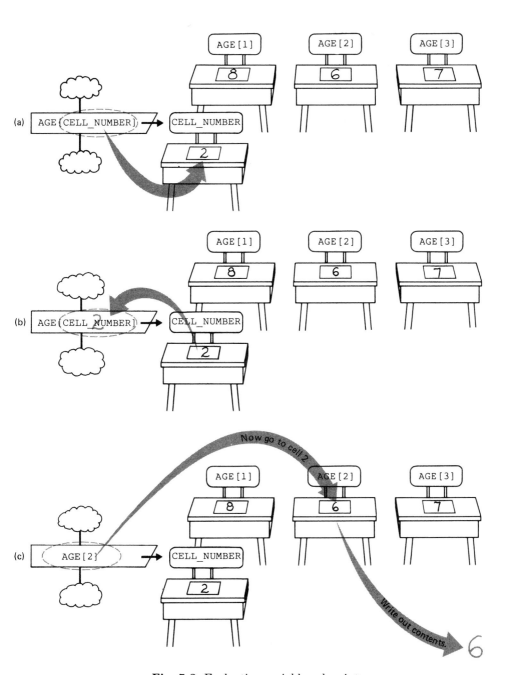

Fig. 5.8 Evaluating variable subscripts.

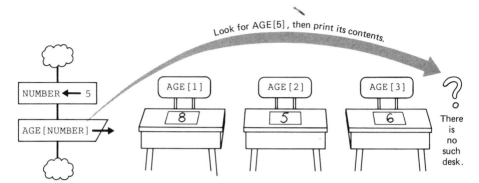

Fig. 5.9 Out-of-bounds subscript value.

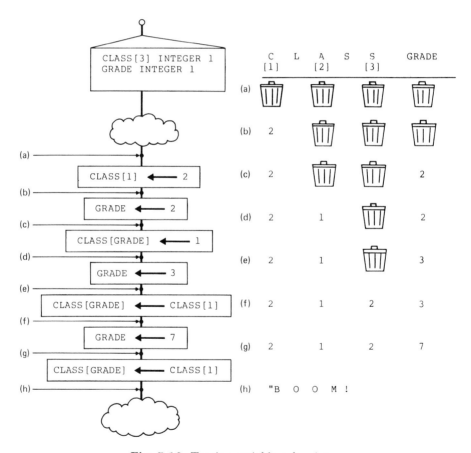

Fig. 5.10 Tracing variable subscripts.

Private Practice

P5.5   Redraw Fig. 5.5 after changing the subscript in the external assignment from 2 to 3. What effect would its execution have upon the person receiving the printout of results?

P5.6   Redraw the sequence shown in Fig. 5.8, after changing the value on desk CELL_NMBR from 2 to 1.

P5.7   Create a desk memory suitable for representing the variables shown in Fig. 5.10.

P5.8   The constant values 2, 3, and 7 are successively assigned to GRADE in the program segment in Fig. 5.10. Change them respectively to 1, 2, and 3. Rerun the program and create a new trace table.

Making Variable Subscripts More Useful

We have considered only one way to change the value of a subscript variable—by assigning a constant to that variable. That value may be changed in other, more dynamic ways. Two variations are shown in Fig. 5.11. Counterparts to each variation are frequently used within WHILE digressions. By using them in that context, a programmer can capitalize on the computer's powerful repetitive capability.

In Fig. 5.11(a), the subscript variable value is determined by directly assigning a data value to the subscript variable through an external assignment. In Fig. 5.11(b), the subscript's value is determined by manipulating a previously established data value and then internally assigning the result of that computation to the subscript variable. Before showing how the reference SEAT [CELL] is evaluated, let's review how these alternate assignments set the value of CELL.

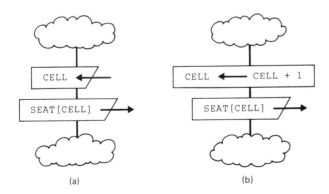

Fig. 5.11 Changing subscript values dynamically.

Figures 5.12 and 5.13 recall the two-step execution of an external assignment. In Fig. 5.12, the type and size declared for the subscript variable are used to extract a value from the input stream. In Fig. 5.13, the declared type and size are used to store the extracted value in the storage location reserved for the particular subscript variable. In this example, the extracted value is 3.

Figures 5.14 through 5.16 recall the three-step execution of an internal assignment. In Fig. 5.14, the values of all needed variables must be retrieved from the named storage locations. In Fig. 5.15, the computation using the retrieved values is performed. In Fig. 5.16, the result of the computation performed is stored as the new value of CELL.

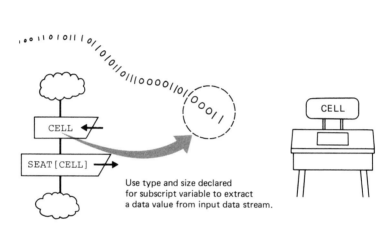

Fig. 5.12 Subscript value set by external assignment—Step One.

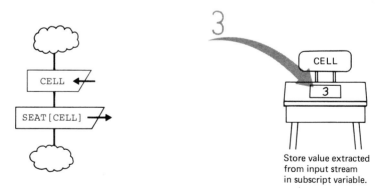

Fig. 5.13 Subscript value set by external assignment—Step Two.

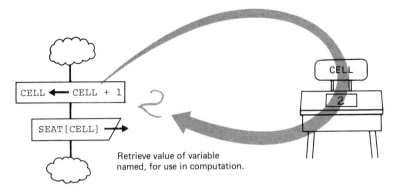

Fig. 5.14 Subscript value set by internal assignment—Step One.

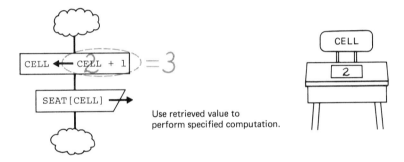

Fig. 5.15 Subscript value set by internal assignment—Step Two.

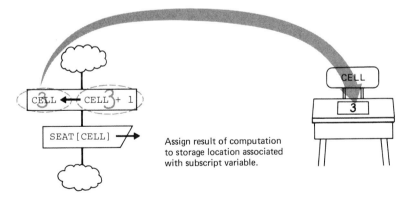

Fig. 5.16 Subscript value set by internal assignment—Step Three.

Figures 5.17–5.19 show how the computer uses the subscript variable's value in handling an array reference.

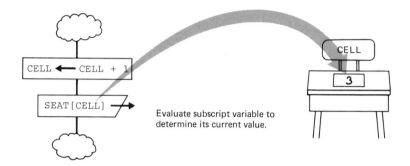

Fig. 5.17 Evaluating the subscript variable—Step One.

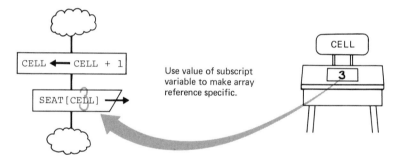

Fig. 5.18 Evaluating the subscript variable—Step Two.

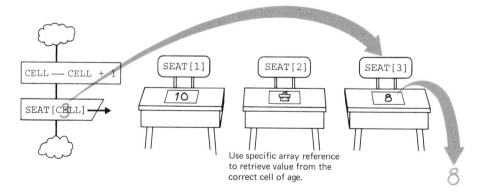

Fig. 5.19 Using the subscript value to retrieve data.

Private Practice

P5.9   Insert and label reference points on each of the segments below. For each, create a complete execution trace table. For the left-hand program below, use the data values 3, 1, and 2; for the center program, the values 11, 13, and 14. If there are errors, your testing should reveal them and you should indicate how such errors can be corrected.

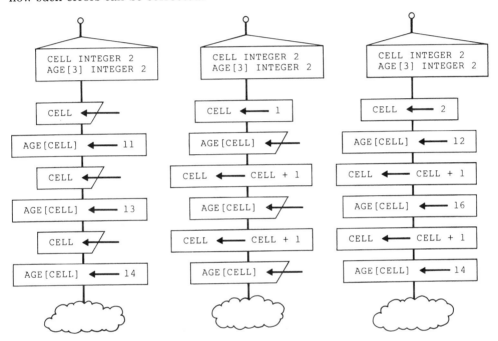

P5.10   Create a series of drawings paralleling Figs. 5.14 through 5.19 but beginning with a value of 0 in CELL, not a value of 2.

P5.11   Instead of basing the series of drawings on Fig. 5.14, create a series based on Fig. 5.13. Assume that the value 2 is initially read in via the external assignment.

More complex subscripting   Subscripts need not be so simple. Indeed, one can name a particular cell by using an expression as a subscript. For example, Fig. 5.20 presents a reference in which (TEST_NUMBER + 1) is used as a subscript to identify one cell of an adjacent pair. Figure 5.21 illustrates how the subscript works in referencing. Note that determining which data values may produce out-of-bounds subscripts is more complex when an expression is used as a subscript. In the illustration, for instance, TEST _NUMBER + 1 is greater than 8 if TEST_NUMBER itself is greater than 7. Thus 7 is the largest value TEST_NUMBER should be permitted to have.

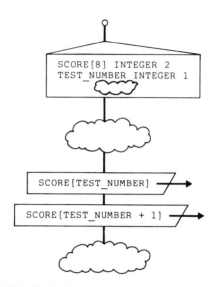

Fig. 5.20 An expression as subscript.

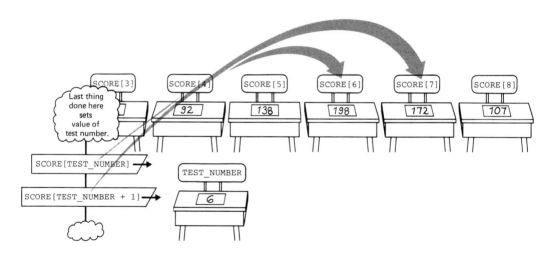

Fig. 5.21 Finding cells by evaluating expressions.

Forming a subscript by an expression that adds (or subtracts) some constant or variable from a subscript variable is a simple and commonly used technique for increasing the flexibility of arrays as a data structure. One can also name a particular array cell by using an array reference as a subscript. An example is shown in Fig. 5.22. There, the value of the fourth cell of IMPROVE-MENT determines which cell of RATINGS is named.

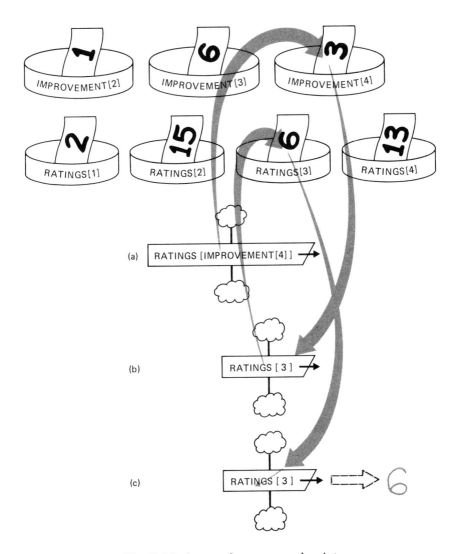

Fig. 5.22 Array references as subscripts.

Private Practice

P5.12   Using the code in Figs. 5.20 and 5.21 as a model, create a trio of assignments that together print out the contents of *three* adjacent cells in the SCORE array. The array reference in the first assignment should use *only the variable* TEST_NUMBER as a subscript; those in the second and third as assignments should use *expressions* involving that variable. Study your code carefully and then indicate the largest and smallest values of TEST_NUMBER that would be acceptable in your trio.

P5.13   Create a trio of assignments alternative to those in (P5.12). In this trio, the array reference in the middle assignment should use only variables; those in the first and third, only expressions. Sketch an accompanying desk memory similar to that in Fig. 5.21. Demonstrate in the sketch that the array reference in the first and third assignments are to cells on either side of the cell referenced in the middle assignment.

P5.14   In Fig. 5.22, what value would be transmitted if the assignment were

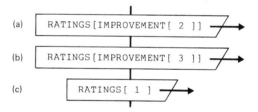

P5.15   Explain how the computer would evaluate the following array reference.

NILOTIC [KEY[INDEX] + 2]

Provide an appropriate set of declarations involving NILOTIC, KEY, and INDEX and indicate the safe subscript ranges which may be assumed by those variables which affect subscript values.

NOTE REVERSAL:
A MUSICAL PROGRAM COMBINING WHILES AND ARRAYS

To illustrate the power of variable subscripting, we will create a program to realize melodic reversal. For this task, we need the special equipment shown in Fig. 5.23: a five-tone *keyboard* and a five-member *trumpet bank*. The connection of this apparatus to the computer need not concern us. We need know only that the connections are such that a program can receive or send notes through appropriate external assignments.

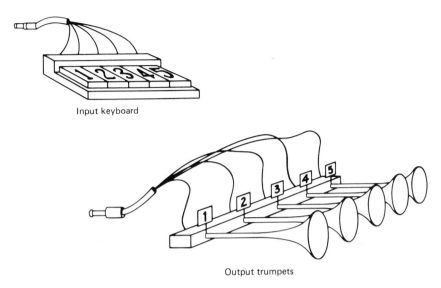

Fig. 5.23 Apparatus for musical composition and playback program.

Each key in the keyboard is set up so that when pressed, its associated numeric value is transmitted into the computer. The value is read by an external assignment statement and appropriately stored. Figure 5.24 presents an example. The fourth key of the keyboard has been pressed so the value 4 is read and stored in the location named NOTE.

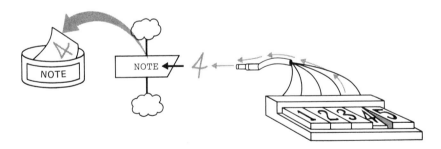

Fig. 5.24 Storing a note in memory.

Each trumpet is pegged to a numeric value; when a particular numeric value is transmitted to the trumpet bank by an external assignment, it sounds a trumpet. Figure 5.25 presents an example. In the example shown, NOTE has contents with a value of 5, so a 5 is transmitted to the trumpet bank, causing trumpet five to be sounded.

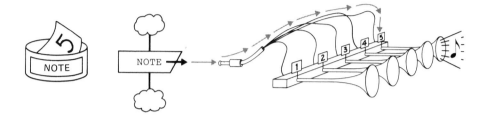

Fig. 5.25 Sounding a trumpet.

A melody can be composed by pressing several of the keys in succession. If the program includes sufficient data variables, the series of notes making up the melody can be stored in an associated series of storage locations. The melody can be played back by transmitting the stored values, one at a time, through a second series of external assignments. Hence a program such as that suggested by Fig. 5.26 could be used to compose and play back a simple three-note melody.

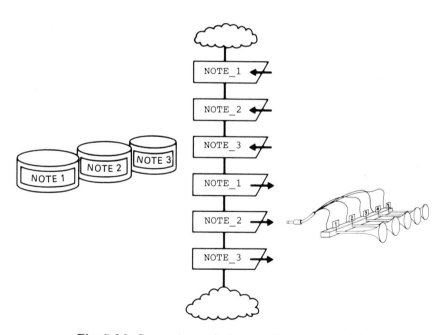

Fig. 5.26 Composing and playing a three-note melody

Our program is a bit more complex because it must *reverse* the order of the keyed-in notes. Thus if the *first note received* originates from key 5, the *last trumpet sounded* must be trumpet 5. Figure 5.27 suggests the most obvious way to modify your earlier program.

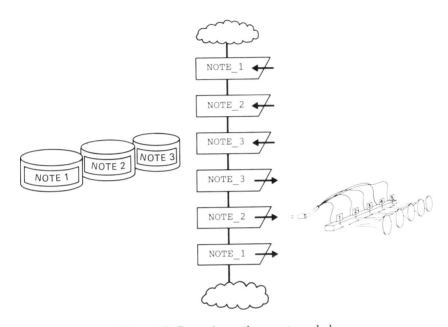

Fig. 5.27 Reversing a three-note melody.

Such a program will work for the three-note example, but it cannot be easily changed to accommodate melodies longer than three notes. For example, 194 additional assignments would have to be added to enable it to handle a 100-note melody! The structure of the program itself suggests that repetitions and an array might provide an improvement.

Our program is repetitious in action and in data. Such repetition can be formalized in a WHILE. The use of an array is suggested by the identical data characteristics (INTEGER 1) of all the note values. These values should be stored in an array.

When we consider just the composition of the original melody, a new structure suggests itself. We need a three-celled array to store the data. The first note value received needs to be stored in cell 1 of the array; the second, in cell 2; and the third, in cell 3. Our WHILE must be designed so that its digression is executed three times. Figure 5.28 shows this. The storing of the three-note melody is represented in Figs. 5.29 to 5.31.

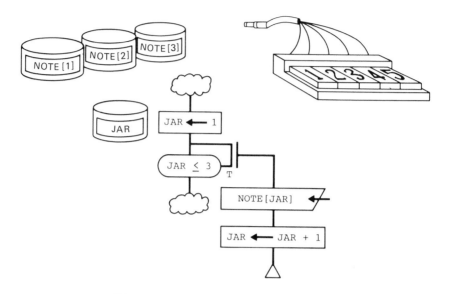

Fig. 5.28 Refining the melody program.

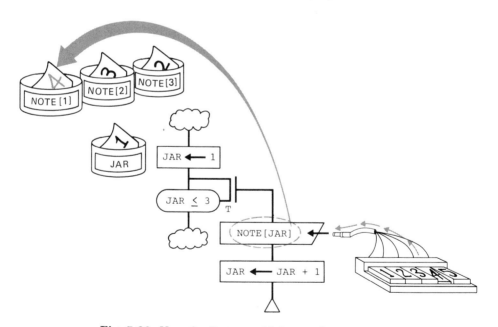

Fig. 5.29 How the first note (4) is stored in NOTE (1).

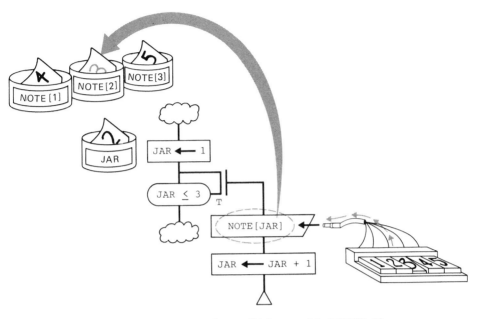

Fig. 5.30 How the second note (3) is stored in NOTE (2).

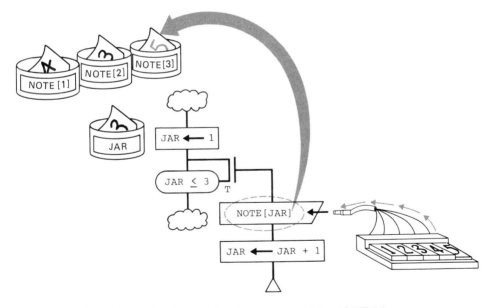

Fig. 5.31 How the third note (5) is stored in NOTE (3).

An internal assignment is used prior to the WHILE to set the value of JAR to 1 before the digression is ever executed. Each time the digression is executed, a note value is read into that cell of NOTE designated by NOTE [JAR]. Another internal assignment is used at the bottom of the digression to set JAR to the next cell number. The assertion is designed so that the digression will be executed exactly as many times as there are cells in the array.

But this much code would only *read in* and *store* the three-note melody from the keyboard. What about *playing back* the melody in reverse? If we modify our original version of the melody reversal program to include the array and WHILE displayed in Figs. 5.28 through 5.31, the result suggests how to finish.

Figure 5.32 presents our modified program. The reversal is accomplished merely by transmitting the stored note values in reverse order. We also see that, except for their subscripts' values, the three transmission assignments are identical. This suggests that another WHILE could be used.

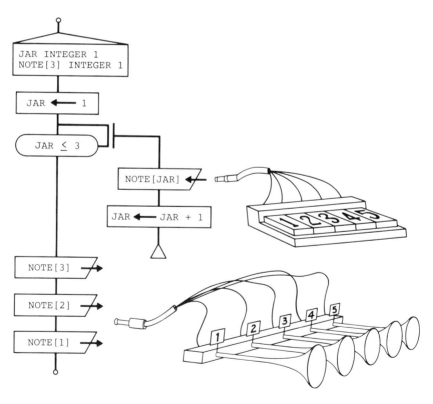

Fig. 5.32 Melodic reversal program.

Its operation should cause NOTE[3] to be referenced the first time the digression is executed; NOTE[2] the second time; and NOTE[1] the third time; and each array reference should transmit a note value to the trumpet bank. A rough version of this WHILE is presented in Fig. 5.33.

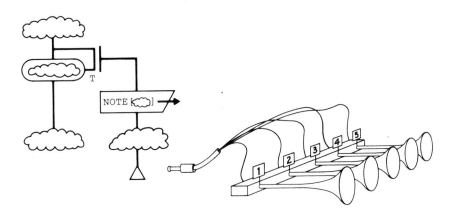

Fig. 5.33 Reversal WHILE inserted.

Because we already have an adequate subscript variable, JAR, we might as well use it again. Because we want the contents of NOTE[3] transmitted the first time the digression is executed, we can refine our WHILE accordingly and arrive at Fig. 5.34.

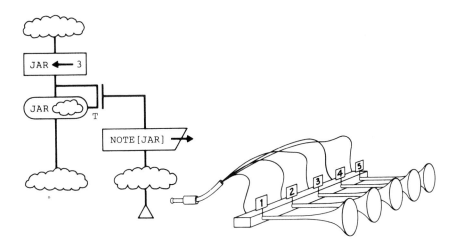

Fig. 5.34 Refining the reversal WHILE.

Next we observe that on the second execution of the digression we want the reference to be to NOTE[2]. Our external assignment refers to NOTE [JAR]. This means that when the second execution of the digression begins, JAR must have a value of 2, *1 less than its value during the previous execution of the digression.* Recalling that we increased the value of JAR by 1 with each execution of the digression, we realize that an assignment is needed that can *decrease the value of JAR by 1 with each execution.* Figure 5.35 presents such a further refinement of our WHILE.

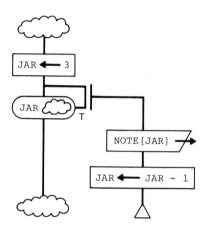

Fig. 5.35 Further refinement of the reversal WHILE.

Now we need only force the digression to be executed the right number of times. Because there are only three cells in NOTE, we want our digression to be executed three times. As the first execution of the digression begins, JAR should have a value of 3; as the second begins, a value of 2; and as the third begins, a value of 1. The internal assignment above the assertion guarantees that JAR starts with a value of 3, so the assertion need only guarantee that its value not sink below 1. The assertion text we need appears in Fig. 5.36.

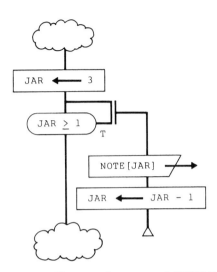

Fig. 5.36 The complete reversal WHILE.

The operation of this reversal is shown in Fig. 5.37. The digression is being executed for the first time and the external assignment has just been executed. This transmits the value 5 to the trumpet bank and causes trumpet 5 to sound. The value of JAR still stands at 3, its initial value before the execu-

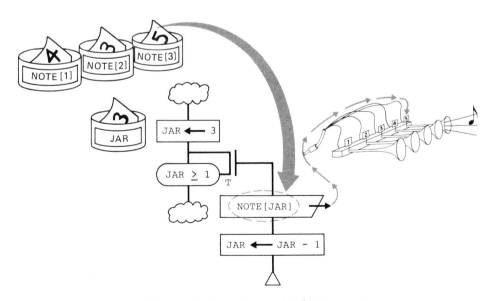

Fig. 5.37 Note being transmitted to trumpet.

tion of the playback WHILE. It will be decremented to 2 as soon as the internal
assignment at the bottom of the digression is executed. This causes the second
cell of NOTE to be accessed the next time the digression is executed. The
complete program, incorporating the second WHILE, appears in Fig. 5.38.

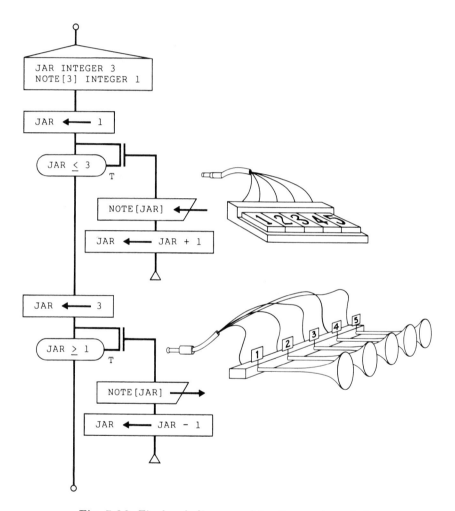

Fig. 5.38 Final melodic reversal for three-note melody.

Does this program overcome the weakness of the original (Fig. 5.27)? It may not be shorter but it is nevertheless better. An appropriate way to show this is to present this new version, modified to handle a 100-note melody. As Fig. 5.39 suggests, modification is fast, simple, and certain. No 194 additional statements are needed!

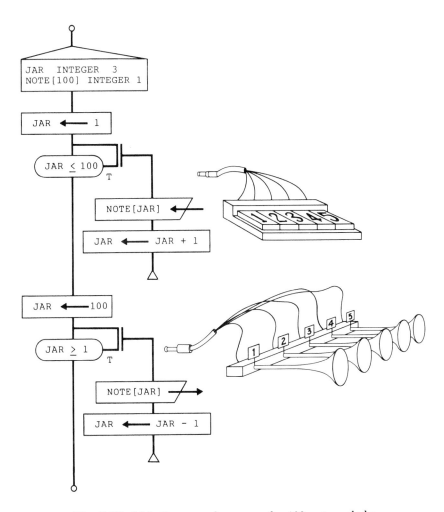

Fig. 5.39 Melodic reversal program for 100-note melody.

Private Practice

P5.16   Expand Fig. 5.37 in the fashion of Figs. 5.29–5.31. Don't forget to show the value of JAR's contents for each figure. (Assume the stored note values shown in Fig. 5.31.)

P5.17   Modify the program in Fig. 5.37 so that it will handle a 45-note melody.

P5.18   Write a program that reads and reverses a series of ten letters of the alphabet.

P5.19   Write a program that successively handles 100 such series before stopping.

P5.20   Write a program that reads in 250 salaries (declared as FIXED 7,2), computes their average, and prints out each salary together with the amount by which it differs from the average. At the top of the list of salaries and differences, print the following.

> Each pair of figures below represents an employee's salary and the amount that salary differs from the average salary for all 250 employees of the firm (left figure is always salary, right is difference).
> (THE AVERAGE SALARY FOR THIS GROUP WAS xxxxx.xx.)

Analyze your external assignments so that the average salary your program computes will appear in the heading in place of the dummy xxxxx.xx.

P5.21   Assume that each employee's salary is part of an employee record that includes the following fields.

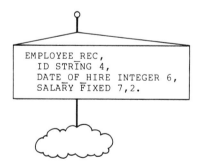

```
EMPLOYEE_REC,
   ID STRING 4,
   DATE_OF_HIRE INTEGER 6,
   SALARY FIXED 7,2.
```

Modify the program created for (P5.20) so that it reads these records, and prints out the ID number of each employee on the line describing his or her salary. Modify the list heading to reflect the addition of ID numbers to the report.

BASIC Interpretation of Chapter 5

THE NOTE REVERSAL PROGRAM
AND ONE-DIMENSIONAL ARRAYS IN BASIC

Arrays are interpreted in BASIC as shown by Fig. B5.1.

```
00100 REM---TRANSLATION OF FIG. 5.38--------------------
00110 REM              JOSEPH CHANG  8/81
00120 REM J% : JAR, 3 DIGITS
00130 REM N%(3) : NOTE [3] , 1 DIGIT
00140 REM--------------------------------------------
00150 DIM N% (3)
00160 J% = 1
00170 PRINT "This program accepts a three note melody and reverses it."
00180 PRINT "At prompt, enter 1,2,3,4, or 5 as note value."
00190 IF J% > 3 GOTO 230
00200     INPUT "NOTE ";N%(J%)
00210     J% = J% + 1
00220     GOTO 190
00230 J% = 3
00240 PRINT
00250 PRINT "The reversed melody follows:"
00260 PRINT
00270 IF J% < 1 GOTO 310
00280     PRINT "NOTE: "; N%(J%)
00290     J% = J% - 1
00300     GOTO 270
00310 END
```

Fig. B5.1 BASIC translation of the note reversal program in Fig. 5.38.

Compare this program to the FPL original and note the following.

1. Every array in a BASIC program must be declared in a DIM (for DIMension) line, indicating the total number of cells in the array. The number of cells must be an integer and must be enclosed in parentheses. The TYPE of the array is indicated in the same DIM, in the usual way, by appending $ for STRING, etc.

00180 DIM N% (3)

As usual in BASIC, there is no way to declare SIZE.

2. The separate cells of the array are accessed, as in FPL, by citing the subscript numbers. However, the lowest cell is always 0 and the highest is the number cited in the DIM; no *range* such as 20:35 may be declared.

3. Assignments involving constants or subscript variables take place as in FPL

00245 INPUT N%(J%) | NOTE[JAR] ◄─────

00250 PRINT N%(J%) | NOTE[JAR] ─────►

or an internal assignment (not shown in this program)

06000 ITEM(3) = ITEM(2) | ITEM[3] ◄──── ITEM[2] |

Private Practice BASIC

BP5.1   Enter the program in Fig. B5.1 into your computer and run it several times, entering a different melody each time.

BP5.2   Modify the program so that it accepts and reverses a ten-note melody and run that modified version several times.

BP5.3   Translate your solution to (P5.20) into BASIC and run it on your computer.

BP5.4   Translate your solution to (P5.21) into BASIC, but design it to handle only three series, not 100. Run the result on your computer.

BP5.5   Translate your solution to (P5.22) into BASIC, but modify it to handle only ten salaries. Run the resulting program on your computer. (The salaries may be entered via a file or directly as the program prompts, whichever you wish.

BP5.6   Translate your solution to (P5.23) into BASIC, create an appropriate file of EMPLOYEE data, and run your program on that file. Again you may limit the data to ten records.

Pascal Interpretation of Chapter 5

THE NOTE REVERSAL PROGRAM
AND ONE-DIMENSIONAL ARRAYS IN PASCAL

Arrays translate into Pascal as suggested in Fig. P5.1.

```
PROGRAM c5f38(input, output);
   (*  Translation of Fig. 5.38 *)
   (*       Clayton Tucker     5/80    *)
   VAR
      jar :INTEGER;
      note : ARRAY[1..3] OF INTEGER;
   BEGIN
      jar := 1;
      WRITELN('This program accepts a three-note melody and reverses it.');
      WRITELN('At prompt, enter 1,2,3,4, or 5 as note value.');
      WHILE jar <= 3 DO
         BEGIN
            WRITELN('NOTE?');
            READLN; READ(note[jar]);
            jar := jar + 1
         END;
      WRITELN(tty);
      WRITELN('The reversed melody follows:');
      WRITELN(tty);
      WRITELN(tty);
      jar := 3;
      WHILE jar >= 1 DO
         BEGIN
            WRITELN(note[jar]);
            jar := jar - 1
         END;
   END. (* c5f38 *)
```

Fig. P5.1 Pascal translation of the note reversal program in Fig. 5.38.

Compare this with the FPL original and note the following.

1. Array dimensions must be declared, citing between square brackets the lowest and the highest value the subscript may assume, and separating the two values by periods.

[1 .. 3]

As in FPL, a range may be specified that does not begin at 1.

[1945 .. 1962]

2. The dimensions must be bracketed by the key words ARRAY and OF.

ARRAY [1 .. 3] OF

3. The declaration must begin with the array name, followed by a colon.

note : ARRAY [1 .. 3] OF

4. The declaration of the array must end with a type specification followed by a semicolon.

note : ARRAY [1 .. 3] OF INTEGER;

5. Assignments are made to or from array cells as in FPL.

READ(note[jar]);

WRITELN(note[jar]);

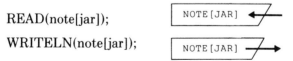

Or, in internal assignment (not shown in this program)

item[3] := item[2]

6. Subscript manipulation is similar to that in FPL in which variable subscripting is used.

7. A string in Pascal is an array of type CHAR. You may wish to confirm this by looking back at the examples of string declaration and manipulation represented in the BITES program.

Private Practice Pascal

PP5.1   Translate the following array declarations into Pascal.

```
AGE [4]  INTEGER  2
YEAR [1945:1962]  INTEGER  4
NAME  STRING  10
SALARY [138]  FIXED  7,2
```

PP5.2   Enter the program c5f38 into your computer and run it.

PP5.3   Translate Fig. 5.10 into Pascal, add an appropriate WRITELN at points (a) through (h), and run it. Compare your trace table with the one shown in Fig. 5.10.

PP5.4   Translate (P5.18) into Pascal and run it.

PP5.5   Translate (P5.19) into Pascal and run it.

PP5.6   Translate (P5.20) into Pascal and run it.

Rows of Similar Data Items– The Multidimensional Array

INTRODUCTION

In Chapter Three, we introduced the record; in Chapter Five, the one-dimensional array. In this chapter, we discuss more elaborate arrays.

Just as one-dimensional arrays can sometimes be more useful than single-item variables, so arrays with more than one subscript can sometimes be more useful than arrays with only a single subscript.

ARRAYS WITH TWO SUBSCRIPTS

For example, suppose we are interested in the ages of six pupils who are seated in two rows with three pupils in each row. As Fig. 6.1 suggests, we could store the ages in a one-dimensional array of six cells. Because there are *six* pupils whose ages must be remembered, the single row of six desk memory locations matches the size of the data collection our program must handle.

Fig. 6.1 Two rows of pupils become one row of data values.

But such a scheme is awkward. It does not fit the two-row arrangement of the data. If we could break the array into rows, we could more comfortably match pupils to stored data values.

Figure 6.2 shows how this can naturally be done by a two-dimensional array. The arrangement of the data in storage then parallels the physical arrangement of the pupils. The pair of subscripts identifies a single-array cell just as specification of a seat and a row in the room identifies a particular pupil. Thus the age of the little girl waving both arms should be stored in AGE[1,3], as suggested by Fig. 6.3.

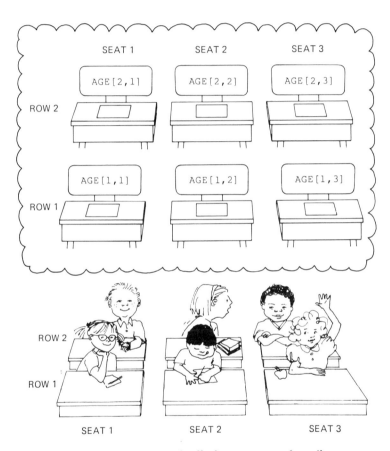

Fig. 6.2 Two rows of cells for two rows of pupils.

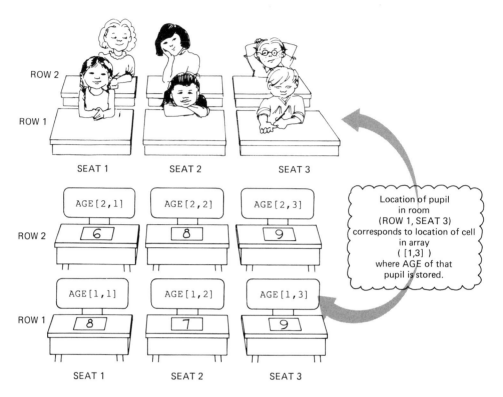

Fig. 6.3 Correspondence between source and array arrangements.

Figures 6.4 and 6.5 illustrate how variable subscripts work in references to two-dimensional arrays. First (Fig. 6.4), the subscripts must be evaluated. To do this, the computer looks up each subscript value in its storage location and replaces each variable subscript dataname with its actual value. Then (Fig. 6.5), the computer goes directly to the cell associated with that set of subscript values. There it retrieves a copy of the value stored in that cell of the array, and replaces the array reference with the retrieved value. (This is symbolized in Fig. 6.5 by the appearance of the value 9 in the final external assignment.)

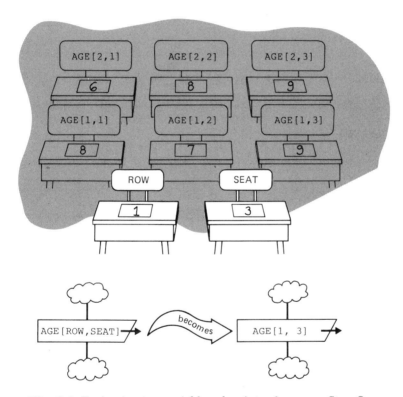

Fig. 6.4 Evaluating two-variable subscript references—Step One.

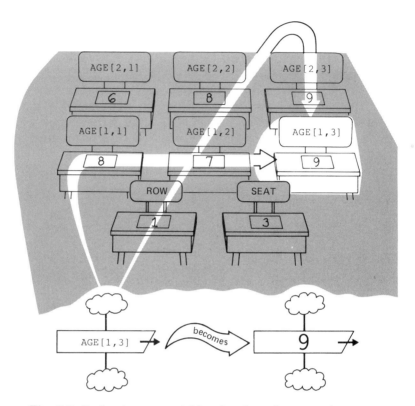

Fig. 6.5 Evaluating two-variable subscript references—Step Two.

Subscript Order—[SEAT, ROW] or [ROW, SEAT]

There is nothing sacred about the order in which subscripts appear within the square brackets or an array reference—so long as the *same* order is maintained throughout the program in which that array is used. In the AGE array, one program might establish that the first subscript refers to the column (SEAT) in the array, and the second to the row (ROW)—thus consistently citing AGE [SEAT,ROW] throughout the program. But another program, using the same collection of data, might establish the reverse and, throughout, cite elements in the array by AGE[ROW,SEAT]. Either order, if used consistently, will produce the same net effect.

Private Practice

P6.1   Make your own copy of the desk memory shown below. Use the letter preceding each reference to label the appropriate desk, and match the following references to memory locations: (a) AGE[2,3], (b) AGE[1,1], (c) AGE[2,2], and (d) AGE[1,3]. As a guide, one desk has already been labeled with the array reference AGE[1,2].

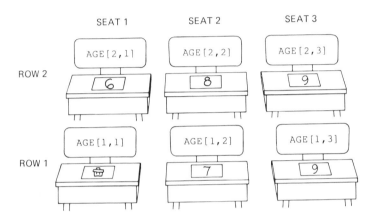

P6.2   Use the memory and contents specified for (P6.1) and complete the following table. For each pair of subscript values, indicate the value that would be written out by the assignment

AGE [ROW, SEAT] $\longrightarrow$

ROW	SEAT	Value assigned to external device
1	3	
2	1	
1	2	
5	2	

P6.3   Redraw the desk memory used for (P6.1). Label the back of each seat to match a *reversal* subscript order appropriate to the reference AGE [SEAT,ROW]. Using the letter preceding the reference to label the appropriate desk, match the following references to memory locations: (a) AGE[3,2], (b) AGE[1,1], (c) AGE[2,2], and (d) AGE[3,1].

P6.4   Copy and complete the trace table below. Use the execution reference points indicated on the superimposed code. Follow the subscript order implied by AGE[SEAT,ROW], *not* AGE[ROW,SEAT].

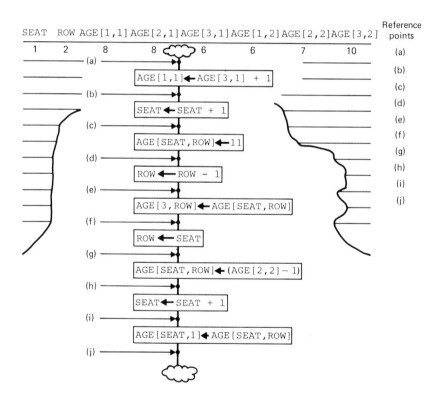

P6.5   Produce a drawing like the one below for the case in which SEAT has a value of 2 and ROW a value of 1. Indicate what would be written by the external assignment once the array reference is fully evaluated by the computer.

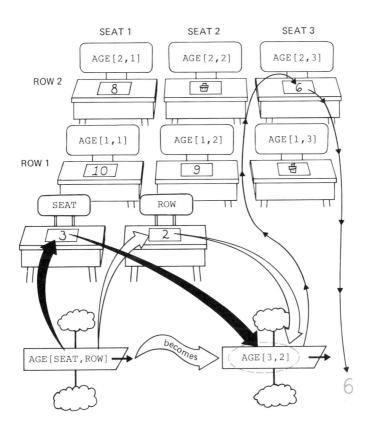

A THREE-DIMENSIONAL ARRAY

But why stop at two dimensions? Some data might be matched better by arrays of three or more dimensions.

For instance, suppose our pupil population expands to *two rooms*. Within a given room we can still use seat and row to identify a particular pupil, but specification of seat and row together can no longer uniquely identify a pupil—we must also specify which *room* the pupil is in. We now need three subscripts to identify completely a cell of our array—SEAT, ROW, and ROOM. This is shown in Fig. 6.6.

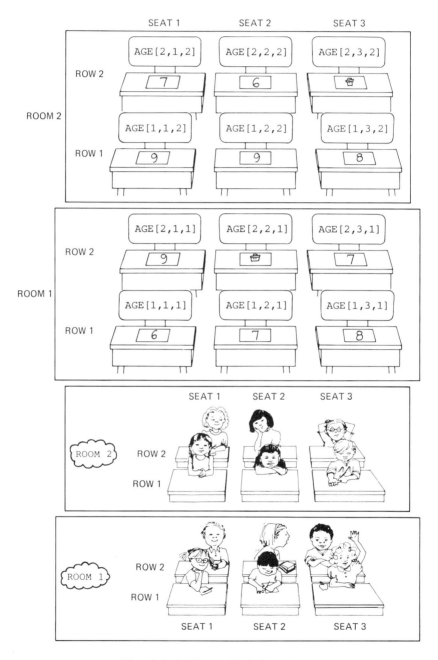

Fig. 6.6 Adding a third dimension.

Figures 6.7 through 6.11 illustrate the evaluation of a three-dimensional array reference. First (Fig. 6.7), the subscript locations are inspected to determine the actual value of each subscript. The variable subscripts are, in effect, replaced by these values in the array reference.

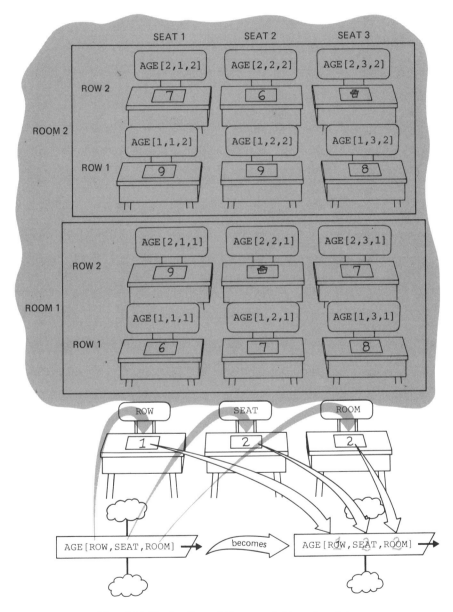

Fig. 6.7 Evaluation of three variable subscripts.

Next (Figs. 6.8–6.10), the computer uses those values to locate the exact cell referred to. Finally (Fig. 6.11), the computer retrieves a copy of the cell's contents and uses its value in place of the actual array reference.

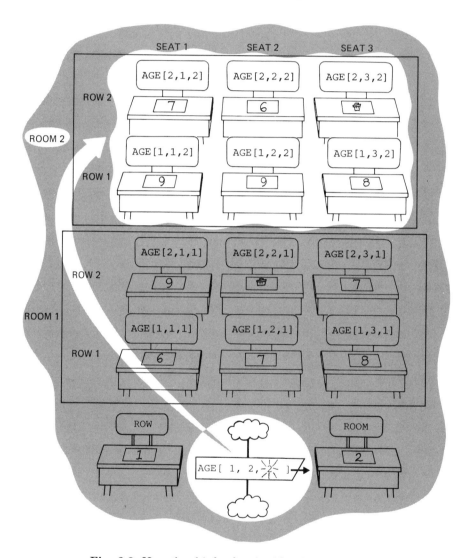

Fig. 6.8 How the third subscript identifies the room.

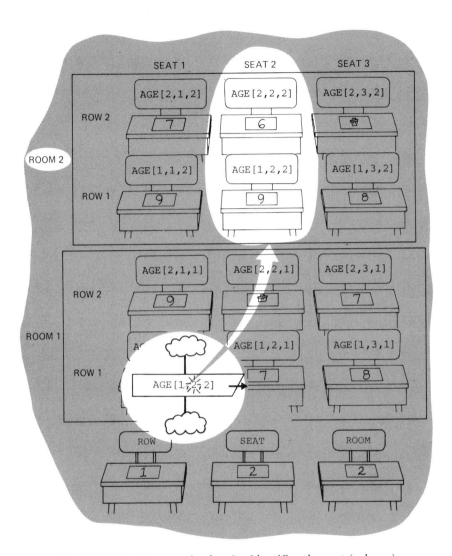

Fig. 6.9 How the second subscript identifies the seat (column).

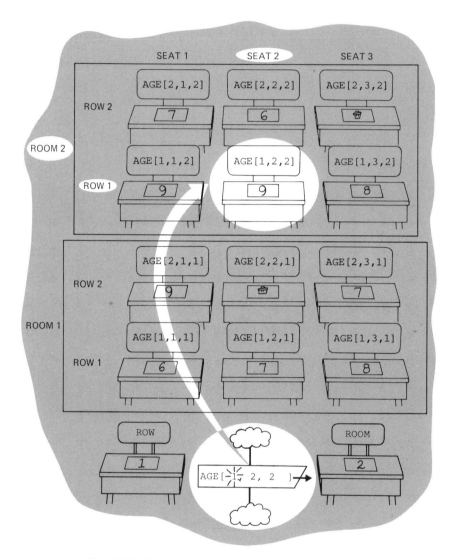

Fig. 6.10 How the first subscript identifies the row.

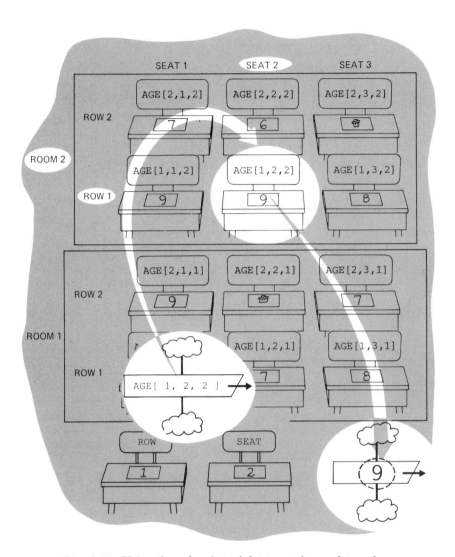

Fig. 6.11 Using the subscript triplet to retrieve a data value.

Private Practice

P6.6   Consider an array used to store the reading score of each of a group of pupils. Call it SCORES. The 20 pupils are seated as shown, five at each of four tables. At each place are two tests that must be completed. The tests are numbered 1 and 2, the seats are numbered 1 to 5, and the tables are numbered 1 to 4. Each score is thus to be identified by test number, seat number, and table number. Draw a three-dimensional desk memory to store the scores. Include three subscript desks: TEST,SEAT,TABLE.

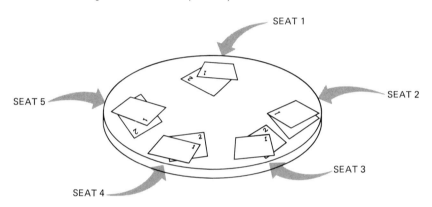

P6.7   Construct a series of figures like Figs. 6.7 through 6.11 to evaluate an array reference of one cell of the array just created for (P6.6). Choose an appropriate set of three values for the subscripts and evaluate the following reference.

SCORES[TABLE,SEAT,TEST]

P6.8   Consider the desk memory array shown in Fig. 6.6. Redraw that memory and relabel the seat backs to establish the first subscript as 'ROOM', the second as 'ROW', and the third as 'SEAT'. On your redrawn desk memory, identity the memory location cited by AGE[2,1,3], AGE[1,1,1], AGE[2,2,2], AGE[1,2,3], and AGE[2,1,1].

P6.9   Rewrite the citations from (P6.8) for the subscript order 'ROW', 'SEAT', 'ROOM'. Identify the memory location of each rewritten array reference. Use the desk layout in Fig. 6.6. Note which four desks are cited and compare their location to those cited in the preceding problem. Do the citations still refer to the same desks?

P6.10   Set up and complete an appropriate execution trace table for the code, desk memory, and suggested contents of a three-dimensional array shown on page 189. Assume the execution has reached reference point (a) of the code. Complete the labeling of each seat-back; follow the subscript order of the second assignment: SEAT,ROW,ROOM.

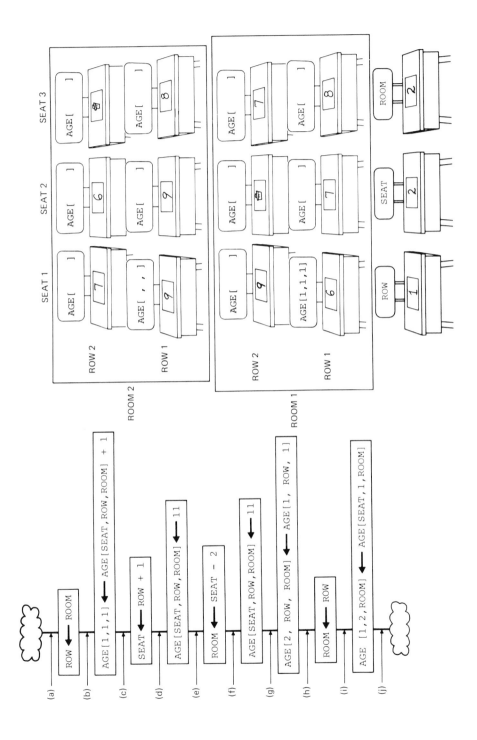

DECLARATION OF MULTIDIMENSIONAL ARRAYS

Two things are established by the declaration of any multidimensional array: (1) the memory space the computer must reserve for the array and (2) the order of the subscripts.

Establishing Storage for the Array

The programmer must tell the computer exactly how many storage locations are required to represent a multidimensional array. Inside the subscript brackets, each dimension must be represented by its own entry, separated from other entries by commas. As with one-dimensional arrays, TYPE and SIZE characteristics follow the structure's dataname. Figure 6.12 illustrates.

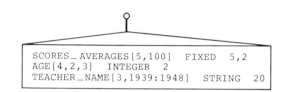

```
SCORES_AVERAGES[5,100]   FIXED   5,2
AGE[4,2,3]   INTEGER   2
TEACHER_NAME[3,1939:1948]   STRING   20
```

Fig. 6.12 Declarations for multidimensional arrays.

SCORES_AVERAGES is a two-dimensional array of decimal data, set up to store five score averages for each of 100 pupils. AGE is a three-dimensional array of integer data, set up to store ages for four rooms of pupils, each containing two three-pupil rows.

TEACHER_NAME is a 30-celled, two-dimensional array of string data, set up to store three teachers' names for each of ten years. But it differs from previous array declarations in that it demonstrates how to set subscript values to a range that does not begin at 1. Its second subscript should only take on values from 1939 through 1948. With such a declaration a reference to TEACHER_NAME[1,4] would be invalid, while a reference to TEACHER_NAME[1,1940] would be fine. Such a range declaration would be useful if the data were already coded with years ranging from 1939 to 1948.

Establishing the Subscript Order through Declaration

The subscript order established in the declaration must be adhered to consistently throughout the program. Though the order declared is strictly up to the programmer, once made, it must be followed religiously thereafter.

The declaration of SCORES_AVERAGES in Fig. 6.12, for example, requires subsequent references to cite subscripts in the order test number, pupil number. Similarly, subsequent references to AGE must use the order room, row, pupil. And references to TEACHER_NAME must use the order teacher, year.

Private Practice

P6.11   For each specification, declare an array and subscript variables, then create a variably subscripted reference to it.

   a. An array to hold 35 pulse readings for each of 2000 patients;
   b. An array to contain the names of 500 employees in each of six locations;
   c. An array to hold 2000 pulse readings for each of 35 patients;
   d. An attendance array for the 10th, 11th, and 12th grades of six high schools in the Central Unified School District.

P6.12   How many cells would be in each of the arrays declared below?

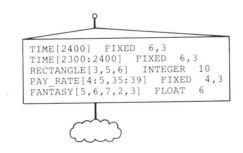

```
TIME[2400]   FIXED   6,3
TIME[2300:2400]   FIXED   6,3
RECTANGLE[3,5,6]   INTEGER   10
PAY_RATE[4:5,35:39]   FIXED   4,3
FANTASY[5,6,7,2,3]   FLOAT   6
```

A DISPLAY PROGRAM: WHILES AND TWO-DIMENSIONAL ARRAYS

Arrays of more than one dimension are very widely used in certain computer applications. As with one-dimensional arrays, their utility depends on repetition. To illustrate, we create a brief program to display large letters on a TV-like screen. The input comes from a device that sends letter-display signals. Our equipment is suggested in Fig. 6.13.

Fig. 6.13 Printing letters on a screen.

Let us first describe the screen. Like our musical apparatus, this screen will be hooked to the computer. Figure 6.14 depicts its face, an arrangement of 63 dots, in nine rows and seven columns. Each dot can be either dark or light.

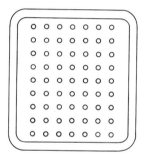

Fig. 6.14 Screen with 63 dots.

A letter may be formed on the screen by lighting some dots and making others dark. A dot is part of the letter formed if that dot is lit; it is not if it is dark. The dots are so arranged that it is natural to represent their location on the screen in array notation. If we declare an array

LETTER[9,7] INTEGER 1

we can store either a 1 or a 0 in each cell, thus specifying the state of each dot on the screen as either light or dark. We refer to any dot by citing LETTER-[LINE,COLUMN]. Each dot's state can be controlled then through a corresponding cell of LETTER.

This relation among screen, dot lighting, array, and cell contents is suggested by Figs. 6.15 and 6.16. The letter "T" is formed by lighting 13 of the 63 dots on the screen. To make any letter appear, our program need only make the right assignments to LETTER and then transmit the contents of the 63 cells to the screen display.

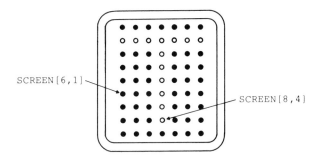

Fig. 6.15 A 13-dot letter T on the screen.

[1,1]	[1,2]	[1,3]	[1,4]	[1,5]	[1,6]	[1,7]
0	0	0	0	0	0	0

[2,1]	[2,2]	[2,3]	[2,4]	[2,5]	[2,6]	[2,7]
1	1	1	1	1	1	1

[3,1]	[3,2]	[3,3]	[3,4]	[3,5]	[3,6]	[3,7]
0	0	0	1	0	0	0

[4,1]	[4,2]	[4,3]	[4,4]	[4,5]	[4,6]	[4,7]
0	0	0	1	0	0	0

[5,1]	[5,2]	[5,3]	[5,4]	[5,5]	[5,6]	[5,7]
0	0	0	1	0	0	0

[6,1]	[6,2]	[6,3]	[6,4]	[6,5]	[6,6]	[6,7]
0	0	0	1	0	0	0

[7,1]	[7,2]	[7,3]	[7,4]	[7,5]	[7,6]	[7,7]
0	0	0	1	0	0	0

[8,1]	[8,2]	[8,3]	[8,4]	[8,5]	[8,6]	[8,7]
0	0	0	1	0	0	0

[9,1]	[9,2]	[9,3]	[9,4]	[9,5]	[9,6]	[9,7]
0	0	0	0	0	0	0

Fig. 6.16 LETTER contents corresponding to a lighted T.

This requires repetition and variable subscripting. Two nested WHILEs are needed. Figure 6.17 presents the inner WHILE; its task is to transmit the contents of a single row of LETTER to the actual screen, one cell at a time. To accomplish this, COLUMN must be varied from 1 through 7, the range of cells per row.

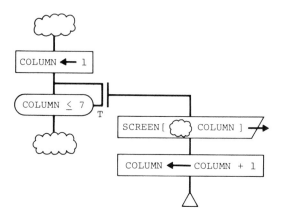

Fig. 6.17 Transmission of light states for one row of dots.

But this WHILE handles only a single row. We need a second WHILE to make the first handle each of nine rows in its turn. Figure 6.18 shows the complete structure. The nine repetitions are accomplished by using LINE as the controlling variable, varying its value from 1 through 9.

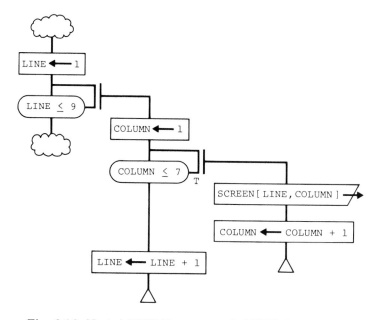

Fig. 6.18 Nested WHILEs to transmit LETTER's contents.

Private Practice

P6.13   Suppose the screen array were ten dots across and ten dots down (10 × 10). Provide a declaration for such an array and modify the code presented in Fig. 6.18 to suit the new screen.

P6.14   Create the nested WHILE code necessary for initializing all cells of Fig. 6.15 to 0 (the dark state).

P6.15   Suppose the screen were 132 dots wide and 66 dots high. What modifications would you need to make to your declaration and nested WHILE code?

P6.16   Assume that the contents of array correspond to those shown in Fig. 6.16. Create an execution trace table for the nested WHILE code in Fig. 6.18. Use five execution reference points, as shown in the code below. Let your execution proceed until LINE assumes the value 3. On each line of the trace table entered for point (D), place a check mark beneath that cell of LETTER whose contents were most recently copied and transmitted.

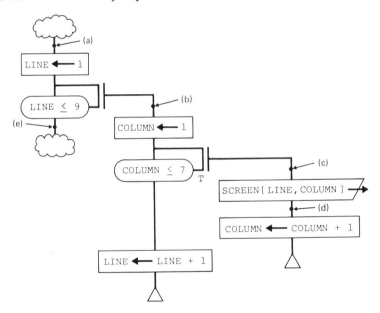

P6.17   A new screen has been developed to produce *colored* letters. This requires that *three* lighting indicator values be transmitted for each dot—one for *red*, one for *blue*, and one for *yellow*. The three values for one dot must be transmitted in sequence (red,blue,yellow) *before* any value is transmitted for the next dot. Write a program to transmit letters to this color screen.

P6.18   Write a program that prints letter patterns on a printer by literally printing LETTER on paper, one line (row) at a time. Enhance the appearance of the printed letter by using blanks and asterisks in place of 0's and 1's.

P6.19   Modify the program created for (P6.18) so that it can read *three* letters, and then print them in *reverse* order. (If the equivalent of R,P,T is read in, the program should print out the pattern for T, then for P, and then for R.)

COMPLETING THE PROGRAM TO DISPLAY THE LETTER T

Let's complete our letter-display program by working out the details of loading the T pattern of 1's and 0's (Fig. 6.16) into LETTER.

Loading the T Pattern into the Array, LETTER

Loading the T into LETTER is tedious but simple. First we assign a 0 to each cell of LETTER (Fig. 6.19), then we define the T by assigning a 1 to those cells forming the actual letter (Fig. 6.20).

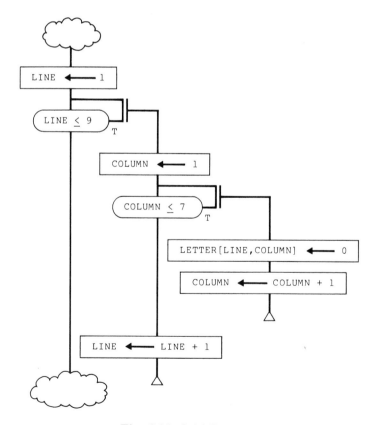

Fig. 6.19 Initialization.

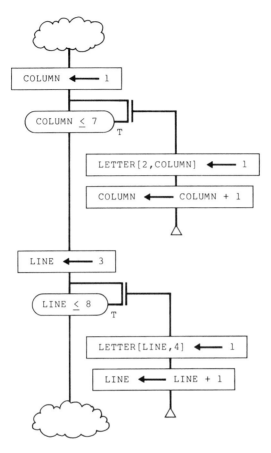

Fig. 6.20 Loading T into LETTER.

Displaying the Letter

The displaying or printing of the letter is done by the FPL in Fig. 6.21, following the pattern of Fig. 6.18. There are two minor differences from that earlier figure because this program is designed to print the pattern as 1's and 0's on a paper or screen; the earlier one was merely transmitting the pattern to a screen which itself interpreted the pattern.

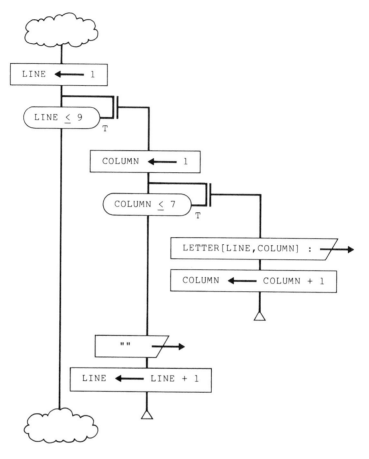

Fig. 6.21 Displaying the letter.

First, a concatenation symbol has been added to

This forces the computer to display the *next* item on the same line used to display this one. This addition is necessary so that each string of 1's and/or 0's constituting a single row in the letter is displayed as a single line on the screen. Second,

has been added. It will be executed once per line, at the end. It terminates the concatenation caused by the (:) in

LETTER[LINE,COLUMN] :

If these two changes were not included, all the 1's and 0's would be displayed in a single column, one per line! On a screen, they would simply flash by in the left-hand column until the last nine of the 63 were visible; those nine would be the only display. On paper, the 63 1's and 0's would be printed in a long column down the left side of the paper.

The Entire Program

The complete program appears in Fig. 6.22.

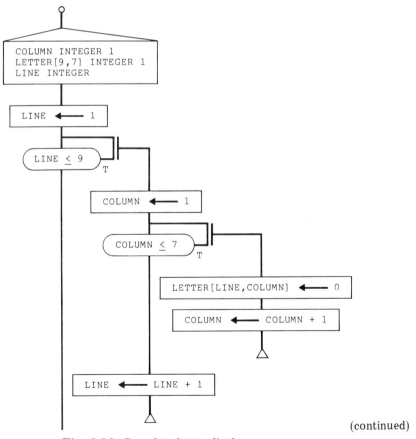

(continued)

Fig. 6.22 Complete letter-display program.

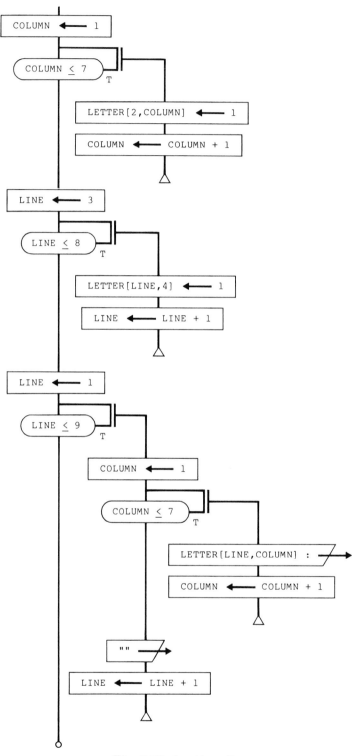

Fig. 6.22 (continued)

Private Practice

P6.20   Modify the program so that the letter loaded and displayed is L rather than T.

P6.21   A larger display screen is available, eleven lines high and nine columns wide. Modify the program so that the same size T is displayed on this larger screen, making the upper and lower borders two lines each and the border on each side, one column.

INCREASING FLEXIBILITY:
STORING THE LETTER PATTERN IN A FILE

There is a weakness in the program as it stands: the data is part of the program. This program would be more flexible if it read the pattern for a letter from a file. Without modification, the program could then print any letter that happened to be represented in the file. Figure 6.23 presents a file-reading version of the program. It assumes that LPATTERN contains 63 integer items, each either a 1 or a 0. Accordingly, it assumes no initialization of the cells of LETTER is required—all will be filled with data from the file. Loading constitutes initialization.

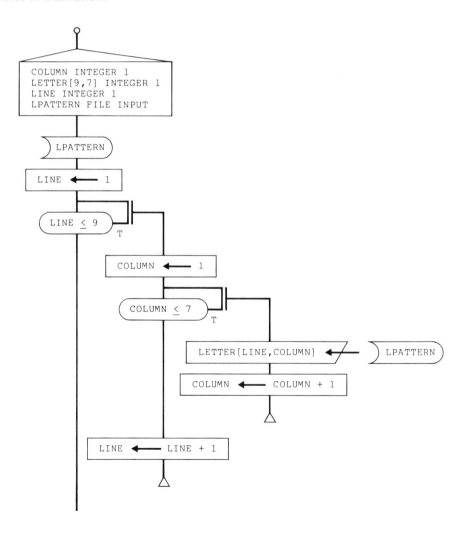

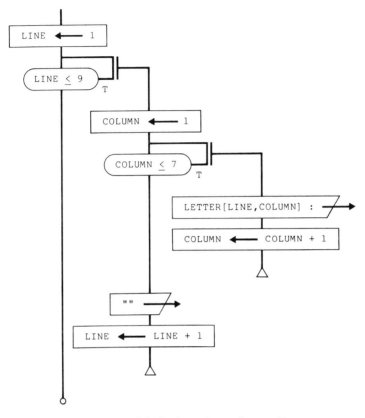

Fig. 6.23 Displaying a letter from a file.

Private Practice

P6.22   Create the program to load the file LPATTERN with a pattern for the letter L.

P6.23   Indicate how both programs should be modified to match the specifications set forth in (P6.21).

BASIC Interpretation of Chapter 6

THE LETTER-DISPLAY PROGRAM
AND TWO-DIMENSIONAL ARRAYS IN BASIC

Multidimensional arrays are interpreted in BASIC as suggested by Fig. B6.1.

```
00100 REM ----- TRANSLATION OF FIG. 6.22 ---------------
00105 REM        EARL SARVEY      JUNE 1980
00110 REM L% : LINE INTEGER 2
00120 REM C% : COLUMN INTEGER 1
00130 REM S%() : SCREEN[9,7] INTEGER 1
00135 REM -------------------------------------------
00140 DIM S%(9,7)
00142 PRINT "THIS PROGRAM PRINTS THE LETTER T AS A PATTERN OF 1'S AND 0'S,"
00144 PRINT "SEVEN COLUMNS WIDE AND NINE LINES HIGH."
00146 PRINT
00160 L% = 1
00170 IF L% > 9 GOTO 250
00180    IC% = 1
00190    IF C% > 7 GOTO 230
00200       S%(L%,C%) = 0
00210       C% = C% + 1
00220       GO TO 190
00230    L% = L% + 1
00240    GOTO 170
00250 L% = 2
00270 C% = 1
00280 IF C% > 7 GOTO 320
00290    S%(L%,C%) = 1
00300    C% = C% + 1
00310    GOTO 280
00320 C% = 4
00330 1% = 3
00340 IF L% >8 GOTO 410
00350    S%(L%,C%) = 1
00360    L% = L% + 1
00370    GOTO 340
00410 L% = 1
00420 IF L% > 9 GOTO 510
00430    C% = 1
00440    IF C% > 7 GOTO 480
00450       PRINT S%(L%,C%);
00460       C% = C% + 1
00470       GOTO 440
00480    PRINT
00490    L% = L% + 1
00500    GOTO 420
00510 PRINT
00520 PRINT
00540 END
```

Fig. B6.1 BASIC translation of the letter-display program in Fig. 6.22.

The translation follows the FPL closely and offers no surprises. Compare this to the original.

Note only the following minor points.

1. The declaration must include all dimensions of the array.

00140 DIM S% (9,7)

2. The ; in line 450 serves the same role as the : in the FPL original, forcing the *next* output to be printed on the same line.

3. Line 480 serves the same role as the

in the FPL original—it forces the computer to skip to a new line.

Private Practice BASIC

BP6.1   Enter the program in Fig. B6.1 into your computer and run it.

BP6.2   Translate the program from (P6.10) into BASIC, inserting an appropriate tracing PRINT at points (a) through (j). In initial assignments, place the values shown in the desk memory into the appropriate cells of AGE and into SEAT and ROOM. Run the program and compare the trace table with the one you originally created by hand.

BP6.3   Translate the program created for (P6.18) into BASIC and run it.

BP6.4   Translate the modification created for (P6.19) into BASIC and run it. Use your own initials for the letters.

BP6.5   Create an FPL program which will read in 20 names, each ten characters long, then print them out with the ten letters of each name in reverse order, and the 20 names in reverse order. For example, if the first name read in is

William∧∧∧

then it should be printed out last and should appear as

∧∧∧mailliW

Translate your program into BASIC and run it.

BP6.6   Translate the solution to (P6.21) into BASIC and run it.

BP6.7   Translate the solution to (P6.22) into BASIC and run it.

BP6.8   Translate the program shown in Fig. 6.23 into BASIC and run it on the file prepared by (BP6.7).

Pascal Interpretation of Chapter 6

THE LETTER-DISPLAY PROGRAM
AND TWO-DIMENSIONAL ARRAYS IN PASCAL

Multidimensional arrays translate into Pascal as suggested in Fig. P6.1.

```
PROGRAM c6f22(output);
  (* Translation of Fig. 6.22 *)
  (*      Earl Sarvey    July 1980 *)
    VAR
      line : INTEGER;
      column : INTEGER;
      letter : ARRAY[1..9,1..7] OF INTEGER;
    BEGIN
      line := 1;
      WHILE line <= 9 DO
          BEGIN
            column := 1;
            WHILE column <= 7 DO
             BEGIN
               letter[line,column] := 0;
               column := column + 1
             END;
             line := line + 1
          END;
      column := 1;
      WHILE column <= 7 DO
          BEGIN
            letter[2,column] := 1;
            column := column + 1
          END;
      line := 3;
      WHILE line <= 8 DO
          BEGIN
            letter[line,4] := 1;
            line := line + 1
          END;
      line := 1;
      WHILE line <= 9 DO
          BEGIN
            column := 1;
            WHILE column <= 7 DO
               BEGIN
                 WRITE(letter[line,column]:1);
                 column := column + 1
               END;
             WRITELN;
             line := line + 1
          END;
    END. (* c6f22 *)
```

Fig. P6.1 Pascal translation of the letter-display program in Fig. 6.22.

Compare this program to the FPL original and note the following.

1. The declaration must include the range of values each subscript may assume, with the respective ranges separated by commas inside the brackets.

letter : ARRAY[1..9,1..7] OF INTEGER;

2. The WRITE(letter[line,column]:1) forces printing to continue on the same line; the WRITELN forces the beginning of a new line. Together, this pair function as do

```
LETTER[LINE,COLUMN] :
```

and

```
" "
```

in the FPL counterpart.

Though this program does not require any string data longer than a single character, this is an appropriate place to remark further about string handling in standard Pascal. You should be aware of the following point.

3. An array of string data must assume one more dimension in Pascal than in FPL because in Pascal a string is itself an array of single characters. For example, the FPL declaration

ANNUAL_PRIZE_FILM [1950:1975] STRING 40

would be translated in Pascal as

annualprizefilm : ARRAY [1950..1975, 1..40] OF CHAR;

Private Practice Pascal

PP6.1   Enter the Pascal letter printing program (c6f22) into your computer and run it.

PP6.2   Translate the program from (P6.10) into Pascal, inserting an appropriate tracing WRITELN at points (a) through (j). In initial assignments, place the values shown in the desk memory into the appropriate cells of AGE and into SEAT and ROOM. Run the program and compare the trace table with the one you originally created by hand.

PP6.3   Translate the program created for (P6.18) into Pascal and run it.

PP6.4   Translate the modification created for (P6.19) into Pascal and run it. Use your own initials for the letters.

PP6.5   Create an FPL program that will read in 20 names, each ten characters long, then print them out with the ten letters of each name in reverse order, and the 20 names in reverse order. For example, if the first name read in is

William∧∧∧

then it should be printed out last and should appear as

∧∧∧mailliW

Translate your program into PASCAL and run it.

PP6.6   Translate the solution to (P6.21) into Pascal and run it.

PP6.7   Translate the solution to (P6.22) into Pascal and run it.

PP6.8   Translate the program shown in Fig. 6.23 into Pascal and run it on the file prepared by (PP6.7).

Synthesizing–
Creating a Survey
Analysis Program

INTRODUCTION

We have covered a number of fundamental programming concepts and constructs. In this chapter, we demonstrate their use by creating a program to analyze a simple set of survey data. The survey concerns student attitudes toward a proposed library improvement.

SURVEYING LIBRARY USE

The questionnaire shown in Fig. 7.1 was given to 643 students enrolled in courses using reserve books. All were returned correctly filled out and each was transformed into a machine-readable record and entered into a file on the computer.

LIBRARY RESERVE SERVICE SURVEY

Student name _____ Age _____ Sex _____

The purpose of this survey is to determine whether students feel reserve book rooms should remain open longer each evening. Please *circle* the number of the item that most nearly expresses your feelings about such a change.

If library reserve room hours were extended to midnight on Monday, Tuesday, Wednesday, and Thursday, it would

(1) considerably increase my use of reserve books;

(2) moderately increase my use of reserve books;

(3) not alter the amount I use reserve books.

Fig. 7.1 The first survey instrument.

Figure 7.2 shows three typical records from that file. Each rates the proposed change differently: Samuelson indicates it would not increase his use of reserve books; Nwankire indicates it would sharply increase hers; and Akai indicates it would moderately increase his.

Name	Age	Sex	Rating of change
Samuelson	21	M	3
Nwankire	23	F	1
Akai	20	M	2

Fig. 7.2 Sample response records.

The required analysis is suggested by Fig. 7.3., a mock-up report based on a sample of 100 input records. It must show how many students rated the proposed change in hours with a 1, how many with a 2, and how many with a 3. In a fourth column, it must provide the average rating. This average is the sum of all the ratings, divided by the number of respondents.

NUMBER OF RESPONDENTS BY RATING			AVERAGE
1	2	3	RATING
21	45	34	2.13

Fig. 7.3 Sample output.

CREATING A PROGRAM TO ANALYZE THE SURVEY DATA

First, we produce an episodic solution as shown in Fig. 7.4. At this rough level, the outline our analysis program must have is obvious: declaration; data reading and tallying; averaging; and reporting.

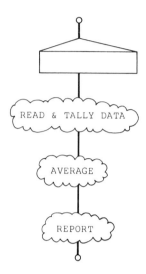

Fig. 7.4 Episodic version of program.

Though we might begin with any one of the episodes, we will start with the final one. In refining it, we will see what is demanded of the earlier episodes, then work our way backwards refining them until the entire program is complete.

Creating the Report

The report mock-up suggests that our program must print a heading above the details. This heading is so simple we can create the assignments to generate it immediately without reference to earlier parts of the program. What we need is shown in Fig. 7.5.

Fig. 7.5 Assignments to produce heading.

To print the factual line we require three counts, one for each of the three possible ratings given the proposed change. Let's assume earlier episodes store those counts in the three cells of an array declared as

COUNT_BY_RATING [3] INTEGER 3

Then the better part of the report detail line would be generated by

COUNT_BY_RATING [1] : COUNT_BY_RATING [2] :
                    COUNT_BY_RATING [3] : $\longrightarrow$

What's missing is the average rating.

Let's assume the preceding episode calculates the average rating and stores it in a variable declared as

AVG_RATING FIXED 3,2

The complete detail report line could then be generated by

COUNT_BY_RATING [1] : COUNT_BY_RATING [2] :
                    COUNT_BY_RATING [3] : AVG_RATING $\longrightarrow$

Combining these declarations and refinements produces the first major refinement toward our finished program, Fig. 7.6.

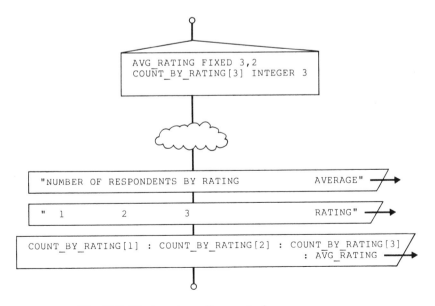

Fig. 7.6 First major refinement of survey program.

Computing the Average Rating

We must calculate an average and assign it to AVG_RATING so that the last segment can print it. To compute the average rating, we must add all the ratings together and divide by the number of respondents. Assume that an earlier episode builds the sum of all ratings and stores it in a variable declared as

TOTAL_OF_RATINGS INTEGER 4

We know that 643 respondents participated so the assignment

AVG_RATINGS ⟵ TOTAL_OF_RATINGS / 643

will compute the average and store it where the final portion of the program expects to find it. This additional refinement extends our program as shown in Fig. 7.7.

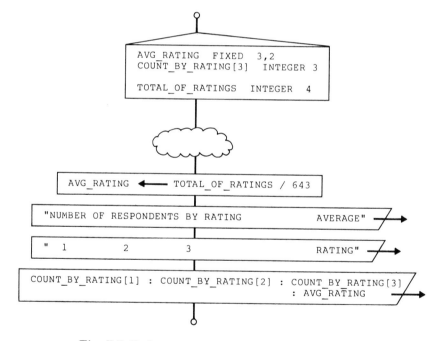

Fig. 7.7 Refinement to include average computation.

Reading All the Ratings

This portion must read the 643 responses, count each, and add its value (1, 2, or 3) to the sum in TOTAL_OF_RATINGS. A record will be necessary, matching the format of the data collected. Assume it is declared as follows

```
RESPONDENT,
        NAME    STRING   20,
        AGE     INTEGER  2,
        SEX     STRING   1,
        RATING  INTEGER  1.
```

To read in all such responses, we will need a WHILE, set to execute its digression 643 times. To control it, assume a counter has been declared as

RESPONSES   INTEGER 3

The WHILE is shown in Fig. 7.8.

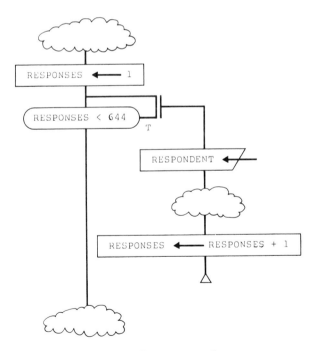

Fig. 7.8 Response reader.

Counting the Ratings and Adding Their Values

To complete the program, we need to refine the digression episode to count the ratings and add their values to the sum in TOTAL_OF_RATINGS. For this refinement, we must use the data in RATING, the last field in the respondent record.

Following the reading of a record into RESPONDENT, RATING is 1, 2, or 3. For example, after reading the record for Samuelson, RATING is 3. This is the value that must be added to TOTAL_OF_RATINGS. The final refinement on one part of this episode then is

$$\text{TOTAL\_OF\_RATINGS} \longleftarrow \text{TOTAL\_OF\_RATINGS} + \text{RATING}$$

The refinement of the rest of the episode also uses RATING, but less directly.

The counts in COUNT_BY_RATING [1], COUNT_BY_ RATING [2], and COUNT_BY_RATING [3] should be the number of respondents who rated the change in hours with a 1, with a 2, and with a 3, respectively. That means the *value* of the RATING read precisely identifies the cell of COUNT_BY_RATING in which that rating should be counted: Samuelson (RATING = 3) should be counted in COUNT_BY_RATING [3], Akai (RAT-ING = 2) in COUNT_BY_RATING [2], and so forth.

Once we've seen that relationship, we arrive at a simple refinement to complete the digression. A single assignment making use of RATING as a subscript will properly count the ratings

$$\text{COUNT\_BY\_RATING[RATING]} \longleftarrow$$
$$\text{COUNT\_BY\_RATING[RATING]} + 1$$

Using input values in this fashion is a very powerful technique, so make sure you understand and remember it. It uses data values to direct the computer to specific cells of an array.

The completely refined section to do all the reading, counting, and totaling appears in Fig. 7.9.

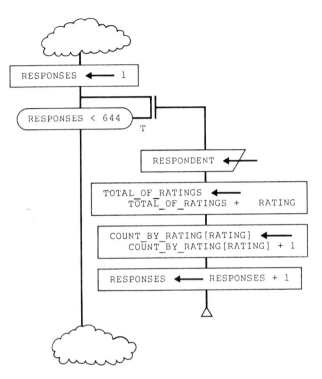

Fig. 7.9 Final refinement to read, count, and total.

Completing the Program

The program is nearly complete but details to initialize TOTAL_OF_RATING and the three cells of COUNT_ BY_RATING must still be added. The first is easily taken care of by inserting

TOTAL_OF_RATING ⟵ 0

Initializing the three array cells requires a single WHILE. This WHILE and the assignment above appear in Fig. 7.10.

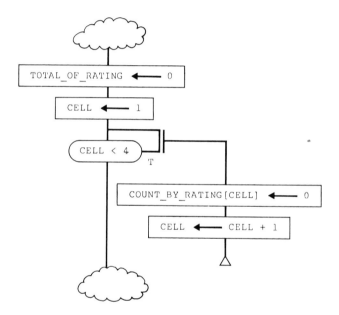

Fig. 7.10 Initialization.

All our refinements combined produce the program product in Fig. 7.11, with execution reference points labeled for testing.

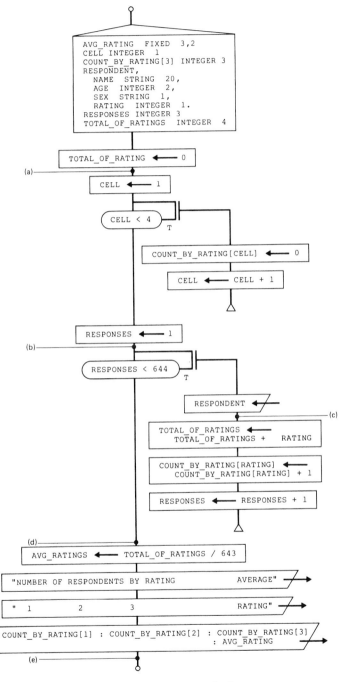

Fig. 7.11 The finished survey analysis program.

Testing the Program

The program is ready to be tested. To simplify, we modify the WHILE assertion to

RESPONSES < 4

the average calculation to

AVG_RATING ⟵ TOTAL_OF_RATINGS / 3

and use the three-record data stream (which has been set in a smaller typeface so that it can remain in an unbroken line)

BILL∧ONUOHA∧∧∧∧∧∧∧∧∧∧∧23M2MARIA∧MEZZINA∧∧∧∧∧∧∧∧25F1JAMES∧CHANG ∧∧∧∧∧∧∧∧∧∧2

The results appear in the table shown in Fig. 7.12. To conserve space, some datanames have been abbreviated and only the first five letters of the name field for each record have been entered.

Point	NAME	RAT	RESPONS	TOTRAT	CNT_RAT			AVG
(a)	*	*	*	0	*	*	*	*
(b)	*	*	*	0	0	0	0	*
(c)	BILL∧	1	1	0	0	0	0	*
(c)	MARIA	1	2	2	0	1	0	*
(c)	JAMES	3	3	3	1	1	0	*
(d)	JAMES	3	4	6	1	1	1	*
(e)	JAMES	3	4	6	1	1	6	2

Fig. 7.12 Program trace table.

Private Practice

P7.1   The same survey is conducted, this time with a questionnaire that allows five different ratings instead of just three. Modify the program to handle this change appropriately.

P7.2   Completely rewrite the survey analysis program, substituting datanames of your own invention for those shown in Fig. 7.11.

P7.3   Modify the report section so that it uses a WHILE to print the three counts, one below the other. It should print the average on a fourth line, below the counts, and each count and the average must be labeled appropriately.

P7.4   The United Nations has prepared a series of brief booklets about UNESCO for school children. Each booklet contains a card to be marked and returned by the reader as soon as he or she has finished reading the booklet. The card allows a reader to indicate which of four aspects of UNESCO seems most important in the booklet. Over 10,000 of the cards have now been completed and returned, and a sample of exactly 1000 has been put in machine-readable form and entered into a computer file. Three typical records from that file are

Name	Age	Country	Aspect
HUMBOLT, HANS	11	53	4
SAMOES, THERESA	11	47	2
CHIN, SHU-MING	13	05	1

The Director of UNESCO wants the sample of 1000 analysed. Write a program that will read all the data and produce a report on the number of respondents choosing each of the four aspects of UNESCO. Design appropriate headings and labels for your report. Assume the record description

```
UN_KID_REC,
        NAME STRING 20,
        AGE INTEGER 2,
        COUNTRY INTEGER 2,
        UNESCO_ ASPECT INTEGER 1.
```

Label your program and use the three sample records above to test it.

MAKING THE PROGRAM MORE
FLEXIBLE AT READING RESPONSES

The survey reflected in Fig. 7.1 is rather simple. Suppose it were more involved, as the questionnaire in Fig. 7.13 suggests. Each response record would include two additional fields as the data in Fig. 7.14 suggests, and the record declaration would have to be modified to match.

LIBRARY RESERVE SERVICE SURVEY

Student name _____ Age _____ Sex _____

The purpose of this survey is to determine whether students feel reserve book rooms should remain open longer each evening, whether students feel the number of book titles currently on reserve is really sufficient, and whether students generally feel the lighting in the west reserve room is adequate. Questions have been repeatedly raised about all three for some time and the Director will take action if student opinion warrants it. Please *circle* the number of the item that most nearly expresses your feelings about each change.

(1) If library reserve room hours were extended to midnight on Monday, Tuesday, Wednesday, and Thursday, it would

>   (1) considerably increase my use of reserve books
>
>   (2) moderately increase my use of reserve books
>
>   (3) not alter the amount I use reserve books

(2) If the number of different titles on reserve regularly were increased, it would

>   (1) considerably increase my use of reserve books
>
>   (2) moderately increase my use of reserve books
>
>   (3) not alter the amount I use reserve books

(3) If the lighting in the west reserve room were significantly improved, it would

>   (1) considerably increase my use of reserve books
>
>   (2) moderately increase my use of reserve books
>
>   (3) not alter the amount I use reserve books

Fig. 7.13 The second survey instrument.

Name	Age	Sex	Rating of Change		
			Hours	Titles	Lights
Samuelson	21	M	3	1	3
Nwankire	23	F	1	2	2
Akai	20	M	2	1	3

Fig. 7.14 Sample response records.

One record alternative would be

RESPONDENT,
      NAME STRING 20,
      AGE INTEGER 2,
      SEX STRING 1,
      HOURS INTEGER 1.
      TITLES INTEGER 1.
      LIGHTS INTEGER 1.

With this record declaration substituted for the original, two additional modifications would render our original program capable of reporting on any one of the three proposed changes. For example, to report on the lighting change, we would substitute LIGHTS for RATING in

      TOTAL_OF_RATINGS ⟵
            TOTAL_OF_RATINGS + LIGHTS

and in

      COUNT_BY_RATING [LIGHTS] ⟵
            COUNT_BY_RATING [LIGHTS] + 1.

An alternative modification to the record declaration that would provide slightly more flexibility would handle the three change ratings as an array within RESPONDENT. This alternative would be declared

RESPONDENT,
      NAME STRING 20,
      AGE INTEGER 2,
      SEX STRING 1,
      CHANGE [3] INTEGER 1.

The totaling and the counting assignments would each need to be modified accordingly. To report on lighting, they should read

TOTAL_OF_RATINGS ⟵—— TOTAL_OF_RATINGS + CHANGE [3]

and

COUNT_BY_RATING [CHANGE [3]] ⟵——
    COUNT_BY_RATING [CHANGE[3]] + 1.

To report on hours instead, only the subscript 3 needs to be changed to 1.

TOTAL_OF_RATINGS ⟵——
    TOTAL_OF_RATINGS + CHANGE [1]

and

COUNT_BY_RATING [CHANGE [1]] ⟵——
    COUNT_BY_RATING [CHANGE [1]] + 1.

Declaring several like fields within a record as an array, then using a reference to some cell of that array as a subscript variable within another array reference is a useful programming trick. Expect to see more of it. The final result here is shown in Fig. 7.15.

Figure 7.15 shows the survey program modified in this fashion. As set, it would report on the hours change; it could be modified to report on a different change merely by modifying the two numeric subscripts in

COUNT_BY_RATING [CHANGE [1]] ⟵——
    COUNT_BY_RATING [CHANGE [1]] + 1.

and

TOTAL_OF_RATINGS ⟵——
    TOTAL_OF_RATINGS + CHANGE [1].

Replacing the 1's with 2's would make the program report on the titles change; with 3's, on the lighting.

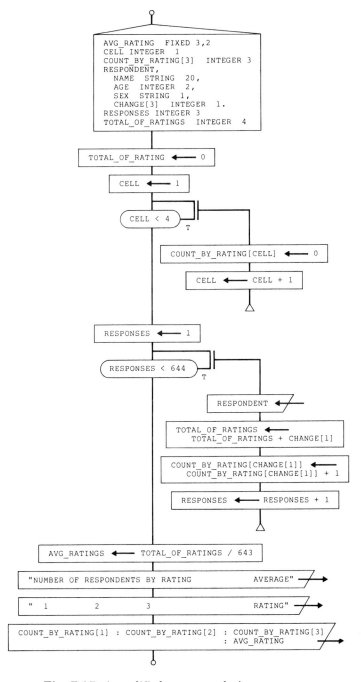

Fig. 7.15 A modified survey analysis program.

Private Practice

P7.5   A fourth change, one about staffing of the reserve room, has been added to the questionnaire. Modify the program so that it can report on that new change.

P7.6   A new, much broader survey about the library has been conducted. It deals with fifteen changes instead of just three, and each change can be rated 1,2,3,4, or 5 rather than just 1,2, or 3. Modify the program so that with minor changes to a single assignment, it can be used to report on any one of the proposed changes.

P7.7   Modify your completely rewritten version of this program (P7.2) so that it works for the fourth change to the survey mentioned in (P7.5). As with (P7.2), use your own datanames for the additions.

P7.8   The UN is so well satisfied with the UNESCO survey that it has designed and run a more complex survey. This survey asks the respondent to pick one of four aspects for *each of five agencies* rather than for UNESCO alone. Use an array within the respondent record to read in the five ratings.

MAKING THE REPORT MORE INFORMATIVE ABOUT THE DATA

Though the program reports different data depending on which change it has been modified to report upon, nothing in the report tells the reader which change is being reported. This shortcoming is easily remedied by use of a further array, the cells of which contain labels for the report. For the program to report on three proposed changes, we declare

REPORT_LABEL [3]   STRING   8

and initialize its cells as follows.

REPORT_LABEL [1] ⟵── "HOURS   "
REPORT_LABEL [2] ⟵── "TITLES   "
REPORT_LABEL [3] ⟵── "LIGHTING"

One additional external assignment can then be inserted to label the report

```
"     CHANGE IN ":REPORT_LABEL[ number ]
```

(*number* must be a 1, 2, or 3.)

To decrease further the amount of modification needed to switch from one CHANGE to another, the subscript identifying the change number can be made into a variable: NUMBER. The assignment

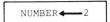

early in the program is the only thing that needs modification to switch from one CHANGE to another. Merely changing the constant completely adapts the program: 1 causes it to report on change 1; 2 (shown), to report on change 2; and 3, on change 3.

These modifications have been incorporated into the version shown in Fig. 7.16. It also includes a modification to read the responses from a file named SURDAT, a more realistic approach when so much data is involved.

Private Practice

P7.9   The survey has been expanded to rate changes in staffing as well as hours, titles, and lighting. Modify the program so that it will properly label the report regardless of which of the four changes is being reported upon.

P7.10   A school election was being held for three offices, each of which has three candidates. It is a very unusual election in that the candidates are known to the voters only by number (1, 2, or 3) and description. The description of each candidate was written by a panel of faculty and students, the numbers assigned to each description by the headmaster. The idea is to see what characteristics students vote for when they do not know the candidates personally. The 432 completed ballots have been entered into a computer file using the following format

```
BALLOT,
     VOTER_NAME   STRING 20,
     HOME_ROOM   INTEGER 3,
     OFFICE[3]      INTEGER 1.
```

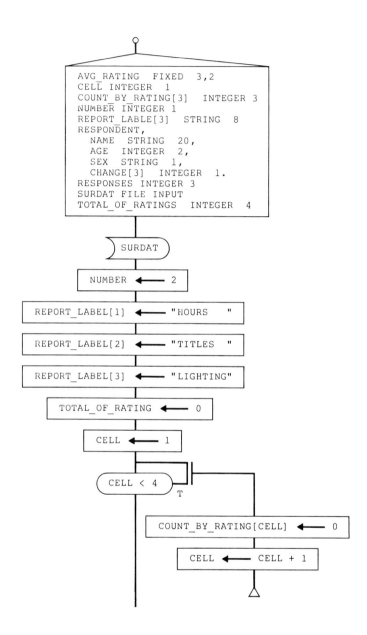

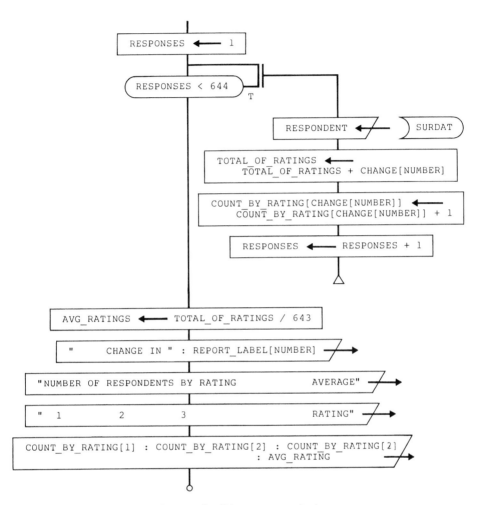

Fig. 7.16 A more flexible survey analysis program.

Write a program that can analyse the results. One run of your program should tally votes for only one of the offices. However, only numerical subscripts changes should be necessary to switch from tallying votes for one office in one run, to tallying votes for another office in another. Like the library survey program, your program is required only to indicate the total number of votes cast for each candidate in a race. Your program should include office-specific labeling of its report. For example, when run to show the results of the presidential race, it should print

RESULTS FOR PRESIDENTIAL RACE

as the first line of the report.

P7.11   Write a program to create the file SURDAT. To test your program, use the three sample records provided earlier to produce the table in Fig. 7.11, i.e.,

BILL∧ONUOHA∧∧∧∧∧∧∧∧∧23M2MARIA∧MEZZINA∧∧∧∧∧∧∧∧25F1JAMES∧CHANG ∧∧∧∧∧∧∧∧∧

BASIC Interpretation of Chapter 7

THE SURVEY ANALYSIS PROGRAM IN BASIC

Figure B7.1 presents the survey analysis program in BASIC.

```
00010 REM -----TRANSLATION OF FIG. 7.16-------------------------
00020 REM        CHARLES YOUNG        FEB 1979
00050 REM A1   : AVG_RATING  FIXED 3,2
00100 REM C1%  : CELL INTEGER   1
00200 REM C2%(3)   : COUNT_RATING[3] INTEGER 3
00300 REM N1%  : NUMBER INTEGER 1
00400 REM R$(3)    : REPORT_LABEL[3]  STRING  20
00500 REM   RESPONDENT,
00600 REM      N2$ :      NAME  STRING  20,
00800 REM      A2% :      AGE   INTEGER  2,
00900 REM      S1$ :      SEX   STRING  1,
00910 REM      C3%(3) :  CHANGE[3]  INTEGER  1.
01100 REM R1%  : RESPONSES INTEGER 3
01200 REM "SURBAS.DAT" : SURDAT FILE INPUT
01300 REM T1%  : TOTAL_OF_RATINGS  INTEGER  4
01500 REM --------------------------------------------------------
01600 DIM R$(3), C2%(3), C3%(3)
01700 OPEN "SURBAS.DAT" FOR INPUT AS FILE #1
01800 N1% = 2
01900 R$(1) = "HOURS    "
02000 R$(2) = "TITLES   "
02100 R$(3) = "LIGHTING"
02200 T1% = 0
02300 C1% = 1
02400 IF C1% > 3 GOTO 2800
02500    C2%(C1%) = 0
02600    C1% = C1% + 1
02700    GOTO 2400
02800 R1% = 1
02900 IF R1% > 3 GOTO 3500
03000    INPUT #1, N2$, A2%, S1$, C3%(1), C3%(2), C3%(3)
03100    T1% = T1% + C3%(N1%)
03200    C2%(C3%(N1%)) = C2%(C3%(N1%)) + 1
03300    R1% = R1% + 1
03400    GOTO 2900
03500 A1 = T1% / 4
03510 PRINT
03600 PRINT "            CHANGE IN "; R$(N1%)
03700 PRINT "NUMBER OF RESPONDENTS BY RATING            AVERAGE"
03800 PRINT "   1              2              3          RATING"
03900 PRINT "   "; C2%(1), C2%(2), C2%(3), "      "; A1
03910 PRINT
04000 END
```

Fig. B7.1 BASIC translation of the survey analysis program in Fig. 7.16.

Figures B7.2 and B7.3 present the test data and the report produced when the program is run on that data.

```
SALLY SHANNON         , 13, F, 1, 1, 3
MARY SMITH            , 14, F, 1, 3, 2
RAYMOND KRAMMAR       , 11, M, 1, 1, 1
FRIEDA LACKMANN       , 15, F, 1, 1, 2
```

Fig. B7.2 Test data in file "SURBAS.DAT".

```
                 CHANGE IN TITLES
NUMBER OF RESPONDENTS BY RATING              AVERAGE
     1           2          3                RATING
     2           0          1                 1.67
```

Fig. B7.3 Report.

Before proceeding to the Private Practice below, study the three figures carefully, comparing Fig. B7.1 to the FPL original (Fig. 7.16). Note that extra PRINT lines have been added to generate a blank line at the beginning and at the end of the report. Note, too, that the items printed by line 3900 depend on a combination of concatenation (;) and tabbing (,) for separation. The programmer must decide the combination to use, considering his or her own convenience and the readability of the resulting program and report.

Private Practice BASIC

BP7.1   Using the program above as a model, translate the program in Fig. 7.11 into BASIC and run it on your computer, using the three test records provided earlier for that program

BILL∧ONUOHA∧∧∧∧∧∧∧∧∧∧23M2MARIA∧MEZZINA∧∧∧∧∧∧∧∧25F1JAMES∧CHANG ∧∧∧∧∧∧∧∧∧∧∴

Include appropriate extra PRINT lines to create a trace table. Compare the table produced with that shown in Fig. 7.12. (Note that unlike the program in Fig. B7.1, this one does not use a file. Your program should be designed to simply accept the data directly, typed in from a terminal.)

BP7.2   Modify your program to match the changes specified in (P7.3).

BP7.3   Translate your solution to (P7.4) into BASIC and run it. Use the sample records provided in that problem.

BP7.4   Through an editor or program of your own, name and create a file containing the test data shown in Fig. B7.2.

BP7.5   Enter the program shown in Fig. B7.1 into your computer and run it on the file created for (BP7.4). (Be sure the name you cite in the OPEN matches the name you gave the data file!) If the resulting report does not match that shown in Fig. B7.3, modify your program until it does produce that report.

BP7.6   Translate your solution to (P7.5) into BASIC and run it.

BP7.7   Translate your solution to (P7.8) into BASIC and run it.

BP7.8   Translate your solution to (P7.9) into BASIC and run it several times, one for each of the different changes being proposed.

BP7.9   Translate your solution to (P7.10) into BASIC and run it.

BP7.10   Modify your solution to (BP7.5) so it transmits the report into a file named SURVAN rather than directly to a display screen or printer. After the program has been executed, examine the contents of SURVAN to see that they agree with those shown in Fig. P7.3.

Pascal Interpretation of Chapter 7

THE SURVEY ANALYSIS PROGRAM IN PASCAL

Figure P7.1 presents the survey analysis program in Pascal. Figures P7.2 and P7.3 present the test data and the report produced when the program is run on that data.

```
PROGRAM c7f16 (input,output,libsur);
    (* Translation of Fig. 7.16 *)
    (*  Donald Young   July 1979 *)
    TYPE
      respondshape =
        RECORD
          name : ARRAY [1 .. 20] OF CHAR;
          age : INTEGER;
          sex : CHAR;
          change : ARRAY [1 .. 3] OF INTEGER
        END;
    VAR
      avgrating : REAL;
      cell : INTEGER;
      countrating : ARRAY [1 .. 3] OF INTEGER;
      libsur : FILE OF respondshape;
      number : INTEGER;
      reportlabel : ARRAY [1 .. 3] OF CHAR;
      respondent : respondshape;
      responses : INTEGER;
      totalofrating : INTEGER;
    BEGIN
        number := 2;
        reportlabel[1] := 'H';
        reportlabel[2] := 'T';
        reportlabel[3] := 'L';
        totalofrating := 0;
        cell := 1;
        WHILE cell < 4 DO
          BEGIN
            countrating[cell] := 0;
            cell := cell + 1
          END;
        RESET(libsur);
        responses := 1;
        WHILE responses < 4 DO
          BEGIN
            respondent := libsur^;
            GET(libsur);
            totalofratings := totalofratings + respondent.change[number];
            countratings[respondent.change[number]] :=
                  countratings[respondent.change[number]] + 1;
            responses := responses + 1
          END;
```

```
avgrating := totalofratings / 3;
WRITELN;
WRITELN('REPORT ON CHANGE: ',reportlabel[1],
        ' (H=HOURS,T=TITLES,L=LIGHTING)');
WRITELN('NUMBER OF RESPONDENTS BY RATING          AVERAGE');
WRITELN('      1          2            3          RATING');
WRITELN(countrating[1]:5, countrating[2]:10, countrating[3]:10,
        '            ', avgrating:10:2);
WRITELN
END. (* c7f16 *)
```

Fig. P7.1 Pascal translation of the survey analysis program in Fig. 7.16.

```
SALLY SHANNON        , 13, F, 1, 1, 3
MARY SMITH           , 14, F, 1, 3, 2
RAYMOND KRAMMAR      , 11, M, 1, 1, 1
FRIEDA LACKMANN      , 15, F, 1, 1, 2
```

Fig. P7.2 Test data in file LIBSUR.

```
REPORT ON CHANGE: T (H=HOURS,T=TITLES,L=LIGHTING)
NUMBER OF RESPONDENTS BY RATING              AVERAGE
    1          2            3                RATING
    2          0            1                 1.67
```

Fig. P7.3 Report.

Study the three figures carefully, comparing Fig. P7.1 to the FPL original (Fig. 7.16). Then do the following Private Practice. Note in particular that the labeling of the three changes has been simplified to avoid using two-dimensional arrays of characters. The result (Fig. P7.3) is specific, but not quite as readable because of the necessary insertion

(H=HOURS,T=TITLES,L=LIGHTING).

Note also that two additional external WRITELNs have been added, the first to create a line of space at the beginning of the report, the second, a line of space at the end.

Private Practice Pascal

PP7.1   Using the program in Fig. P7.1 as a model, translate the program in Fig. 7.11 into Pascal and run it on your computer, using the three test records provided earlier for that program.

BILL∧ONUOHA∧∧∧∧∧∧∧∧∧∧23M2MARIA∧MEZZINA∧∧∧∧∧∧∧∧25F1JAMES∧CHANG ∧∧∧∧∧∧∧∧∧∧

Design and insert an appropriate number of extra WRITELNs, so that a trace table will be created as the program is executed. Compare the table produced with that shown in Fig. 7.12. (Note that unlike the program in Fig. P7.1, this one does not use a file. Your program should be designed simply to accept the data directly, typed in from a terminal.)

PP7.2   Modify your program to match the changes specified in (P7.3).

PP7.3   Translate your solution to (P7.4) into Pascal and run it. Use the sample records provided in that problem.

PP7.4   Through a program of your own, name and create a file containing the test data shown in Fig. P7.2. (If you need a model, study Fig. 3.1.)

PP7.5   Enter the program shown in P7.1 into your computer and run it on the file created for (PP7.4). (Be sure the name you cite in the program matches the name you gave the data file!) If the resulting report does not match that shown in Fig. P7.3, modify your program until it does produce that report.

PP7.6   Modify your survey program so that it uses the labels "HOURS", "TITLES", and "LIGHTING" as in the original FPL (for example, modify reportlabel[..] so that it includes far more than the first initial of each proposed change).

PP7.7   Translate your solution to (P7.5) into Pascal and run it.

PP7.8   Translate your solution to (P7.8) into Pascal and run it.

PP7.9   Translate your solution to (P7.9) into Pascal and run it several times, once for each of the different changes being proposed.

PP7.10   Translate your solution to (P7.10) into Pascal and run it.

PP7.11   Modify your solution to (PP7.5) so it transmits the report into a file named SURVAN rather than directly to a display screen or printer. After the program has been executed, examine the contents of SURVAN to see that they agree with those shown in Fig. P7.3.

Forcing the Computer to Choose – the EITHER

INTRODUCTION

In Chapter One we learned how to force the computer to execute a series of statements by means of the NEXT. In Chapter Four we learned how to make the computer repeat such executions by means of the WHILE. In this chapter, we show how to force the computer to choose between alternatives by means of the EITHER. This is the third of the basic control structures used in FPL. To begin, we will present three different problems involving choice.

THREE PROBLEMS REQUIRING CHOICES

The Tea Party: Plain or with Milk?

Consider the choices afforded guests at a tea party. The host is rigid, dictating what shall be served, and limiting the choices. A liveried servant announces that tea is ready.

Four carts pass each guest in succession and each guest must serve himself or herself something from each cart. The first cart contains cups of tea on one shelf and cups of coffee on another. Each guest must take one or the other. The second cart contains only two large pitchers, one filled with milk, one filled with air (the eccentric host's way of allowing the guest to drink the coffee black). Each guest must pour something from one pitcher or the other into his or her cup. The third cart carries slices of brown bread on one shelf and crackers wrapped in packets of two on the other shelf. Each guest must take either one slice of bread or one packet of crackers. The last cart contains a large slab of butter with a knife beside it on one shelf and on the other shelf, a jar of honey with a spoon in it. Each guest must take either some honey or some butter.

This situation is represented in Fig. 8.1. The rough program suggests several things that will prove useful in our formal definition of the EITHER. First, at the selection of decision point, a choice between two alternatives *must* be made. Second, the execution of either alternative represents an aside or digression that must be taken *before* the program below the decision point can be followed. Third, once the alternative has been executed, control returns to the point *below* the decision and not above it.

The Machine Condition Problem: Up or Down?

Two computers have been set up so that the first sends messages to the second that, in turn, translates and prints them out. We will consider the problem of writing a program that will read one message from the first computer and print "Sending machine is still down" on the second computer if the message is the numeral zero. If the message is not zero, it prints instead "Sending machine is up and transmitting." A program for this problem appears in Fig. 8.2. Without

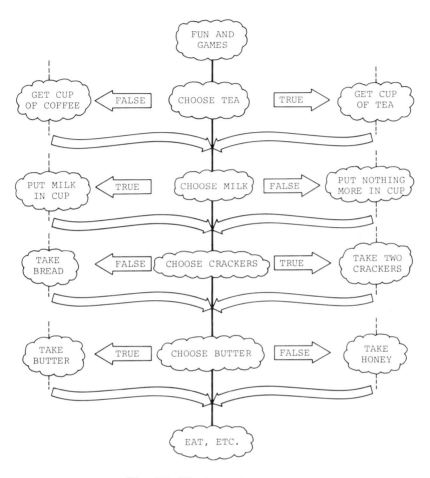

Fig. 8.1 The tea party program.

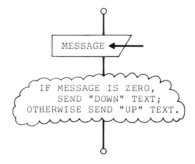

Fig. 8.2 Machine condition program.

further work, this first version could be refined as in Fig. 8.3. To refine it further, we need a definition of the EITHER.

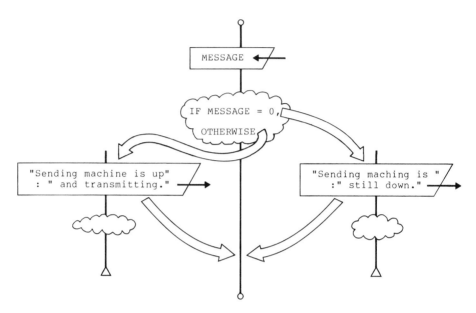

Fig. 8.3 Refining the machine condition program.

The Age Selection Problem: 13 Years Old or Not?

In this problem the program must guide the computer in finding and analyzing every occurrence of a specific record. Such occurrences are distributed randomly in a large collection, which includes other records as well. For example, suppose that mathematics scores have been collected for each of the 36,756 pupils in School District 18. The superintendent needs to know the average mathematics score for all 13-year-olds. The *order* of the computer-readable records does not help because they are arranged by school and grade, not by age. We need to write a program that will read the records, pick out the ones belonging to 13-year-olds, and compute and print out their average score.

Because it requires repetition, this program appears more complicated than did the preceding one. But Fig. 8.4 shows how to place the selection episode so as to guarantee the required repetition. The unrefined remainder appears no more complicated than did the unrefined solution to the decision problem. Three sample records appear beneath the program.

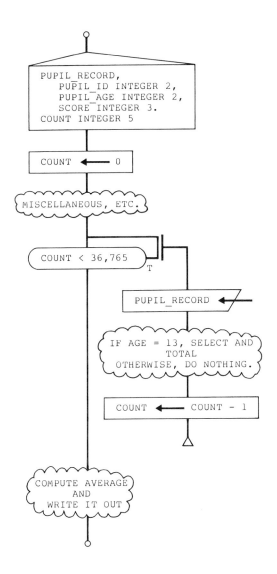

Fig. 8.4 Age selection program.

	Pupil Identification Number	Pupil age	Pupil math score
First record	1456	11	132
Second record	1223	13	109
Third record	3347	12	115

Because we've already had some experience with averaging, we deduce that the "COMPUTE AVERAGE" episode needs three variables: one for the average value itself, one to count the 13-year-olds there were, and, one in which to accumulate their total score. If we name them respectively: AVERAGE, NMBR_13_YROLDS, and TOTAL_13_YROLDS-SCORES, we can replace that particular episode with the code shown in Fig. 8.5.

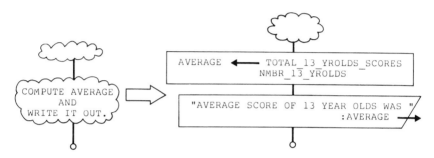

Fig. 8.5 Refining the COMPUTE AVERAGE episode.

We see immediately that the "MISCELLANEOUS, ETC." episode must include the initialization of both TOTAL_13_YROLDS_SCORES and NMBR_13_YROLDS. We refine that episode in Fig. 8.6. However, other initializations might be needed. Without formal definition of the EITHER, the refinement of the selection episode shown in Fig. 8.7 represents the furthest we can go, and leaves our entire programming effort for that problem at the stage shown in Fig. 8.8.

Private Practice

P8.1   Assume you have at your disposal some machine-readable records with the fields suggested by the following declaration.

```
PEOPLE_RECORD,
     NAME   STRING   20,
     SEX   INTEGER   1,
     DATE   INTEGER   6,
     WEIGHT   FIXED   3,2,
     ROOM   STRING   4.
```

As far as you can, rough out and refine a program that will read in one of these records and print a message indicating which sex appears on the record. "IT'S

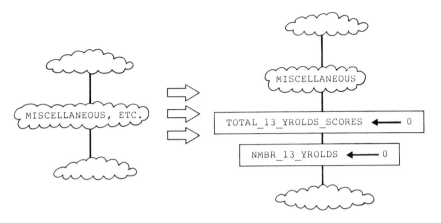

Fig. 8.6 Refining the MISCELLANEOUS, ETC, episode.

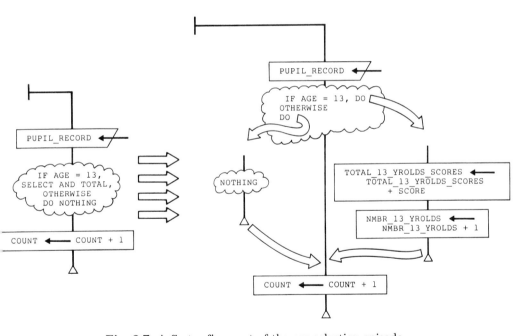

Fig. 8.7 A first refinement of the age selection episode.

A BOY!" should be printed if the value of SEX is 2 and "IT'S A GIRL!" otherwise.

P8.2   Create a rough FPL program to represent an everyday situation in which several successive decision points characterize alternative choices.

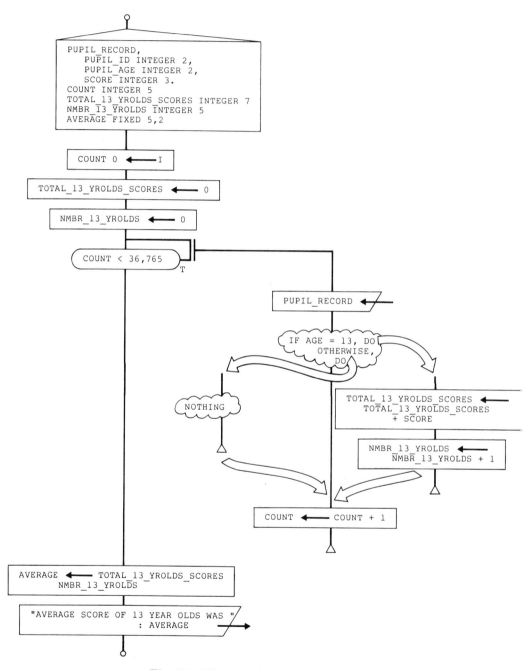

Fig. 8.8 The age selection program so far.

THE EITHER

Figure 8.9 represents the EITHER in FPL. Like the WHILE, this construct must include an assertion that is either true or false. But unlike the WHILE, the EITHER must have *two* digressions and *two* sets of entering and returning paths. One digression is executed if the assertion is true, the other if it is false. The various components of the EITHER are identified by label as follows.

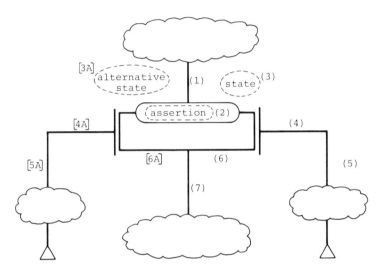

Fig. 8.9 EITHER components.

(1) A NEXT leading into the construct,

(2) An assertion,

(3) , [3A] the state (T or F) that the evaluated assertion must match if the digression is executed,

(4) , [4A] the path leading from the assertion to the digression,

(5) , [5A] the digression,

(6) , [6A] the return path from the digression,

(7) the NEXT existing from the EITHER.

In executing an EITHER, the computer is forced to

Step One: Evaluate the assertion.

Step Two: Execute the digression associated with the T state if the assertion is true; execute the other digression if the digression is false.

Step Three: Return from the digression and proceed down the NEXT, which exists from the EITHER construct, and then execute the next portion of the program.

When the computer encounters an EITHER, only one of the two digressions will be executed; which one depends on the way the programmer has stated the assertion and specified the T and F, and on the current value of each variable named in the assertion. Execution of the rest of the program proceeds as soon as the chosen EITHER digression has been completely executed.

The EITHER's two alternative execution paths are illustrated in Fig. 8.10. If the assertion is true, execution moves as in (a); if false, as in (b). By including it inside a WHILE digression the same EITHER may of course be executed more than once in the same program. Note, however, that in such a situation the assertion might be true one time and false the next, depending on the value of the variable named in the assertion. Thus one digression might be executed one time; the other, the next.

It is clear why the construct is called the EITHER. The two digressions are alternatives, and the computer must choose and do *either* one or the other on any execution of the construct itself. Recall that with the WHILE, digression execution need not occur at all.

There is another important difference between the EITHER and the WHILE. After a digression is executed in the EITHER, the assertion is *not* reevaluated and execution instead proceeds to the next portion of the program. Hence the EITHER itself has no power to force repetition.

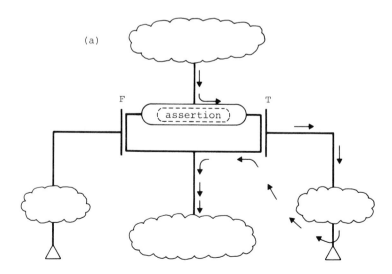

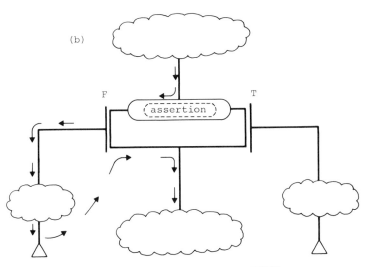

Fig. 8.10 Execution of the EITHER.

THE EITHER IN THE MACHINE CONDITION PROGRAM

Let's apply the EITHER to the decision problem introduced at the beginning of this chapter. An FPL program to solve that problem appeared in Fig. 8.2, and its first refinement in Fig. 8.3. We complete the refinement by introducing the formal EITHER. We need only make specific the general representation of the EITHER shown in Fig. 8.9. Figures 8.3 and 8.9 together suggest the specifics shown in Fig. 8.11.

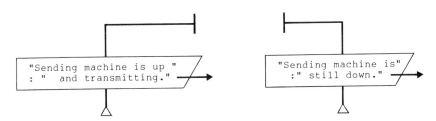

Fig. 8.11 EITHER digressions for the machine conditions.

But what assertion will guide the choice between these digressions? There are several possible ways to phrase the assertion so that the program will accomplish its objective. We consider two. One is shown in Fig. 8.12. That phrasing forces the programmer to place the states and the digressions in the relative positions shown.

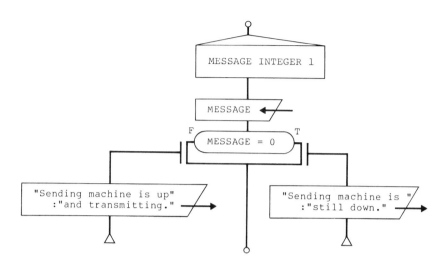

Fig. 8.12 Final version of the machine condition program.

We can relate this version of the decision program to the three-step analysis for EITHER executions presented a few paragraphs ago.

Step One: Enter assertion box from the top and evaluate the claim that the message is zero.

Step Two: If true, execute the digression on the right, if false, execute the digression on the left.

Step Three: Return from the digression executed and proceed down the NEXT.

An alternative way to produce the same results in the problem is shown in Fig. 8.13. You should realize that such alternatives are usually possible; which the programmer chooses to employ may be largely a matter style. In choosing your alternative, write for those who may have to read your program later. Make it as self-evident and simple as possible to understand. Before going on to the next section, study Fig. 8.13 and do the problems in the Private Practice.

Private Practice

P8.3   Write out the relevant three-step execution analysis for the version of the decision problem program shown in Fig. 8.13.

P8.4   Create a final version of the same program, so that the "down" digression is on the left and the "up" digression is on the right.

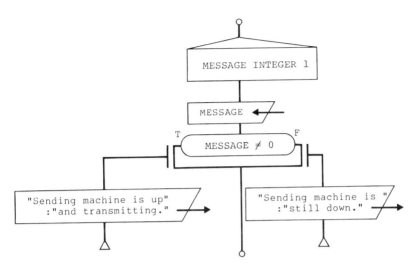

Fig. 8.13 An alternative version.

Watching the EITHER Work

To be certain you understand the EITHER, let's run some data through the program. Two messages are traced through this code, the first in Fig. 8.14, the

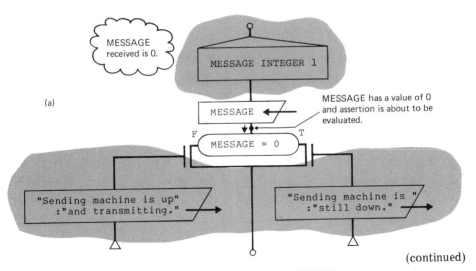

(continued)

Fig. 8.14 EITHER execution—MESSAGE – 0.

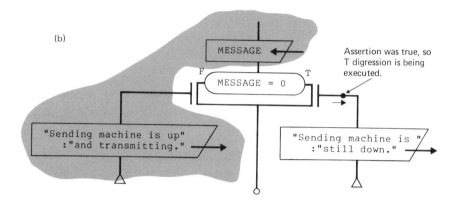

(b)

MESSAGE

MESSAGE = 0

Assertion was true, so
T digression is being
executed.

"Sending machine is up"
 :"and transmitting."

"Sending machine is "
 :"still down."

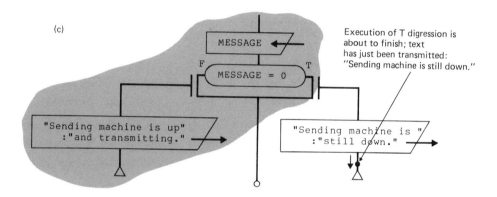

(c)

MESSAGE

MESSAGE = 0

Execution of T digression is
about to finish; text
has just been transmitted:
"Sending machine is still down."

"Sending machine is up"
 :"and transmitting."

"Sending machine is "
 :"still down."

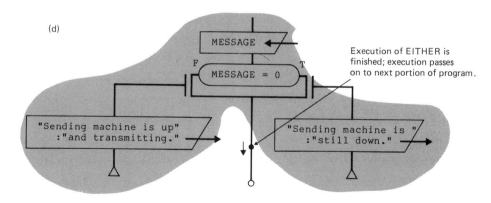

(d)

MESSAGE

MESSAGE = 0

Execution of EITHER is
finished; execution passes
on to next portion of program.

"Sending machine is up"
 :"and transmitting."

"Sending machine is "
 :"still down."

Fig. 8.14 (continued)

second in Fig. 8.15. Each figure includes several snapshots of the code, each snapshot freezing the execution at the exact point indicated. The direction of execution at that instant is also indicated by a miniature arrow.

Note which digression is executed in each run and how the value of the particular piece of data determines the digression chosen. After being certain that you understand what each figure represents, work the associated Private Practice before continuing on to the next section.

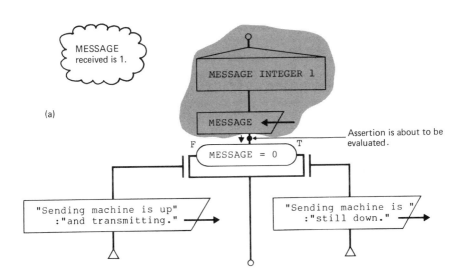

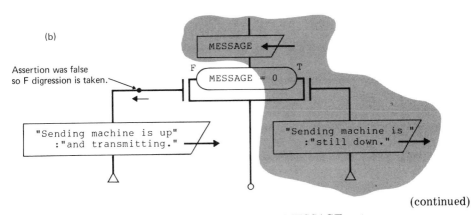

(continued)

Fig. 8.15 EITHER execution—MESSAGE − 1.

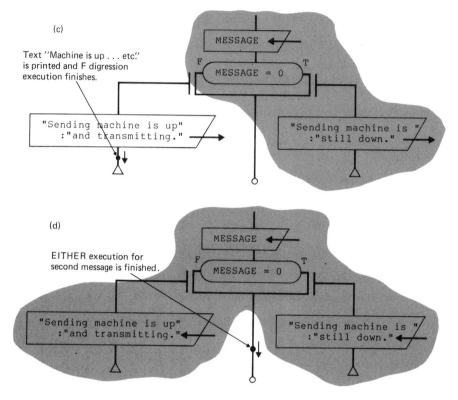

Fig. 8.15 (continued)

Private Practice

P8.5   Assume a message of "8" is sent from the first computer to the second. Create a series of snapshots, analogous to those in Fig. 8.14 and 8.15, that traces this third value through the program.

P8.6   Use the test data and labeled version of the decision program provided to answer questions (a) through (g). Note that the condition under which the "down" message is to be printed has been altered. In this version, the slave computer will send a "6" if it is still not working properly (in all earlier versions of this program we expected a zero if the slave was "down").

   a. What will the contents of MESSAGE be when the execution reaches point A during the run on the first piece of data?
   b. On the first run, will execution successively pass through points A–B–C–D or through points A–E–F–D?
   c. Will the evaluated assertion be true or false on the second run?
   d. How many times in all will the execution pass through point B if we consider all three runs?

e. If the execution is to pass through point E on a given run, must the assertion be true, or must it be false?

f. Can the execution ever pass through point C without first passing through point B?

g. Which message will be printed on the third run?

TEST DATA

Messages Received upon Running Program		
First Run	Second Run	Third Run
0	13	6

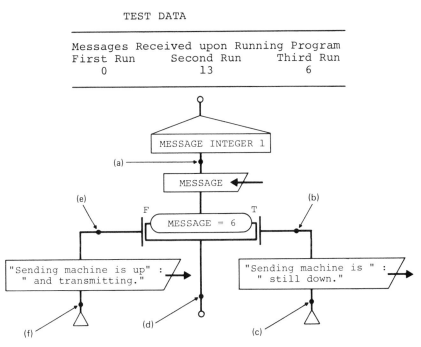

P8.7   Is the following program equivalent to the program shown in Fig. 8.12? (Does it accomplish the same result in every case?) Justify your answer.

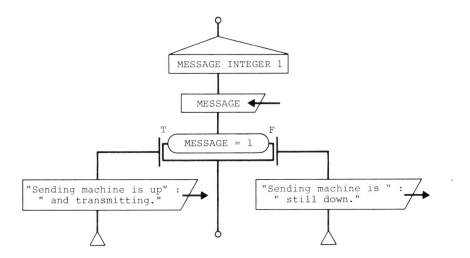

EITHERs inside EITHERs: More Machine Conditions

The situation above is simple: the message can have only one of two possible values. Only one EITHER is needed. Other situations may be more complex; for them, multiple EITHERs may be required, one inside another. Consider one illustration.

The sending computer has been modified to monitor the color drivers on a two-color TV screen. It sends a message periodically to the other computer, but the message is more complex: 3 if both drivers are up; 2 if blue is up and red is down; 1 if blue is down and red is up; and 0 if both drivers are down. The FPL to analyse the receipt of such a message requires multiple EITHERs, one "nested" inside another, as shown in Fig. 8.16.

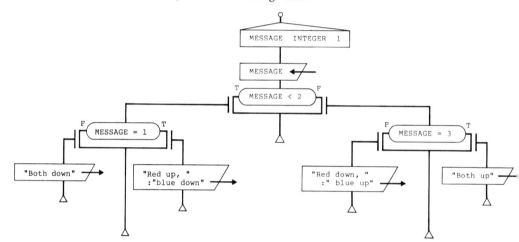

Fig. 8.16 Multiple EITHERS, nested one inside another.

Private Practice

P8.8   One microcomputer is sending a message to another about what a human being is typing into the first computer. The message can be a 1, 2, or 3. The receiving computer is to act as follows: print "hotter" if the message received is a 1; "got it!" if a 2; and "colder" if a 3. Write a program to do this.

P8.9   Modify the program to include the handling of two additional message values: print "warm" if a 4 is received and "cool" if a 5.

A SPECIFIC EITHER FOR THE AGE SELECTION PROGRAM

Now that we have seen how the EITHER works, let's return to the selection problem program (Fig. 8.8). Inside the digression, repeated until all pupil records are read, a question is asked. We must rephrase the question as an EITHER assertion. When we extend our refinement that way, we arrive at Fig. 8.17.

On the left side of the assertion, this version still includes the "NOTHING" episode that triggers the selection. It represents the fact that we are interested only in 13-year-old pupils. The simplest way to code a digression that does nothing is shown in Fig. 8.18. We often use such digressions: there are many situations calling for a choice between action and inaction. In such cases, one of the digressions tells the computer to do nothing but move on.

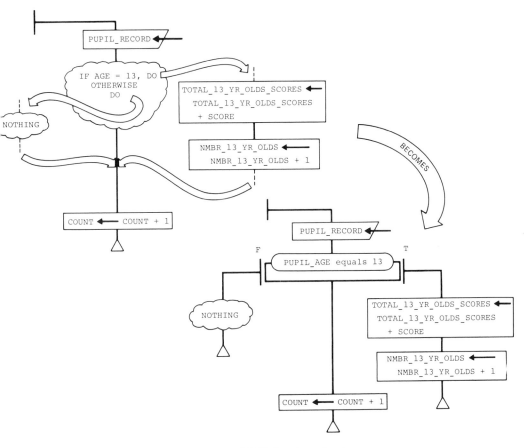

Fig. 8.17 The exact EITHER for the selection program.

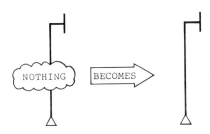

Fig. 8.18 The do-nothing digression.

Figure 8.19 represents the final version of the age selection episode. Each time the digression is executed, it is to read a record and count it. If that record *is not* for a 13-year-old, the digression does nothing more. If the record *is* for a 13-year-old, the digression adds the score from that record into the total for all 13-year-olds and then adds 1 to the count of all 13-year-olds selected.

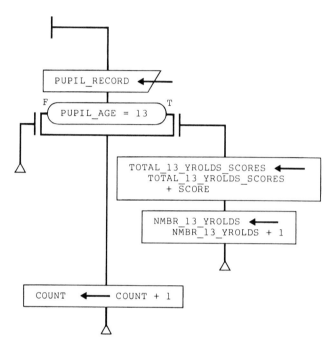

Fig. 8.19 Record-handling code for the selection program.

Testing a Digression

We can test this digression with two pieces of data: the record of a child who *is* 13 and the record of one who *is not*. For each, lets assume that the values of all data variables in the program have been initialized to zero.

Figure 8.20 includes two such data records and presents the digression labeled with execution reference points. Figure 8.21 shows a trace table for the first record; Fig. 8.22, a trace table for the second. As we would expect, for the first record the computer executes the T digression of the EITHER; for the second, the F digression. Each raises the count of all records (COUNT), but only the 13-year-old's record changes the other variables (TOTAL_13_YR-OLDS_SCORES and NMBR_13_YROLDS).

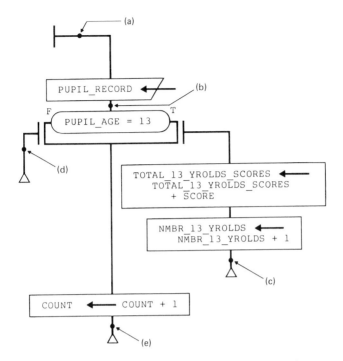

Fig. 8.20 Data and labeled record-handling code.

Point	SCORE	PUPIL_AGE	TOTAL_13_YROLDS_SCORES	NMBR_13_YROLDS	COUNT
(a)	🗑	🗑	0	0	0
(b)	97	13	0	0	0

At this point, the assertion is true (the age is 13), and the T digression of the EITHER is executed. Our next point of reference is therefore point C, and point D will not be passed at all on this execution of the EITHER......

Point	SCORE	PUPIL_AGE	TOTAL_13_YROLDS_SCORES	NMBR_13_YROLDS	COUNT
(c)	97	13	97	1	0
(e)	97	13	97	1	1

Fig. 8.21 Trace table following record one.

Point	SCORE	PUPIL_AGE	TOTAL_13_YROLDS_SCORES	NMBR_13_YROLDS	COUNT
(a)	🗑	🗑	0	0	0
(b)	108	11	0	0	0

At this point, the assertion is false (the age is 11), and the F digression of the EITHER is executed. Our next point of reference is therefore (d), and (c) will not be passed at all on this execution of the EITHER........

Point	SCORE	PUPIL_AGE	TOTAL_13_YROLDS_SCORES	NMBR_13_YROLDS	COUNT
(d)	108	11	0	0	0
(e)	108	11	0	0	1

Fig. 8.22 Trace table following record two.

Private Practice

P8.10   The following digression is supposed to count all pupils whose scores are greater than 103, and add their scores to a total of high-scoring pupils. Create some reasonable data records and test this digression. Create tables similar to those in Figs. 8.21 and 8.22 as you carry out the testing. Assume the records are in the same format as those we have been using throughout.

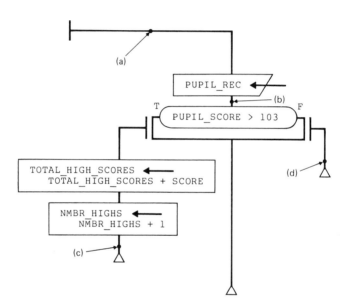

P8.11   By incorporating an appropriate EITHER, design a modification to the first version of the survey analysis program (Fig. 7.11) which will cause it to total and count a response only if the respondent is older than 20.

Testing the Entire Program

The completion of this WHILE digression introduced no more variables. Hence we can eliminate the remaining MISCELLANEOUS episode because it was inserted only to leave room should further initialization prove necessary. A final version of the program appears in Fig. 8.23, ready for testing.

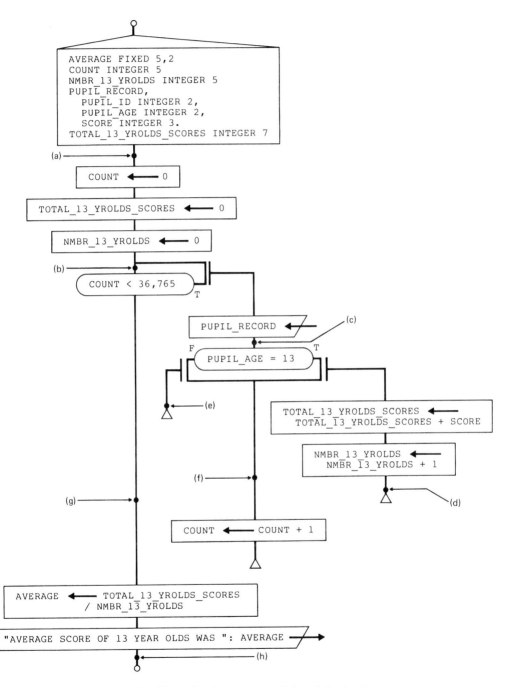

Fig. 8.23 The selection program, labeled for testing.

We have already tested the selection mechanism built into the WHILE, so we need now test only the WHILE itself. To do this, we had best look at the first and last few records read in. If this program begins properly and ends properly, there's not much that can go wrong in the middle.

Figure 8.24 provides the records for our test. We will run the first two records through the program and then skip to the last two records. Figure 8.25 is a trace table for the first two records; Fig. 8.26, a trace table for the last two.

	Pupil identification	Pupil age	Pupil score
First record	123	11	102
Second record	135	13	110
	* * * * * * * * * * *		
36754th record	28325	13	95
36755th record	26314	13	95
36756th record	22778	14	113

Fig. 8.24 Records for testing the selection problem program.

Execution Reference Points	PUPIL_ID	PUPIL_AGE	SCORE	COUNT	NMBR_13_YROLDS	TOTAL_13_YROLDS_SCORES	AVERAGE
a	🗑	🗑	🗑	🗑	🗑	🗑	🗑
b	-	-	-	0	0	0	-
( )	WHILE assertion evaluates to true, so WHILE digression is executed (COUNT is less than36,75						
c	123	11	102	0	0	0	-
( )	EITHER assertion evaluates to false, so F digression of EITHER is executed (PUPIL_AGE ≠ 13!						
e	123	11	102	0	0	0	-
f	123	11	102	0	0	0	-
b	123	11	102	1	0	0	-
( )	WHILE assertion evaluates to true, so WHILE digression is executed (COUNT is less than 36,7						
c	135	13	110	1	0	0	-
( )	EITHER assertion evaluates to true (PUPIL_AGE = 13!), so T digression of EITHER is executed						
d	135	13	110	1	1	110	-
f	135	13	110	1	1	110	-
b	135	13	110	2	1	110	-
( )	WHILE assertion again evaluates to true (COUNT is less than 36,756), so WHILE digression is again executed.........etc						
	THIS PROCESS CONTINUES FOR MANY RECORDS IN THE SAME FASHION						

Fig. 8.25 Tracing the first two test records.

In its first line, Fig. 8.26 assumes arbitrary sums for the contents of both TO-TAL_13_YROLDS_SCORES and NMBR_13_YROLDS, so that the checking of addition and average calculation can proceed.

More EITHERs inside EITHERs: Finer Selection

As we saw with the message problem, choices of more complexity can be handled by incorporating additional EITHERs. Another example follows.

The school superintendent who requested the selection program wants additional information. Besides the average now reported, she wants three totals reported: (1) the number of 13-year-olds who scored above 120 on the test; (2) the total number of 13-year-olds tested; and (3) the total number of children other than 13-year-olds who were tested.

A solution is shown in Fig. 8.27. It uses two additional variables compared with our earlier solution (Fig. 8.23). Each is declared, initialized, incremented, and reported upon. To select the high-scoring 13-year-olds, an additional assertion has also been included. Note where that assertion has been placed—in the digression already reserved for handling 13-year-olds! Note too that each additional counting assignment has been inserted in a digression where it will be executed only when an appropriate data value has been read into the record.

Execution Reference points	PUPIL_ID	PUPIL_AGE	SCORE	COUNT	NMBR_13_YROLDS	TOTAL_13_YROLDS_SCORES	AVERAGE
b	28325	13	95	36754	10999	1099903	–
	WHILE assertion again evaluates to true (COUNT is less than 36,756), so WHILE digression is again executed						
c	26314	13	97	36754	10999	1099903	–
	EITHER assertion evaluates to true (PUPIL_AGE = 13!), so T digression of EITHER is executed						
d	26314	13	97	36754	11000	1100000	–
f	26314	13	97	36754	11000	1100000	–
b	26314	13	97	36755	11000	1100000	–
	WHILE assertion still evaluates to true (COUNT is less than 36,756), so WHILE digression is again executed						
c	22778	14	113	36755	11000	1100000	–
	EITHER assertion evaluates to false (PUPIL_AGE ≠ 13), so F digression of EITHER is executed						
e	22778	14	113	36755	11000	1100000	–
f	22778	14	113	36755	11000	1100000	–
b	22778	14	113	36756	11000	1100000	–
	WHILE assertion finally evaluates to false (COUNT is no longer less than 36756, it now equals that value), so WHILE digression is not executed						
g	22778	14	113	36756	11000	1100000	–
h	22778	14	113	36756	11000	1100000	100
STOP	STOP	STOP	STOP	STOP	STOP	STOP	STOP	STOP

Fig. 8.26 Tracing the last two test records.

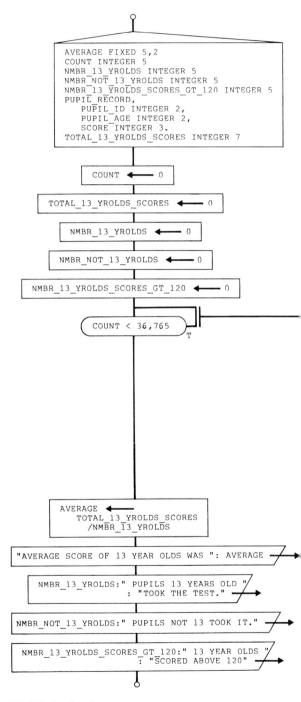

Fig. 8.27 Modified selection program.

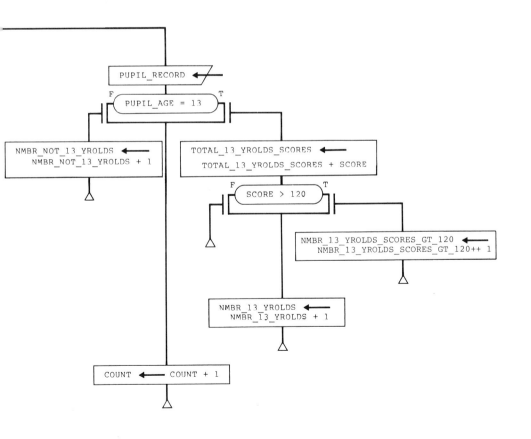

Private Practice

P8. 12   Assume that 4001 pupil records are prepared for computer analysis. Write a program that will read all 4001 records and compile the average age of those pupils who scored at least 100. (Finding the average means printing it as well!) Design test data and test your program by creating a trace table.

P8. 13   The director of pupil information has just determined that she must have the average age of all pupils and the average age of those who scored less than 100. Modify your program to meet the new requirements. Demonstrate that it works.

P8. 14   Modify the survey analysis program so that it reports improvement ratings only from records of those respondents who were at least twenty-five years old. You need not rewrite the entire program.

P8. 15   Modify the survey analysis program so that it reports only on females.

P8. 16   Modify the survey program so that it reports only on females who are over 26 years old.

P8. 17   Modify the survey program so that it produces a separate report for *each* sex. Both reports must be produced by a single run of the program. To do this, you may want to introduce some different variables to count and total the ratings: one pair for males, one pair for females.

USING THE EITHERS TO EDIT AND ENSURE DATA VALIDITY

It is wise to make sure your program can exclude any unreasonable data values included in the input stream. Good programs always include a segment that scrutinizes the incoming data and screens out unreasonable values. Such segments are referred to as *editors* because of the function they perform. An editor typically includes one or more EITHERs, each making an assertion about the range of some particular data value.

Figure 8.28 shows an editor designed to screen out unreasonable rating values for the survey analysis program. The first assertion screens out values below 1; the second, values above 3. With this editor in place, the program prevents out-of-bounds array references to CHANGE_RATINGS when CHANGE is used as the subscript. This is important because the value of CHANGE is taken from a response; there is no guarantee that all such values will be reasonable. However if the value of CHANGE [1] is smaller or larger than allowed by the declared dimension of CHANGE_RATINGS (e.g., less than 1 or greater than 3), the editor will detect it and skip the troublesome assignment.

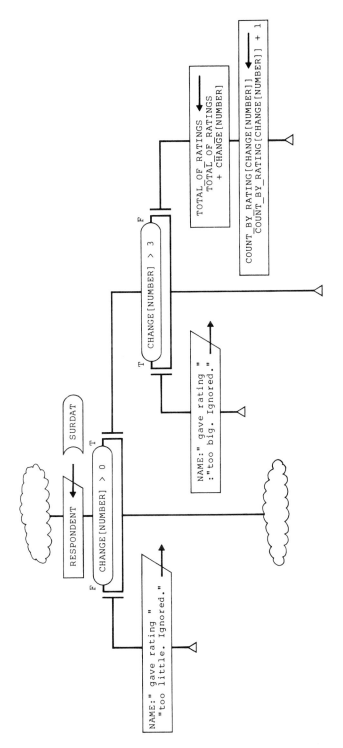

Fig. 8.28 An EITHER to "edit" data.

Earlier we learned that division by zero is meaningless to the computer and that attempts to divide by zero cause errors. Editing computed results in midprogram can prevent such division. For example, in the selection program (Fig. 8.23), some editing should be done *before* the average calculation is attempted. It is always possible that *no* 13-year-olds will be represented in a particular set of data fed to this program; in that case, NMBR_13_YROLDS will remain 0. To avoid dividing by zero in such an event, the program should be modified by the addition shown in Fig. 8.29.

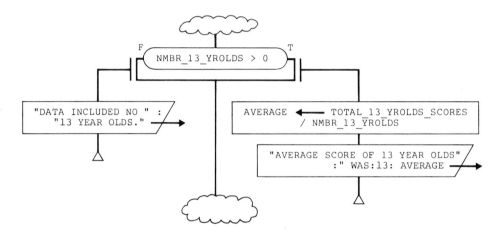

Fig. 8.29 An EITHER to avoid division by zero.

Private Practice

P8.18   Assume the acceptable ratings a respondent can give are 3, 4, 5, 6, 7, or 8. Modify the editor in Fig. 8.26 to trap data with values outside this new range of acceptability.

P8.19   Modify the survey program to edit the sex value. Your editor should reject any response record if its sex value is neither 0 nor 1.

P8.20   Modify the program you created to handle the UNESCO data concerning children's perceptions so that the program screens out bad data values.

P8.21   A *palindrome* (from the Greek word *palindromos*—running back again) is a string of letters or words that reads the same from back to front as from front to back. For example, consider the following palindromes.

   1. AMA

2. Dad

3. A man, a plan, a canal, Panama

(The last takes a little straining of commas, etc., but is fun.)

Create a program capable of detecting palindromes. Your palindromic program should allow the user to type in any string to be analysed; it should examine the string and determine if it is or is not a palindrome; and if it is, fill and display an entire print line with the palindrome. For example, if the palindrome TUT were entered, your program would immediately (within two microseconds) display:

TUTTUTTUTTUTTUTTUTTUTTUTTUTTUTTUTTUTTUTTUTTUT

Hint: You may want to ask the user to enter the letters one at a time so your program can store them in an array and easily remember just how many letters are in the string. If you use this approach, you will want to have the user type in a signal to indicate when he or she has entered the last letter (a . or an ! will do nicely). Alternatively, you can ask the user to type in how many letters long the string will be.

BASIC Interpretation of Chapter 8

THE AGE SELECTION PROGRAM AND THE EITHER IN BASIC

Figure B8.1 presents the EITHER from the selection problem program and its translation into BASIC. Figure B8.2 presents the entire program in BASIC.

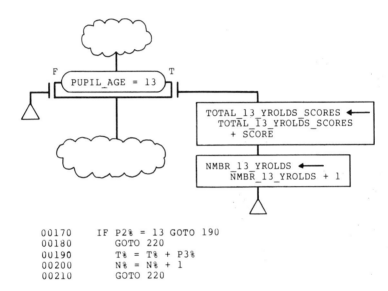

```
00170      IF P2% = 13 GOTO 190
00180         GOTO 220
00190         T% = T% + P3%
00200         N% = N% + 1
00210         GOTO 220
```

Fig. B8.1 BASIC translation of the EITHER in Fig. 8.23.

Note the following.

1. The assertion is formed as in FPL

P2% = 13

2. The EITHER places the assertion immediately after the key word IF rather than inside a graphic symbol

IF P2% = 13

3. The digressions must be written one below the other and cannot be placed to either side of the assertion as in FPL.

```
00010 REM ----- TRANSLATION OF FIG. 8.23 --------------------------
00015 REM     PAT OWENS    /    SEPT 1981
00020 REM PUPIL_RECORD,
00025 REM    P1%  : PUPIL_ID, 2 DIGITS
00030 REM    P2%  : PUPIL_AGE, 2 DIGITS
00035 REM    P3%  : SCORE, 3 DIGITS
00040 REM C%  : COUNT, 5 DIGITS
00045 REM T%  : TOTAL_13_YROLDS_SCORES, 7 DIGITS
00050 REM N%  : NMBR_13_YROLDS, 5 DIGITS
00055 REM A  :  AVERAGE, FIXED 5,2
00060 REM -------------------------------------------------------
00070 PRINT "At prompt, enter pupil record : ID, AGE, SCORE"
00075 PRINT "Use commas to separate thus: 31, 13, 132"
00080 PRINT "ID & AGE can't exceed 99; SCORE can't exceed 999."
00085 PRINT "The program expects exactly 5 records to be entered."
00100 C% = 1
00105 T% = 0
00110 N% = 0
00150 IF C% >= 6 GOTO 300
00160     INPUT P1%, P2%, P3%
00170     IF P2% = 13 GOTO 190
00180        GOTO 220
00190          T% = T% + P3%
00200          N% = N% + 1
00210        GOTO 220
00220     C% = C% + 1
00230     GOTO 150
00300 A = T% / N%
00310 PRINT "Average score of 13 year olds was ";A
00500 END
```

Fig. B8.2 BASIC translation of the age selection program in Fig. 8.23.

4. The location of the first line of the true digression is indicated in the GOTO directive following the assertion.

$$120 \quad \text{IF P2\% } = 13 \ \textit{GOTO 190}$$
$$(\qquad)$$
$$(\qquad)$$
$$\textit{190} \quad \text{T\% } = \text{T\% } + \text{P3\%}$$
$$(\qquad)$$

5. The false digression always begins on the line immediately beneath the assertion

$$170 \quad \text{IF P2\% } = 13 \ \text{GOTO 190}$$
$$\textit{180} \qquad\qquad \textit{GOTO 220}$$

6. The body of each digression is indented the same depth with respect to the assertion. Each ends with a GOTO directive citing the line number of the first line subsequent to the entire EITHER

```
170   IF   P2% = 13 GOTO 190
180        GOTO 220
190        T% = T% + P3%
200        N% = N% + 1
210        GOTO 220
```

7. The first line of the program subsequent to the EITHER should align with the assertion's IF, and not be indented to align with the digressions. (See Fig. B8.2)

```
170   IF   P2% = 13 GOTO 190
180   ∧    GOTO 220
190        T% = T% + P3%
200        N% = N% + 1
210        GOTO 220
220        C% = C% + 1
```

8. Either digression may be empty as is the false digression in this EITHER. If empty, a digression should contain nothing but its ending GOTO.

```
180   GOTO 220
```

Private Practice BASIC

PB8.1   Create a BASIC version of the program in Fig. 8.13. It should read the message from the keyboard rather than from another computer. Run the program four times, once for each of the following messages: 0, 1, 2, 3.

PB8.2   Verify the conclusion you reached on (P8.7) by translating that alternative version into BASIC and running it on some appropriate test values of your own creation.

PB8.3   Enter the program in Fig. B8.2 into your computer and run it on the first two records provided in Fig. 8.24. (Modify the WHILE assertion to reflect the presence of only two records.)

PB8.4   Translate your solution to (P8.11) into BASIC and run it on your computer. (Make use of the translation you've already developed for the survey analysis program.)

THE FINER SELECTION PROGRAM
AND EITHERS INSIDE EITHERS IN BASIC

Figure B8.3 presents the translation of an EITHER inside the digression of another EITHER. Compare this translation with the original FPL.

```
00005 REM -----TRANSLATION OF FIG. 8.27 --------------------------
00010 REM   BARBARA MACENALLEN / OCT 1980
00020 REM PUPIL_RECORD,
00025 REM    P1% : PUPIL_ID, 2 DIGITS
00030 REM    P2% : PUPIL_AGE, 2 DIGITS
00035 REM    P3% : SCORE, 3 DIGITS
00040 REM C% : COUNT, 5 DIGITS
00041 REM N% : NMBR_13_YROLDS, 5 DIGITS
00042 REM N1% : NMBR_NOT_13_YROLDS   5 DIGITS
00044 REM N2% : NMBR_13_YROLDS_SCORES_GT_120    4 DIGITS
00045 REM T% : TOTAL_13_YROLDS_SCORES, 7 DIGITS
00055 REM A :   AVERAGE, FIXED 5,2
00060 REM ---------------------------------------------------------
00070 PRINT "At prompt, enter pupil record : ID, AGE, SCORE"
00075 PRINT "Use commas to separate thus: 31, 13, 132"
00080 PRINT "ID & AGE can't exceed 99; SCORE can't exceed 999."
00085 PRINT "The program expects exactly 5 records to be entered."
00100 C% = 1
00105 T% = 0
00110 N% = 0
00120 N1% = 0
00125 N2% = 0
00150 IF C% >= 6 GOTO 300
00160    INPUT P1%, P2%, P3%
00170    IF P2% = 13 GOTO 190
00175       N1% = N1% + 1
00180       GOTO 220
00190       T% = T% + P3%
00200       N% = N% + 1
00206       IF P3% > 120 GOTO 208
00207          GOTO 210
00208          N2% = N2% + 1
00209          GOTO 210
00210       GOTO 220
00220    C% = C% + 1
00230    GOTO 150
00300 A = T% / N%
00310 PRINT "Average score of 13 year olds was ";A
00320 PRINT N%; " PUPILS 13 YEARS OLD TOOK THE TEST."
00325 PRINT N1%; " PUPILS WHO TOOK THE TEST WERE NOT 13."
00330 PRINT N2%; " OF THE 13 YEAR OLDS SCORED ABOVE 120."
00500 END
```

Fig. B8.3 BASIC translation of the selection program in Fig. 8.27.

Note the following.

1. The same format for indenting holds for the interior EITHER, i.e., both digressions are indented the same amount with respect to the assertion.

```
00206    IF P3% > 120 GOTO 208
00207        GOTO 210
00208        N2% = N2% + 1
00209        GOTO 210
```

2. The entire interior EITHER is indented to the degree required by its inclusion within a digression of the main EITHER.

```
00170   IF P2% = 13 GOTO 190
00175       N1% = N1% + 1
00180       GOTO 220
00190       T% = T% + P3%
00200       N% = N% + 1
00206       IF P3% > 120 GOTO 208
00207           GOTO 210
00208           N2% = N2% + 1
00209           GOTO 210
00210       GOTO 220
```

Private Practice BASIC

BP8.5   Translate the EITHERs in Fig. 8.16 into BASIC and run the program on your computer.

BP8.6   Translate (P8.8) into BASIC and run it on your computer.

BP8.7   Enter the program in Fig. B8.3 into your computer and run it. Use the same test data you used to test the simpler program shown in Fig. B8.2.

BP8.8   Translate your solution to (P8.12) into BASIC and run it on your computer.

BP8.9   Translate your solution to (P8.13) into BASIC and run it on your computer.

BP8.10   Translate your solution to (P8.14) into BASIC and run it on your computer.

BP8.11   Translate your solution to (P8.16) into BASIC and run it on your computer.

BP8.12   Translate your solution to (P8.17) into BASIC and run it on your computer.

BP8.13   Translate your solution to (P8.18) into BASIC and run it on your computer.

BP8.14   Translate your solution to (P8.19) into BASIC and run it on your computer.

BP8.15   Translate your solution to (P8.20) into BASIC and run it on your computer.

BP8.16   Translate your solution to (P8.21) into BASIC and run it on your computer.

Pascal Interpretation of Chapter 8

THE AGE SELECTION
PROGRAM AND THE EITHER IN PASCAL

Figure P8.1 presents the EITHER from the selection problem program and its translation into Pascal. Figure P8.2 presents the entire program in Pascal.

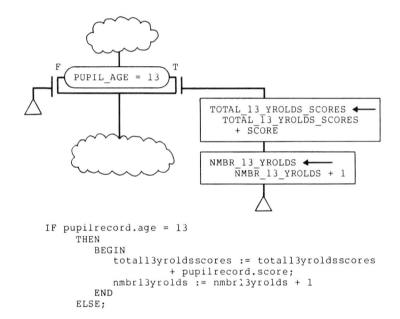

```
IF pupilrecord.age = 13
     THEN
          BEGIN
              totall3yroldsscores := totall3yroldsscores
                       + pupilrecord.score;
              nmbr13yrolds := nmbr13yrolds + 1
          END
     ELSE;
```

Fig. P8.1 Pascal translation of the EITHER in Fig. 8.23.

Note the following.

1. The EITHER assertion is formed as in FPL:

pupilrecord.age = 13

2. The EITHER places the assertion immediately after the key word *IF* rather than inside a graphic symbol as in FPL.

IF pupilrecord.age = 13

```
PROGRAM c8f23 (pupils, output);
   (* Translation of Fig. 8.23 *)
   (*   Don Young       March 1981 *)
   TYPE
     pupilrecshape =
         RECORD
           id : INTEGER;
           age : INTEGER;
           score : INTEGER
         END;
   VAR
       pupils : FILE OF pupilrecshape;
       pupilrecord : pupilrecshape;
       count, total13yroldsscores, nmbr13yrolds : INTEGER;
       average : REAL;
   BEGIN
       count := 0;
       total13yroldsscores := 0;
       nmbr13yrolds := 0;
       RESET(pupils);
       WHILE count < 13 DO
          BEGIN
            pupilrecord := pupils^;
            GET(pupils);
            IF pupilrecord.age = 13
               THEN
                 BEGIN
                   total13yroldsscores := total13yroldsscores
                                       + pupilrecord.score;
                   nmbr13yrolds := nmbr13yrolds + 1
                 END
               ELSE;
             count := count + 1
          END;
       average := total13yroldsscores / nmbr13yrolds;
       WRITELN ('Average score of 13 year olds was ', average:6:2)
   END. (* c8f23 *)
```

Fig. P8.2 Pascal translation of the age selection program in Fig. 8.23.

3. The true digression follows beneath the assertion. It begins with the key word THEN.

4. The false digression follows beneath the true, and begins with the key word ELSE.

5. A digression may contain details, or it may be empty. If it contains details, the digression is formed exactly like a WHILE digression. For example, in this program, the THEN (true) digression contains details

```
THEN
  BEGIN
    total13yroldscores : = ... etc ... ;
    numbr13yrolds : = ... etc ...
  END
```

6. An empty digression is represented by the key word THEN or ELSE alone. For example, in this program, the ELSE (false) digression is empty.

ELSE;

7. The true digression must *not* end in a semicolon when it is empty.

THEN
ELSE

or not

THEN
    BEGIN

etc.
etc.

    END
ELSE

8. The false digression must end in a semicolon unless the entire EITHER is contained (nested) within another construct and is followed immediately either by the key word END or ELSE.

Private Practice Pascal

PP8.1   Create a Pascal version of the program in Fig. 8.13. It should read the message from the keyboard rather than from another computer. Run the program four times, once for each of the following messages: 0, 1, 2, 3.

PP8.2   Verify the conclusion you reached on (P8.7) by translating that alternative version into Pascal and running it on some appropriate test values of your own creation.

PP8.3   Enter the program in Fig. B8.2 into your computer and run it on the first two records provided in Fig. 8.24. (Modify the WHILE assertion to reflect the presence of only two records.)

PP8.4   Translate your solution to (P8.11) into Pascal and run it on your computer. (Make use of the translation you've already developed for the survey analysis program.)

THE FINER SELECTION PROGRAM
AND EITHERS INSIDE EITHERS IN PASCAL

Figure P8.3 presents the translation of an EITHER inside the digression of another EITHER. Compare this translation with the original FPL.

```
PROGRAM c8f27 ( pupils, output);
   (* Translation of Fig. 8.27 *)
   (*    Don Young    April 1981  *)
   TYPE
     pupilrecshape =
         RECORD
            id : INTEGER;
            age : INTEGER;
            score : INTEGER
         END;
   VAR
       pupils : FILE OF pupilrecshape;
       pupilrecord : pupilrecshape;
       count, total13yroldsscores, nmbr13yrolds : INTEGER;
       nmbrnot13yrolds, nmbrhighscore13yrolds : INTEGER;
       average : REAL;
   BEGIN
       count := 0;
       total13yroldsscores := 0;
       nmbr13yrolds := 0;
       RESET(pupils);
       WHILE count < 13 DO
         BEGIN
           pupilrecord := pupils^;
           GET(pupils);
           IF pupilrecord.age = 13
             THEN
                 BEGIN
                    total13yroldsscores := total13yroldsscores
                                     + pupilrecord.score;
                    nmbr13yrolds := nmbr13yrolds + 1;
                    IF pupilrecord.score > 120
                        THEN
                          BEGIN
                             nmbrhighscore13yrolds :=
                                   nmbrhighscore13yrolds + 1
                          END
                        ELSE
                 END
             ELSE
                BEGIN
                   nmbrnot13yrolds := nmbrnot13yrolds + 1
                END;
             count := count + 1
           END;
       average := total13yroldsscores / nmbr13yrolds;
       WRITELN(nmbr13yrolds:4, ' 13 year old pupils took the test.');
       WRITELN(nmbrhighscored13yrolds:4, ' of them scored above 120');
       WRITELN ('The average score of all 13 year olds was ',
                average:6:2);
       WRITELN(nmbrnot13yrolds:4,
                  ' pupils not 13 years old took the test.');
   END. (* c8f27 *)
```

Fig. P8.3 Pascal translation of the selection program in Fig. 8.27.

Note the following.

1. The EITHER inside is written in the format described above for any EITHER.

```
IF pupilrecord.score > 120
   THEN
     BEGIN
       nmbrhighscore13yrolds :=
           nmbrhighscore13yrolds + 1
     END
   ELSE
```

(Though marking an empty digression, its closing ELSE takes no semicolon because the key word END follows immediately.)

2. This nested EITHER is itself totally indented to show its status within the true digression of the larger EITHER.

```
IF pupilrecord.age = 13
   THEN
     BEGIN
       total13yroldsscores := total13yroldsscores
         + pupilrecord.score;
       nmbr13yrolds := nmbr13yrolds + 1;
       IF pupilrecord.score > 120
         THEN
           BEGIN
             nmbrhighscore13yrolds :=
                 nmbrhighscore13yrolds + 1
           END
         ELSE
     END
   ELSE
     BEGIN
       nmbrnot13yrolds := nmbrnot13yrolds + 1
     END;
```

(The final END is followed by a semicolon because it marks the end of the entire EITHER.)

Private Practice Pascal

PP8.5   Translate the EITHERs in Fig. 8.16 into Pascal and run the program on your computer.

PP8.6   Translate (P8.8) into Pascal and run it on your computer.

PP8.7   Enter the program in Fig. P8.3 into your computer and run it. Use the same test data you used to test the simpler program shown in Fig. P8.2.

PP8.8   Translate your solution to (P8.12) into Pascal and run it on your computer.

PP8.9   Translate your solution to (P8.13) into Pascal and run it on your computer.

PP8.10   Translate your solution to (P8.14) into Pascal and run it on your computer.

PP8.11   Translate your solution to (P8.16) into Pascal and run it on your computer.

PP8.12   Translate your solution to (P8.17) into Pascal and run it on your computer.

PP8.13   Translate your solution to (P8.18) into Pascal and run it on your computer.

PP8.14   Translate your solution to (P8.19) into Pascal and run it on your computer.

PP8.15   Translate your solution to (P8.20) into Pascal and run it on your computer.

PP8.16   Translate your solution to (P8.21) into Pascal and run it on your computer.

Two Embellishments— Compound Assertions and ENDFILE

INTRODUCTION

This chapter adds to what we have already learned, and provides a large number of problems for practice. Our first embellishment enables the programmer to combine two or more assertions within a single assertion oval; our second enables the programmer to use a special EITHER assertion to handle the reading of data more flexibly.

COMBINING ASSERTIONS

While single assertions are adequate in some programming contexts, there are other contexts that require multiple assertions functioning together. Such multiple assertions become convenient when a given record is to be selected only if several quite independent criteria are met, or a given digression executed only

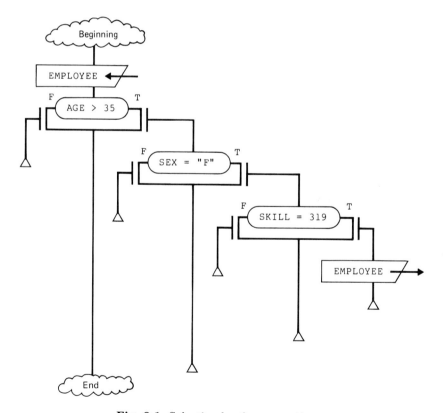

Fig. 9.1 Selection by three assertions.

if several conditions have not yet occurred. It is so frequently necessary to link several assertions together in such contexts that a formal shorthand for combining assertions exists. Two or more assertion texts should be linked if the result is easier to understand.

Two Examples

Figure 9.1 presents a program segment that must print a copy of a record if, and only if, (1) the value of AGE is greater than 35; (2) the value of SEX is F; and (3) the value of SKILL is 319. Figure 9.2 presents a program segment that must assign a value of 1 to the variable STOPPER if *either* (1) the value of COUNT is greater than 100 *or* (2) the value of TIME is equal to or greater than 1630.

Although we could clearly write each segment in other ways, the need to use several selection criteria *simultaneously* makes a single EITHER assertion inconvenient.

Instead, a compound text such as that shown in Fig. 9.3 is more appropriate. We are not, after all, going to do anything to the record unless *all three* criteria are met simultaneously. The compound text is extensive, but the resulting code looks much simpler. Similarly, Fig. 9.4 rather markedly simplifies Fig. 9.2.

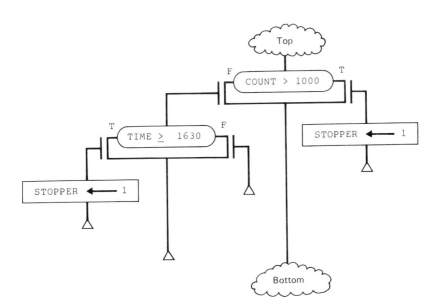

Fig. 9.2 Selection through alternative assertions.

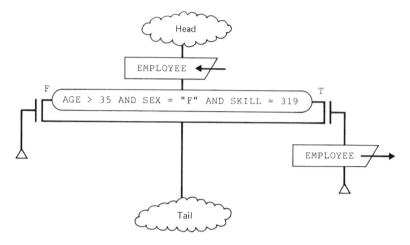

Fig. 9.3 Selection by compound assertion.

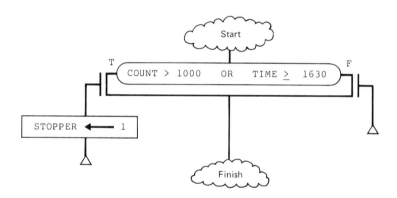

Fig. 9.4 Assignment via compound assertion.

Compound Assertion "AND"

Figure 9.3 displays the compound assertion known as an "AND." Each component of the compound assertion must be true for the computer to treat the compound as true. In the code shown in Fig. 9.3, the entire compound assertion would be false if AGE were 33, even though SEX had the value F and SKILL the value of 319. Similarly, if the value of SEX were M, the compound would be false even if the value of AGE were 40, and that of SKILL, 319.

In what follows, we use the ampersand symbol "&" in place of the word AND. Figure 9.5 shows the use of the ampersand, and Fig. 9.6 shows how compound assertions are evaluated.

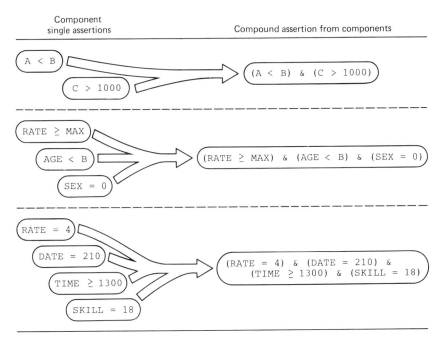

Fig. 9.5 Compound assertions using the ampersand to stand for "AND."

Compound Assertions: "OR"

The program segment presented in Fig. 9.4 features an example of a different compound assertion—the "OR." For an OR to be considered true, it is sufficient that one of its components be true. In the code shown in Fig. 9.4, the compound assertion is true, just so long as COUNT has a value of 1000 or more, *or* TIME has a value greater than 1630.

The space-saving symbol used for OR is a vertical bar (|). Figure 9.7 presents a table of data variable values, and single and compound assertion evaluations based on those values.

A Caution about Combining Assertions

Though considerable space may be saved by combining assertions, the result may be more difficult to modify or harder to understand. The greater the number of assertions combined, the more either or both of these facts will be true, so be prudent. Combine only when it makes good sense.

COMPOUND ASSERTION : (A < B) & (C > 1000)

Content values of data storage locations			Component evaluations		Compound assertion evaluation
A	B	C	(A < B)	(C > 1000)	
1	4	2000	true	true	true
1	4	1000	true	false	false
3	2	2000	false	true	false
5	2	15	false	false	false

COMPOUND ASSERTION : (RATE = 4) & (DATE = 210) & (TIME ≥ 1300) & (SKILL = 18)

Content values of data storage locations				Component evaluations				Compound assertion evaluation
RATE	DATE	TIME	SKILL	(RATE=4)	(DATE=210)	(TIME ≥ 1300)	(SKILL=18)	
4	210	1300	18	true	true	true	true	true
4	210	2200	18	true	true	true	true	true
4	211	2200	18	true	false	true	true	false
3	210	1800	37	false	true	true	false	false
3	208	1300	35	false	false	true	false	false
1	200	0800	48	false	false	false	false	false

Fig. 9.6 Evaluating "AND" assertions.

Private Practice

P9.1   Complete the table below as it relates to

(A ≤ B) & (C = 1000)

Content values of data storage locations			Component evaluations		Compound assertion evaluation
A	B	C	(A ≤ B)	(C = 1000)	
10	11	1000	____	true	____
30	10	1000	____	____	false
9	13	100	____	____	____
14	13	0	____	____	____
11	11	0	____	____	____

COMPOUND ASSERTION: ("or-ing")	(COUNT > 1000) I (TIME ≥ 1630)		Compound assertion evaluation
Content values of data storage locations	Component evaluations		
COUNT TIME	COUNT > 1000	TIME ≥ 1630	
2000 1972	true	true	true
2000 1492	true	false	true
100 1972	false	true	true
100 1099	false	false	false

COMPOUND ASSERTION: ("or-ing")	(A < B) I (RATE > 10) I (HT ≤ 6)			Compound assertion evaluation
Content values of data storage locations	Component evaluations			
A B RATE HT	A < B	RATE > 10	HT ≤ 6	
0 0 19 5	true	true	true	true
1 0 19 5	false	true	true	true
1 0 4 5	false	false	true	true
1 0 4 10	false	false	false	false

Fig. 9.7 Evaluating "OR" assertions.

P9.2   Complete the table below as it relates to

(RATE ≥ 5) I (DATE < 181) I (TIME = 19)			Compound assertion evaluation
Content values of data storage locations	Component evaluations		
RATE DATE TIME	RATE ≥ 5	DATE < 181	TIME = 19	

RATE	DATE	TIME	RATE ≥ 5	DATE < 181	TIME = 19	Compound assertion evaluation
4	200	20	_____	_____	_____	_____
5	137	19	_____	true	_____	true
6	181	17	_____	_____	_____	true
3	181	17	_____	_____	_____	_____
1	190	19	_____	_____	_____	_____
2	182	09	_____	_____	_____	false

P9.3   Complete the table below as it relates to

(((AGE < 10) & (HT < 50)) | (WT < NORM_WT))

Note: ((AGE < 10) & (HT < 50)) is itself a conjunction. Its components must be evaluated separately before one can determine the truth of this compound. Its truth value must then be used to determine the truth of the overall compound assertion

[((AGE < 10) & (HT <50)) & (WT <NORM_WT)].

Content values of data storage locations				Component evaluations and one compound evaluation				Overall compound assertion evaluation
AGE	HT	WT	NORM_WT	AGE < 10	HT < 50	the &	WT < NORM_WT	
8	47	62	62	true	true	true	false	true
8	60	62	61	___	___	___	___	___
11	48	70	70	___	___	___	___	___
11	60	70	73	___	___	___	___	___
7	49	63	65	___	___	___	___	___

P9.4   Parts (a) through (f) require a single, compound assertion to accomplish the stated selection. Design a compound assertion for each. Use a record called CANDIDATE, which includes the following fields: NAME, AGE, HT_IN_INCHES, SEX, and VISION (assume VISION is STRING 5).
    a. Select the record for further processing if the person is 18 years or older and has 20/20 vision.
    b. Select the record for further processing if the person is over 18 but not over 30 years of age.
    c. Select the record for further processing if the person is under 60 inches or over 77 inches in height.
    d. Select the record for further processing if the person is at least 60 inches but not more than 77 inches in height, provided the person is also at least 18 years and has a 20/15 vision.
    e. Select the record for further processing if the person is between 20 and 24 years or between 36 and 38 years.
    f. Select for rejection any record if the person is under 12 years, or female (F), or blind (vision score is 00/00).

P9.5   For each of the six compound assertions created in (P9.4), create and complete a test table to be sure your compound assertion does what it is supposed to do. In each case, include in the "Content values of data storage locations" section the values from at least four sample records. Two should be selected by each of your compound assertions.

P9.6   Assume that, for each Martian, a computer-readable record of Martian behavior exists in the following format

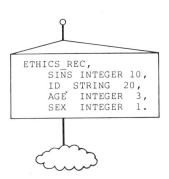

where SINS keeps score of the number of sins committed; ID is the Martian's identification code; AGE is the age of the Martian in hours (few Martians live more than 380 hours); and SEX is the Martian's sex type, designated by a number from 1 to 7 (there are seven different sexes on Mars). Write a program that reads a single record. If the sin score is less than 27, a message is to be written out saying "Score one for the forces of Light." If the sin score is 27 or greater, the message "Score one for the forces of Darkness." is to be printed instead. Develop an execution trace table, design several different data records, and complete the trace table by running your program on the test data. If the testing uncovers errors in your code, correct them and retest. Continue until all is well.

P9.7   Write a program that will execute 1000 times the episode,

TOP_SECRET_ANALYSIS.

P9.8   Write a program to read 1000 records of the sort described in (P9.6); the program should treat each record exactly as the program in (P9.6) treated a single record. In programming this solution, you may find it helps to use the code developed to solve (P9.7).

Develop a trace table and test data, and then run the data through your program; use the results to complete the table. Appropriate data tests the selection criteria built into the EITHER: the program should at least be tested with respect to the first and last two or three records read.

P9.9   Modify your program from (P9.8) so that it prints out the Darkness message even for those who have a sin score of less than 27, unless such Martians also happen to be over 275 hours old and have a sex designation of either 1 or 3. Develop an execution trace table just for your modified digression, run the digression on at least three suitably designed test records, and complete the table. If errors are discovered during testing, modify and retest your code. Continue until all is well.

P9.10   Create a WHILE digression to read the following record.

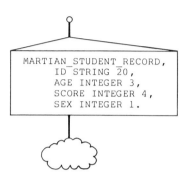

```
MARTIAN_STUDENT_RECORD,
     ID STRING 20,
     AGE INTEGER 3,
     SCORE INTEGER 4,
     SEX INTEGER 1.
```

P9.11   Rewrite the WHILE digression so that it will read the record and then add one (1) to the count of records read, CNT_RECORDS_READ.

P9.12   Modify the digression from (P9.11) so that it also examines the value of the AGE field; if its value is greater than 127 hours, have the computer add one (1) to the count of those Martians who are over 127 hours old, CNT_OVER_127_HOURS.

P9.13   Modify the digression from (P9.12) so that, *in addition to what it already does,* it also prompts the computer to add one (1) to the count of those Martians whose score (in field SCORE) on the ammonia absorption test is greater than 140 points (CNT_SCORES_GT_140).

Develop an execution trace table for this digression and all its variables. Create three test records and execute the digression on each.

P9.14   Further modify the digression so that it only adds scores over 140 if the Martian has a sex designation of either one (1) or five (5). Test your work in the usual way.

P9.15   Incorporate the final version of the digression (from P9.14) into a complete program that repeats the digression's execution 5000 times, and then prints out the various count values. (Assume that there are exactly 5000 records ready to be read by the program!) Since a Martian sex designation of one (1) refers to an ork and a five (5) to an erk, the final program should automatically meet the following program requirement specifications.

Create a program that will read 5000 Martian student records and print out the count of the number read, the count of those read which belonged to Martians over 127 hours old, and the count of all orks and erks who had an ammonia absorption score greater than 140 points.

Test your program with the usual trace table technique.

P9.16   Modify the program created in (P9.15) so that it computes and prints the average ammonia absorption score of *all* orks and erks. Test your program in the usual manner.

ENDFILE: PROGRAMMATICALLY HANDLING DATA FILES OF ANY SIZE

We have worked with many programs that read many data items or records from an input file. To work properly, most had to include an exact count of the number of records or items expected. For example, the averaging problem in Fig. 4.13 expected 30,000 scores and was written to process exactly that number—not more, not less. As our test version of that program (Fig. 4.14) suggested, to read a different size data file, one with fewer items, the program had to be modified. Such programs place unnecessary demands on their users: every variation in file size requires a count be made of the number of items or records in the file, and every variation requires a modification of the program to reflect that count.

Example One: A Modified Score Averaging Program

Figure 9.8 shows a more flexible approach. It makes the computer read every item in the file regardless of how many may be present, and then pass smoothly on to execute the rest of the program. This approach requires the incorporation of an EITHER whose assertion includes nothing but the single, special variable name, ENDFILE. Located immediately after the external assignment to read data, this special assertion depends on two characteristics of ENDFILE. First, ENDFILE's value is logical (either *true* or *false*) rather than string or numeric. Second, its value can be assigned only by the computer, not by the program.

    The computer's assignments to ENDFILE work as follows. When it begins executing the program, the computer assigns a value of *false* to END-FILE. Each time execution of an external assignment

forces the computer to seek more data from the file, the disk drive or other device where the file has been stored responds either with the requested data or with a signal indicating that all data in that file has already been read. If the computer receives data, no new assignment is made to ENDFILE. If the computer receives the signal instead, ENDFILE is assigned a value of *true*.

    To control the WHILE, the programmer introduces a variable of his or her own choice (e.g., ALL_BEEN_READ). It is initialized so that the first

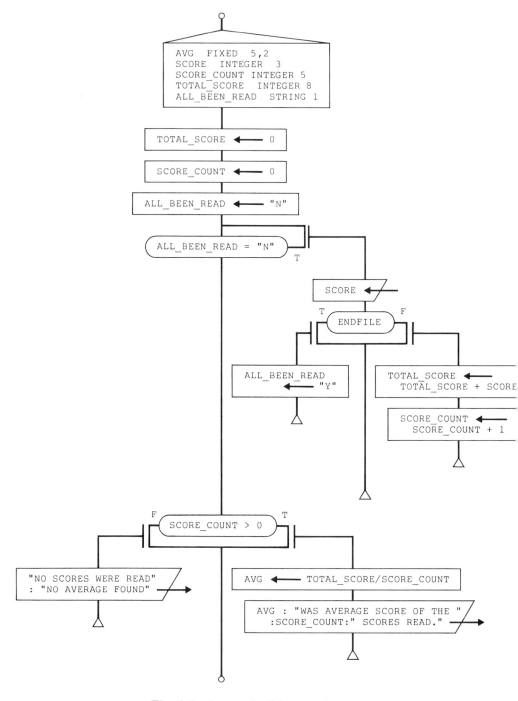

Fig. 9.8. A more flexible averaging program.

repetition of the WHILE and hence the first attempt to read from the data file will take place. It is not assigned the value that terminates the WHILE until the ENDFILE assertion becomes true. This terminating assignment is located in the T digression of the ENDFILE EITHER and will be executed only once per WHILE. By contrast, *all* details appropriate for processing a data item are located in the other digression of the ENDFILE EITHER and will be executed each time an item is successfully read.

Note that *no* details are located directly beneath the ENDFILE assertion—anything there would be executed whether or not the end of the data had been reached.

The EITHER at the end of the program is a further change from the original Fig. 4.13. With an ENDFILE EITHER added, the program would successfully reach the average calculation even if *no* data were presented, (ENDFILE would be true, so no execution of the WHILE digression would take place.) This second EITHER is necessary to prevent the computer from trying to divide by the resulting SCORE_COUNT of 0 in such a case, and to inform the program's user of what happened.

Example Two: A Modified ID Search Program

A second example of increasing program flexibility is the modified version of the search program in Fig. 9.9. Unlike the averaging program, the original search program (Fig. 4.7) did not include a count of the number of items in file. However, it assumed a record with an ID of 3453 was *somewhere* in the file. Unlike the original, this version works predictably even when the data includes no record with an ID of 3453.

The compound WHILE assertion will terminate repetition as soon as the specified ID is found or the data has all been read, whichever occurs first. The EITHER added at the end of this program notifies the user if no ID of 3453 is encountered.

Example Three: A Modified Age Selection Program

A third, slightly more elaborate ENDFILE example is shown in Fig. 9.10. The original (Fig. 8.23) included an EITHER within the WHILE digression, so this modification includes that EITHER within the F digression of its ENDFILE EITHER. Note again that all details to be executed when data is successfully read (e.g., when ENDFILE is false) are placed in the F digression of that ENDFILE EITHER. Note also that an editing EITHER has been added to the end of the program, for the same reasons such editing was added in Figs. 9.8 and 9.9. This program has further been modified to use a named file, PUPILS.

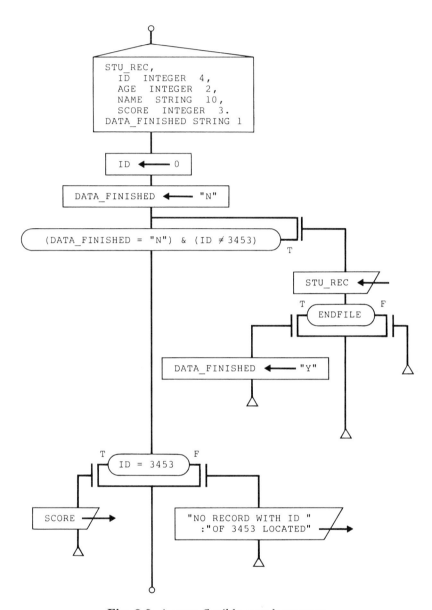

Fig. 9.9 A more flexible search program.

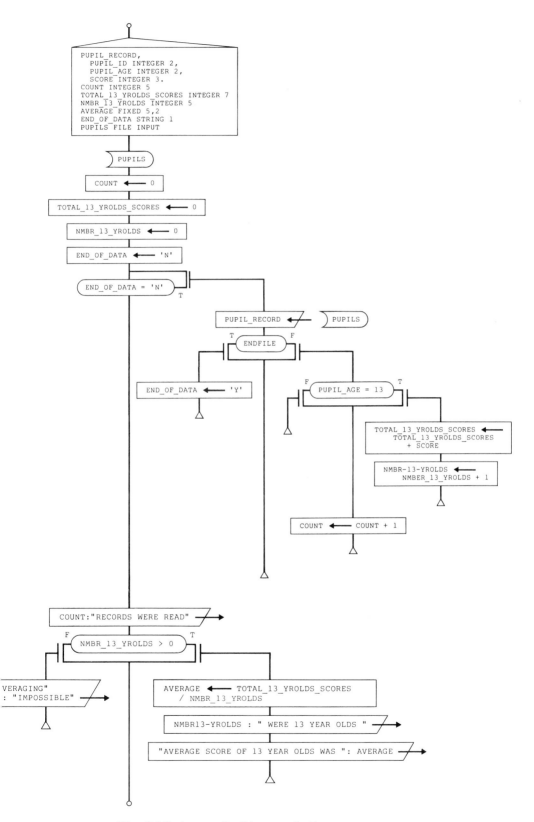

Fig. 9.10 A more flexible age selection program.

HANDLING THE AMOUNT OF DATA
SUBMITTED INTERACTIVELY: QUIT NOW?

An analogous structure for handling the end of data situation is required for interactive programs, as shown in Fig. 9.11. Like the original (Fig. 2.15), this version assumes the program user is interacting with the program while it is executing, typing in the data requested, item by item, according to the prompting of the computer. Unlike the original, this version assumes the user may want to repeat the analysis for several countries, in a single run of the program. At the start of each round, it asks the user if he or she wants to continue. The resulting response is used to control repetition in much the same way as END-FILE values are in other programs.

In effect, the file being read by such an interactive program is of a dynamic size, specifiable at the user's wish. The file is not stored on a device that automatically signals the computer when the last of the data has been read; instead it is stored in or beside the user, and the user signals the end whenever he or she has reached it.

Private Practice

P9.17   Write a program that will read a file of student names and list them, followed by a count of the number listed. Each name is 20 characters long (padded when necessary with blanks), and the number of names in the file varies from week to week.

P9.18   Modify the program for (P9.17) to function interactively, so that it reads the names one at a time as they are submitted from a terminal.

P9.19   Modify the melody reversal program (Fig. 5.39) so that the melody entered can be of any length up to 200 notes, but not longer.

P9.20   Modify your program for (P9.19) so that it can interactively read the notes, storing each in the appropriate array cell as the composer enters it. (It must still accept any length up to 200 notes but not longer.)

P9.21   Modify your program for (P9.19) so that it reads the notes from a file named NOTES and transmits the reversed melody's notes to a file named RNOTES.

P9.22   Modify the averaging program (Fig. 4.13) so that it reads the scores interactively from a terminal, and lets the user submit as many scores as he or she wishes.

P9.23   Modify the program shown in Fig. 8.27 so that it can smoothly read a data file called PUPS whose size varies from day to day.

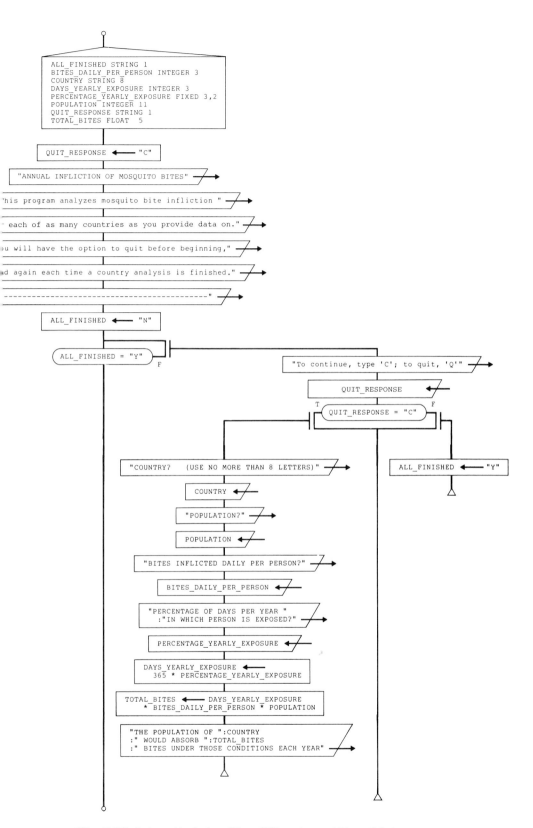

Fig. 9.11 Interactively handling different quantities of data.

P9.24   Modify the program you created for (P2.15) so users can analyze as many cities per run as desired.

P9.25   Using ENDFILE, modify the survey analysis program (Fig. 7.11) to enable it to handle any number of records. **Note:** Dividing by 643 in the averaging section will no longer work—the computer must keep count of how many records contribute to the total in each run.

BASIC Interpretation of Chapter 9

COMPOUND ASSERTIONS IN BASIC

Figure B9.1 presents the translations of two representative compound assertions.

```
(A < B) & (C > 1000)          1002 IF (A < B) AND (C > 100) GOTO ....

(COUNT > 1000) | (TIME ≥ 1630)  155 IF (COUNT > 1000) OR (TIME >= 1630) GOTO ...
```

Fig. B9.1 Translating compound assertions.

Some versions of BASIC allow compound assertions; some don't. If your version does, study the documentation and do some experimenting to determine the specifics. If your version does not support compound assertions, you will simply have to substitute successive single assertions as appropriate.

The BASIC translation of an EITHER that employs a compound assertion follows the same format as one that employs a single assertion. Your programs will remain easier to read if you combine no more than two assertions in any one compound, even though three, four, or more could be combined. To see why, and to better understand compound assertions in general, experiment with them through toy programs like the one shown in (BP9.1).

Private Practice BASIC

BP9.1   Explore the compound assertion in (P9.1) by entering the following toy program into your computer, then running it once on each set of A, B, and C values provided in (P9.1).

```
 10 REM TOY TO TEST COMPOUND ASSERTIONS
 90 INPUT, A, B, C
100 IF (A<=B) AND (C=1000) GOTO 200
110         PRINT "compond not true"
120         GOTO 300
200         PRINT "compound true"
210         GOTO 300
300 END
```

BP9.2   Modify lines 90 and 100 to match the variables and assertion in (P9.2), then run the model on each of the six sets of values provided in P9.2.

BP9.3   Translate your solution to (P9.4) into BASIC.

BP9.4   Translate your solution to (P9.6) into BASIC and run it on your computer.

BP9.5   Reread your solutions to (P9.6) through (P9.9) then translate the solution to the problem into BASIC, incorporating all the modifications represented.

BP9.6   Translate your solution to (P9.15) into BASIC and run it on your computer.

THREE ENDFILE EXAMPLES IN BASIC

Versions of BASIC that permit the programmer to read files typically include some facility analogous to ENDFILE. Figures B9.2, B9.3, and B9.4 present three examples in one version of BASIC. Your version may employ a somewhat different approach. You should explore what is provided by your version after studying these examples and the brief discussion of them which follows.

```
00005 REM  -------- TRANSLATION OF FIGURE 9.8 -----
00008 REM            JAMES ALEXANDER / NOV 1981
00010 REM   A$  : ALL_BEEN_READ STRING 1
00020 REM   A   : AVG FIXED 5,2
00030 REM   S1% : SCORE INTEGER 3
00040 REM   S2% : SCORE_COUNT INTEGER 5
00050 REM   T%  : TOTAL_SCORE INTEGER 8
00060 REM   SCORES.DAT FILE INPUT
00070 REM  --------------------------------------------
00100 OPEN "SCORES.DAT" FOR INPUT AS FILE #3
00110 T% = 0
00120 S2% = 0
00130 A$ = "N"
00200 IF A$ <> "N" GOTO 1000
00210     IFEND #3 GOTO 300
00220        INPUT #3, S1%
00230        T% = T% + S1%
00240        S2% = S2% + 1
00250        GOTO 500
00300        A$ = "Y"
00350        GOTO 500
00500     GOTO 200
01000 IF S2% > 0 GOTO 1200
01100     PRINT "NO SCORES WERE READ, NO AVERAGE FOUND."
01150     GOTO 1500
01200     A = T% / S2%
01250     PRINT A; " WAS AVERAGE SCORE OF THE ";
01255     PRINT S2%; " SCORES READ"
01280     GOTO 1500
01500 END
```

Fig. B9.2 ENDFILE translation—Example 1.

Note the following about the program in Fig. B9.2.

1. Just as its FPL counterpart does, the BASIC WHILE digression encompasses the reading of the file.

```
00200 IF A$ <> "N" GOTO 1000
00210     IFEND #3 GOTO 300
00220       INPUT #3, S1%
00230       T% = T% + S1%
00240       S2% = S2% + 1
00250       GOTO 500
00300       A$ = "Y"
00340       CLOSE #3
00350       GOTO 500
00500     GOTO 200
```

2. The assertion to test for ENDFILE (IFEND in this particular version of BASIC) *precedes* the external assignment to read a record from the file. That external assignment is placed first in the false digression and is followed in that digression by whatever is to be done if the end of the file has not been reached.

```
00210     IFEND #3 GOTO 300
00220       INPUT #3, S1%
00230       T% = T% + S1%
00240       S2% = S2% + 1
00250       GOTO 500
00300       A$ = "Y"
00350       GOTO 500
```

The IFEND in this BASIC in effect makes the computer ask of the disk or other device storing the file, "Will there be a score if I try to read one?"

Note the following about the program in Fig. B9.3.

The overall WHILE structure parallels that used with any single assertion even though a compound assertion is used in the WHILE

```
01000 IF (D$ <> "N") OR (I% = 3453) GOTO 2000.
```

```
00100 REM TRANSLATION OF FIG. 9.9 WITH FILE ADDED------
00120 REM        PAUL KAISER     OCT 1980
00140 REM   STU_REC, RECORD ----
00160 REM       I% : ID INTEGER 4,
00180 REM       A% : AGE INTEGER 4,
00200 REM       N$ : NAME STRING 10,
00220 REM       S% : SCORE INTEGER 5.
00240 REM D$ : DATA_FINISHED  STRING 1
00260 REM "STUDENT:DAT" FILE INPUT (STUDENT_RECORDS)
00280 REM ------------------------------------------
00500 OPEN "STUDENT.DAT" FOR INPUT AS FILE #6
00510 I% = 0
00530 D$ = "N"
01000 IF (D$ <> "N") OR (I% = 3453) GOTO 2000
01020    IFEND #6 GOTO 1100
01040       INPUT #6, I%, A%, N$, S%
01060       GOTO 1300
01100       D$ = "Y"
01200       GOTO 1300
01300    GOTO 1000
02000 CLOSE# 6
02010 IF I% = 3453 GOTO 2100
02030    PRINT "NO RECORD WITH ID OF 3453 LOCATED."
02060    GOTO 2600
02100    PRINT "SCORE FOR # 3453 WAS "; S%
02160    GOTO 2600
02600 END
```

Fig. B9.3 ENDFILE translation—Example 2.

Note the following about Fig. B9.4.

As in FPL, the complete EITHER to select the records of pupils 13 years old is incorporated in the *false* digression where it will be executed only if ENDFILE has not occurred.

```
00290      IFEND #1 GOTO 380
00300         INPUT #1, P1%, P2%, P3%
00310      IF P2% = 13 GOTO 330
00320         GOTO 360
00330         T = T + P3%
00340         N% = N% + 1
00350         GOTO 360
00360      C% = C% +1
00370      GOTO 410
00380      E$ = .. etc ...
```

```
00100 REM -------TRANSLATION OF FIGURE 9.10---------
00110 REM            ALICE WARDELL   FEB 1981
00120 REM PUPIL RECORD,
00130 REM    P1% : PUPIL_ID, 2 DIGITS
00140 REM    P2% : PUPIL_AGE, 2 DIGITS
00150 REM    P3% : SCORE, 3 DIGITS
00160 REM A :   AVERAGE, FIXED 5,2
00170 REM C% : COUNT, 5 DIGITS
00180 REM E$ : END_OF_DATA STRING 1
00190 REM N% : NMBR_13_YROLDS, 5 DIGITS
00200 REM T : TOTAL_13_YROLDS_SCORES, 7 DIGITS
00210 REM PUPILS.BAT : PUPILS_FILE INPUT
00220 REM ------------------------------------------
00230 OPEN "PUPILS.BAT" FOR INPUT AS FILE #1
00240 C% = 0
00250 E$ = "N"
00260 N% = 0
00270 T = 0
00280 IF E$ <> "N" GOTO 420
00290     IFEND #1 GOTO 380
00300        INPUT #1, P1%, P2%, P3%
00310        IF P2% = 13 GOTO 330
00320           GOTO 360
00330           T = T + P3%
00340           N% = N% + 1
00350           GOTO 360
00360        C% = C% + 1
00370        GOTO 410
00380        E$ = "Y"
00390        CLOSE #1
00400        GOTO 410
00410     GOTO 280
00420 PRINT C%; " RECORDS WERE READ."
00430 IF N% > 0 GOTO 460
00440     PRINT "AVERAGING IMPOSSIBLE; NO 13 YEAR OLDS"
00450     GOTO 500
00460     A = T / N%
00470     PRINT N%; " WERE 13 YEARS OLD "
00480     PRINT "AVERAGE SCORE OF 13 YEAR OLDS WAS "; A
00490     GOTO 500
00500 END
```

Fig. B9.4 ENDFILE translation—Example 3.

INTERACTIVE ANALOG TO ENDFILE IN BASIC

Figure B9.5 presents a translation of the program that gracefully allows the program's user to quit entering data from the keyboard whenever he or she desires.

```
00100     REM  -----TRANSLATION OF FIG. 9.11---------------------
00110     REM         R. TAYLOR     AUG 1980
00200     REM
00210     REM A1$ : ALL FINISHED, STRING 1
00220     REM B 1% BITES INFLICTED DAILY, 3 DIGITS
00300     REM C1$ : COUNTRY, 8 LETTERS
00400     REM P1% : POPULATION 11 DIGITS
00500     REM Q1$ : QUIT RESPONSE, STRING 1
00600     REM E1  : PERCENTAGE_YEARLY_EXPOSURE, FIXED 3,2
00700     REM E2 : DAYS_YEARLY_EXPOSURE, 3 DIGITS
00800     REM T1  : TOTAL_BITES, 5 SIGNIFICANT DIGITS (FLOAT)
00900     REM --------------------------------------------------
01000     PRINT "Annual Infliction of Mosquito Bites"
01010     PRINT "This program analyzes mosquito bite infliction "
01020     PRINT "for each of as many countries as you provide data on."
01030     PRINT "You will have the option to quit before beginning,"
01040     PRINT "and again each time a country analysis is finished."
01100     PRINT "----------------------------------"
01110     A1$ = "N"
01120     Q1$ = "C"
01130     IF A1$ = "Y" GOTO 2800
01140        PRINT "To continue, enter 'C'; to quit, enter 'Q'."
01145        INPUT Q1$
01150        IF Q1$ = "Q" GOTO 2650
01200           PRINT "Country (use no more than 8 letters)"
01300           INPUT C1$
01400           PRINT "Population"
01500           INPUT P1%
01600           PRINT "Bites inflicted daily per person"
01700           INPUT B1%
01800           PRINT "Percentage of days per year in which person is exposed"
01900           PRINT "     (Enter as decimal, eg, for 73%, enter .73)"
02000           INPUT E1
02100           E2 = 365 * E1
02200           T1 = E2 * B1% * P1%
02300           PRINT "The population of ";C1$; " would absorb ";T1; " bites";
02400           PRINT " annually under those conditions."
02600           GOTO 2750
02650           A1$ = "Y"
02660           GOTO 2750
02750     GOTO 1130
02800     END
```

Fig. B9.5 Translation of interactive end of data entry.

Note the following.

Instead of incorporating IFEND or any special variable into an assertion to determine if any more data is present in some file stored on a disk or other storage device, the program asks the user if he or she wants to enter any more data.

Private Practice BASIC

BP9.7   Using your editor or a simple program you write (modeled on Fig. B3.1), create a file of scores called "SCORE.DAT" suitable for use with the program presented in Fig. B9.2. Enter that program into your computer and run it, using the file "SCORE.DAT".

BP9.8   Using your editor or a simple program you write (modeled on Fig. B3.1), create a file of records called "STUDENT.DAT" appropriate for use with the program shown in Fig. B9.3.

BP9.9   Enter the program in Fig. B9.3 into your computer and run it, using the file "STUDENT.DAT" created in (BP9.8).

BP9.10   Using your editor of a simple program you write (modeled on Fig. B3.1), create a file of records called "PUPILS.DAT" appropriate for use with the program shown in Fig. B9.4.

BP9.11   Enter the program in Fig. B9.4 into your computer and run it, using the file "PUPILS.DAT" created in (BP9.10).

BP9.12   Using your editor or a simple program you write, create a file of student names as required by (P9.17). Then translate your solution to that problem into BASIC and run it, using the file. Create a second file of the same kind but with a different number of names in it and run that file through your BASIC translation of (P9.17).

BP9.13   Using (Fig. P9.5) as a model, translate your solution to (P9.18) into BASIC and run it.

BP9.14   Translate your solution to (P9.20) into BASIC and run it.

BP9.15   Translate your solution to (P9.22) into BASIC and run it.

BP9.16   Translate your solution to (P9.24) into BASIC and run it.

BP9.18   Translate your solution to (P9.25) into BASIC and run it.

BP9.19   Translate your solution to (P9.26) into BASIC and run it.

Pascal Interpretation of Chapter 9

COMPOUND ASSERTIONS IN PASCAL

Figure P9.1 presents the translations of two representative compound assertions.

```
(A < B) & (C > 1000)              IF A < B AND C > 1000
                                     THEN
                                         BEG.....

(COUNT > 1000) | (TIME ≥ 1630)    IF COUNT > 1000 OR TIME >= 1630
                                     THEN
                                         BEG....
```

Fig. P9.1 Translating compound assertions.

The Pascal translation of an EITHER that employs a compound assertion follows the same format as one that employs a single assertion. Your programs will remain easier to read if you combine no more than two assertions in any one compound, even though three, four, or more could be combined. To see why, and to better understand compound assertions in general, experiment with them through toy programs like the one shown in (PP9.1).

Private Practice Pascal

PP9.1   Explore the compound assertion in (P9.1) by entering the following toy program into your computer, then running it once on each set of A, B, and C values provided in (P9.1).

```
PROGRAM toy(input,output);
    (* Toy program to experiment with compound assertions*)
    VAR
        a,b,c, : INTEGER;
    BEGIN
        WRITELN ('Enter A, B, C as separate values');
        READLN; READ (a);
        READLN; READ (b);
        READLN; READ (c);
        IF a <= b AND c=1000
         THEN WRITELN('Compound false');
         ELSE WRITELN('Compound true');
        (* toy *)
```

PP9.2   Modify the READs and the assertion in *toy* to match the variables and assertion in (P9.2), then run the model on each of the six sets of RATE, DATE, and TIME values provided in (P9.2).

PP9.3   Translate your solution to (P9.4) into Pascal.

PP9.4   Translate your solution to (P9.6) into Pascal and run it on your computer.

PP9.5   Reread your solutions to (P9.6) through (P9.9) then translate the solution to the problem into Pascal, incorporating all the modifications represented.

PP9.6   Translate your solution to (P9.15) into Pascal and run it on your computer.

```
PROGRAM c9f8(scores,input,output);
  (* Translation of Fig. 9.8 *)
  (*     Ralph McKenzie    Mar 1980     *)
  VAR
    score, scorecount, totalscore : INTEGER;
    avg : REAL;
    allread : CHAR;
    scores : FILE OF CHAR;
  BEGIN
    totalscore := 0;
    scorecount := 0;
    allread := 'n';
    RESET(scores);
    WHILE allread = 'n' DO
        BEGIN
          READ (scores,score);
          IF EOF(scores)
              THEN allread := 'y'
              ELSE
                BEGIN
                  totalscore := totalscore + score;
                  scorecount := scorecount + 1
                END
        END;
    WRITELN(scorecount, ' scores were read, and');
    IF scorecount = 0
        THEN WRITELN('so no average could be calculated.')
        ELSE
          BEGIN
            avg := totalscore / scorecount;
            WRITELN(avg:5:2, ' was average of all scores.')
          END
  END. (* c9f8 *)
```

Fig. P9.2 ENDFILE translation—Example 1: (text file).

THREE ENDFILE EXAMPLES IN PASCAL

Because there are two different kinds of files in Pascal, text and binary, there are two different translations of ENDFILE handling. As shown by Fig. P9.2, the translation for text files closely parallels its FPL counterpart. As shown by Figs. P9.3 and P9.4, the translation for binary files does not.

Note the following about ENDFILE translation for text files.

1. As in FPL, the variable used to control the WHILE must be initialized to indicate that the end of data has not been reached.

allread := 'n';

2. The Pascal counterpart to ENDFILE is EOF and must be followed immediately by the name in parentheses of the file in question.

EOF (scores)

3. With a text file like (scores), the EITHER to test for ENDFILE comes, like its FPL counterpart, immediately after the external assignment attempting to read the data.

```
READ (scores, score);
IF EOF (scores)
    THEN all . . . .
    ELSE . . . .
```

4. As in FPL, all details pertaining to the end of data encounter must be housed in the *true* digression;

```
READ (scores,score);
IF EOF (scores)
  THEN allread := 'y'
    ELSE
        BEGIN
            totalsc . . . . . .
```

all details pertaining to the handling of a successfully read piece of data must be housed in the *false* digression.

READ (scores, score);
IF EOF (scores)
   THEN allread := 'y'
   ELSE
     BEGIN
       totalscore := totalscore + score;
       scorecount := scorecount+ 1
     END

As we learned in Chapter Three, an external assignment to get data from a binary file is a two-step rather than a one-step procedure. Copy the data from the file to a buffer, then copy the data from the buffer to the storage location named for the data. Figure P9.3 illustrates. Compare it with the structure of the original FPL in Fig. 9.9.

```
PROGRAM c9f9 (stusch,output);
   (* Translation of Fig. 9.9 *)
   (* Barbara Rinehart    Nov 1980 *)
   TYPE
     sturecshape =
         RECORD
           id : INTEGER;
           age : INTEGER;
           name : PACKED ARRAY [1 .. 10] OF CHAR;
           score : INTEGER
         END;
   VAR
       stusch : FILE OF sturecshape;
       sturec : sturecshape;
       soughtscore : INTEGER;
       allbeenread : CHAR;
   BEGIN
     sturec.id := 0;
     RESET(stusch);
     IF EOF(stusch)
           THEN allbeenread := 'y'
           ELSE allbeenread := 'n';
     WHILE (allbeenread = 'n') AND (sturec.id <> 3453) DO
         BEGIN
           sturec := stusch^;
           GET(stusch);
           IF EOF(stusch)
               THEN allbeenread := 'y'
               ELSE;
         END;
     WRITELN(sturec.score,' was score for student 3453.')
   END. (* c9f9 *)
```

Fig. P9.3 ENDFILE translation—Example 2: (binary file).

Note the following about ENDFILE translation for binary files.

1. The assertion about the end of the data parallels its counterpart for text files

IF EOF (stusch)

2. Because the RESET which opens the file also attempts to copy one record from the file to the temporary storage area reserved for use by that file during the program's execution, a test for end of file must be made immediately following that RESET.

IF EOF (stusch)
    THEN allbeenread := 'y'
    ELSE allbeenread := 'n';

This EITHER initializes the variable that controls the WHILE: if the file is empty, the value assigned prevents any repetitions at all; otherwise, a value to force repetition is assigned.

3. Because the RESET (if the file is not initially empty) will copy a first record to the buffer, the first part of the WHILE digression must deal with processing that data. In this program, the processing of a record amounts to no more than examining the *id* to see if it equals 3453, a task performed by the WHILE assertion itself. The only thing in the first part of the digression is therefore the assignment to copy the data from the buffer into the record

sturec := stusch∧;

4. The rest of the digression must attempt the next copy of data from file to buffer, test for success, and assign the appropriate value to the WHILE-controlling variable if EOF occurred.

GET(stusch);
IF EOF(stusch)
    THEN allbeenread := 'y'
    ELSE;

Figure P9.4 presents a second example of ENDFILE translation for a binary file, illustrating a situation where more processing takes place per record than in the earlier search program (Fig. P9.3).
translation—Example 3 (binary file)

```
PROGRAM c9f10 ( pupils, output);
      (* Translation of Figure 9.10 *)
      (* Dick Owens    April 1980 *)
      TYPE
        pupilrecshape =
            RECORD
              id : INTEGER;
              age : INTEGER;
              score : INTEGER
            END;
      VAR
          average : REAL;
          count, total13yroldsscores, nmbr13yrolds : INTEGER;
          endofdata : CHAR;
          pupilrecord : pupilrecshape;
          pupils : FILE OF pupilrecshape;
      BEGIN
          count := 0;
          total13yroldsscores := 0;
          nmbr13yrolds := 0;
          RESET(pupils);
          IF EOF (pupils)
              THEN endofdata := 'y'
              ELSE endofdata := 'n';
          WHILE endofdata = 'n' DO
              BEGIN
                pupilrecord := pupils^;
                IF pupilrecord.age = 13
                  THEN
                    BEGIN
                      total13yroldsscores := total13yroldsscores
                          + pupilrecord.score;
                      nmbr13yrolds := nmbr13yrolds + 1
                    END
                  ELSE;
                  count := count + 1;
                  GET(pupils);
                  IF EOF (pupils)
                      THEN endofdata := 'y'
                      ELSE;
              END;
          WRITELN(COUNT:5, ' records were read.');
          IF nmbr13yrolds > 0
            THEN
             BEGIN
               WRITELN(nmbr13yrolds:5, ' were 13 year olds.');
               average := total13yroldsscores / nmbr13yrolds;
               WRITELN ('Average score of 13 year olds was ', average:6:2)
             END
            ELSE
             WRITELN('Averaging impossible; no 13 year olds.');
      END. (* c9f10 *)
```

Fig. P9.4 ENDFILE—Example 3: (binary file).

Note the following about Fig. P9.4.

1. The processing of a record follows the copying of that record from the buffer to the named location.

```
                    pupilrecord := pupils∧;
                IF pupilrecord.age = 13
                    THEN
                        BEGIN
                            totall3yroldsscores :=
totall3yroldsscores
                                + pupilrecord.score;
                            nmbrl3yrolds := nmbrl3yrolds + 1
                    END

        ELSE;
        count :=   count+ 1;
```

2. The attempt to copy another record from the file to the buffer follows the record processing, at the bottom of the WHILE digression.

```
        count := count + 1;
        GET (pupils);
        IF EOF (pupils)
            THEN endofdata := 'y'
            ELSE;
```

INTERACTIVE ANALOG TO ENDFILE IN PASCAL

Figure P9.5 presents a translation of the program that gracefully allows the program's user to quit entering data from the keyboard whenever he or she desires.

```
PROGRAM c9fll(input,output);
     (* Translation of Fig. 9.11 *)
     (*  Earl Sarvey    Jan 1981    *)
   VAR
     allfinished : CHAR;
     bitesdailyperperson : INTEGER;
     country : ARRAY[1..8] OF CHAR;
     daysyearlyexposure : REAL;
     percentageyearlyexposure : REAL;
     population : INTEGER;
     quitresponse : CHAR;
     totalbites : REAL;
   BEGIN
     quitresponse := 'C';
     WRITELN('Annual infliction of mosquito bites');
     WRITELN('This program analyses mosquito bite infliction');
     WRITELN('for each of as many countries as you provide data on.');
     WRITELN('You will have the option to quit before beginning,');
     WRITELN('and again each time a country analysis is finished.');
     WRITELN('--------------------------');
     allfinished := 'n';
     WHILE allfinished = 'n' DO
       BEGIN
         WRITELN('To continue, type "C"; to quit, "Q".');
         READLN;READ(quitresponse);
         IF quitresponse = 'C'
           THEN
            BEGIN
             WRITELN('Country?  (exactly 8 letters -- if too long, ',
                                 'abbreviate');
             WRITELN('      if too short, add blanks)');
             READLN;
             READ(country[1]);
             READ(country[2]);
             READ(country[3]);
             READ(country[4]);
             READ(country[5]);
             READ(country[6]);
             READ(country[7]);
             READ(country[8]);
             WRITELN('Population?');
             READ(population);
             WRITELN('Bites inflicted daily per person (estimate)?');
             READ(bitesdailyperperson);
             WRITELN('Percentage of days per year in which ',
                                 'person is exposed ');
             WRITELN('   to mosquitoes? (Use decimal, eg, .73 for 73%, etc)');
             READ(percentageyearlyexposure);
             daysyearlyexposure := 365.0 * percentageyearlyexposure;
             totalbites := daysyearlyexposure * bitesdailyperperson
                             * population;
             WRITELN('The population of ',country, ' would absorb ',
                         totalbites:4,' bites under such conditions.');
            END
         ELSE allfinished := 'y';
       END;
   END. (* c9fll *)
```

Fig. P9.5 Translation of interactive end of data entry.

Note the following.

Instead of incorporating EOF or any special variable into an assertion to determine if any more data is present in some file stored on a disk or other storage device, the program asks the user if he or she wants to enter any more data.

Private Practice Pascal

PP9.6   Using your editor or a simple program you write (modeled on Fig. P3.1), create a file of scores called *scores* suitable for use with the program presented in Fig. P9.2.

PP9.7   Enter the program in Fig. P9.2 into your computer and run it, using the file *scores* created in (PP9.6).

PP9.8   Using your editor or a simple program you write (modeled on Fig. B3.1), create a file of records called *stusch* appropriate for use with the program shown in Fig. P9.3.

PP9.9   Enter the program in Fig. P9.3 into your computer and run it, using the file *stusch* created in (PP9.8).

PP9.10   Using your editor or a simple program you write (modeled on Fig. P3.1) create a file of records called *pupils* appropriate for use with the program shown in Fig. P9.4.

PP9.11   Enter the program in Fig. P9.4 into your computer and run it, using the file *pupils* created in (PP9.10).

PP9.12   Using your editor or a simple program you write, create a file of student names as required by (P9.17). Then translate your solution to that problem into Pascal and run it, using the file. Create a second file of the same kind but with a different number of names in it and run that file through your Pascal translation of (P9.17).

PP9.13   Using Fig. P9.5 as a model, translate your solution to (P9.18) into Pascal and run it.

PP9.14   Translate your solution to (P9.20) into Pascal and run it.

PP9.15   Translate your solution to (P9.22) into Pascal and run it.

PP9.16   Translate your solution to (P9.24) into Pascal and run it.

PP9.17   Translate your solution to (P9.25) into Pascal and run it.

PP9.18   Translate your solution to (P9.26) into Pascal and run it.

Keeping Programs Easy to Read, Repair, and Modify— The Program Block

INTRODUCTION

Once written, a program is going to be read, perhaps only a few times, perhaps many, perhaps only by its author, perhaps by a wide range of people. In any case, the reading will be easier if the program's creator writes with the human reader and not just the computer in mind. Wise use of logic structures such as WHILES and EITHERs, of data structures such as arrays and records, and of descriptive datanames all help to make the program readable. This chapter presents another construct whose appropriate use can make the resulting program dramatically easier to read: the program block.

USING OUTLINES TO ORGANIZE
AND SIMPLIFY: A SIMPLE EXAMPLE

Suppose you are leaving for a vacation and want someone to take care of your apartment. You work out general and detailed lists of things to be done (Figs. 10.1 and 10.2). When you ask a friend to do the work, you don't give details. The friend probably asks one or two questions "How many chairs?" or "You don't have a spider plant, do you?"

Fig. 10.1 Major duties.

Your friend counts on learning details later. In fact, *if* you begin to recite the details, the friend may become irritated and say, "Yes, I'll do it. Never mind the details. I'll look at them later." He or she has enough of an idea of what's wanted just from the rough list and assumes details will be available when required. No one would want all the details in *one* long list: watering the plants has nothing to do with collecting the mail. At most, a list like the one in Fig. 10.3 would be appropriate.

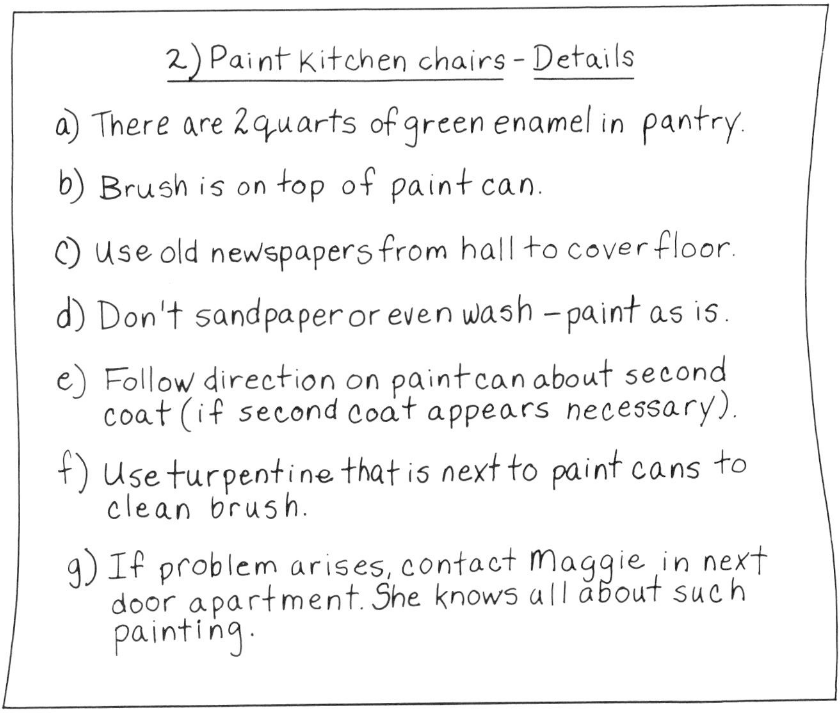

2) Paint Kitchen chairs - Details

a) There are 2 quarts of green enamel in pantry.

b) Brush is on top of paint can.

c) Use old newspapers from hall to cover floor.

d) Don't sandpaper or even wash - paint as is.

e) Follow direction on paint can about second coat (if second coat appears necessary).

f) Use turpentine that is next to paint cans to clean brush.

g) If problem arises, contact Maggie in next door apartment. She knows all about such painting.

Fig. 10.2 Detailed instructions for one task.

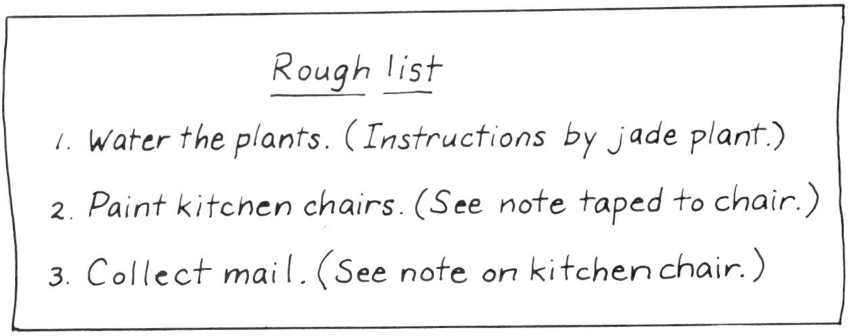

Rough list

1. Water the plants. (*Instructions by jade plant.*)

2. Paint kitchen chairs. (*See note taped to chair.*)

3. Collect mail. (*See note on kitchen chair.*)

Fig. 10.3 Amended list of major duties.

Now suppose that someone you knew wanted *you* to watch an apartment for *them*. Instead of a rough, major item list you are given a list much like that in Fig. 10.4. Such a set of instructions is difficult to follow and obscures the major tasks. You can use it only by looking at every item, regardless of whether you intend to water plants or paint chairs. And how do you suppose the creator of such a list usually adds a new item? Right! By tacking it to the bottom of the list or finding something vaguely related in midlist and inserting the new item there. And how do you suppose the creator finds an item in order to change it? Right! With great difficulty!

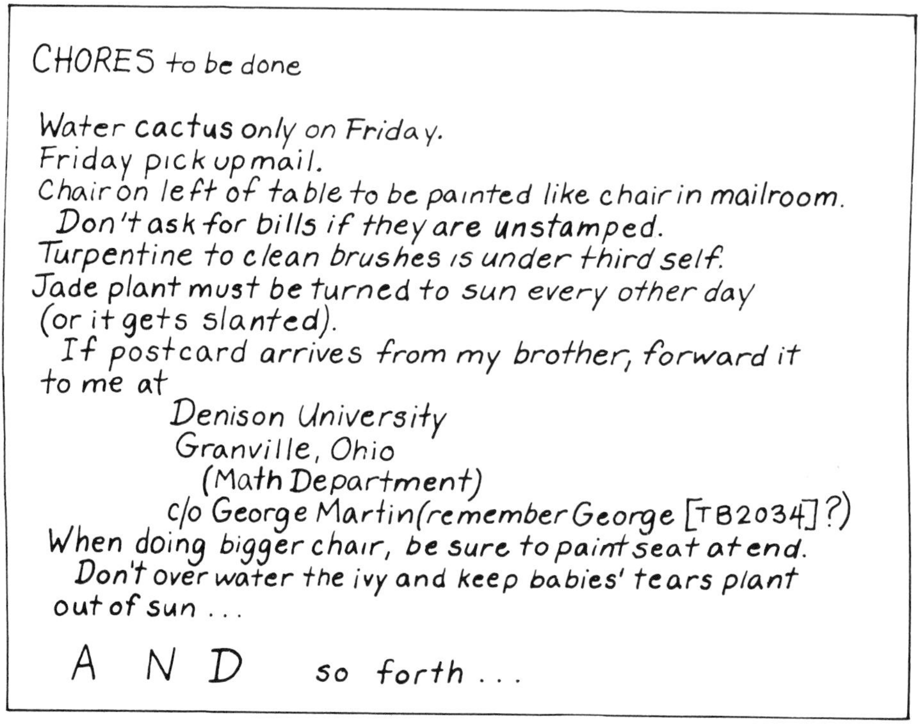

Fig. 10.4 Disorganized list of details.

Yet this is precisely the way many, many computer programs are written. Programs should have clear rough structure so that people can read them and quickly find just those details they need. We can emphasize their structure by using program blocks.

MAKING A PROGRAM EASIER TO READ BY ORGANIZING IT IN BLOCKS.

What Is a Block?

The *Program Block* in FPL has a lot in common with an item in a rough-outline list. Its name, written inside a double-sided block name box,

```
INITIALIZE_ALL
```

appears in at least two places in any program in which it appears at all (1) as a *block reference* or *call* and (2) as a *block detail heading.* The block detail heading may occur only once in a program but the block reference may appear more than once. Figure 10.5 illustrates both occurrences and how they are related during execution of a program containing them.

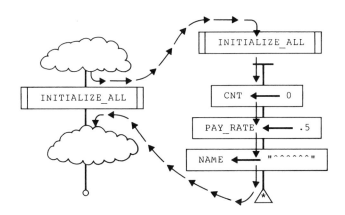

Fig. 10.5 Dual occurrence of the block name box.

When the block reference is encountered, the computer stops executing the code containing the reference, finds the block details referenced, and executes them. When finished, the computer returns to executing the referencing code, just below the referencing block's name box.

A block's details may include any valid FPL constructs except a START or STOP circle. The code constituting the block must end with one and only one ENDBLOCK triangle, aligned directly below the heading box. Block execution begins immediately below the detail heading box and proceeds until the triangle is reached.

As Fig. 10.6 suggests, one block may call another. In fact, it is sometimes appropriate to create a block whose details are nothing but calls to other blocks. For instance, in addition to the call shown in Fig. 10.6, COMPUTE_ALL_RATES might call a block to computer newspaper rates, one to compute letter rates, and one to compute oversize item rates.

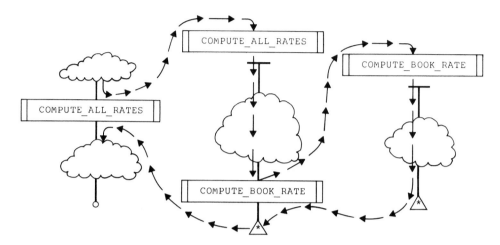

Fig. 10.6 The calling of one block from another.

Private Practice

P 10.1   Assume you are going away for three weeks and must leave your apartment empty while you are away. Make a well-structured list of the main things a housekeeper or friend would have to do in your absence to keep things ready for your return. Take one of these things and expand it into a set of details such as would be required by anyone actually trying to fulfill the task involved.

P 10.2   Refine each rough program below, replacing each of the episodes shown by a block reference box and appropriately named block details. Leave block details in episode form, as you would if you were not yet sure of the exact details.

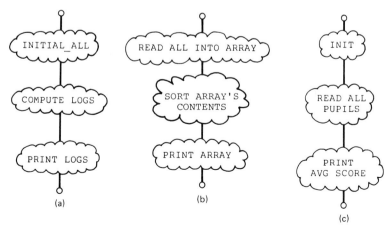

P 10.3   Arrange the following details into a well-structured list, placing the details under one of three major headings (you must deduce the headings). Make sure your headings are broad enough to encompass all the details and be sure to "throw away" any redundant (duplicated) details, indicating below your list what such details were.

Mark sections to be deleted from new math book.
Put on shoes.
Put on trousers.
Get underwear from hall closet.
Put on green stockings.
Don't score too often against Henry's backhand.
Buy new math book, *Easy Adding.*
Work problems 2.3, 2.2, 2.10 in math book.
Look in phone book to find which bookstore sells math book, *Easy Adding.*
Cover new math book with plastic from under bed.
Play tennis with Henry.
Call Henry about time of match and about new tennis shoes.
Finish off dressing with new necktie.

Simplifying an Existing Program by "Blocking" It

Consider the program in Fig. 10.7. It is neither exceptionally long nor particularly complex, yet it is difficult to comprehend at a glance. What does it do? How does it do it? We can not easily say; we must study it for some minutes before answering.

In all its detail, it generates the same reader confusion as the disorganized list of duties in Fig. 10.4. That list was clarified by imposing some organization upon it and announcing that organization through an outline. This program can be clarified by subdividing it into coherent pieces and treating each as a block.

Figure 10.8 shows the result of a first-phase reorganization. The major activities stand out clearly to the reader, as the major duties did with the vacation list; initialization, reading, and analyzing a file; and reporting. Figure 10.9 shows the process carried further, subdividing the most complicated of the original blocks. The result is easier to follow. You can pick up the program's structure at a glance and quickly go to details of interest.

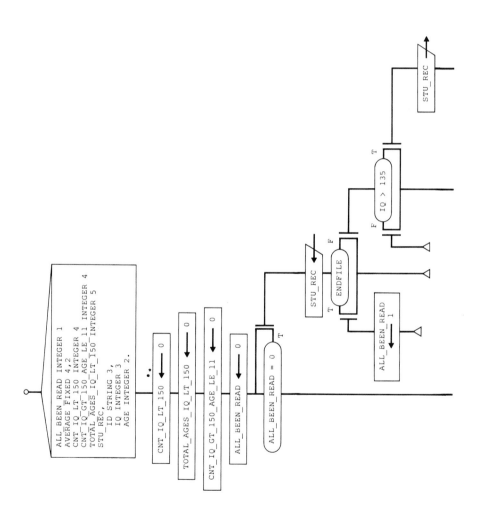

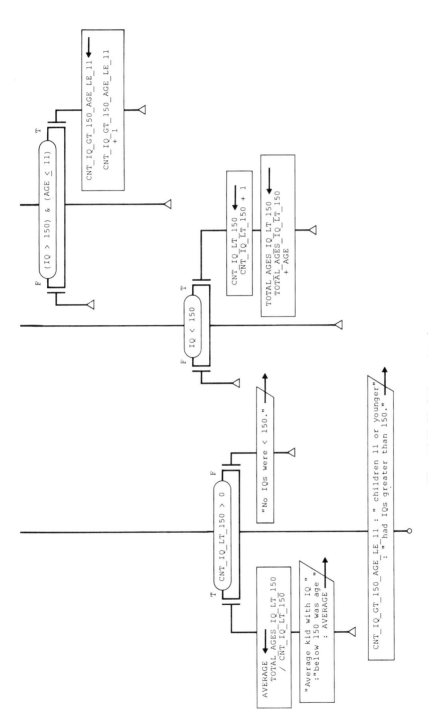

Fig. 10.7 Undifferentiated program mass.

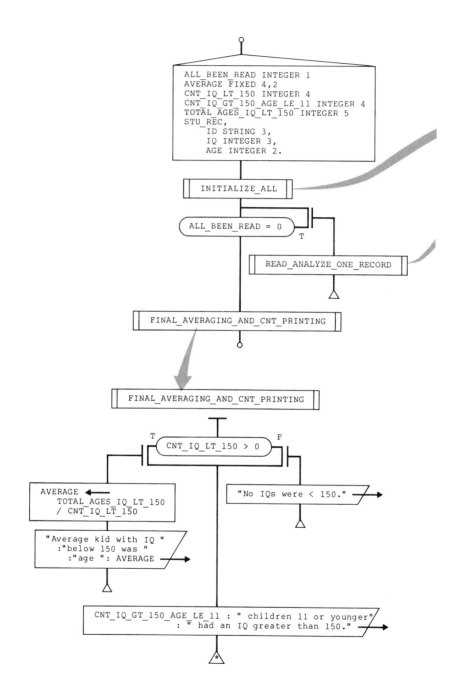

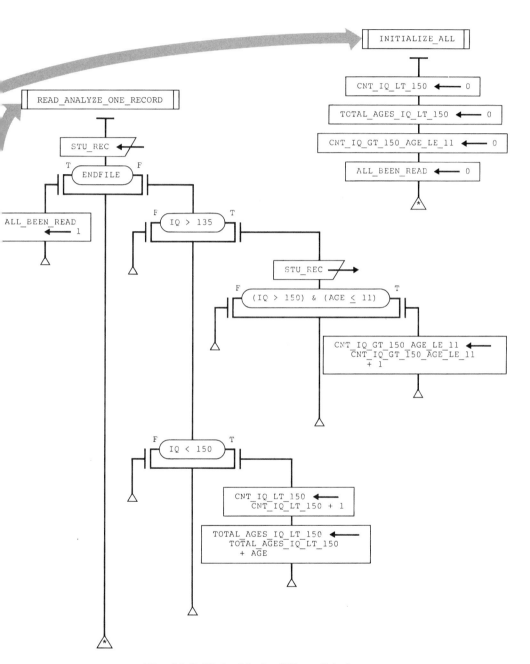

Fig. 10.8 Major blocks differentiated.

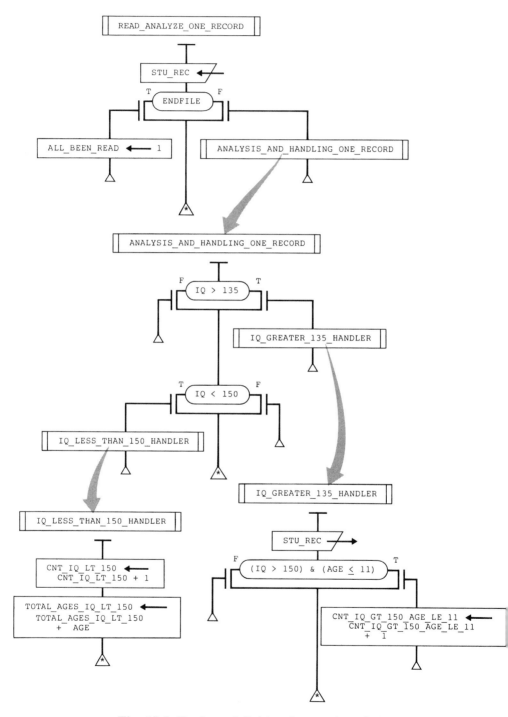

Fig. 10.9 Further subdivision, increased revelation.

Private Practice

P10.4   Rewrite the note reversal program (Fig. 5.39), subdividing it into blocks.

P10.5   Rewrite the modified selection program (Fig. 8.27), subdividing it into blocks.

P10.6   Rewrite your original UNESCO program (P7.4), subdividing it into blocks.

P10.7   Rewrite your election analysis program (P7.10), subdividing it into blocks.

BLOCKS AS AN AID IN PROGRAM MODIFICATION: TWO EXAMPLES

The primary reason for making a program more readable is not to please the casual reader; it is to reduce the work of any person charged with modifying the program. If a program proves useful once it has been created, it is almost certain to require modification. The more clearly it is structured, the more easily it can be modified. Let's look at an example.

An Example: Modifying the Letter-display Program

Figure 10.10 shows the letter-display program (Fig. 6.22) rewritten using blocks.

The letter-display program has worked well. However, a new, bigger screen has been developed and the program must be modified to make use of it. Making the modification will demonstrate further the utility of blocks.

The larger screen,

SCREEN [25,11] INTEGER 1

is capable of displaying three letters, as shown in Fig. 10.11. Our program will still print a T, but it will be so designed that, at the cost of very minor modification, the T can be printed in any one of three locations shown: (1), (2), or (3).

The approach we shall take is evident. We will need two arrays: SCREEN and LETTER, the first 25 × 11, the second 9 × 7. SCREEN will be used to display the letter after it has been loaded into LETTER.

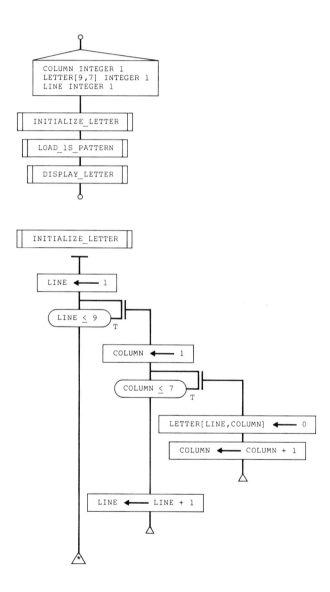

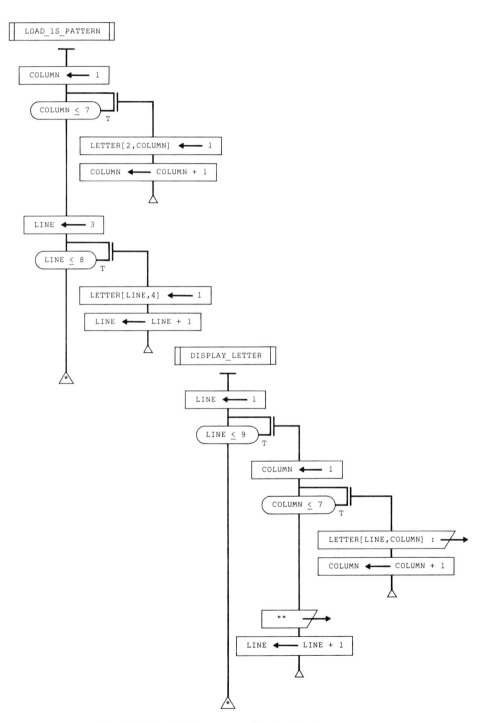

Fig. 10.10 Block-structured letter-display program.

	(1)									(2)									(3)					
	1	2	3	4	5	6	7	8	9	0	1	2	3	4	5	6	7	8	9	0	1	2	3	4	5
1	0	0	0	0	0	0	0	0	0	0	0	0	0	0	0	0	0	0	0	0	0	0	0	0	0
2	0	0	0	0	0	0	0	0	0	0	0	0	0	0	0	0	0	0	0	0	0	0	0	0	0
3	0	0	0	0	0	0	0	0	0	0	0	0	0	0	0	0	0	0	0	0	0	0	0	0	0
4	0	0	0	0	0	0	0	0	0	0	0	0	0	0	0	0	0	0	0	0	0	0	0	0	0
5	0	0	0	0	0	0	0	0	0	0	0	0	0	0	0	0	0	0	0	0	0	0	0	0	0
6	0	0	0	0	0	0	0	0	0	0	0	0	0	0	0	0	0	0	0	0	0	0	0	0	0
7	0	0	0	0	0	0	0	0	0	0	0	0	0	0	0	0	0	0	0	0	0	0	0	0	0
8	0	0	0	0	0	0	0	0	0	0	0	0	0	0	0	0	0	0	0	0	0	0	0	0	0
9	0	0	0	0	0	0	0	0	0	0	0	0	0	0	0	0	0	0	0	0	0	0	0	0	0
0	0	0	0	0	0	0	0	0	0	0	0	0	0	0	0	0	0	0	0	0	0	0	0	0	0
1	0	0	0	0	0	0	0	0	0	0	0	0	0	0	0	0	0	0	0	0	0	0	0	0	0

Fig. 10.11 The big screen.

Figure 10.12 presents the approach in episodic form. Initialize all cells of both arrays. Assign to LETTER the T pattern of 1's and 0's shown in Fig. 6.16. Transfer a copy of LETTER to the screen location (1), (2), or (3). Print the entire SCREEN, using details based on Fig. 6.18. We will refine each episode into a block, copying where possible from the simpler program in Fig. 10.10.

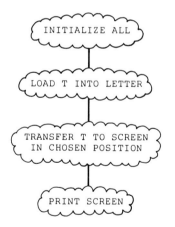

Fig. 10.12 The letter-display program.

The transfer   Let's refine the transfer episode first; it has no analogue in our simpler program. Assume initializations: a 0 has been assigned to each cell of SCREEN and the pattern in Fig. 6.16 has been set in LETTER.

Were both arrays the same size, the transfer could be accomplished through repeated execution of an assignment using common subscripting across arrays.

SCREEN [LINE, COLUMN] ⟵⎯ LETTER [LINE, COLUMN]

Since SCREEN is actually larger than LETTER, this would not work; it would transfer the letter into a corner of the screen.

By superimposing a layout of LETTER on SCREEN, in each of the three possible positions, we see the relationship between them (Fig. 10.13). For increased clarity, each cell of SCREEN not overlayed appears as a dot.

```
              (1)              (2)              (3)
      1 2 3 4 5 6 7 8 9 0 1 2 3 4 5 6 7 8 9 0 1 2 3 4 5

 1  . . . . . . . . . . . . . . . . . . . . . . . . . .
 2  . 0 0 0 0 0 0 0 . 0 0 0 0 0 0 0 . 0 0 0 0 0 0 0 .
 3  . 1 1 1 1 1 1 1 . 1 1 1 1 1 1 1 . 1 1 1 1 1 1 1 .
 4  . 0 0 0 1 0 0 0 . 0 0 0 1 0 0 0 . 0 0 0 1 0 0 0 .
 5  . 0 0 0 1 0 0 0 . 0 0 0 1 0 0 0 . 0 0 0 1 0 0 0 .
 6  . 0 0 0 1 0 0 0 . 0 0 0 1 0 0 0 . 0 0 0 1 0 0 0 .
 7  . 0 0 0 1 0 0 0 . 0 0 0 1 0 0 0 . 0 0 0 1 0 0 0 .
 8  . 0 0 0 1 0 0 0 . 0 0 0 1 0 0 0 . 0 0 0 1 0 0 0 .
 9  . 0 0 0 1 0 0 0 . 0 0 0 1 0 0 0 . 0 0 0 1 0 0 0 .
10  . 0 0 0 0 0 0 0 . 0 0 0 0 0 0 0 . 0 0 0 0 0 0 0 .
11  . . . . . . . . . . . . . . . . . . . . . . . . . .
```

Fig. 10.13 LETTER in relation to SCREEN.

We assume that a cell-by-cell copy of LETTER's entire contents into a subset of SCREEN's cells is required; into (1) if the letter is to appear in the left position, into (2) if in the center, and into (3) if in the right position. The copying assignment would have the form

SCREEN [*line , column*] ⟵⎯ LETTER [LINE,COLUMN]

and *line* and *column* would be respectively related to LINE and COLUMN through a simple formula.

Discovering the formula for *line* is simple; Fig. 10.13 reveals it. The value of *line* is always 1 more than that of LINE because line 1 of the screen is left blank to form a top border. Incorporating that fact, a first refinement of the copying assignment is

SCREEN [1 + LINE, *column*] ⟵⎯ LETTER [LINE,COLUMN].

To discover the appropriate expression for *column*, we must consider the horizontal displacement of the superimposed positions. The question is: How much must we add to the value of COLUMN for a particular cell in one of the superimposed LETTER positions to get the value of the SCREEN *column* underneath it? Again, Fig. 10.13 provides all we need to know: add 1 for every border to the left of the cell's position; add 7 for every superimposed letter position to its left. An approximate formula for *column* in terms of COLUMN would then be

1 * number   7 * number
of borders to   + of positions to   +   COLUMN value
COLUMN's left   COLUMN's left

From studying Fig. 10.13, we see that the number of border widths to the left of (1) is 1, of (2) is 2, and of (3) is 3. Thus the position number is also the number of borders to any COLUMN's left. Similarly we see that the number of positions to the left is always 1 less than the position number: 2 positions are to the left of (3), 1 to the left of (2), 0 to the left of (1). Declaring an appropriate dataname for position:

POSITION INTEGER 1

we use it to complete refinement of the column transformation

POSITION * 1 + ((POSITION - 1) * 7) + COLUMN

The completely refined copying assignment then is:

SCREEN[1+LINE,POSITION+((POSITION-1) *7)+COLUMN]
←—— LETTER [LINE,COLUMN]

The final refinement of the transfer episode is the block TRANSFER _LETTER shown in Fig. 10.14. It combines this assignment with the nested WHILEs from Fig. 6.18 and an intial assignment to set the letter position.

Loading the *T* into *LETTER*   Loading the T into LETTER can be done exactly as in Fig. 10.10. We simply copy the block LOAD_1S_ PATTERN into our new program.

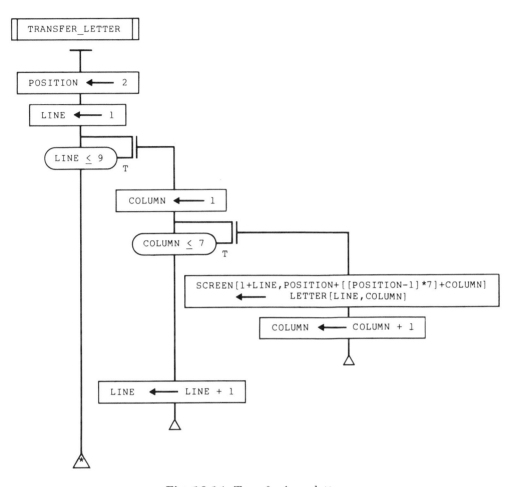

Fig. 10.14 Transferring a letter.

Initialization   Initialization parallels that in the simpler program except there are *two* arrays rather than one. From the earlier program, we copy the details to initialize LETTER and add a similar set to initialize SCREEN. The new initialization block appears in Fig. 10.15.

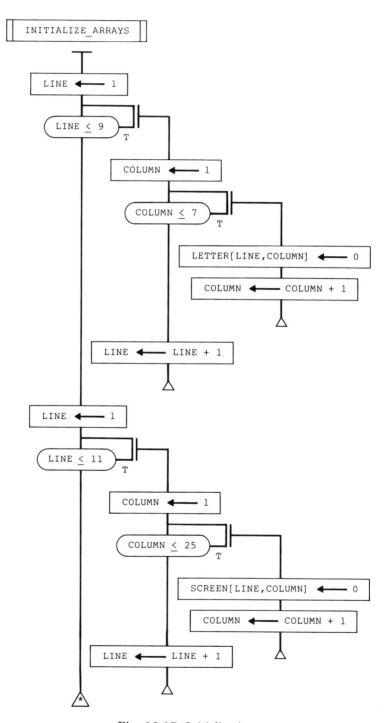

Fig. 10.15 Initialization.

Displaying the letter   The block to display the screen appears in Fig. 10.16. It is only a slight modification of the simpler DISPLAY_LETTER seen earlier: the array is called SCREEN rather than LETTER and the associated assertions reflect SCREEN's greater dimensions. The entire screen is displayed by this block though only a portion is occupied by the T.

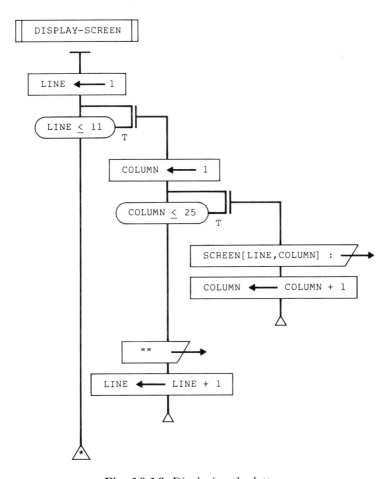

Fig. 10.16 Displaying the letter.

The heart of the screen-display program   The main part or root of the new program is shown in Fig. 10.17. We did not need to create a new block to load the T; the others are the blocks just worked out.

Not only did blocks help us avoid some unnecessary work in creating this program but they also make the result easy to follow. If the reader wants

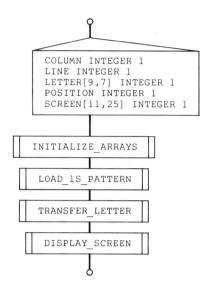

```
COLUMN INTEGER 1
LINE INTEGER 1
LETTER[9,7] INTEGER 1
POSITION INTEGER 1
SCREEN[11,25] INTEGER 1
```

```
INITIALIZE_ARRAYS
```

```
LOAD_1S_PATTERN
```

```
TRANSFER_LETTER
```

```
DISPLAY_SCREEN
```

Fig. 10.17 The root of the screen-display program.

detail, he or she can turn to the respective block of interest. If not, the reader can ignore the details with ease and still come away with a clear idea of the major structure of the program.

Testing by block   Block structure also simplifies testing by making it possible to focus on one small segment (i.e., a block) of the program at a time. Such focused scrutiny hastens the pinpointing of discrepancies, omissions, and errors. It usually increases the tester's understanding of the block, too.

Figure 10.18 illustrates using the most complex block in this program. Note how few trace points are needed. Initial values for 14 of LETTER's cells are provided and the transfer of these values to SCREEN is traced in the table. Entries under the heading (1+LINE) represent the first subscript value for SCREEN; entries under the next, the second subscript, including its computation (the number following the = is the value). Entries under SCREEN[*,*] show the two subscript values in place (i.e., [3,10]) and the value stored in the cell (i.e.,1).

Private Practice

P 10.8   Modify the letter-display program to use a bigger screen five letters wide and three letters high. Set it to print the letter in the bottom right-hand position on the screen. Indicate the changes needed to make it print the letter in the second position from the left, middle row.

P10.9   Modify the three-position, letter-display program so that it prints the letter in all three positions in one run of the program.

P10.10   Modify the three-position program so that it can print TO, using the first two positions. One way is to make LETTER three-dimensional and use LETTER[1,LINE,COLUMN] for T and LETTER[2, LINE,COLUMN] for O. There are other ways. Feel free to discover them.

P10.11   Modify your solution to (P10.9) so that it reads the T from a file called LPATTERNS (see Fig. 6.23).

P10.12   Modify your solution to (P10.11) so that it reads from a sequential file containing the patterns for three different letters.

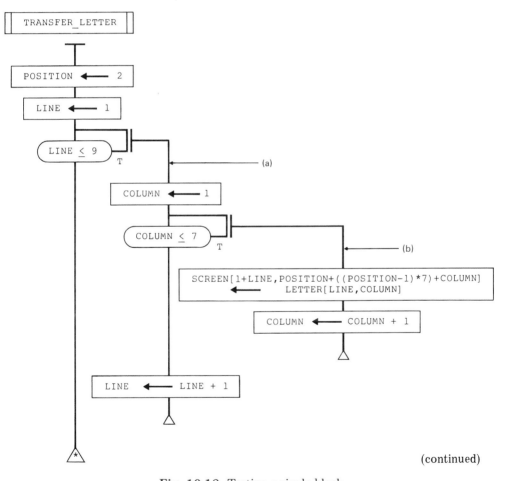

Fig. 10.18 Testing a single block.

```
Initial Values for Selected Cells of LETTER
[2,1]  [2,2]  [2,3]  [2,4]  [2,5]  [2,6]  [2,7]
  1      1      1      1      1      1      1

[3,1]  [3,2]  [3,3]  [3,4]  [3,5]  [3,6]  [3,7]
  0      0      0      1      0      0      0
```

				Trace Table	
point	LINE	COLUMN	(1+LINE)	(POSITION+((POSITION-1)*7)+COLUMN)	SCREEN[*,*]
(a)	2				
(b)	2	1	3	2 + ((2-1)*7) + 1 = 10	[3,10] : 1
(b)	2	2	3	2 + ((2-1)*7) + 2 = 11	[3,11] : 1
(b)	2	3	3	2 + ((2-1)*7) + 3 = 12	[3,12] : 1
(b)	2	4	3	2 + ((............	
(b)	2	5	....		
(b)	2	....			
(b)	3	......			
(b)	3	4	4	2 + ((2-1)*7) + 4 = 13	[4,13] : 1
(b)	3	5	4	2 + ((2-1)*7) + 5 = 14	[4,14] : 0
(b)	3	6	4	2 + ((2-1)*7) + 6 = 15	[4,15] : 0
(b)	3	7	4	2 + ((2-1)*7) + 7 = 16	[4,16] : 0

Fig. 10.18 (continued)

P 10.13 Test the block LOAD_1S_PATTERN. Check the appropriateness of each trace table LETTER entry by plotting each 1 or 0 on a 9 × 7 array pattern arranged like a screen.

P 10.14 Test DISPLAY_SCREEN by tracing execution while LINE = 2 and LINE = 3. Indicate where each of the 50 values would be printed on an 11 × 25 screen.

A Second Example: Modifying the Survey Analysis Program

The survey analysis program from Chapter Seven provides a second clear example of how block structuring makes a program readable and easier to modify. Figure 10.19 is a block-structured version of the program from Fig. 7.15. Before proceeding further, you should review the specifications this version was designed to satisfy.

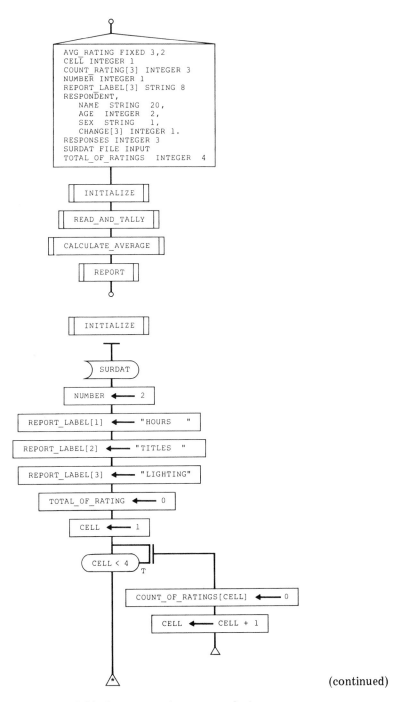

(continued)

Fig. 10.19 A block-structured survey analysis program.

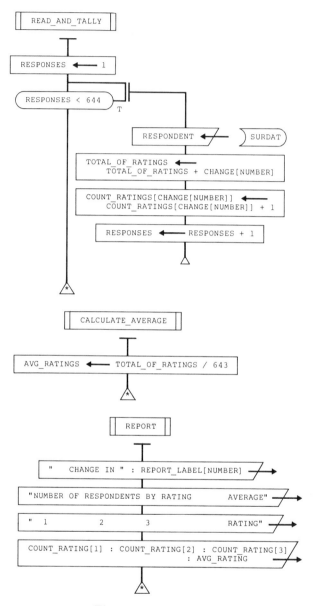

Fig. 10.19 (continued)

Adding ENDFILE handling and data editing Let's bring the program up to date by adding ENDFILE handling and data editing. These activities will be associated primarily with the block READ_AND_TALLY, requiring it to be split into subblocks.

The ENDFILE modification is shown in Fig. 10.20. Both the average and the report block must be modified to handle the possibility that no valid responses were read.

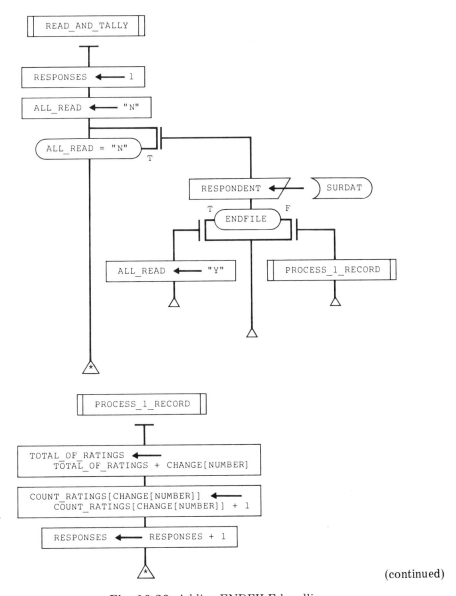

Fig. 10.20 Adding ENDFILE handling.

(continued)

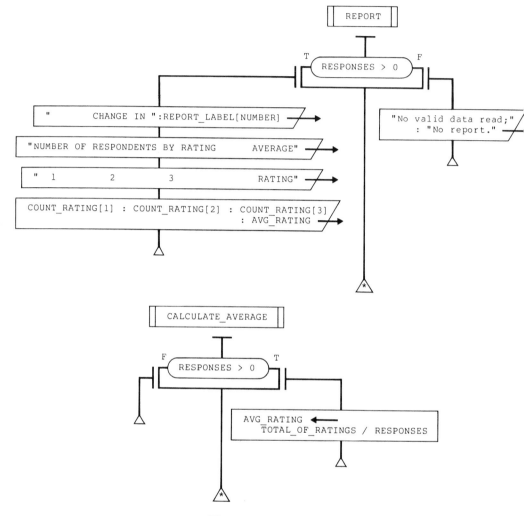

Fig. 10.20 (continued)

To add editing of the data, we merely modify the block that processes one record. Figure 10.21 shows how. We create a separate block to do the editing, and separate blocks to handle rejected and accepted responses, respectively. The editing block begins by assigning "OKAY" to the result indicator (VALUES). If the rating on the response (CHANGE[NUMBER]) is not a 1, 2, or 3, the "OKAY" is changed to "NONO." PROCESS_1_RECORD then handles the response accordingly: if "OKAY," the rating is processed; if "NONO," it's ignored and a warning message is issued.

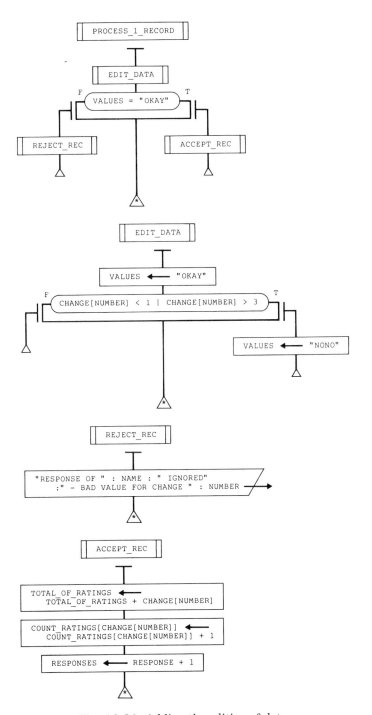

Fig. 10.21 Adding the editing of data.

Increasing the scope—three changes in one run   Suppose we are faced with more comprehensive specifications: redesign the program to report on all *three* changes (hours, titles, lights) in one run. To meet this new requirement, the program must be modified. Its block structure will make it easier to modify.

To handle all three changes in one run, three change ratings must be edited, three totals must be built, three counts kept, three averages calculated, and three reports issued. For example, ACCEPT_REC would have to include the three assignment triplets shown in Fig. 10.22.

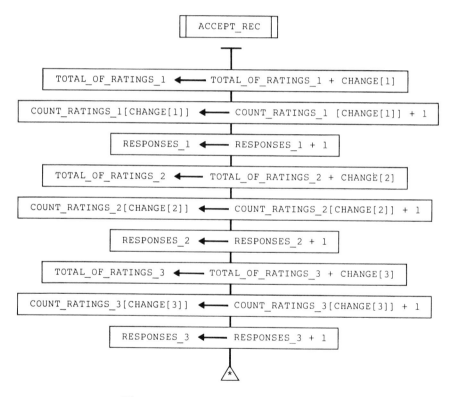

Fig. 10.22 Three assignment triplets.

The patterns of 1's, 2's, and 3's correspond to the first, second, and third triplets and suggest a neater format: transform RESPONSES and TOTAL_OF_RATINGS into one-dimensional arrays and add a second dimension to COUNT_RATINGS. For example, the last triplet could be written

TOTAL_OF_RATINGS [3] ⟵
TOTAL_OF_RATINGS [3] +
    CHANGE [3]
COUNT_RATINGS [3,CHANGE [3]] ⟵ COUNT_RATINGS
    [3,CHANGE [3]] + 1
RESPONSES [3] ⟵ RESPONSES[3] + 1

The three triplets could then be represented by a single, variably subscripted triplet in a WHILE as in Fig. 10.23. For the first execution of the digression (N = 1), the assignments would be equivalent to the first triplet in Fig. 10.22, for the second execution (N = 2), the second triplet, and so forth. To maintain reasonable brevity, NUMBER has been shortened to N.

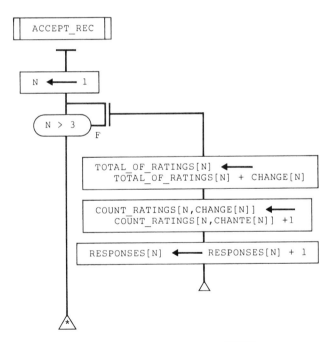

Fig. 10.23 New ACCEPT_REC.

One long-range benefit to this approach is its suitability for easily handling many more than three changes. For example, if there were five changes (hours, titles, lights, staff, and security) rather than three, this block would work just as well, provided only that the assertion were changed to

N > 5

A more immediate benefit of this approach is its appropriateness as a model for modifying other parts of the program. Figures 10.24, 10.25, 10.26, and 10.27 illustrate.

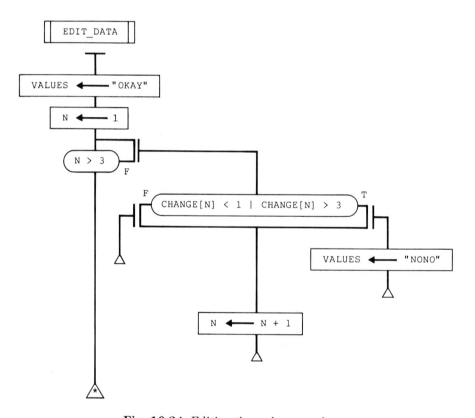

Fig. 10.24 Editing three change ratings.

Testing by block   To illustrate block testing on this program, let's test the block ACCEPT_REC. The labeled block, various initial values, three sample ratings, and the resulting trace table appear in Fig. 10.28.

We note immediately that something is wrong because the entries refer repeatedly to the same cells of the arrays and the same data value is used over and over again. The problem is quickly pinpointed: we forgot the assignment to increment N. A corrected version appears in Fig. 10.29, along with a correct trace table. This test suggests the block is now correct.

The complete, revised survey analysis program   Figure 10.30 presents the modified version of the survey analysis program, incorporating all the changes discussed in this chapter.

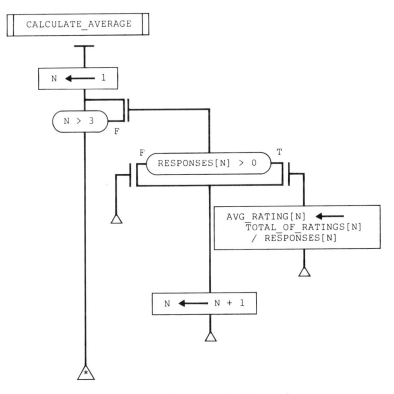

Fig. 10.25 Averaging for each of three changes.

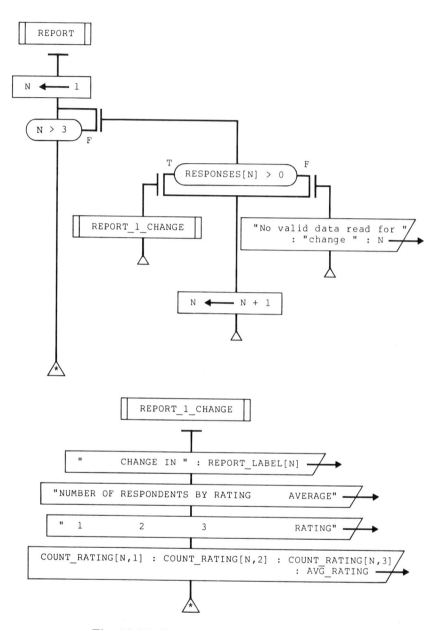

Fig. 10.26 Reporting each of three changes.

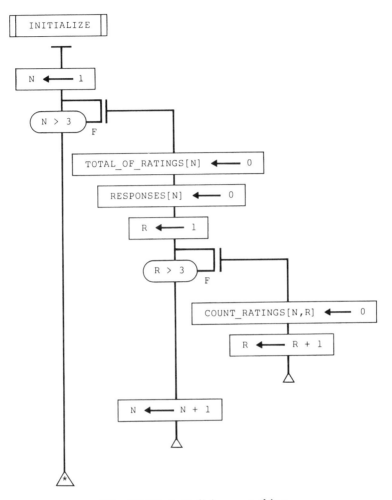

Fig. 10.27 Initializing everything.

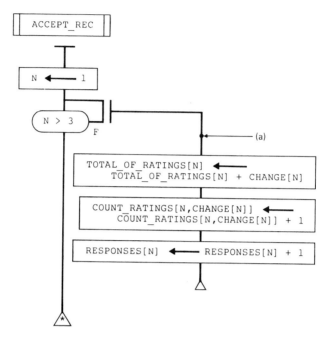

S a m p l e   R a t i n g s

CHANGE[1]	CHANGE[2]	CHANGE[3]
1	3	3

T r a c e   T a b l e

Pt	N	TOTAL [1]	[2]	[3]	COUNT [1,1]	[1,2]	[1,3]	[2,1]	[2,2]	[2,3]	[3,1]	[3,2]	[3,3]	RESPONSES [1]	[2]	[3]
a)	1	46	39	61	10	6	8	15	3	6	3	5	16	24	24	24
a)	1	47			11									25		
a)	1	48			12									26		
a)	1	49			13									27		
a)	1	50			14									28		
a)	1	51			........etc											

Fig. 10.28 Block and trace table.

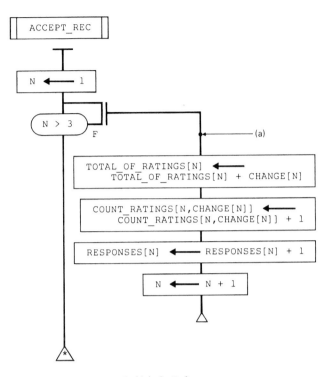

Initial Values

	CHANGE[1]	CHANGE[2]	CHANGE[3]
	1	3	3

Trace Table

Pt	N	TOTAL [1]	[2]	[3]	COUNT [1,1]	[1,2]	[1,3]	[2,1]	[2,2]	[2,3]	[3,1]	[3,2]	[3,3]	RESPONSES [1]	[2]	[3]
a)	1	46	39	61	10	6	8	15	3	6	3	5	16	24	24	24
a)	1	47			11									25		
a)	1		42							7					25	
a)	1			64									17			25

Fig. 10.29 Corrected block and trace table.

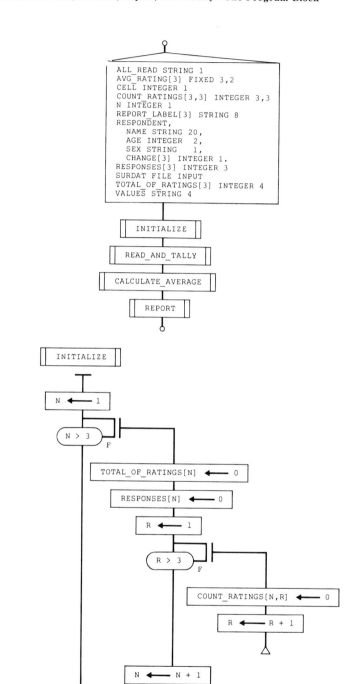

Fig. 10.30 Modified version of the survey analysis program.

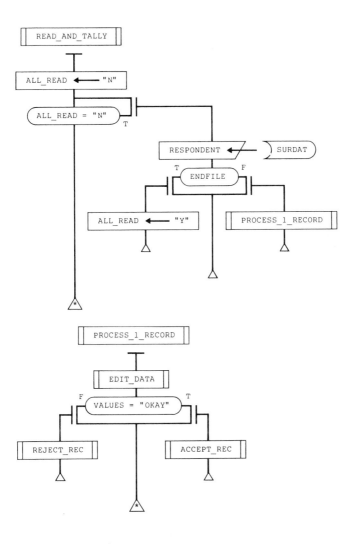

(continued)

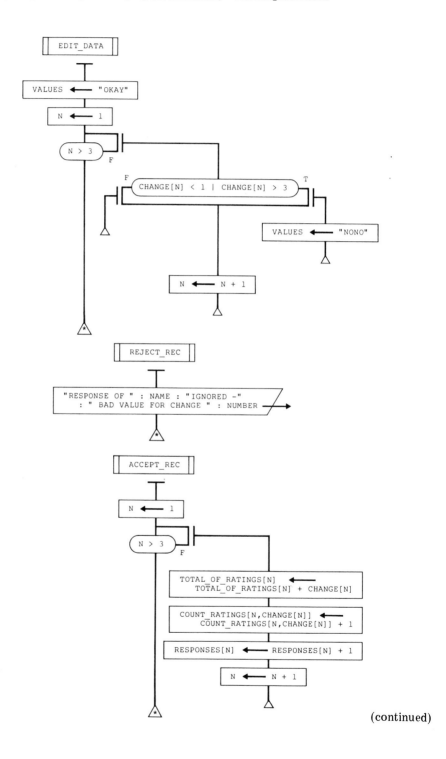

(continued)

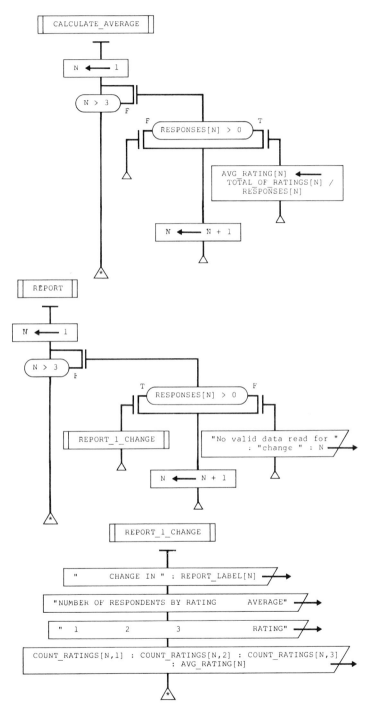

Fig. 10.30 (continued)

Private Practice

P10.15   Inspect the new version of the survey program carefully. Then indicate how many assignments would be required to do the same thing if the modifications had all used only the limited array structure represented in Fig. 10.22. (COUNT_RATINGS was the only array; it was one-dimensional.)

P10.16   Indicate all modifications needed to transform the survey analysis program so that it could report in one run on 15 different changes in the library.

P10.17   Modify your version of the UNESCO five-agency reporting program (P7.8) so that it reports on all five agencies in one run of the program.

P10.18   Modify the school election program (P7.10) so that it reports on all three offices in one run.

P10.19   Modify the survey program so that it produces six reports in a single run—three reflecting the male respondents; three, the female respondents.

BASIC Interpretation of Chapter 10

THE PROGRAM BLOCK IN BASIC

Figure B10.1 illustrates the translation of both block reference and block details, using a block introduced in the letter display program. That program is translated in its entirety in Fig. B10.2 and the library survey program in its entirety in Fig. B10.3.

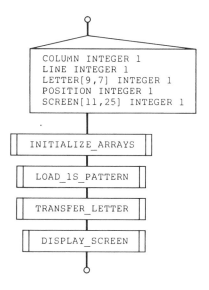

```
00010 REM -----TRANSLATION OF FIG. 10.17--------------------
00015 REM           WILLIAM MCMAHON    MAY 1981
00020 REM C1% : COLUMN INTEGER 1
00024 REM L1% : LINE INTEGER 1
00026 REM L2%(9,7) : LETTER[9,7] INTEGER 1
00028 REM P1% : POSITION INTEGER 1
00030 REM S1%(11,25) : SCREEN[11,25] INTEGER 1
00050 DIM L2%(9,7), S1%(11,25)
00060 REM -------------------------------------------------
01000 GOSUB 10000   \ REM INITIALIZE ARRAYS
02000 GOSUB 20000   \ REM LOAD 1S PATTERN
03000 GOSUB 30000   \ REM TRANSFER LETTER
04000 GOSUB 40000   \ REM DISPLAY SCREEN
09000 GOTO 90000    \ REM END PROGRAM
09010 REM -------------------------------------------------
```

Fig. B10.1 Translating the block.   (continued)

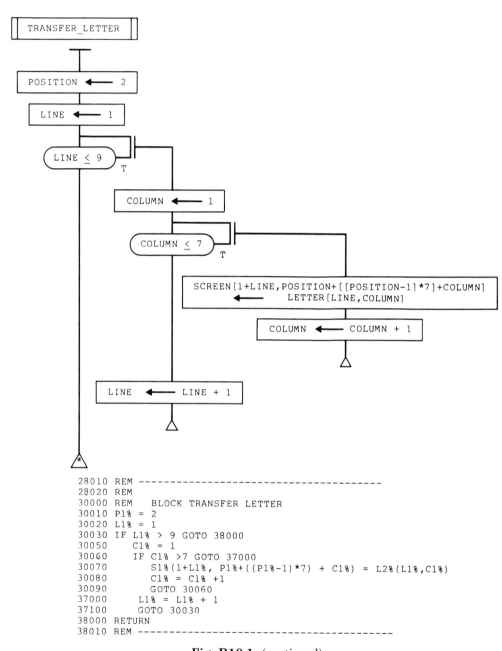

```
28010 REM -------------------------------------
28020 REM
30000 REM    BLOCK TRANSFER LETTER
30010 P1% = 2
30020 L1% = 1
30030 IF L1% > 9 GOTO 38000
30050    C1% = 1
30060    IF C1% >7 GOTO 37000
30070       S1%(1+L1%, P1%+((P1%-1)*7) + C1%) = L2%(L1%,C1%)
30080       C1% = C1% +1
30090       GOTO 30060
37000    L1% = L1% + 1
37100    GOTO 30030
38000 RETURN
38010 REM -------------------------------------
```

Fig. B10.1 (continued)

Note the following about translating block references and block details.

1. A block is referenced by citing the key word GOSUB and the number of the line where the details begin.

GOSUB 30000

2. Because the block is referenced by number rather than by name, the name of the block should be included in a REM, immediately after the reference

REM TRANSFER LETTER

3. The block naming REM should appear on the same line as the reference if the BASIC version in use allows. For example, this version permits the two to be entered on the same line but requires that a back slash (\) separate them.

GOSUB 30000 \ REM TRANSFER LETTER

Otherwise, the REM should appear on the line following the reference

03000 GOSUB 30000
03005 REM TRANSFER LETTER

4. The block's details should be located elsewhere in the program, beginning with the line number cited in the GOSUB. To keep the program easy to read, that first line of the details should be a REM identifying the block by name.

30000 REM BLOCK TRANSFER LETTER

5. Details in the block translate in the normal fashion.

6. The block ends with BASIC's counterpart to the ENDBLOCK TRIANGLE, the key word RETURN.

38000 RETURN

7. As upon reaching the ENDBLOCK TRIANGLE, upon reaching the RETURN, the computer is automatically routed to the point immediately after the reference

   03000 GOSUB 30000 \ REM TRANSFERLETTER
→ 04000 GOSUB 40000 \ REM DISPLAY SCREEN

THE BLOCK-STRUCTURED
LETTER-DISPLAY PROGRAM IN BASIC

Figure B10.2 presents a translation of the entire block-structured letter-display program.

```
00010 REM -----TRANSLATION OF FIG. 10.17--------------------
00015 REM            WILLIAM MCMAHON    MAY 1981
00020 REM C1% : COLUMN INTEGER 1
00024 REM L1% : LINE INTEGER 1
00026 REM L2%(9,7) : LETTER[9,7] INTEGER 1
00028 REM P1% : POSITION INTEGER 1
00030 REM S1%(11,25) : SCREEN[11,25] INTEGER 1
00050 DIM L2%(9,7), S1%(11,25)
00060 REM ----------------------------------------------------
01000 GOSUB 10000    \ REM INITIALIZE ARRAYS
02000 GOSUB 20000    \ REM LOAD 1S PATTERN
03000 GOSUB 30000    \ REM TRANSFER LETTER
04000 GOSUB 40000    \ REM DISPLAY SCREEN
09000 GOTO 90000     \ REM END PROGRAM
09010 REM ----------------------------------------------------
09020 REM
09030 REM ---------------------------------------------
10000 REM   BLOCK INITIALIZE ARRAYS
10100 L1% = 1
10200 IF L1% > 9 GOTO 15000
10300    C1% = 1
10400    IF C1% > 7 GOTO 14000
10500       L2%(L1%,C1%) = 0
10600       C1% = C1% + 1
10700       GOTO 10400
14000    L1% = L1% + 1
14100    GOTO 10200
15000 L1% = 1
15100 IF L1% > 11 GOTO 16000
15200    C1% = 1
15300    IF C1% > 25 GOTO 15500
15320       S1%(L1%,C1%) = 0
15330       C1% = C1% + 1
15340       GOTO 15300
15500    L1% = L1% + 1
15520    GOTO 15100
16000 RETURN
16010 REM---------------------------------------------
16020 REM
20000 REM   BLOCK LOAD 1S PATTERN
21000 REM SET CELLS IN T TO 1
21010 L1% = 2
21020 C1% = 1
21030 IF C1% > 7 GOTO 21070
21040    L2%(L1%,C1%) = 1
21050    C1% = C1% + 1
21060    GOTO 21030
21070 C1% = 4
21080 L1% = 3
21090 IF L1% > 8 GOTO 28000
21100    L2%(L1%,C1%) = 1
21110    L1% = L1% + 1
21120    GOTO 21090
28000 RETURN
```

```
28010 REM -------------------------------------
28020 REM
30000 REM    BLOCK TRANSFER LETTER
30010 P1% = 2
30020 L1% = 1
30030 IF L1% > 9 GOTO 38000
30050    C1% = 1
30060    IF C1% >7 GOTO 37000
30070       S1%(1+L1%, P1%+((P1%-1)*7) + C1%) = L2%(L1%,C1%)
30080       C1% = C1% +1
30090      GOTO 30060
37000     L1% = L1% + 1
37100      GOTO 30030
38000 RETURN
38010 REM -------------------------------------
38020 REM
40000 REM    BLOCK DISPLAY SCREEN
40100 L1% = 1
40110 IF L1% > 11 GOTO 40200
40120    C1% = 1
40130    IF C1% > 25 GOTO 40170
40140       PRINT S1%(L1%,C1%);
40150       C1% = C1% + 1
40160      GOTO 40130
40170    PRINT
40180    L1% = L1% + 1
40190     GOTO 40110
40200 PRINT
48000 RETURN
48010 REM -------------------------------------
48020 REM
90000 END
```

Fig. B10.2 Block-structured letter-display program.

Note the following in terms of an entire program.

1. All block details are grouped together below the end of the main part of the program, beginning with the details of the first block referenced in the program. (See line 10000 for the beginning of the details of the very first block in this program.)

2. The main part of the program ends with a GOTO directive pointing to the END statement of the program.

09000 *GOTO 90000*   REM END PROGRAM

09010 REM ---

09020 REM

This directive prevents the computer from inadvertently beginning to execute the details of the first block again, upon reaching the end of the main part of the program.

3. A separating comment should be inserted between each set of details, to aid the reader.

REM ---

THE BLOCK-STRUCTURED SURVEY ANALYSIS PROGRAM

Figure B10.3 presents the BASIC translation of the block-structured version of the survey analysis program.

```
00010 REM -----TRANSLATION OF FIG. 10.30 ----------------------
00015 REM         GERALD ALSTON        APRIL 1980
00030 REM --------------------------------------------------------
00032 REM    NOTE THAT THE TOTAL AND COUNT MUST BE FORCED TO
00034 REM    A REAL VALUE (MULTIPLIED BY 1.0) TO PRODUCE AN
00036 REM    AVERAGE NOT AN INTEGER. LINE 43530
00038 REM --------------------------------------------------------
00050 REM A1(3)   : AVG_RATING   FIXED 3,2
00070 REM A2$ : ALL_READ STRING 1
00100 REM C1%   : CELL INTEGER  1
00200 REM C2%(3,3)   : COUNT__RATING[3,3] INTEGER 3
00300 REM N1%   : NUMBER INTEGER 1
00400 REM R$(3)    : REPORT__LABEL[3]   STRING   20
00500 REM RESPONDENT,
00600 REM      N2$ :      NAME  STRING   20,
00800 REM      A2% :      AGE  INTEGER  2,
00900 REM      S1$ :      SEX  STRING  1,
00910 REM      C3%(3) :  CHANGE[3]   INTEGER  1.
01100 REM R1%(3)   : RESPONSES[3] INTEGER 3
01200 REM "SURBAS.DAT" : SURDAT FILE INPUT
01300 REM T1%(3)   : TOTAL__OF__RATINGS[3]   INTEGER   4
01500 REM --------------------------------------------------
01600 DIM A1(3), C2%(3,3), C3%(3), R1%(3), R$(3), T1%(3)
01700 GOSUB 21650  \ REM INITIALIZE
01800 GOSUB 32790  \ REM READ_AND_TALLY
01900 GOSUB 43460  \ REM CALCULATE_AVERAGE
02000 GOSUB 50000  \ REM REPORT
03000 GOTO 90000   \ REM            END
03001 REM ------------------------------------------------
03005 REM
21650 REM    BLOCK INITIALIZE
21700 OPEN "SURBAS.DAT" FOR INPUT AS FILE #1
21900 R$(1) = "ANALYSIS OF HOURS CHANGE"
22000 R$(2) = "ANALYSIS OF TITLES CHANGE"
22100 R$(3) = "ANALYSIS OF LIGHTING CHANGE"
22200 N1% = 1
22300 IF N1% > 3 GOTO 22710
22310    T1%(N1%) = 0
22320    R1%(N1%) = 0
22330    C1% = 1
22400    IF C1% > 3 GOTO 22600
22410       C2%(N1%,C1%) = 0
22420       C1% = C1% + 1
22430       GOTO 22400
22600    N1% = N1% + 1
22610    GOTO 22300
22710 RETURN
22720 REM ------------------------------------------------
```

Fig. B10.3 Block-structured survey analysis program.

```
22730 REM
32790 REM      BLOCK READ_AND_TALLY
32800 R1% = 1
32805 A2$ = "N"
32810 IF A2$ = "Y" GOTO 32860
32813    IFEND #1 GOTO 32830
32815       INPUT #1, N2$, A2%, S1$, C3%(1), C3%(2), C3%(3)
32820       GOSUB 32870 \ REM PROCESS_1_RECORD
32825       GOTO 32840
32830       A2$ = "Y"
32835       GOTO 32840
32840    GOTO 32810
32860 RETURN
32862 REM -------------------------------------
32870 REM     BLOCK PROCESS_1_RECORD
32874 GOSUB 40000\   REM EDIT_DATA
32878 IF V1$ = "OKAY" GOTO 32886
32880    GOSUB 33000 \ REM REJECT_REC
32882    GOTO 32896
32886    GOSUB 33090 \  REM ACCEPT_REC
32888    GOTO 32896
32896 RETURN
32898 REM -------------------------------------
32899 REM
33000 REM     BLOCK REJECT-REC
33010 PRINT "RESPONSE OF ";N2$; " IGNORED DUE TO BAD DATA VALUE"
33020 RETURN
33030 REM -------------------------------------
33090 REM     BLOCK ACCEPT_REC
33092 N1% = 1
33094 IF N1% > 3 GOTO 33450
33100    T1%(N1%) = T1%(N1%) + C3%(N1%)
33200    C2%(N1%,C3%(N1%)) = C2%(N1%,C3%(N1%)) + 1
33300    R1%(N1%) = R1%(N1%) + 1
33302    N1% = N1% + 1
33306    GOTO 33094
33450 RETURN
33500 REM -------------------------------------
33504 REM
40000 REM     BLOCK EDIT_DATA
40010 V1$ = "OKAY"
40020 N1% = 1
40030 IF N1% >  3 GOTO 40100
40040    IF C3%(N1%) < 1 OR C3%(N1%) > 3 GOTO 40060
40050       GOTO 40080
40060       V1$ = "NONO"
40070       GOTO 40080
40080    N1% = N1% + 1
40090    GOTO 40030
40100 RETURN
40110 REM -------------------------------------
40120 REM
43460 REM     BLOCK CALCULATE AVERAGE
43480 N1% = 1
43490 IF N1% > 3 GOTO 43550
43500    IF R1%(N1%) > 0 GOTO 43530
43510       GOTO 43540
43530       A1(N1%) = T1%(N1%) * 1.0  / R1%(N1%)
43535       GOTO 43540
43540    N1% = N1% + 1
43545    GOTO 43490
43550 RETURN
43600 REM -------------------------------------
```

(continued)

```
43700 REM
50000 REM     BLOCK REPORT
50010 N1% = 1
50100 IF N1%> 3 GOTO 51000
50110    IF R1%(N1%) > 0 GOTO 50200
50150       PRINT "NO VALID DATA READ FOR CHANGE "; N1%
50160       GOTO 50300
50200       GOSUB 53570  \ REM REPORT_1_CHANGE
50210       GOTO 50300
50300    N1% = N1% + 1
50310    GOTO 50100
51000 RETURN
51100 REM ---------------------------------------
51110 REM
53570 REM     BLOCK REPORT_1_CHANGE
53600 PRINT "          "; R$(N1%)
53700 PRINT "NUMBER OF RESPONDENTS BY RATING           AVERAGE"
53800 PRINT "     1          2          3         RATING"
53900 PRINT "  "; C2%(N1%,1), C2%(N1%,2), C2%(N1%,3), "   "; A1(N1%)
53950 RETURN
54000 REM ---------------------------------------
90000 END
```

Fig. B10.3 (continued)

Note the following.

As in FPL, blocks can reference other blocks. For example, from within READ_AND_TALK, PROCESS_1_RECORD is referenced

    32820   GOSUB 32870 \REM PROCESS_1_RECORD

and from within PROCESS_1_RECORD, EDIT_DATA, ACCEPT_REC, and REJECT_REC are all referenced.

Note again the order in which the details are listed and how the readability is enhanced by judicious use of REMs. These are crucial to keeping the program intelligible despite its complexity.

Private Practice BASIC

BP10.1   Enter the program in Fig. B10.2 into your computer and run it.

BP10.2   Enter the program in Fig. B10.3 into your computer and run it using the file originally prepared for (BP7.4).

BP10.3   Study Figs. 10.8 and 10.9. Then translate a block-structured version of the program involved into BASIC. Create an appropriate file of records for use by the program. Then run it on your computer.

BP10.4   Translate your solutions to (P10.4) into BASIC and run it on your computer.

BP10.5   Translate your solution to (P10.5) into BASIC and run it on your computer.

BP10.6   Translate your solution to (P10.6) into BASIC and run it on your computer. Use the file you created for the original UNESCO program.

BP10.7   Translate your solutions to (P10.7) into BASIC and run it on your computer.

BP10.8   Translate your solution to (P10.8) into BASIC and run it on your computer.

BP10.9   Translate your solution to (P10.9) into BASIC and run it on your computer.

BP10.10   Translate your solution to (P10.10) into BASIC and run it on your computer.

BP10.11   Translate your solution to (P10.11) into BASIC, create a file suitable for its use, and run the program on that file.

BP10.12   Translate your solution to (P10.12) into BASIC, create a suitable file for its use, and run the program on that file.

BP10.13   Translate your solution to (P10.17) into BASIC, create a file suitable for its use, and run the program on your computer.

BP10.14   Translate your solution to (P10.18) into BASIC, create a file suitable for its use, and run the program on your computer.

BP10.15   Translate your solution to (P10.19) into BASIC, create a file suitable for its use, and run the program on your computer.

Pascal Interpretation of Chapter 10

THE PROGRAM BLOCK IN PASCAL

Figure P10.1 illustrates the translation of both block reference and block details, using a block introduced in the letter display program. That program is translated in its entirety in Fig. P10.2 and the library survey program in its entirety in Fig. P10.3.

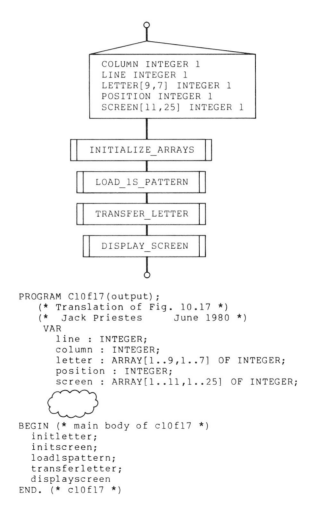

```
PROGRAM C10f17(output);
    (* Translation of Fig. 10.17 *)
    (* Jack Priestes      June 1980 *)
    VAR
      line : INTEGER;
      column : INTEGER;
      letter : ARRAY[1..9,1..7] OF INTEGER;
      position : INTEGER;
      screen : ARRAY[1..11,1..25] OF INTEGER;


BEGIN (* main body of c10f17 *)
    initletter;
    initscreen;
    load1spattern;
    transferletter;
    displayscreen
END. (* c10f17 *)
```

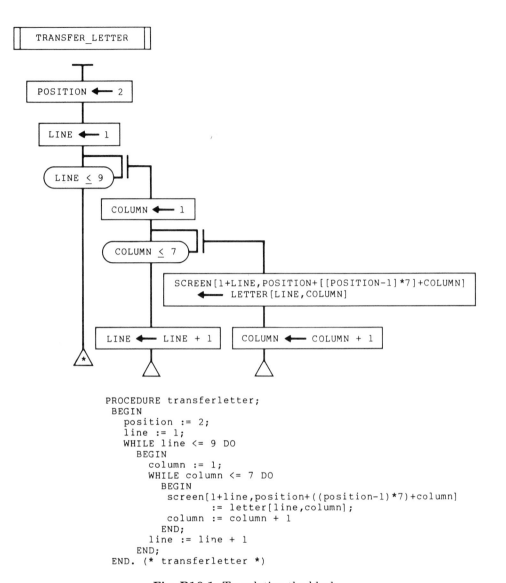

```
PROCEDURE transferletter;
 BEGIN
   position := 2;
   line := 1;
   WHILE line <= 9 DO
     BEGIN
       column := 1;
       WHILE column <= 7 DO
         BEGIN
          screen[1+line,position+((position-1)*7)+column]
                    := letter[line,column];
          column := column + 1
         END;
       line := line + 1
     END;
END. (* transferletter *)
```

Fig. P10.1 Translating the block.

Note the following about translating block references and block details.

1. A block is called a *procedure* and a procedure name, like a Pascal dataname, cannot include any underscores.

2. The procedure's name must be cited with the key word PROCE-DURE, at the head of its details.

PROCEDURE transferletter;

3. The actual details of a procedure start following the key word BE-GIN, terminate with the key word END, and are indented with respect to those two key words. Additional indentation within the details may be necessary to represent included digressions and so on. Both basic and additional indentation are illustrated in *transferletter.*

```
PROCEDURE transferletter;
 BEGIN
    position := 2;
    line := 1;
    WHILE line <= 9 DO
      BEGIN
        column := 1;
        WHILE column <= 7 DO
          BEGIN
            screen[1+line,position+((position-1)*7)+column]
                   := letter[line,column];
            column := column + 1
          END;
        line := line + 1
      END;
 END. (* transferletter *)
```

4. A procedure is referenced simply by citing its name.

transferletter;

THE BLOCK-STRUCTURED
LETTER-DISPLAY PROGRAM IN PASCAL

Figure P10.2 presents a translation of the entire block-structured letter-display program.

```
PROGRAM c10f17(output);
    (* Translation of Fig. 10.17 *)
    (* Jack Priestes  June 1980 *)*)
    VAR
      line : INTEGER;
      column : INTEGER;
      letter : ARRAY[1..9,1..7] OF INTEGER;
      position : INTEGER;
      screen : ARRAY[1..11,1..25] OF INTEGER;

    PROCEDURE initletter;
     BEGIN
      line := 1;
      WHILE line <= 9 DO
         BEGIN
           column := 1;
           WHILE column <= 7 DO
            BEGIN
              letter[line,column] := 0;
              column := column + 1
            END;
           line := line + 1
         END;
     END; (* initall *)

    PROCEDURE initscreen;
     BEGIN
      line := 1;
      WHILE line <= 11 DO
         BEGIN
           column := 1;
           WHILE column <= 25 DO
            BEGIN
              screen[line,column] := 0;
              column := column + 1
            END;
           line := line + 1
         END;
     END; (* initscreen *)

    PROCEDURE load1spattern;
     BEGIN
      column := 1;
      WHILE column <= 7 DO
         BEGIN
           letter[2,column] := 1;
           column := column + 1
         END;
```

(continued)

Fig. P10.2 The block-structured letter-display program.

```
          line := 3;
         WHILE line <= 8 DO
            BEGIN
              letter[line,4] := 1;
              line := line + 1
            END;
       END; (* load1spattern *)

     PROCEDURE transferletter;
      BEGIN
         position := 2;
         line := 1;
         WHILE line <= 9 DO
            BEGIN
              column := 1;
              WHILE column <= 7 DO
                BEGIN
                  screen[1+line,position+((position-1)*7)+column]
                         := letter[line,column];
                  column := column + 1
                END;
              line := line + 1
            END;
       END; (* transferletter *)

     PROCEDURE displayscreen;
      BEGIN
         line := 1;
         WHILE line <= 11 DO
            BEGIN
              column := 1;
              WHILE column <= 25 DO
                 BEGIN
                   WRITE(screen[line,column]:1);
                   column := column + 1
                 END;
              WRITELN;
              line := line + 1
            END;
       END; (* displayscreen *)

     BEGIN (* main body of c10f17 *)
        initletter;
        initscreen;
        load1spattern;
        transferletter;
        displayscreen
     END. (* c10f17 *)
```

Fig. P10.2 (continued)

Note the following.

The details of all procedures in the program appear between the end of the VAR section and the BEGIN of the program's main section.

THE BLOCK-STRUCTURED
SURVEY ANALYSIS PROGRAM IN PASCAL

Figure P10.3 presents the complete translation of the block-structured version
of the survey analysis program.

```
PROGRAM c10f30(surdat,input,output);
   (*Translation of Fig. 10.30 *)
   (*      Willis Kaiser        July 1980   *)
   TYPE
     respndshape =
       RECORD
         name : ARRAY[1..20] OF CHAR;
         age : INTEGER;
         sex : CHAR;
         change : ARRAY[1..3] OF INTEGER;
       END;
   VAR
    allread : CHAR;
    avgrating : ARRAY[1..3] OF REAL;
    countofratings : ARRAY[1..3,1..3] OF INTEGER;
    n : INTEGER;
    r : INTEGER;
    reportlabel : ARRAY[1..20,1..3] OF CHAR;
    respondent : respndshape;
    responses : ARRAY[1..3] OF INTEGER;
    surdat : FILE OF respndshape;
    totalofratings : ARRAY[1..3] OF INTEGER;
    values : CHAR;

   PROCEDURE initialize;
     BEGIN
       n := 1;
       WHILE n <= 3 DO
         BEGIN
           totalofratings[n] := 0;
           responses[n] := 0;
           r := 1;
           WHILE r <= 3 DO
             BEGIN
               countofratings[n,r] := 0;
               r := r + 1
             END;
           n := n + 1
         END;
     END; (* initialize *)

   PROCEDURE readandtally;
     PROCEDURE process1record;
       PROCEDURE editdata;
         BEGIN
           values := 'O';
           n := 1;
           WHILE (n <= 3) AND (values = 'O') DO
             BEGIN
               IF (respondent.change[n] < 1) OR (respondent.change[n] > 3)
                 THEN values := 'N'
                 ELSE;
               n := n + 1
             END;
         END; (* editdata *)                                    (continued)
```

Fig. P10.3 The block-structured survey analysis program.

```
    PROCEDURE rejectrec;
      BEGIN
        WRITELN('Response of ', respondent.name, ' ignored - bad value ',
            'for change ', n);
      END; (* rejectrec *)

    PROCEDURE acceptrec;
      BEGIN
        n := 1;
        WHILE n <= 3 DO
          BEGIN
          totalofratings[n] := totalofratings[n] + respondent.change[n];
          countofratings[n,respondent.change[n]] :=
              countofratings[n,respondent.change[n]] + 1;
          responses[n] := responses[n] + 1;
          n := n + 1
          END;
      END; (* acceptrec *)

    BEGIN
      editdata;
      IF values = '0'
          THEN acceptrec
          ELSE rejectrec;
    END; (* process1rec *)

  BEGIN
    RESET(surdat);
    IF EOF(surdat)
        THEN allread := 'Y'
        ELSE allread := 'N';
    WHILE allread = 'N' DO
      BEGIN
      respondent := surdat^;
      GET (surdat);
      IF EOF(surdat)
          THEN allread := 'Y'
          ELSE process1record;
      END;
        responses[2] := 1;
        totalofratings[2] := 2
  END; (* readandtally *)

PROCEDURE calculateaverage;
  BEGIN
    n := 1;
    WHILE n <= 3 DO
      BEGIN
      IF (responses[n] > 0)
          THEN avgrating[n] := totalofrating[n] / responses[n]
          ELSE;
      n := n + 1
      END;
  END; (* calculateaverage *)
```

(continued)

```
PROCEDURE report;
  PROCEDURE report1change;
    BEGIN
      WRITELN(' -------------------------------------------');
      WRITELN('            ANALYSIS FOR CHANGE ',n:1);
      WRITELN('NUMBER OF RESPONDENTS BY RATING        AVERAGE');
      WRITELN('        1          2          3       RATING');
      WRITELN(countofratings[n,1]:10, countofratings[n,2]:10,
              countofratings[n,3]:10,  avgrating[n]:13:2);
    END; (* report1change *)

  BEGIN
    n := 1;
    WHILE n <= 3 DO
      BEGIN
        IF (responses[n] > 0)
          THEN report1change
          ELSE WRITELN('No valid data read for change ',n:1);
        n := n + 1
      END;
  END; (* report *)

BEGIN (* main body of c10f30 *)
  initialize;
  readandtally;
  calculateaverage;
  report
END. (* c10f30 *)
```

Fig. P10.3 (continued)

Note the following further points.

1. Details for one procedure may be nested *inside* another procedure that references it. For example, *readandtally* includes the details for *process1record.*

2. The details of a procedure must physically precede any reference to that procedure. For example, in this program *process1record* need not have been included within *readandtally* even though it is referenced only by *readandtally;* it could have been listed outside just like *initall, calculateaverage* and *report.* Had its details been housed outside, however, they would have to *precede* the details of *readandtally.*

Private Practice Pascal

PP10.1   Enter the program in Fig. P10.2 into your computer and run it.

PP10.2   Enter the program in Fig. P10.3 into your computer and run it using the file originally prepared for (PP7.4).

PP10.3   Study Figs. 10.8 and 10.9. Then translate a block-structured version of the program involved into Pascal. Create an appropriate file of records for use by the program, then run it on your computer.

PP10.4   Translate your solutions to (P10.4-19) into Pascal and run them on your computer.

PP10.5   Translate your solution to (P10.5) into Pascal and run it on your computer.

PP10.6   Translate your solution to (P10.6) into Pascal and run it on your computer. Use the file your created for the original UNESCO program.

PP10.7   Translate your solution to (P10.7) into Pascal and run it on your computer.

PP10.8   Translate your solution to (P10.8) into Pascal and run it on your computer.

PP10.9   Translate your solution to (P10.9) into Pascal and run it on your computer.

PP10.10   Translate your solution to (P10.10) into Pascal and run it on your computer.

PP10.11   Translate your solution to (P10.11) into Pascal, create a file suitable for its use, and run the program on that file.

PP10.12   Translate your solution to (P10.12) into Pascal, create a suitable file for its use, and run the program on that file.

PP10.13   Translate your solution to (P10.17) into Pascal, create a file suitable for its use, and run the program on your computer.

PP10.14   Translate your solution to (P10.18) into Pascal, create a file suitable for its use, and run the program on your computer.

PP10.15   Translate your solution to (P10.19) into Pascal, create a file suitable for its use, and run the program on your computer.

Simplifying Program Creation – The Parametric Block

INTRODUCTION

Blocks provide a direct, simple means for creating programs that are more readable. *Parametric Blocks* extend the means through two capabilities not found in regular blocks. The parametric block is able to (1) communicate with any referencing program through one or more special channels called parameters, and (2) declare its own storage locations, independent of, and therefore protected from changes made by the referencing program.

In this chapter, we will concentrate primarily on (1). The context of discussion will be the creation of a graphic name display program for use by young children. The primary objective will be to illustrate how program clarity is enhanced by appropriate use of even a simple parametric block. A full discussion of (2) will be deferred to the following chapter in which the program will be extended to animate the display.

Though it can alternatively be solved without using parametric blocks, the name-display problem provides a good context for our discussion for the following reasons.

1. It provides a simple, appropriate context for presenting the new construct.

2. Many elements of its solution (letter displaying, etc.) are already familiar to us.

3. The entire discussion provides a good background for presenting animation later (Chapter Twelve).

Let's begin with the context.

THE NAME-DISPLAY PROGRAM

An interactive program is needed to attract children to the computer as a tool for manipulating words and letters. For a child, the program wanted must do the following.

1. Get the child to type in his or her name;

2. Display the name in large letters on a screen;

3. Maintain the display for ten seconds;

4. Display the letters of the name in reverse order;

5. Maintain the display for ten seconds;

6. Return to name display;

7. Maintain the display for ten seconds;

8. Clear the screen.

Figure 11.1 presents the main steps in this sequence.

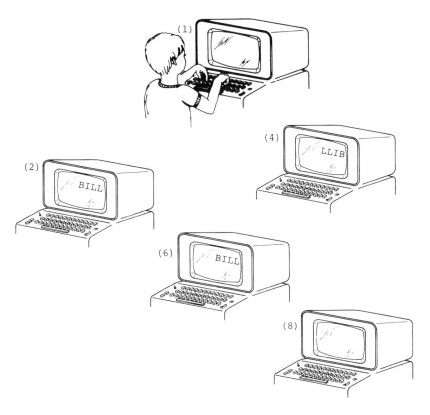

Fig. 11.1 Name display sequence.

The program is to assume the child knows how to spell his or her name but is probably incapable as yet of reading anything more than that. The computer used therefore must be able to speak aloud in a clearly recognizable simulation of human speech. It also assumes the constant presence of an older, supervising student familiar with computers and fluent in English. The program is to be used by a number of children and should terminate only if the older student types in the symbol @. The screen and letters are modeled on those discussed in Chapter Ten except that the screen is ten letters wide (11 × 81) instead of 3 (11 × 25). The letter size remains unchanged (9 × 7).

APPROACH

We will create a two-part solution—(1) a subsidiary part to display the letters on the screen, and (2) a main part to control (1) and to do everything else. Part (1) will be a parametric block based on our previous letter display program (Fig. 10.17); part (2) will be the main line of the program, along with all the blocks it requires to handle everything not done by (1).

We'll call the new parametric block LETTER_DISPLAYER. Since our letter display program already does much of what we want the subsidiary part of this new system to do, we'll use it as a basis from which to construct LETTER_DISPLAYER. This parametric block will be used over and over again, once for each letter of the child's name, for each of the three displays of that name. Its job is simply stated: display a specified letter of the alphabet on a specified location on the screen. For example, if the pair (A,3) were specified, this block should make a large A appear in position 3 on the screen; if (B,8) were specified, a B in position 8, and so forth. Though it provides a start, our letter-display program (Fig. 10.17) has some limitations. For example, it needs more letter patterns and a means for automatically selecting the appropriate screen-display position. Such limitations must be overcome in building LETTER_DISPLAYER.

The main part of the program will have to do everything else. For any child, it will have to collect the name as a set of letters. Then, for each of three displays, pass each letter and its position to LETTER_DISPLAYER for inclusion in the name display and, when each display is complete, generate a pause to prolong it. This part will also have to provide the @ facility for shutting down the program.

Because the tasks will be divided between the main program and the parametric block, each will be considerably easier to comprehend than would their combination into a single large program. In fact, using a parametric block and dividing the work in this fashion will make it possible to work out the two solution parts independently.

THE PARAMETRIC BLOCK

Figure 11.2 presents the parametric block reference (a) and its details as they would appear in the name display program (b).

How a Parametric Block Works

Note the two differences from regular blocks: (1) the name box includes a bin beneath, to list parameters, and (2) the details include declarations. Each parameter in the reference bin must have a counterpart in the details bin (i.e.,

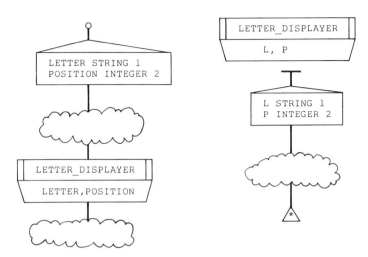

Fig. 11.2 Parametric block reference and rough details.

LETTER and L; POSITION and P) because reference parameter and counterpart alternately name the *same* storage location. For that reason, the parameters listed in the details bin must appear in the same order as their counterparts in the reference bin and the declaration of TYPE and SIZE for counterparts must agree (i.e., both LETTER and L are declared as STRING 1). Figure 11.3 shows how the alternative naming works.

Before execution of the parametric block begins (a), the storage is known by the reference bin names (LETTER and POSITION). While execution of the parametric block is underway (b), the same storage is known by the details bin names (L and P). When execution of the parametric block is finished (c), the original names are restored (LETTER and POSITION).

Declarations within the block add a powerful new dimension that we will discuss more fully in the next chapter. It is important to understand one thing about such declaration here though. Unless separately declared in the parametric block's own declaration box, all datanames used in the parametric block are synonymous with (refer to the same storage locations as) identically spelled datanames in the main program.

Developing the software for name displaying will clarify matters further. We'll begin by creating the parametric block out of the old letter-display program (Fig. 10.17).

Like that program, this parametric block will use a frame the size of one letter, will initialize that frame entirely to 0's, will load an appropriate letter pattern of 1's into selected cells, will transfer its contents to SCREEN and will display the SCREEN's contents. Unlike the earlier letter-display program, the parametric block made from it must use a larger screen, must include

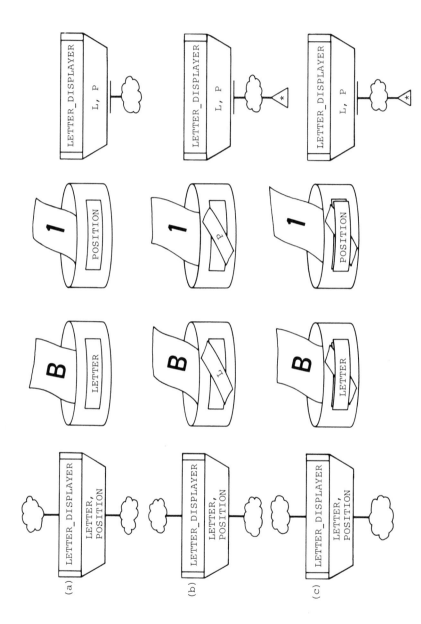

Fig. 11.3 Communicating by renaming storage.

26 letter patterns, and must be able to select a specified letter pattern and assign it to a specified letter position on the screen. We will take all this into account as we proceed.

Private Practice

P11.1   A program is needed that can accept a number from a child and display it on the screen, with a size specified (1 or 2), in a position specified (1 = left, 2 = center, 3 = right). Based on Fig. 11.2, create an analogous parametric block call and details heading box for such a program. Create appropriate parameter names and include them in the two bins.

P11.2   Create a drawing similar to Fig. 11.3 for the number display (P11.1) program, illustrating how the number and size parameters cause storage to be renamed and restored to original names as the program executes.

The Bigger Screen

The screen size change presents no problem; we merely redeclare SCREEN as

SCREEN [11,81] INTEGER 1

and accordingly modify the WHILE assertion of DISPLAY_SCREEN to

COLUMN ≤ 81

An Alphabet of Blocks

The old program included a block (LOAD_ls_PATTERN) to load a T pattern of 1's into LETTER, the frame. It assumed every cell in LETTER was initially set to 0. We need 25 more such blocks, one for each letter of the alphabet, as suggested in Fig. 11.4.

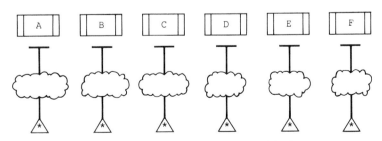

Fig. 11.4 The first six alphabet blocks.

We know T; its details appeared in LOAD_IS_PATTERN. Those of I are shown in Fig. 11.5. To conserve space, no details of any of the other blocks will be shown. Note we have given LETTER a new name, FRAME.

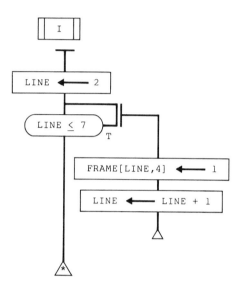

Fig. 11.5 I block details.

Selecting the Specified Block

The value of the parameter L will be a single letter: "A," "B," "C," etc. How can this be used to select the appropriate block from the alphabet? Figure 11.6 shows the approach in SELECT_LETTER. It is lengthy but easy to follow. For example, if C were the letter specified via L, only the third assertion would be true, only block C of the 26 would be executed, and only the C pattern would be loaded into the frame.

What will happen if the character passed is not a letter of the alphabet? No letter pattern will be selected. What should the parametric block display in that case?

There are various options but the simplest is best: display a blank. We'll implement this option by initializing the letter frame to blank (all 0's), immediately before executing SELECT_LETTER. Then if none of the 26 letters is selected, the pattern for a blank will remain in the frame and subsequently be displayed. Before developing that initialization, let's make sure the letter pattern will be transferred to the specified screen position.

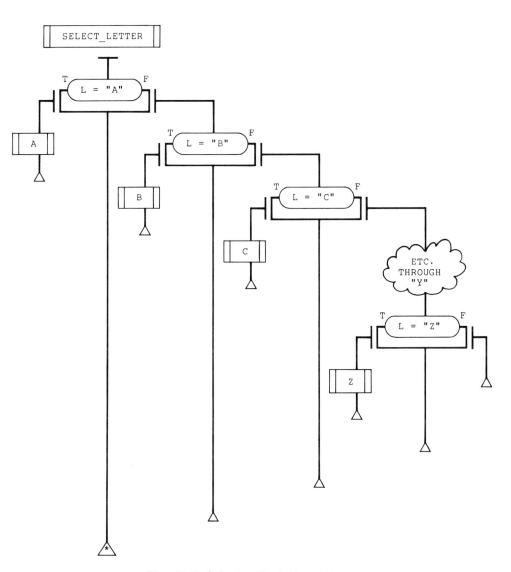

Fig. 11.6 Selecting the letter pattern.

Private Practice

P11.3   Design a screen high enough to accommodate two different number sizes: 9 × 7 (like the letter frame) and 14 × 11. Make it wide enough to accommodate three numbers displayed side by side in the 14 × 11 format. Allow the following extras: one row at the top, one row at the bottom, one column at the left, one column at the right, and a column between adjoining numbers. Your screen should thus be 37 wide by 16 high.

P11.4 Following the model in Fig. 11.6, create a block that can select a number and size to match the parameters passed to it by the program suggested in (P11.1) to (P11.3). Create the two subblocks for displaying the digit 1; call the larger ONE_14×11, the smaller ONE_9×7.

Transferring the Letter to SCREEN

In our program, TRANSFER_LETTER (Fig. 10.14) copies the pattern from the letter frame to SCREEN. The same block will do here, with slight modification: delete the first assignment

$$\text{POSITION} \longleftarrow 2$$

and replace every occurrence of the dataname POSITION by the parameter P. P's value will then determine the SCREEN location into which the frame is copied. There is no need to reproduce the borrowed block here; except for this one change we will copy it, name and all, unaltered.

Initializing

Figure 11.7 shows the position of INIT_FRAME within the parametric block. Its details are copied unchanged from INIT_LETTER as it appeared in Fig. 10.10.

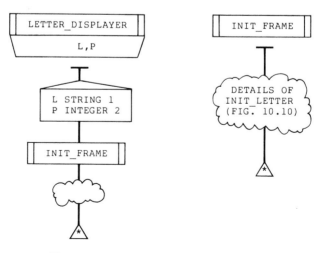

Fig. 11.7 Initializing the letter frame.

Locating the reference to INIT_FRAME here will always initialize the frame before it is used. If a letter of the alphabet is passed, 0's will be changed to 1's where appropriate before the frame is transferred to SCREEN and displayed. If any character not a letter of the alphabet is passed, no 0's will be changed before transfer and a blank will subsequently be displayed.

The parametric block needs no further initialization details. The program calling it will need to clear the screen at specific points but that is best handled elsewhere. It will be done on a whole-screen basis, not frame by frame.

Display

Figure 11.8 reproduces the first four displays for the name Tim.

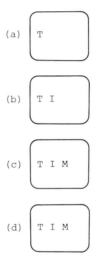

Fig. 11.8 Successive SCREEN displays.

The process behind those successive displays is as follows. The calling program sends the parametric block the first letter, T.; its pattern is loaded into the letter frame; the frame is copied into position 1 on the screen; and the screen is displayed (a). The second letter, I, is sent and loaded into the frame; the frame is copied into position 2 on the screen; and the screen is displayed a second time (b). Because the T pattern already in position 1 in the screen array is not disturbed by copying the I pattern into position 2, both letters appear. The process for the third letter, M, is analogous and results in (c).

Because the calling program *always* calls ten times, regardless of the length of the name, the displaying continues until ten characters have been passed. If the name is shorter than ten characters, the difference must be passed in blanks. For TIM, seven blanks must be passed after the M. Figure 11.8 (d) shows the display generated by the passing of the first of these seven blanks; six more would follow.

Such redundant displaying not only simplifies program construction but it also provides a base for simple animation. Though the programming is detailed and the description lengthy, the computer can generate the series of ten displays in very rapid succession, a prerequisite to any animation. We will return to this topic later.

The display can be accomplished by a duplicate of DISPLAY _SCREEN (Fig. 10.16), with the assertion constant altered to 81. We need not reproduce it here.

The Complete Parametric Block LETTER_DISPLAYER

The completed parametric block is shown in Fig. 11.9. Except for SELECT _LETTER (Fig. 11.6), the details of every block referenced are shown also.

The usefulness of this construct is obvious—this one block will work for any letter of the alphabet and can thus be reused many times in the same program. While its function could be replaced by carefully designed regular blocks, this form of parametric block simplifies the design, making it easy to design this part of the program almost independently of the rest. As we complete the program, the design independence this construct provides will become increasingly clear.

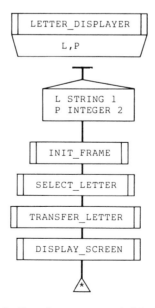

Fig. 11.9 Complete parametric block details.

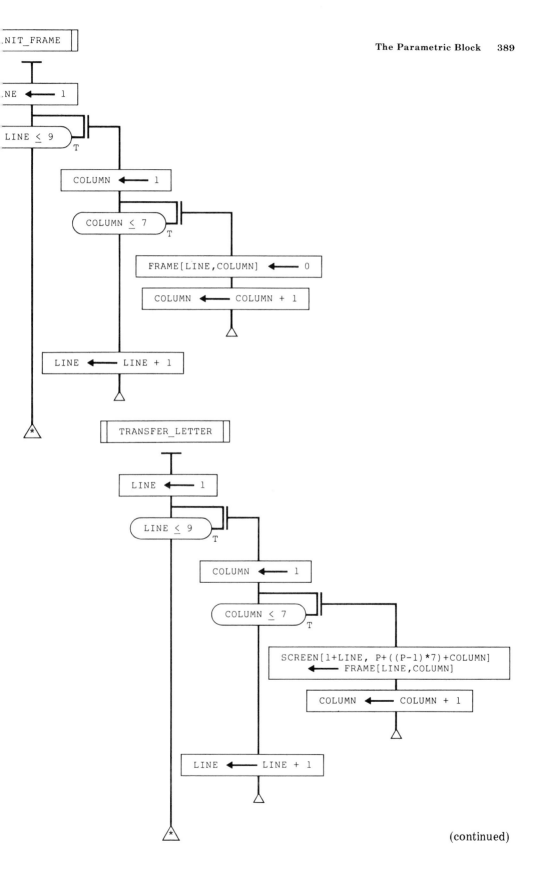

(continued)

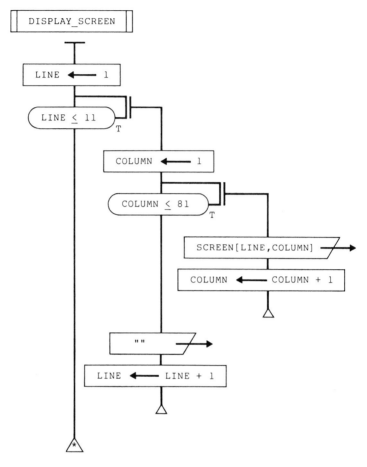

Fig. 11.9 (continued)

Now we must return to complete the program that uses this parametric block.

Private Practice

P11.5   Create the transfer, initialization, and display details for the number-display program.

P11.6   Following the example in Fig. 11.9, write the main line or root of the parametric block for number displaying.

THE MAIN PROGRAM

By specification, our program must remain active between names. For instance, after displaying the name of one child, the program should not terminate execution; it should be ready for the next name, whether entered immediately or some minutes later. It must continue to run so long as the supervisor is willing. Without worrying about details, we know such continuous running involves repetition. Assume we can add that repetition later by superimposing a WHILE. Let's solve the simpler problem of one name first.

A first draft of a single-child version is shown in Fig. 11.10. Its block structure makes it briefer and easier to read than might otherwise be the case. Let's run through what it does.

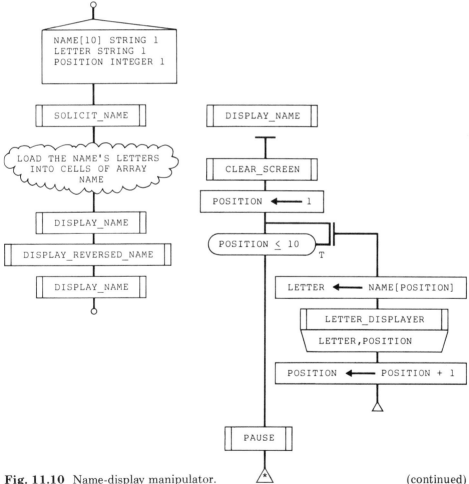

Fig. 11.10 Name-display manipulator.

(continued)

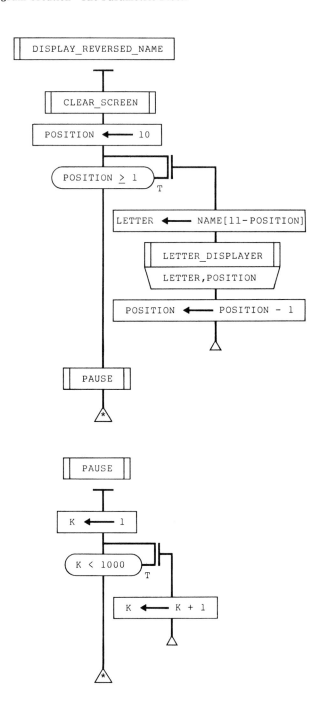

(continued)

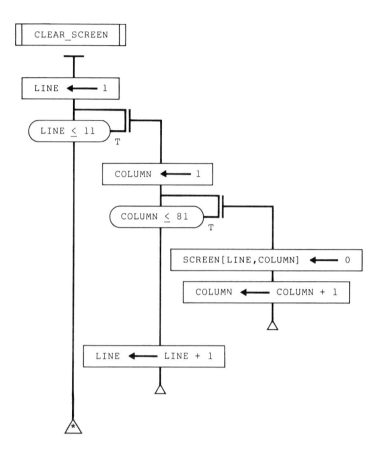

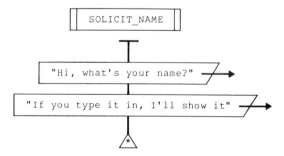

Fig. 11.10 (continued)

1. A name is solicited aloud, the file represented by a speaker.

2. The name is entered and stored as individual characters in the array NAME. We will refine this process into an appropriate block shortly.

3. DISPLAY_NAME calls CLEAR_SCREEN to clear out the garbage in SCREEN; passes ten letter/position pairs to the parametric block for display; and generates a pause of reasonable duration to hold the display in view.

4. DISPLAY_REVERSED_NAME follows a similar pattern except that it cycles *backward* through the frame display positions. It passes the first letter but the tenth position on the first call, the second letter but the ninth position on the second call, and so on. The appropriate letter is selected for each call by subscript arithmetic.

$$\text{LETTER} \longleftarrow \text{NAME [11–POSITION]}$$

Before proceeding further, we will comment on pause generation and discuss testing by block.

Pause Generation

PAUSE represents one way to generate a delay. Because it takes the computer a finite amount of time to repeat even the most trivial WHILE digression, a pause can be generated by a "do-nothing" WHILE of the sort shown. For a longer pause, the number of repetitions must be increased; for a shorter one, decreased. Many computers provide an alternative to this approach, one that allows the programmer to accurately time the length of any delay desired. Details for such alternatives depend on the particular computer and will not be considered here.

Testing by Block

This time, we choose DISPLAY_REVERSED_NAME for demonstration testing. Testing it should increase our understanding of the most complex of the blocks in this program. Figure 11.11 presents a labeled version of the block, and Fig. 11.12, the resulting trace table. The table includes initial values but no subsequent entries for NAME because it uses but does not modify those values. Nor does it include any entries due to calling CLEAR_SCREEN or PAUSE. Because these do not affect detail values in DISPLAY_REVERSED_NAME, they can be tested separately. Whether or not they work does not affect the correctness of the details in this block.

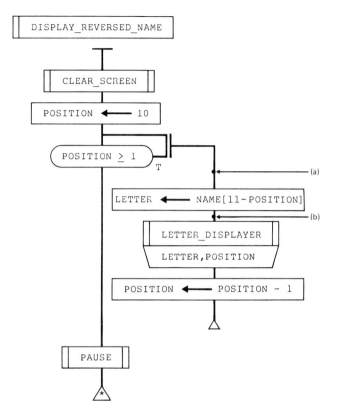

Fig. 11.11 Testable version of block.

Private Practice

P11.7   As a parallel to the name-display manipulator, write a program that will thrice call your parametric block for number displaying. First it should display the solicited digit in screen position 1 (screen left), then position 3 (screen right), and then position 2 (screen center). It must be able to display the digit in either size 14 × 11 or 9 × 7.

P11.8   Label and test DISPLAY_NAME using the name SAMUEL as provided in Fig. 11.12.

				N	A	M	E	(initial values)
[1]	[2]	[3]	[4]	[5]	[6]	[7]	[8]	[9]	[10]
S	A	M	U	E	L	^	^	^	^

T R A C E   T A B L E

	POSITION	LETTER	(11-POSITION)
(a)	10		
(b)	–	S	1
(a)	9	–	–
(b)	–	A	2
(a)	8	–	–
(b)	–	M	3
(a)	7	–	–
(b)	–	U	4
(a)	6	–	–
(b)	–	E	5
(a)	5	–	–
(b)	–	L	6
(a)	4	–	–
(b)	–		7

Fig. 11.12 Trace table testing DISPLAY_REVERSED_NAME.

Loading the solicited name into the cells of NAME

Ordinarily a solicited string such as the child's name would be assigned to a string variable of appropriate length. In this case, however, because we want to pass the letters one at a time to the parametric block, we will collect the child's name letter by letter, in the cells of an array declared as

NAME [10] STRING 1

The basic approach is evident in Fig. 11.13. It simply collects ten letters from the person and stores them in NAME. It assumes that exactly ten characters (possibly some of them blanks) will be entered; no more, no less.

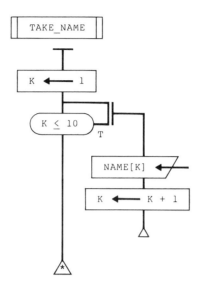

Fig. 11.13 Collecting ten characters.

A less rigid approach would be that in Fig. 11.14: indicate the end of a name shorter than ten characters by typing a period. To incorporate this approach, we will have to modify SOLICIT_NAME accordingly (e.g., tell the child how and when to use the period). The approach assumes the computer examines the letters *as each one is typed* and collects letters until ten have been entered or a period has been typed. It also assumes the keyboard being used includes a "RETURN" key that sends the computer its own unique signal, different from that sent by any other key.

With declarations modified appropriately and the reference TAKE_NAME added, our program appears as in Fig. 11.15. SOLICIT_NAME is included, modified to provide the child with more prompting. As indicated, this is only a single-child version.

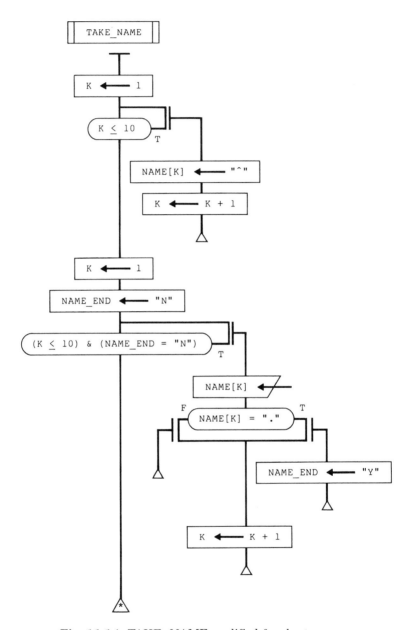

Fig. 11.14 TAKE_NAME modified for short names.

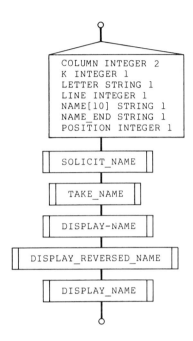

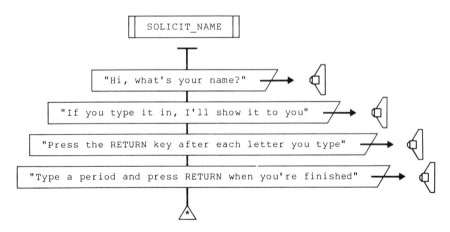

Fig. 11.15 Main program for single child.

Private Practice

P11.9   To your number design program, add the block and details needed to take in the number and size from the child.

P11.10   Modify your program so that by three successive displays (screen left, center, and right), it crudely "walks" the number across the screen. (Clear the screen between displays.)

The Program Modified to Handle a Series of Children

Now we can add repetition to accommodate a succession of children. Following the original specifications, we use detection of the supervisor's entry of an at the rate of sign @ to control the WHILE. The result appears in Figs. 11.16 and 11.17.

TAKE_NAME has been modified further, this time to detect the @ if it occurs. With respect to terminating the collection of characters for a name, the @ functions like the period (.). Normally, we would expect the supervisor to type in an @ when no name is being entered, hence it would go into NAME [1].

Because the @ might be entered inadvertently, we build into our main program a confirmation check. This allows the supervisor to override the termination pending and go back to accepting and displaying names.

The main structure of our program is nothing more than we anticipated—the superimposition of repetition over our single-child version. Further block structuring has been added for simplicity's sake, collecting the entire display cycle into one block, DO_3_DISPLAYS.

Apart from the parametric block and the blocks it references, the remainder of this program is shown below in Figs. 11.16, 11.17, and 11.18.

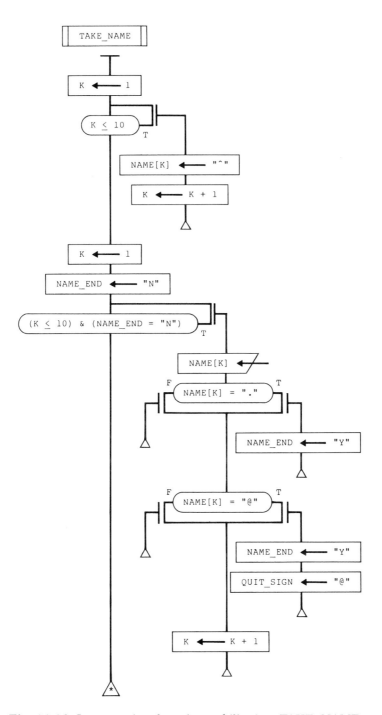

Fig. 11.16 Incorporating the quit capability into TAKE_NAME.

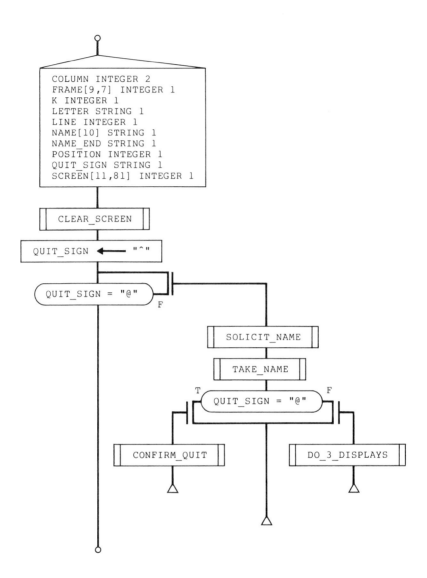

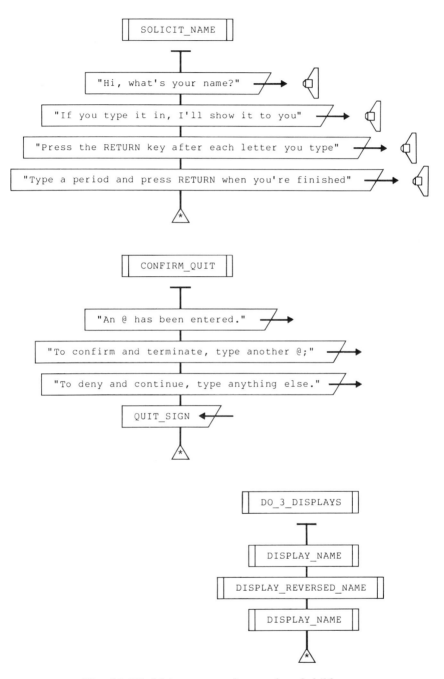

Fig. 11.17 Main program for a series of children.

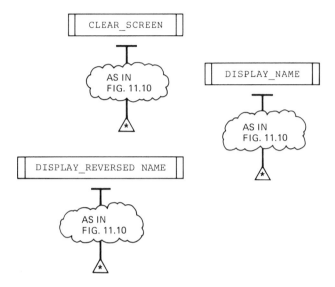

Fig. 11.18 Remaining blocks.

A FINAL NOTE: REUSING THE SCREEN

Throughout this presentation we have assumed that each cycle of LET-TER_DISPLAYER will cause the new display to be superimposed upon the position occupied by the preceding display, replacing it. (See Figs. 11.1 and 11.8.) Specifically if the 81 values in line 1 for the display of the first letter appear on the topmost line on the screen, the 81 values on line 1 for the display of the second letter will also appear in that line.

In fact, such an assumption would be unwarranted, given the way most screen devises are constructed. Figure 11.19 suggests what would be more likely to happen. Instead of replacing one image with the next, our program would produce a series of separate displays, one below the other, filling the screen.

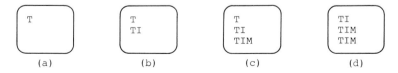

Fig. 11.19 Successive displays without screen reuse.

The screen would become full before the requisite number of displays had all been made, and at that point, overflow of some sort would occur, probably resulting in a scrolling of the images upward and off the top of the screen as suggested in (d). The result would not be what we want.

The solution is to communicate to the display screen whenever a display cycle begins that it must begin at the *top* of the screen. The manner of communicating this is specified by the manufacturer of the display device and is accessible to the programmer.

Let's assume our screen's manufacturer specifies that such communication be made through a sequence of special characters, transmittable in any external assignment. Its form is

$$\$\$\$=4,10.$$

The number pair must specify a line on the screen and a column within that line so that the very next thing displayed will begin at that point. In this example, the next display would begin in the tenth column of the fourth line from the top of the screen. The entire string must be enclosed in quotes inside the external assignment.

"$\$\$\$=4,10$".

(We assume our screen has 20 lines on its face, that the topmost line is designated 1, the bottommost, 20.) By means of such a communication at appropriate points in the program, we can force the display to reuse the screen as we want.

Figure 11.20 shows where we would want to use this string—as an initial assignment in DISPLAY_SCREEN.

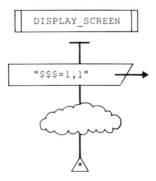

Fig. 11.20 Screen reuse modification.

Private Practice

P11.11   Modify your number display program so that the quitsign is a question mark (?). Unlike the letter program, make the confirmation character different (i.e., not a second (?)).

P11.12   Modify the final letter display program (Fig. 11.16) so that it *begins* with an attractive display. This should consist of displaying the letters of the word NAME as though they were a child's name: regular display, pause, reverse, pause, regular.

P11.13   Modify the program so that it always displays the child's name (and name reverse) as near the *center* of the screen as the length of the name allows.

P11.14   Modify the program so that it prints characters, not 1's and 0's on the screen. Use blanks instead of 0's, and ?'s instead of 1's.

P11.15   Modify the program so that DISPLAY_NAME and DISPLAY_RE-VERSED_NAME do not uselessly display trailing or leading blanks on short names. For example, if BOB is entered, DISPLAY_NAME is to force only three displays of the screen.

B∧∧∧∧∧∧∧∧∧

BO∧∧∧∧∧∧∧∧

BOB∧∧∧∧∧∧∧

P11.16   Create a new SELECT_LETTER block that works more efficiently because it employs a "binary" search to identify the letter passed. A binary search is one that at each stage of the search cuts in two the set of data (in this case, the letters of the alphabet) to be searched further. It should begin by deciding if the letter passed is one of the letters (a) through (m) or one of the letters (n) through (z). It should proceed by further cutting in half until the letter is positively identified. For example, if the letter is one of (a) through (m), the block should then check to see if it is one of the letters (a) through (g) or one of the letters (h) through (m). Binary searching of this sort can save considerable time for the computer (no more than five assertion evaluations will be required to positively identify any letter of the alphabet). The original version of SELECT_LETTER is easier to understand at a glance, but probably not much easier, particularly to an experienced programmer. Your choice of whether to use the alternative ought to be based on whether there is a definite need to cut the time required by the computer to identify the letter.

BASIC Interpretation of Chapter 11

THE PARAMETRIC BLOCK IN BASIC

Most versions of BASIC do not include any parametric block construct. Nevertheless, using a BASIC that does, we present a translation of this construct. The parametric block is so important for good programming that those having access to a BASIC that includes the construct should know how to utilize it. The interpretation that follows should serve as an adequate translation model for anyone using a BASIC with parametric blocks.

Figure B11.1 presents the translation of a parametric block reference; Fig. B11.2, of a parametric block's details. Both are extracted from a complete translation of the name display program.

```
07550    CALL LETTERDISPLAYER (L1$, P1%, S1% (,))

09000    END
```

Fig. B11.1 Translating the parametric block reference.

Note the following.

1. A parametric block reference begins with the key word CALL, names the block, and lists the parameters.

07555 CALL LETTERDISPLAYER(L1$,P1%,S1%(,)))

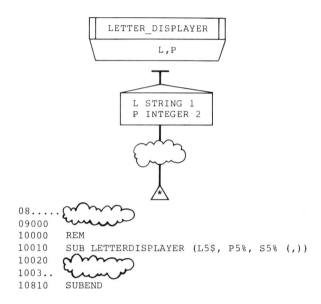

```
08.....
09000
10000    REM
10010    SUB LETTERDISPLAYER (L5$, P5%, S5% (,))
10020
1003..
10810    SUBEND
```

Fig. B11.2 Translating the parametric block's details.

2. A parametric block's details begin with an identifying first line similar in form to the call but differing in *key word* and in the *names* of the parameters.

10010 SUB LETTERDISPLAYER(L5$,P5%,S5%(,))

3. A parametric block's details end with the key word last line

10810 SUBEND

4. A third parameter representing the 11 × 81 screen array has been added to the list of parameters in the BASIC.

7555 CALL LETTERDISPLAYER(L1$,P1%,S1%(,))
10010 SUB LETTERDISPLAYER(L5$, P5%, S5%(,))

(In this context, the (,) means *all* cells of the array) This addition to the parameter list is necessary because of the way this version of BASIC handles storage for parametric blocks. An explanation follows.

First, except for parameters, no dataname cited in the parametric block's details refers to any storage location associated with any dataname cited in the referencing program; even if the datanames are identical, they are *distinct* to the computer and *represent different variables.* Second, each time a parametric block is called, all its variables except for the parameters are automatically initialized (numerics to zero, strings to blank). Because only a parameter can refer to a storage location accessible to both program and parametric block, and because only such storage is accessible to the block yet *not* automatically initialized by it, we must treat the screen array as a parameter. Only by doing so can we preserve the name pattern constructed in it through ten calls of LETTERDISPLAYER.

Private Practice BASIC

BP11.1   Enter the toy program shown into your computer and run it with various modifications to explore how parametric blocks work on your computer.

```
00100 REM TOY PROGRAM TO PLAY WITH PARAMETRIC
BLOCKS
00200 S1$ = "BILL"
00250 L1$ = S1$
00260 PRINT "S1 AND L1 BEFORE CALL WERE ";S1$;", ";L1$
00300 CALL PRINTER (L1$)
00340 PRINT "S1 AND L1 AFTER CALL WERE ";S1$;", ";L1$
00500 END
01000 REM.............................................................................................
02000 SUB PRINTER (L3$)
02100 PRINT "............................. START BLOCK ............................."
02200 PRINT "L3 WAS ";L3$
02300 PRINT "S1 WAS "; S1$
02400 PRINT "L1 WAS "; L1$
02500 PRINT "............................... END BLOCK ..............................."
02600 SUBEND
```

BP11.2   Modify the toy program so that the parametric block changes the value of L3$ and so that both the block and the main program subsequently print out the value of that variable. (Together with (BP11.1), this problem should give you a clear picture of how your BASIC handles storage for parametric block and main block variables.)

CREATING A BASIC TRANSLATION IN EASY STAGES

Figures B11.3 and B11.4 suggest how the development of a complex program can be translated and checked out in stages. They represent "stubs" or "embryos" of what will become the two parts of the final solution. Figure B11.3 is the beginning of the parametric block; Fig. B11.4, the main program that calls it. Both stubs will execute as is and produce useful output for determining if the development so far is on the right track.

```
00010 REM     STUB1 OF PARAMETRIC BLOCK
00015 REM          ROCCO MARZARELLA     JUNE 1981
00020 REM
00030 REM L1$ : LETTER STRING 1
00035 REM P1% : POSITION INTEGER 2
00040 REM S1%(11,81) : SCREEN[11,81] INTEGER 1
00045 REM -------------------------------
00048 DIM S1%(11,81)
00040 INPUT "LETTER,POSITION";L1$,P1%
00050 CALL LETTERDISPLAYER(L1$,P1%,S1%(,))
00055 END
00075 REM ------------------------------------------------
10000 SUB LETTERDISPLAYER(L5$,P5%,S5%(,))
10015 REM L5$ : L STRING 1
10020 REM P5% : P INTEGER 2
10025 REM S5%(11,81) : SCREEN(11,81) INTEGER 1
10030 REM -------------------------------------------
10100 GOSUB 15000      \REM INIT FRAME
10200 GOSUB 17000      \REM SELECT LETTER
10300 GOSUB 19000      \REM TRANSFER LETTER
10400 GOSUB 21000      \REM DISPLAY SCREEN
10500 GOTO  30000      \REM END PARAMETRIC BLOCK
15000 REM
15001 REM -------------------------------------------
15002 REM          BLOCK INIT FRAME
15500   PRINT "FRAME INITIALIZED"
15900 RETURN
15990 REM -------------------------------------------
15992 REM
17000 REM          BLOCK SELECT LETTER
17500 PRINT "LETTER SELECTED"
17990 RETURN
17992 REM -------------------------------------------
17995 REM
19000 REM          BLOCK TRANSFER LETTER
19075 PRINT "LETTER TRANSFERRED TO SCREEN ARRAY"
19990 RETURN
19992 REM -------------------------------------------
19995 REM
21000 REM          BLOCK DISPLAY SCREEN
21500 PRINT "SCREEN DISPLAYED"
21990 RETURN
21992 REM -------------------------------------------
21995 REM
30000 SUBEND
```

Fig. B11.3 A stub translation of the parametric block.

Note the following about Fig. B11.3.

1. A very minimal (ten lines) main program is used to power or drive the stub of the parametric block.

```
00010 REM STUB OF PARAMETRIC BLOCK
00020 REM
00030 REM L1$ : LETTER STRING 1
00035 REM P1% : POSITION INTEGER 2
00040 REM S1% (11,81) : SCREEN [11,81] INTEGER 1
00045 REM ..................................................................................................
00048 DIM S1% (11,81)
00040 INPUT "LETTER, POSITION"; L1$, P1%
00050 CALL LETTERDISPLAYER (L1$, P1%, S1%(,))
00055 END
```

All it can test is that the embryonic parametric block is callable and receives the parametric values passed to it.

2. The parametric block follows the END of the main program, separated from it only by a REM inserted to help the reader.

3. The main line of the parametric block is complete

```
10000 SUB LETTERDISPLAYER (L5$,P5%,S5%(,))
10015 REM L5$ : L STRING 1
10020 REM P5% : P INTEGER 2
10025 REM S5% (11,81) : SCREEN (11,81) INTEGER 1
10030 REM ....................................
10100 GOSUB 15000      \REM INIT FRAME
10200 GOSUB 17000      \REM SELECT LETTER
10300 GOSUB 19000      \REM TRANSFER LETTER
10400 GOSUB 21000      \REM DISPLAY SCREEN
10500 GOTO   30000     \REM END PARAMETRIC BLOCK
10900    (        )
```

but only stubs are present to represent its four blocks.

4. Each block stub within the embryonic parametric block contains sufficient detail only to demonstrate whether or not it is called when it should be. SELECT_LETTER for example, if called, merely verifies the call by printing

"LETTER SELECTED"

It is left to a later stage, once all the stubs appear to be referenced and responding in the correct order, to flesh out the details of the stubs so that each actually performs its appointed tasks.

```
00100 REM     STUB1 OF MAIN PROGRAM
00110 REM          ROCCO MARZARELLA     AUG 1981
00170 REM Q1$ : QUITSIGN STRING 1
00190 REM ------------------------------------------
01001 REM
01002 REM --------- BODY OF MAIN PROGRAM -----------
01010 REM
01020 GOSUB 2000               \REM CLEAR SCREEN
01030 Q1$ = " "
01050 IF Q1$ = "@" GOTO 1900
01060    GOSUB 3000            \ REM SOLICIT NAME
01070    GOSUB 4000            \ REM TAKE NAME
01080    IF Q1$ = "@" GOTO 1200
01090       GOSUB 6000         \ REM DO 3 DISPLAYS
01100       GOTO 1500
01200       GOSUB 6500         \ REM CONFIRM QUIT
01210       GOTO 1500
01500    GOTO 1050
01900 GOTO 90000               \ REM END
01910 REM
01920 REM ------------------------------------------
02000 REM            BLOCK CLEAR SCREEN
02500 PRINT "CLEARED SCREEN"
02990 RETURN
02992 REM------------------------------------------
02995 REM
03000 REM            BLOCK SOLICIT NAME
03980 INPUT "GIVE SIGNAL TO QUIT (@) OR CONTINUE";Q1$
03990 RETURN
03992 REM------------------------------------------
03995 REM
04000 REM            BLOCK TAKE NAME
04500 PRINT "TOOK NAME"
05990 RETURN
05992 REM ------------------------------------------
05995 REM
06000 REM              BLOCK DO 3 DISPLAYS
06250 PRINT "DID 3 DISPLAYS"
06490 RETURN
06492 REM------------------------------------------
06495 REM
06500 REM              BLOCK CONFIRM QUIT
06600 PRINT "An @ has been entered."
06620 PRINT "To confirm and terminate, type another @."
06640 PRINT "To deny and continue, type anything else."
06660 INPUT Q1$
06700 RETURN
06750 REM------------------------------------------
90000 END
```

Fig. B11.4 Embryonic main program.

Note the following about the stub of the main program.

1. The embryonic main program is complete in its main line, but only the details of CONFIRM_QUIT and SOLICIT_NAME amount to more than verifying stubs. (SOLICIT_NAME includes only enough detail to provide CONFIRM_QUIT with a value to test itself.)

2. The major block DO_3_DISPLAYS is represented by a stub but at this stage no calls to DISPLAY_NAME or DISPLAY_REVERSED_NAME have been inserted, and so no calls from them to LETTERDISPLAYER have yet been put in place either. All this will follow in a subsequent stage or two.

Creating such embryonic translations is a simple and effective way to progress toward a properly functioning finished product. Just as episodes allow the programmer to defer consideration of some details in order to concentrate upon others, so the development of translation in terms of stubs allows concentration to be focused on different parts and levels of the system at different stages. By such controlling of focus, a properly functioning final product can efficiently and surely be developed.

Private Practice BASIC

BP11.3   Enter the parametric block stub (Fig. B11.3) into your computer and run it.

BP11.4   Modify the stub so that while executing the parametric block it prints out the value of the letter and position passed to it from the main program. Run your modification on the computer.

BP11.5   Enter the main program stub (Fig. B11.4) into your computer and run it.

A FURTHER STAGE

Figure B11.5 presents the stub of the main program after it has been developed a bit further. This one is shown as representative of the many created along the way to producing the finished translation in Fig. 11.6. Each stub should expand upon its predecessor by adding details to finish off some portion of the stub. By developing the details in stages, a considerable amount of confusion and consequent wasted work can be avoided. A mistake can be isolated and corrected easily when its origin is a newly created, small addition to an already correctly functioning stub. By contrast, a mistake may be hard to isolate and correct when its source might be any one of a large number of additions, all made to a stub since the last time it was executed. Confusion is maximized if the entire program is translated before any testing is done on the computer!

Other stubs will not be shown but were created *en route* to producing the final product. The Private Practice will encourage you to create some of these intermediate stages yourself. You should use this general approach liberally whenever you develop your own complex programs.

```
00100 REM STUB2 OF MAIN PROGRAM
00105 REM      ROCCO MARZARELLA     AUG 1981
00110 REM C1% : COLUMN INTEGER 2
00120 REM  K% : K INTEGER
00130 REM L1$ : LETTER STRING 1
00140 REM L1% : LINE INTEGER 1
00145 REM N1$(10) : NAME[10] STRING 1
00150 REM N2$ : NAME END STRING 1
00160 REM P1% : POSITION INTEGER 1
00170 REM Q1$ : QUITSIGN STRING 1
00180 REM S1%(11,81) : SCREEN[11,81] INTEGER 1
00190 REM -------------------------------------------
00200 DIM N1$(10), S1%(11,81)
01001 REM
01002 REM -------- BODY OF MAIN PROGRAM -----------
01010 REM
01020 GOSUB 2000                \REM CLEAR SCREEN
01030 Q1$ = " "
01050 IF Q1$ = "@" GOTO 1900
01060    GOSUB 3000             \REM SOLICIT NAME
01070    GOSUB 4000             \REM TAKE NAME
01080    IF Q1$ = "@" GOTO 1200
01090       GOSUB 6000          \REM DO 3 DISPLAYS
01100       GOTO 1500
01200       GOSUB 6500          \REM CONFIRM QUIT
01210       GOTO 1500
01500    GOTO 1050
01900 GOTO 09000                \REM END
01910 REM
01920 REM ------------------------------------------
02000 REM           BLOCK CLEAR SCREEN
02005 PRINT "^Z"      \ REM SIGNAL TO DEVICE TO CLEAR SCREEN
02100 L1% = 1
02110 IF L1% > 11 GOTO 2990
02120    C1% = 1
02130    IF C1% > 81 GOTO 2400
02200       S1%(L1%,C1%) = 0
02210       C1% = C1% + 1
02220       GOTO 2130
02400    L1% = L1% + 1
02410    GOTO 2110
02990 RETURN
02992 REM-------------------------------------------
02995 REM
03000 REM            BLOCK SOLICIT NAME
03100 PRINT "Hi, what's your name?"
03110 PRINT "If you type it in, I'll show it to you"
03120 PRINT "Press the RETURN key after each letter you type."
03130 PRINT "Type a period and press RETURN when you're finished."
03990 RETURN
03992 REM-------------------------------------------
03995 REM
04000 REM            BLOCK TAKE NAME
04010 K% = 1
```

```
04020 IF K% > 10 GOTO 4100
04030    N1$(K%) = " "
04040    K% = K% + 1
04050    GOTO 4020
04100 K% = 1
04150 N2$ = "N"
04200 IF (K% > 10) OR (N2$ = "Y") GOTO 5990
04210 INPUT N1$(K%)
04220 IF N1$(K%) = "." GOTO 4300
04230    GOTO 4500
04300    N2$ = "Y"
04310    GOTO 4500
04500 IF N1$(K%) = "@" GOTO 4600
04510    GOTO 4700
04600    N2$ = "Y"
04610    Q1$ = "@"
04620    GOTO 4700
04700 K% = K% + 1
05000 GOTO 4200
05990 RETURN
05992 REM --------------------------------------------
05995 REM
06000 REM                 BLOCK DO 3 DISPLAYS
06100 GOSUB 7500          \REM DISPLAY NAME
06200 GOSUB 8000          \REM DISPLAY REVERSED NAME
06300 GOSUB 7500          \REM DISPLAY NAME
06490 RETURN
06492 REM--------------------------------------------
06495 REM
06500 REM                 BLOCK CONFIRM QUIT
06600 PRINT "An @ has been entered."
06620 PRINT "To confirm and terminate, type another @"
06640 PRINT "To deny and continue, type anything else."
06660 INPUT Q1$
06700 RETURN
06750 REM--------------------------------------------
07495 REM
07500 REM                 BLOCK DISPLAY NAME
07510 GOSUB 2000          \REM CLEAR SCREEN
07550    PRINT "LETTERDISPLAYER CALLED 10 TIMES"
07700 GOSUB 7900          \REM PAUSE
07790 RETURN
07792 REM --------------------------------------------
07795 REM
07900 REM                 BLOCK PAUSE
07950 PRINT "PAUSED"
07990 RETURN
07992 REM --------------------------------------------
07995 REM
08000 REM                 BLOCK DISPLAY REVERSED NAME
08010 GOSUB 2000          \REM CLEAR SCREEN
08200    PRINT "LETTERDISPLAYER CALLED 10 TIMES"
08400 GOSUB 7900          \REM PAUSE
08490 RETURN
08492 REM --------------------------------------------
08495 REM
09000 END
```

Fig. B11.5 A more developed stub of the main program.

Note the following.

1. The declarations have been added.

2. The details of CLEAR_SCREEN, SOLICIT_NAME, TAKE_-NAME, and DO_3_DISPLAYS have been translated.

3. Stubs for DISPLAY_NAME, DISPLAY_REVERSED_NAME, and PAUSE have been added.

4. No details to call LETTERDISPLAYER have yet been added, so no trace of the parametric block appears yet either.

Private Practice BASIC

BP11.6   Enter the stub in Fig. B11.5 into your computer and run it.

BP11.7   Develop a next stage of the stub by completing DISPLAY_NAME and DISPLAY_REVERSED_NAME *except* for the call to the parametric block. In place of that call, substitute

PRINT "LETTERDISPLAYER CALLED"

(If you have trouble, check your details against those shown in Fig. B11.6)

BP11.8   Complete a further stage by adding the embryonic parametric block shown in Fig. B11.3 to this version of the main program and replacing the

PRINT "LETTERDISPLAYER CALLED"

with an actual call to that embryonic parametric block. (Once again, if you have trouble, check your addition against Fig. B11.6.)

BP11.9   Complete the parametric block by developing and executing at least three more stages of it, leaving the driver portion as shown in Fig. B11.3. (You need not translate the assignment that forces screen reuse.)

BP11.10   Put the two finished parts together by attaching the parametric block (minus the ten driver lines) to the end of the main program. Run the result on your computer.

THE COMPLETE PROGRAM AND PARAMETRIC BLOCK

Figure B11.6 presents the translation of the entire program and parametric block.

```
00100 REM NAME DISPLAY PROGRAM AND PARAMETRIC BLOCK
00120 REM        ROCCO MARZARELLA    SEPT 1981
00140 REM C1% : COLUMN INTEGER 2
00160 REM  K% : K INTEGER
00180 REM L1$ : LETTER STRING 1
00200 REM L1% : LINE INTEGER 1
00220 REM N1$(10) : NAME[10] STRING 1
00240 REM N2$ : NAME END STRING 1
00260 REM P1% : POSITION INTEGER 1
00280 REM Q1$ : QUITSIGN STRING 1
00300 REM S1%(11,81) : SCREEN[11,81] INTEGER 1
00320 REM ------------------------------------------
00340 DIM N1$(10), S1%(11,81)
00360 REM ------------------------------------------
00380 REM
00400 REM --------- BODY OF MAIN PROGRAM ------------
00420 REM
00440 GOSUB 720                \REM CLEAR SCREEN
00460 Q1$ = " "
00480 IF Q1$ = "@" GOTO 660
00500    GOSUB 1000            \REM SOLICIT NAME
00520    GOSUB 1160            \REM TAKE NAME
00540    IF Q1$ = "@" GOTO 600
00560       GOSUB 1640         \REM DO 3 DISPLAYS
00580       GOTO 640
00600       GOSUB 1780         \REM CONFIRM QUIT
00620       GOTO 640
00640    GOTO 480
00660 GOTO 2520                \REM END
00680 REM
00700 REM ------------------------------------------
00710 REM
00720 REM            BLOCK CLEAR SCREEN
00740 PRINT "^Z"      \ REM SIGNAL TO DEVICE TO CLEAR SCREEN
00760 L1% = 1
00780 IF L1% > 11 GOTO 940
00800    C1% = 1
00820    IF C1% > 81 GOTO 900
00840       S1%(L1%,C1%) = 0
00860       C1% = C1% + 1
00880       GOTO 820
00900    L1% = L1% + 1
00920    GOTO 780
00940 RETURN
00960 REM----------------------------------------------
00980 REM
01000 REM            BLOCK SOLICIT NAME
01020 PRINT "Hi, what's your name?"
01040 PRINT "If you type it in, I'll show it to you"
01060 PRINT "Press the RETURN key after each letter you type."
01080 PRINT "Type a period and press RETURN when you're finished."
01100 RETURN
01120 REM----------------------------------------------
01140 REM
01160 REM            BLOCK TAKE NAME
01180 K% = 1
01200 IF K% > 10 GOTO 1280
01220    N1$(K%) = " "
01240    K% = K% + 1
01260    GOTO 1200
01280 K% = 1
01300 N2$ = "N"
01320 IF (K% > 10) OR (N2$ = "Y") GOTO 1580
```

(continued)

Fig. B11.6 The entire program and parametric block.

```
01340 INPUT N1$(K%)
01360 IF N1$(K%) = "." GOTO 1400
01380    GOTO 1440
01400    N2$ = "Y"
01420    GOTO 1440
01440 IF N1$(K%) = "@" GOTO 1480
01460    GOTO 1540
01480    N2$ = "Y"
01500    Q1$ = "@"
01520    GOTO 1540
01540 K% = K% + 1
01560 GOTO 1320
01580 RETURN
01600 REM ------------------------------------------
01620 REM
01640 REM              BLOCK DO 3 DISPLAYS
01660 GOSUB 1940              \REM DISPLAY NAME
01680 GOSUB 2280              \REM DISPLAY REVERSED NAME
01700 GOSUB 1940              \REM DISPLAY NAME
01720 RETURN
01740 REM------------------------------------------
01760 REM
01780 REM              BLOCK CONFIRM QUIT
01800 PRINT "An @ has been entered."
01820 PRINT "To confirm and terminate, type another @"
01840 PRINT "To deny and continue, type anything else."
01860 INPUT Q1$
01880 RETURN
01900 REM------------------------------------------
01920 REM
01940 REM              BLOCK DISPLAY NAME
01960 GOSUB 720              \REM CLEAR SCREEN
01980 P1% = 1
02000 IF P1% > 10 GOTO 2100
02020    L1$ = N1$(P1%)
02040    CALL LETTERDISPLAYER(L1$,P1%,S1%(,))
02060    P1% = P1% + 1
02080    GOTO 2000
02100 GOSUB 2180              \REM PAUSE
02120 RETURN
02140 REM ------------------------------------------
02160 REM
02180 REM              BLOCK PAUSE
02190 K = 1
02200 IF K > 1000 GOTO 2230
02210    K = K + 1
02220    GOTO 2200
02230 RETURN
02240 REM ------------------------------------------
02260 REM
02280 REM              BLOCK DISPLAY REVERSED NAME
02300 GOSUB 720              \REM CLEAR SCREEN
02320 P1% = 10
02340 IF P1% < 1 GOTO 2440
02360    L1$ = N1$(11 - P1%)
02380    CALL LETTERDISPLAYER(L1$,P1%,S1%(,))
02400    P1% = P1% - 1
02420    GOTO 2340
02440 GOSUB 2180              \REM PAUSE
02460 RETURN
02480 REM ------------------------------------------
02500 REM
02520 END
02540 REM -----      END MAIN PROGRAM      ------------
02560 REM ***                                        ***
```

Fig. B11.6 (continued)

```
02600 REM -----   START PARAMETRIC BLOCK   -----------
02620 REM
02640 SUB LETTERDISPLAYER(L5$,P5%,S5%(,))
02660 REM C5% : COLUMN INTEGER 2
02680 REM L5$ : LETTER STRING 1
02700 REM L5% : LINE INTEGER 2
02720 REM F2%(9,7) : FRAME[9,7]
02740 REM P5% : POSITION INTEGER 2
02760 REM S5%(11,81) : SCREEN[11,81]
02780 REM ------------------------------------------
02800 REM
02820 GOSUB 2940        \REM INIT FRAME
02840 GOSUB 3200        \REM SELECT LETTER
02860 GOSUB 4880        \REM TRANSFER LETTER
02880 GOSUB 5140        \REM DISPLAY SCREEN
02900 GOTO  12040       \REM END PARAMETRIC BLOCK
02910 REM ------------------------------------------
02920 REM
02940 REM           BLOCK INIT FRAME
02960 L5% = 1
02980 IF L5% > 9 GOTO 3140
03000    C5% = 1
03020    IF C5% > 7 GOTO 3100
03040       F2%(L5%,C5%) = 0
03060       C5% = C5% + 1
03080       GOTO 3020
03100    L5% = L5% + 1
03120    GOTO 2980
03140 RETURN
03160 REM ---------------------------------------
03180 REM
03200 REM           BLOCK SELECT LETTER
03220  IF (L5$ <> 'a') AND (L5$ <> 'A') GOTO 3280
03240   GOSUB 5440      \REM ABLK
03260   GOTO 4780
03280   IF (L5$ <> 'b') AND (L5$ <> 'B') GOTO 3340
03300     GOSUB 5720      \REM BBLK
03320     GOTO 4780
03340    IF (L5$ <>'c') AND (L5$ <>'C') GOTO 3400
03360      GOSUB 6100     \REM CBLK
03380      GOTO 4780
03400     IF (L5$ <>'d') AND (L5$ <>'D') GOTO 3460
03420       GOSUB 6400      \REM DBLK
03440       GOTO 4780
03460      IF (L5$ <> 'e') AND (L5$ <> 'E') GOTO 3520
03480       GOSUB 6600       \REM  EBLK
03500       GOTO 4780
03520       IF (L5$ <>'f') AND (L5$ <>'F') GOTO 3580
03540        GOSUB 6880      \REM FBLK
03560        GOTO 4780
03580        IF (L5$ <>'g') AND (L5$ <>'G') GOTO 3640
03600         GOSUB 7160     \REM GBLK
03620         GOTO 4780
03640         IF (L5$ <>'h') AND (L5$ <>'H') GOTO 3700
03660          GOSUB 7320      \REM HBLK
03680          GOTO 4780
03700          IF (L5$ <>'i') AND (L5$ <>'I') GOTO 3760
03720           GOSUB 7580      \REM IBLK
03740           GOTO 4780
03760           IF (L5$ <>'j') AND (L5$ <>'J') GOTO 3820
03780            GOSUB 7840      \REM JBLK
03800            GOTO 4780
03820            IF (L5$ <>'k') AND (L5$ <>'K') GOTO 3880
03840             GOSUB 8100     \REM KBLK
03860             GOTO 4780
```

(continued)

```
03880            IF (L5$ <>'l') AND (L5$ <>'L') GOTO 3940
03900            GOSUB 8460     \REM LBLK
03920            GOTO 4780
03940            IF (L5$ <> 'm') AND (L5$ <> 'M') GOTO 4000
03960             GOSUB 8700     \REM MBLK
03980             GOTO 4780
04000            IF (L5$ <>'n') AND (L5$ <>'N') GOTO 4060
04020             GOSUB 8960     \REM NBLK
04040             GOTO 4780
04060             IF (L5$ <> 'o') AND (L5$ <> 'O') GOTO 4120
04080             GOSUB 9220     \REM OBLK
04100             GOTO 4780
04120              IF (L5$ <>'p') AND (L5$ <>'P') GOTO 4180
04140              GOSUB 9500     \REM PBLK
04160              GOTO 4780
04180              IF (L5$ <>'q') AND (L5$ <>'Q') GOTO 4240
04200              GOSUB 9800     \REM QBLK
04220              GOTO 4780
04240              IF (L5$ <>'r') AND (L5$ <>'R') GOTO 4300
04260              GOSUB 9880     \REM RBLK
04280              GOTO 4780
04300              IF (L5$ <>'s') AND (L5$ <>'S') GOTO 4360
04320              GOSUB 10000     \REM SBLK
04340              GOTO 4780
04360              IF (L5$ <> 't') AND (L5$ <> 'T') GOTO 4420
04380              GOSUB 10220     \REM TBLK
04400              GOTO 4780
04420             IF (L5$ <>'u') AND (L5$ <>'U') GOTO 4480
04440             GOSUB 10460     \REM UBLK
04460             GOTO 4780
04480              IF (L5$ <>'v') AND (L5$ <>'V') GOTO 4540
04500              GOSUB 10720     \REM VBLK
04520              GOTO 4780
04540              IF (L5$ <>'w') AND (L5$ <>'W') GOTO 4600
04560              GOSUB 10980     \REM WBLK
04580              GOTO 4780
04600             IF (L5$ <>'x') AND (L5$ <>'X') GOTO 4660
04620             GOSUB 11260     \REM XBLK
04640             GOTO 4780
04660              IF (L5$ <>'y') AND (L5$ <>'Y') GOTO 4720
04680              GOSUB 11460     \REM YBLK
04700              GOTO 4780
04720              IF (L5$ <>'z') AND (L5$ <>'Z') GOTO 4780
04740               GOSUB 11720     \REM ZBLK
04760               GOTO 4780
04780 RETURN
04840 REM ----------------------------------------
04860 REM
04880 REM         BLOCK TRANSFER LETTER
04900 L5% = 1
04920 IF L5% > 9 GOTO 5080
04940    C5% = 1
04960    IF C5% >7 GOTO 5040
04980       S5%(1+L5%, P5%+((P5%-1)*7) + C5%) = F2%(L5%,C5%)
05000       C5% = C5% +1
05020       GOTO 4960
05040      L5% = L5% + 1
05060     GOTO 4920
05080 RETURN
05100 REM ----------------------------------------
05120 REM
05140 REM         BLOCK DISPLAY SCREEN
05160 PRINT "^^"
```

Fig. B11.6 (continued)

```
05180 L5% = 1
05200 IF L5% > 11 GOTO 5380
05220    C5% = 2
05240    IF C5% > 81 GOTO 5320
05260       IF S5%(L5%,C5%) = 1 THEN PRINT "0"; ELSE PRINT " ";
05280       C5% = C5% + 1
05300       GOTO 5240
05320    PRINT
05340    L5% = L5% + 1
05360    GOTO 5200
05380 PRINT
05400 RETURN
05420 REM ----------------------------------------
05440 REM ----   ABLK
05460    L5% = 3
05480    IF L5% > 8 GOTO 5580
05500       F2%(L5%,1) = 1
05520       F2%(L5%,7) = 1
05540       L5% = L5% + 1
05560       GOTO 5480
05580    C5% = 2
05600    IF C5% > 6 GOTO 5700
05620       F2%(2,C5%) = 1
05640       F2%(5,C5%) = 1
05660       C5% = C5% + 1
05680       GOTO 5600
05700 RETURN
05720 REM ----   BBLK
05740    L5% = 2
05760    IF L5% > 8 GOTO 5840
05780       F2%(L5%,1) = 1
05800       L5% = L5% + 1
05820       GOTO 5760
05840    C5% = 2
05860    IF C5% > 6 GOTO 6000
05900       F2%(2,C5%) = 1
05920       F2%(5,C5%) = 1
05940       F2%(8,C5%) = 1
05960       C5% = C5% + 1
05980       GOTO 5860
06000    F2%(3,7) = 1
06020    F2%(4,7) = 1
06040    F2%(6,7) = 1
06060    F2%(7,7) = 1
06080 RETURN
06100 REM ----   CBLK
06120    C5% = 2
06140    IF C5% > 6 GOTO 6240
06160       F2%(2,C5%) = 1
06180       F2%(8,C5%) = 1
06200       C5% = C5% + 1
06220       GOTO 6140
06240    L5% = 3
06260    F2%(L5%,7) = 1
06280    IF L5% > 7 GOTO 6360
06300       F2%(L5%,1) = 1
06320       L5% = L5% + 1
06340       GOTO 6280
06360    F2%(7,7) = 1
06380 RETURN
06400 REM ----   DBLK
```

(continued)

```
06420    GOSUB 6100        \REM CBLK
06440  F2%(2,1) = 1
06460  F2%(8,1) = 1
06480  L5% = 4
06500  IF L5% > 6 GOTO 6580
06520     F2%(L5%,7) = 1
06540     L5% = L5% + 1
06560     GOTO 6500
06580 RETURN
06600 REM ----  EBLK
06620  L5% = 2
06640  IF L5% > 8 GOTO 6720
06660     F2%(L5%,1) = 1
06680     L5% = L5% + 1
06700     GOTO 6640
06720  C5% = 2
06740  IF C5% > 7 GOTO 6860
06760     F2%(2,C5%) = 1
06780     F2%(5,C5%) = 1
06800     F2%(8,C5%) = 1
06820     C5% = C5% + 1
06840     GOTO 6740
06860 RETURN
06880 REM ----  FBLK
06900  L5% = 2
06920  IF L5% > 8 GOTO 7000
06940     F2%(L5%,1) = 1
06960     L5% = L5% + 1
06980     GOTO 6920
07000  C5% = 2
07020  IF C5% > 7 GOTO 7120
07040     F2%(2,C5%) = 1
07060     F2%(5,C5%) = 1
07080     C5% = C5% + 1
07100     GOTO 7020
07120        F2%(5,7) = 0
07140 RETURN
07160 REM ----  GBLK
07180 GOSUB 6100       \REM CBLK
07200  C5% = 4
07220  IF C5% > 7 GOTO 7300
07240     F2%(6,C5%) = 1
07260     C5% = C5% + 1
07280     GOTO 7220
07300  RETURN
07320 REM ----  HBLK
07340  L5% = 2
07360  IF L5% > 8 GOTO 7460
07380     F2%(L5%,1) = 1
07400     F2%(L5%,7) = 1
07420     L5% = L5% + 1
07440     GOTO 7360
07460  C5% = 2
07480  IF C5% > 6 GOTO 7560
07500     F2%(5,C5%) = 1
07520     C5% = C5% + 1
07540     GOTO 7480
07560 RETURN
07580 REM ----  IBLK
07600  L5% = 3
07620  IF L5% > 7 GOTO 7700
07640     F2%(L5%,4) = 1
07660     L5% = L5% + 1
07680     GOTO 7620
```

Fig. B11.6 (continued)

```
07700   C5% = 3
07720   IF C5% > 5 GOTO 7820
07740      F2%(2,C5%) = 1
07760      F2%(8,C5%) = 1
07780      C5% = C5% + 1
07800      GOTO 7720
07820   RETURN
07840   REM ----   JBLK
07860   L5% = 2
07880   IF L5% > 7 GOTO 7960
07900      F2%(L5%,7) = 1
07920      L5% = L5% + 1
07940      GOTO 7880
07960   C5% = 2
07980   IF C5% > 6 GOTO 8060
08000      F2%(8,C5%) = 1
08020      C5% = C5% + 1
08040      GOTO 7980
08060   F2%(7,1) = 1
08080   RETURN
08100   REM ----   KBLK
08120   L5% = 2
08140   IF L5% > 8 GOTO 8220
08160      F2%(L5%,1) = 1
08180      L5% = L5% + 1
08200      GOTO 8140
08220   C5% = 2
08240   IF C5% > 4 GOTO 8320
08260      F2%(5,C5%) = 1
08280      C5% = C5% + 1
08300      GOTO 8240
08320   F2%(6,5) = 1
08340   F2%(7,6) = 1
08360   F2%(8,7) = 1
08380   F2%(4,5) = 1
08400   F2%(3,6) = 1
08420   F2%(2,7) = 1
08440   RETURN
08460   REM ----   LBLK
08480   L5% = 2
08500   IF L5% > 8 GOTO 8580
08520      F2%(L5%,1) = 1
08540      L5% = L5% + 1
08560      GOTO 8500
08580   C5% = 2
08600   IF C5% > 7 GOTO 8680
08620      F2%(8,C5%) = 1
08640      C5% = C5% + 1
08660      GOTO 8600
08680   RETURN
08700   REM ----   MBLK
08720   F2%(3,2) = 1
08740   F2%(3,6) = 1
08760   F2%(4,3) = 1
08780   F2%(4,5) = 1
08800   F2%(5,4) = 1
08820   L5% = 2
08840   IF L5% > 8 GOTO 8940
08860      F2%(L5%,1) = 1
08880      F2%(L5%,7) = 1
08900      L5% = L5% + 1
08920      GOTO 8840
```

(continued)

```
08940   RETURN
08960   REM ----   NBLK
08980   L5% = 2
09000   IF L5% > 8 GOTO 9100
09020      F2%(L5%,1) = 1
09040      F2%(L5%,7) = 1
09060      L5% = L5% + 1
09080      GOTO 9000
09100   C5% = 2
09120   IF C5% > 6 GOTO 9200
09140      F2%(C5%+1,C5%) = 1
09160      C5% = C5% + 1
09180      GOTO 9120
09200 RETURN
09220      REM ----   OBLK
09240   C5% = 2
09260   IF C5% > 6 GOTO 9360
09280      F2%(2,C5%) = 1
09300      F2%(8,C5%) = 1
09320      C5% = C5% + 1
09340      GOTO 9260
09360   L5% = 3
09380   IF L5% > 7 GOTO 9480
09400      F2%(L5%,1) = 1
09420      F2%(L5%,7) = 1
09440      L5% = L5% + 1
09460      GOTO 9380
09480 RETURN
09500 REM ----   PBLK
09520   L5% = 2
09540   IF L5% > 8 GOTO 9620
09560      F2%(L5%,1) = 1
09580      L5% = L5% + 1
09600      GOTO 9540
09620   C5% = 2
09640   IF C5% > 6 GOTO 9740
09660      F2%(2,C5%) = 1
09680      F2%(5,C5%) = 1
09700      C5% = C5% + 1
09720      GOTO 9640
09740   F2%(3,7) = 1
09760   F2%(4,7) = 1
09780 RETURN
09800 REM ----QBLK
09820   GOSUB 9220      \REM   OBLK
09840   F2%(7,5) = 1
09860   RETURN
09880 REM ----   RBLK
09900    GOSUB 9500
09920   F2%(6,5) = 1
09940   F2%(7,6) = 1
09960   F2%(8,7) = 1
09980 RETURN
10000 REM ----   SBLK
10020   GOSUB 6100      \REM   CBLK
10040   F2%(5,1) = 0
10060   F2%(6,1) = 0
10080   F2%(6,7) = 1
10100   C5% = 2
10120   IF C5% > 6 GOTO 10200
10140      F2%(5,C5%) = 1
10160      C5% = C5% + 1
10180      GOTO 10120
```

Fig. B11.6 (continued)

```
10200 RETURN
10220 REM ----    TBLK
10240  C5% = 1
10260  IF C5% > 7 GOTO 10340
10280     F2%(2,C5%) = 1
10300     C5% = C5% + 1
10320     GOTO 10260
10340 L5% = 3
10360 IF L5% > 8 GOTO 10440
10380     F2%(L5%,4) = 1
10400     L5% = L5% + 1
10420     GOTO 10360
10440 RETURN
10460 REM ----    UBLK
10480  C5% = 2
10500  IF C5% > 6 GOTO 10580
10520     F2%(8,C5%) = 1
10540     C5% = C5% + 1
10560     GOTO 10500
10580 L5% = 2
10600 IF L5% > 7 GOTO 10700
10620     F2%(L5%,1) = 1
10640     F2%(L5%,7) = 1
10660     L5% = L5% + 1
10680     GOTO 10600
10700 RETURN
10720 REM ----    VBLK
10740  L5% = 2
10760  IF L5% > 5 GOTO 10860
10780     F2%(L5%,1) = 1
10800     F2%(L5%,7) = 1
10820     L5% = L5% + 1
10840     GOTO 10760
10860  F2%(6,2) = 1
10880  F2%(7,3) = 1
10900  F2%(8,4) = 1
10920  F2%(7,5) = 1
10940  F2%(6,6) = 1
10960 RETURN
10980 REM ----    WBLK
11000        L5% = 2
11020  IF L5% > 7 GOTO 11120
11040     F2%(L5%,1) = 1
11060     F2%(L5%,7) = 1
11080     L5% = L5% + 1
11100     GOTO 11020
11120  F2%(5,4) = 1
11140  F2%(6,4) = 1
11160  F2%(7,3) = 1
11180  F2%(7,5) = 1
11200  F2%(8,2) = 1
11220  F2%(8,6) = 1
11240 RETURN
11260 REM ----    XBLK
11280  C5% = 1
11300  L5% = 2
11320  IF L5% > 8 GOTO 11440
11340     F2%(L5%,C5%) = 1
11360     F2%(L5%,8-C5%) = 1
11380     C5% = C5% + 1
11400     L5% = L5% + 1
11420     GOTO 11320
11440 RETURN
```

(continued)

```
11460 REM ----   YBLK
11480   F2%(2,1) = 1
11500   F2%(2,7) = 1
11520   F2%(3,2) = 1
11540   F2%(3,6) = 1
11560   F2%(4,3) = 1
11580   F2%(4,5) = 1
11600   L5% = 5
11620   IF L5% > 8 GOTO 11700
11640       F2%(L5%,4) = 1
11660       L5% = L5% + 1
11680       GOTO 11620
11700 RETURN
11720 REM ----   ZBLK
11740   C5% = 1
11760   IF C5% > 7 GOTO 11860
11780       F2%(2,C5%) = 1
11800       F2%(8,C5%) = 1
11820       C5% = C5% + 1
11840       GOTO 11760
11860   L5% = 7
11880   C5% = 2
11900   IF C5% > 6 GOTO 12000
11920       F2%(L5%,C5%) = 1
11940       C5% = C5% + 1
11960       L5% = L5% - 1
11980       GOTO 11900
12000 RETURN
12040 SUBEND
```

Fig. B11.6 (continued)

Note the following.

1. To avoid any misunderstanding and to emphasize the distinction between program and parametric block in this BASIC, no dataname in the parametric block duplicates any dataname in the main program.

2. An external assignment is inserted in CLEAR_SCREEN to clear the display to blanks.

00740 PRINT "∧Z" \ REM SIGNAL TO DEVICE TO CLEAR SCREE▮

This is an example of a command to the screen device, according to the manufacturer's specifications. It is peculiar to a particular display terminal. To use this program, you should look up the specification for clearing the screen on your terminal and substitute it for the string quoted. They may require something as complex as this, or they may require something simpler such as the citation of a key word like CLEAR.

3. A external assignment is inserted in DISPLAY_SCREEN to force the next display to begin in the upper left-hand corner of the screen.

05160 PRINT "∧∧"

Use of this command involves the same kind of considerations discussed for CLEAR_SCREEN in (2) above. The same advice holds.

Private Practice BASIC

BP11.11 Create one or more toy programs in your version of BASIC to experiment with controlling your display screen. In particular, discover how to clear the screen, how to direct the display to next begin in the upper left-hand corner of the screen, and how to direct the display to next begin at some specific point other than that upper corner (i.e., line 13, column 8).

BP11.12 Enter the complete program and parametric block from Fig. B11.6 into your computer and run the system.

BP11.13 Use your work on the number display program to produce a BASIC translation of (P11.11).

BP11.14 Use your work on (P11.13) to produce a BASIC program that centers the name displays. Run the result on your computer.

BP11.15 Translate your modified program from (P11.15) into BASIC and run the result on your computer.

BP11.16 Translate your new version of SELECT_LETTER into BASIC, substitute it for the version shown in Fig. B11.6, and run the result on your computer. Insert a counter to demonstrate the number of searches necessary to identify a particular letter.

BP11.17 Using your work on two different sizes of displays, (P11.3) and (P11.4), modify your BASIC version of the number display program so that it allows the user to choose one of two sizes for the displayed numbers.

Pascal Interpretation of Chapter 11

THE PARAMETRIC BLOCK IN PASCAL

Figure P11.1 presents the translation of a parametric block reference; Fig. P11.2, of a parametric block's details. Both are extracted from a complete translation of the name display program.

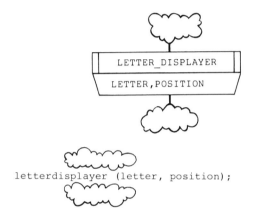

Fig. P11.1 Translating the parametric block reference.

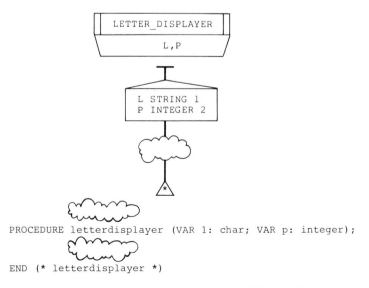

Fig. P11.2 Translating the parametric block's details.

Note the following.

1. A parametric block reference names the block, and lists the parameters.

letterdisplayer(letter,position);

2. A parametric block's details begin with an identifying first line that cites the *key word* PROCEDURE, names the block, and lists the *names* of the parameters.

PROCEDURE letterdisplayer(VAR 1:CHAR;VAR p:INTEGER);

3. Each parameter must be declared in that first line list, and each must be preceded with the key word VAR.

(*VAR* 1:CHAR; *VAR* p:INTEGER)

An explanation of this preceding key word is provided below, following (4).

4. A parametric block's details end with the same key word last line used to end a regular block's details

END;   (* letterdisplayer *)

The key word VAR listed before each parameter means that it is a *variable* parameter; such a parameter uses storage exactly as suggested in the FPL explanation. (See Fig. 11.3.) Pascal provides other types of parameters you may wish to explore. One type, *value* parameters is presented informally through (PP11.2). That type functions differently from the variable parameter and has quite different results—the value of a parameter in the referencing program or block *is the same after the parametric block is executed as it was before!* The reason is simple. For each value parameter (any parameter not preceded by the key word VAR in the parameter list), the parametric block sets up a *separate storage location,* copies the value of the parameter as passed from the referencing program, and stores all changes it may make to that value in the new location. That location is not known to the referencing program. So far as it is concerned, the new location and any value it contains do not exist. Consequently, when control returns to the referencing program after the parametric block's execution is completed, the referencing program knows only the location and value it set up, the value that it passed to the parametric block. There are occasions when value parameters are useful, but it will be up to you to explore how they work and determine if and when you wish to use them. We will use variable parameters only.

Private Practice Pascal

PP11.1 Enter the toy program shown into your computer and run it with various modifications to explore how parametric blocks work on your computer.

```
PROGRAM toy12(input,output);
VAR
  letter1, letter2, lt2 : char;
PROCEDURE letterchanger (VAR lt1:char);
BEGIN
  WRITELN('....... start block ......');
  WRITELN('lt1 was ',lt1, 'letter2 was ',letter2);
  lt1 := 'C';
  letter2 := 'D';
  WRITELN('lt1 was ',lt1, 'letter2 was ',letter2);
  WRITELN('....... end block ......')
END; (* letterchanger *)
BEGIN (* main *)
  letter1 := 'A';
  letter2 := 'B';
  lt2 := letter 1;
  WRITELN ('letter1, letter2, and lt2 before',
           ' reference were ',letter1, ', ',letter2, ', ',lt2);
  letterchanger(letter1);
  WRITELN('letter1, letter2, and lt2 after',
           ' reference were ',letter1, ', ',letter2, ', ',lt2);
END. (* toy12 *)
```

PP11.2 Delete the key word VAR in the parameter list cited for the first line of the parametric block's details, run the program again, and observe the results for letter1 and lt1. Experiment with the toy further and find out more about the difference between variable parameters (PP11.1) and value parameters (PP11.2).

CREATING A PASCAL TRANSLATION IN EASY STAGES

Figures P11.3 and P11.4 suggest how the development of a complex program can be translated and checked out in stages. They represent "stubs" or "embryos" of what will become the two parts of the final solution. Figure P11.3 is the beginning of the parametric block; Fig. P11.4 is the main program that calls it. Both stubs will execute as is and produce useful output for determining if the development so far is on the right track.

```
PROGRAM cllpbl(input,output);
  (* Stubl of parametric block *)
  (* Elaine Weed    July 1981 *)
  VAR
       letter  : CHAR;
       position : INTEGER;

PROCEDURE letterdisplayer(VAR l:CHAR; VAR p:INTEGER);

  PROCEDURE initframe;
    BEGIN
    WRITELN('Frame initialized');
    END; (* initframe *)

  PROCEDURE selectletter;
    BEGIN
    WRITELN('Letter selected');
    END; (* selectletter *)

  PROCEDURE transferletter;
    BEGIN
    WRITELN('Letter transferred');
    END; (* transferletter *)

  PROCEDURE displayscreen;
    BEGIN
    WRITELN('Screen displayed');
    END; (* displayscreen *)

  BEGIN (* main body of letterdisplayer *)
    initframe;
    selectletter;
    transferletter;
    displayscreen;
  END; (* letterdisplayer *)

  BEGIN (* main body of cllpbl *)
    WRITELN('Enter a letter');
    READLN;READ(letter);
    WRITELN('Enter a position (1 to 10)');
    READLN;READ(position);
    letterdisplayer(letter, position);
  END. (* program cllpbl *)
```

Fig. P11.3 A stub translation of the parametric block.

Note the following about Fig. P11.3.

1. A very minimal (12 lines) main program is used to power or drive the stub of the parametric block.

```
BEGIN
  WRITELN('Enter a letter');
  READLN;READ(letter);
  WRITELN('Enter a position (1 to 10)');
  READLN;READ(position);
  letterdisplayer(letter, position);
END. (* program cllstub1 *)
```

All it can test is that the embryonic parametric block is callable.

2. Like the details of any other Pascal procedure, those of a parametric block must be listed *after* the END of the VAR section and *before* the BEGIN of the main program.

3. The main line of the parametric block is complete but only stubs are present to represent its four blocks.

```
PROCEDURE letterdisplayer(VAR 1:CHAR; VAR p:INTEGER);
  PROCEDURE initframe;
  BEGIN
  WRITELN('Frame initialized');
  END;
```

```
BEGIN
  initframe;
  selectletter;
  transferletter;
  displayscreen;
END; (* letterdisplayer *)
```

4. Each block stub within the embryonic parametric block contains sufficient detail only to demonstrate whether or not it is called when it should be. SELECT LETTER for example, if called, merely verifies the call by printing

'Letter selected'

It is left to a later stage, once all the stubs appear to be referenced and re-sponding in the correct order, to flesh out the details of the stubs so that each actually performs its appointed tasks.

```
PROGRAM cllml(input,output);
   (* Stubl of main program *)
   (* Elaine Weed      Aug 1981 *)
   VAR
        quitsign  : CHAR;

   PROCEDURE clearscreen;
      BEGIN
        WRITELN('Screen cleared');
      END; (* clearscreen *)

   PROCEDURE confirmquit;
      BEGIN
        WRITELN('An  @  has been entered.');
        WRITELN('To confirm and quit, type another @');
        WRITELN('To deny and continue, type anything else.');
        READLN; READ(quitsign)
      END; (* confirmquit *)

   PROCEDURE do3displays;
      BEGIN
        WRITELN('Did 3 displays');
      END; (* do3displays *)

   PROCEDURE solicitname;
      BEGIN
        WRITELN('Give signal to quit or continue');
        READLN;READ(quitsign);
      END; (* solicitname *)

   PROCEDURE takename;
      BEGIN
        WRITELN('Took name');
      END; (* takename *)

   BEGIN (* main body of cllstub2 *)
     quitsign := ' ';
     WHILE quitsign <> '@' DO
       BEGIN
         solicitname;
         takename;
         IF quitsign = '@'
            THEN confirmquit
            ELSE do3displays
       END;
   END. (* cllml *)
```

Fig. P11.4 Embryonic main program.

Note the following about the stub of the main program.

1. The embryonic main program is complete in its main line, but only the details of CONFIRM_QUIT and SOLICIT_NAME amount to more than verifying stubs. (SOLICIT_NAME includes enough detail only to provide CONFIRM_QUIT with a value to test itself.)

2. The major block DO_3_DISPLAYS is represented by a stub but at this stage no calls to DISPLAY_NAME or DISPLAY_REVERSED_NAME have been inserted, and so no calls from them in LETTERDISPLAYER have yet been put in place either. All this will follow in a subsequent stage or two.

Creating such embryonic translations is a simple and effective way to progress toward a properly functioning finished product. Just as episodes allow the programmer to defer consideration of some details in order to concentrate upon others, so the development of translation in terms of stubs allows concentration to be focused on different parts and levels of the system at different stages. By such controlling of focus, a properly functioning final product can efficiently and surely be developed.

Private Practice Pascal

PP11.3   Enter the parametric block stub (Fig. P11.3) into your computer and run it.

PP11.4   Modify the stub so that while executing the parametric block it prints out the value of the letter and position passed to it from the main program. Run your modification on the computer.

PP11.5   Enter the main program stub (Fig. P11.4) into your computer and run it.

A FURTHER STAGE

Figure P11.5 presents the stub of the main program after it has been developed a bit further. This one is shown as representative of the many created along the way to producing the finished translation in Fig. P11.6. Each stub should expand upon its predecessor by adding details to finish off some portion of the stub. By developing the details in stages, a considerable amount of confusion and consequent wasted work can be avoided. A mistake can be isolated and corrected easily when its origin is a newly created, small addition to a stub that is already functioning correctly. By contrast, a mistake may be hard to isolate and correct when its source might be any one of a large number of additions, all made to a stub since the last time it was executed. Confusion is maximized if the entire program is translated before any testing is done on the computer!

Other stubs will not be shown but were created *en route* to producing the final product. The Private Practice will encourage you to create some of these intermediate stages yourself. You should use this general approach liberally whenever you develop your own complex programs.

```
PROGRAM cllm2(input,output);
   (* stub2 of main program *)
   (* Elaine Weed            September 1981 *)
   VAR
        column, k, line, position : INTEGER;
        letter, nameend, quitsign  : CHAR;
        ESC : CHAR;
        frame : ARRAY[1..9,1..7] OF INTEGER;
        name : ARRAY [1..10] OF CHAR;
        screen : ARRAY[1..24,1..81] OF INTEGER;

   PROCEDURE clearscreen;
      BEGIN
         line := 1;
         WHILE line <= 24 DO
            BEGIN
               column := 1;
               WHILE column <= 81 DO
                  BEGIN
                     screen[line,column] := 0;
                     column := column + 1
                  END;
               line := line + 1
               END;
   END; (* clearscreen *)

PROCEDURE confirmquit;
   BEGIN
      WRITELN('An  @   has been entered.');
      WRITELN('To confirm and quit, type another @');
      WRITELN('To deny and continue, type anything else.');
      READLN; READ(quitsign)
   END; (* confirmquit *)

PROCEDURE displayname;
   BEGIN
      clearscreen;
      WRITELN('Letterdisplayer called 10 times');
   END; (* displayname *)

PROCEDURE displayreversedname;
   BEGIN
      clearscreen;
      WRITELN('Letterdisplayer called 10 times');
   END; (* displayreversedname *)

PROCEDURE pause;
   BEGIN
      WRITELN('Pause called for');
   END; (* pause *)

PROCEDURE do3displays;
   BEGIN
      displayname;
      displayreversedname;
      displayname
   END; (* do3displays *)

PROCEDURE solicitname;
   BEGIN
      WRITELN(' What''s your name?');
      WRITELN('If you type it in, I''ll show it to you.');
      WRITELN('Press the RETURN key after each letter you type.');
      WRITELN('Type a period ( . ) to end your name.')
   END; (* solicitname *)
```
                                                      (continued)

Fig. P11.5 More developed stub of main program.

```
PROCEDURE takename;
   BEGIN
     k := 1;
     WHILE k <= 10 DO
       BEGIN
         name[k] := ' ';
         k := k + 1
       END;
     k := 1;
     nameend := 'N';
     WHILE (k <= 10) and (nameend = 'N') DO
       BEGIN
         READLN; READ(name[k]);
         IF name[k] = '.' THEN nameend := 'Y';
         IF name[k] = '@'
           THEN
             BEGIN
               nameend := 'Y';
               quitsign := '@'
             END;
         k := k + 1
       END;
   END; (* takename *)

BEGIN (* main body of cllstub3 *)
   quitsign := ' ';
   WHILE quitsign <> '@' DO
     BEGIN
       solicitname;
       takename;
       IF quitsign = '@'
         THEN confirmquit
         ELSE do3displays
     END;
END. (* cllm2 *)
```

Fig. P11.5 (continued)

Note the following.

1. The declarations have been added.

2. The details of CLEAR_SCREEN, SOLICIT_NAME, TAKE_-NAME, and DO_3_DISPLAYS have been translated.

3. Stubs for DISPLAY_NAME, DISPLAY_REVERSED_NAME, and PAUSE have been added.

4. No details to call LETTERDISPLAYER have yet been added, so no trace of the parametric block appears yet either.

Private Practice Pascal

PP11.6   Enter the stub in Fig. P11.5 into your computer and run it.

PP11.7   Develop a next stage of the stub by completing DISPLAY_NAME and DISPLAY_REVERSED_NAME *except* for the call to the parametric block. In place of that call, substitute

WRITELN('Letterdisplayer called once');

(If you have trouble, check your details against those shown in Fig. P11.6.)

PP11.8   Complete a further stage by adding the embryonic parametric block shown in Fig. P11.3 to this version of the main program and replacing the

WRITELN('Letterdisplayer called once');

with an actual call to that embryonic parametric block. (Once again, if you have trouble, check your addition against Fig. P11.6.)

PP11.9   Complete the parametric block by developing and executing at least three more stages of it, leaving the driver portion as shown in Fig. P11.3. (You need not translate the assignment that forces screen reuse.)

PP11.10 Put the two finished parts together by attaching the parametric block (minus the 12 driver lines) to the end of the main program. Run the result on your computer.

THE COMPLETE PROGRAM AND PARAMETRIC BLOCK

Figure P11.6 presents the translation of the entire program and parametric block.

```
PROGRAM c11(input,output);
   (* translation of letter display program from Chapter 11 *)
   (* Elaine Weed Oct 1981 *)
   VAR
        column, k, line, position : INTEGER;
        letter, nameend, quitsign  : CHAR;
        ESC : CHAR;
        frame : ARRAY[1..9,1..7] OF INTEGER;
        name : ARRAY [1..10] OF CHAR;
        screen : ARRAY[1..24,1..81] OF INTEGER;

   PROCEDURE letterdisplay(VAR l:CHAR; VAR p:INTEGER);
      PROCEDURE initframe;
      BEGIN
        line := 1;
        WHILE line <= 9 DO
           BEGIN
             column := 1;
             WHILE column <= 7 DO
              BEGIN
                frame[line,column] := 0;
                column := column + 1
              END;                              (continued)
```

Fig. P11.6 The entire program and the parametric block.

```
                    line := line + 1
            END;
    END; (* initframe *)
PROCEDURE selectletter;
    PROCEDURE ablk;
      BEGIN
        line := 3;
        WHILE line <= 8 DO
         BEGIN
          frame[line,1] := 1;
          frame[line,7] := 1;
          line := line + 1
         END;
        column := 2;
        WHILE column <= 6 DO
         BEGIN
          frame[2,column] := 1;
          frame[5,column] := 1;
          column := column + 1
         END;
      END; (* ablk *)
    PROCEDURE bblk;
      BEGIN
        line := 2;
        WHILE line <= 8 DO
         BEGIN
          frame[line,1] := 1;
          line := line + 1
         END;
        column := 2;
        WHILE column <= 6 DO
         BEGIN
          frame[2,column] := 1;
          frame[5,column] := 1;
          frame[8,column] := 1;
          column := column + 1
         END;
        frame[3,7] := 1;
        frame[4,7] := 1;
        frame[6,7] := 1;
        frame[7,7] := 1;
      END; (* bblk *)
    PROCEDURE cblk;
      BEGIN
        column := 2;
        WHILE column <= 6 DO
          BEGIN
            frame[2,column] := 1;
            frame[8,column] := 1;
            column := column + 1
          END;
        line := 3;
        frame[line,7] := 1;
        WHILE line <= 7 DO
          BEGIN
            frame[line,1] := 1;
            line := line + 1
          END;
        frame[7,7] := 1;
      END; (* cblk *)
    PROCEDURE dblk;
```

Fig. P11.6 (continued)

```
      BEGIN
        cblk;
        frame[2,1] := 1;
        frame[8,1] := 1;
        line := 4;
        WHILE line <= 6 DO
         BEGIN
           frame[line,7] := 1;
           line := line + 1;
         END;
  END; (* dblk *)
  PROCEDURE eblk;
    BEGIN
      line := 2;
      WHILE line <= 8 DO
       BEGIN
         frame[line,1] := 1;
         line := line + 1
       END;
      column := 2;
      WHILE column <= 7 DO
       BEGIN
         frame[2,column] := 1;
         frame[5,column] := 1;
         frame[8,column] := 1;
         column := column + 1
       END;
    END; (* eblk *)
  PROCEDURE fblk;
    BEGIN
      line := 2;
      WHILE line <= 8 DO
       BEGIN
         frame[line,1] := 1;
         line := line + 1
       END;
      column := 2;
      WHILE column <= 7 DO
       BEGIN
         frame[2,column] := 1;
         frame[5,column] := 1;
         column := column + 1
       END;
      frame[5,7] := 0
    END; (* fblk *)
  PROCEDURE gblk;
    BEGIN
      cblk;
      column := 4;
      WHILE column <= 7 DO
        BEGIN
          frame[6,column] := 1;
          column := column + 1
        END;
      END; (* gblk *)
    PROCEDURE hblk;
      BEGIN
        line := 2;
        WHILE line <= 8 DO
         BEGIN
           frame[line,1] := 1;
           frame[line,7] := 1;
           line := line + 1
         END;
```

(continued)

```
         column := 2;
         WHILE column <= 6 DO
          BEGIN
           frame[5,column] := 1;
           column := column + 1
          END;
       END; (* hblk *)
   PROCEDURE iblk;
     BEGIN
         line := 3;
         WHILE line <= 7 DO
          BEGIN
           frame[line,4] := 1;
           line := line + 1
          END;
         column := 3;
         WHILE column <= 5 DO
          BEGIN
           frame[2,column] := 1;
           frame[8,column] := 1;
           column := column + 1
          END;
       END; (* iblk *)
   PROCEDURE jblk;
     BEGIN
         line := 2;
         WHILE line <= 7 DO
          BEGIN
           frame[line,7] := 1;
           line := line + 1
          END;
         column := 2;
         WHILE column <= 6 DO
          BEGIN
           frame[8,column] := 1;
           column := column + 1
          END;
         frame[7,1] := 1
       END; (* jblk *)
   PROCEDURE kblk;
     BEGIN
         line := 2;
         WHILE line <= 8 DO
          BEGIN
           frame[line,1] := 1;
           line := line + 1
          END;
         column := 2;
         WHILE column <= 4 DO
          BEGIN
           frame[5,column] := 1;
           column := column + 1
          END;
         frame[6,5] := 1;
         frame[7,6] := 1;
         frame[8,7] := 1;
         frame[4,5] := 1;
         frame[3,6] := 1;
         frame[2,7] := 1;
       END; (* kblk *)
   PROCEDURE lblk;
     BEGIN
         line := 2;
         WHILE line <= 8 DO
```

Fig. P11.6 (continued)

```
      BEGIN
       frame[line,1] := 1;
       line := line + 1
      END;
     column := 2;
     WHILE column <= 7 DO
      BEGIN
       frame[8,column] := 1;
       column := column + 1
      END;
  END; (* lblk *)
PROCEDURE mblk;
  BEGIN
     frame[3,2] := 1;
     frame[3,6] := 1;
     frame[4,3] := 1;
     frame[4,5] := 1;
     frame[5,4] := 1;
     line := 2;
     WHILE line <= 8 DO
      BEGIN
        frame[line,1] := 1;
        frame[line,7] := 1;
        line := line + 1
      END;
  END; (* mblk *)
PROCEDURE nblk;
  BEGIN
     line := 2;
     WHILE line <= 8 DO
      BEGIN
       frame[line,1] := 1;
       frame[line,7] := 1;
       line := line + 1
      END;
     column := 2;
     WHILE column <= 6 DO
      BEGIN
        frame[column+1,column] := 1;
        column := column + 1
      END;
   END; (* nblk *)
PROCEDURE oblk;
 BEGIN
  column := 2;
  WHILE column <= 6 DO
     BEGIN
       frame[2,column] := 1;
       frame[8,column] := 1;
       column := column + 1
     END;
  line := 3;
  WHILE line <= 7 DO
     BEGIN
       frame[line,1] := 1;
       frame[line,7] := 1;
       line := line + 1
     END;
 END; (* oblk *)
 PROCEDURE pblk;
   BEGIN
     line := 2;
     WHILE line <= 8 DO
```

(continued)

```
               BEGIN
                frame[line,1] := 1;
                line := line + 1
               END;
              column := 2;
              WHILE column <= 6 DO
               BEGIN
                frame[2,column] := 1;
                frame[5,column] := 1;
                column := column + 1
               END;
              frame[3,7] := 1;
              frame[4,7] := 1;
            END; (* pblk *)
         PROCEDURE qblk;
          BEGIN
           oblk;
           frame[7,5] := 1
          END; (*qblk *)
         PROCEDURE rblk;
          BEGIN
           pblk;
           frame[6,5] := 1;
           frame[7,6] := 1;
           frame[8,7] := 1;
          END; (* rblk *)
         PROCEDURE sblk;
          BEGIN
           cblk;
           frame[5,1] := 0;
           frame[6,1] := 0;
           frame[6,7] := 1;
           column := 2;
           WHILE column <= 6 DO
              BEGIN
                frame[5,column] := 1;
                column := column + 1
              END;
          END; (* sblk *)
         PROCEDURE tblk;
          BEGIN
           column := 1;
           WHILE column <= 7 DO
              BEGIN
                frame[2,column] := 1;
                column := column + 1
              END;
           line := 3;
           WHILE line <= 8 DO
              BEGIN
                frame[line,4] := 1;
                line := line + 1
              END;
          END; (* tblk *)
         PROCEDURE ublk;
          BEGIN
           column := 2;
           WHILE column <= 6 DO
              BEGIN
                frame[8,column] := 1;
                column := column + 1
              END;
```

Fig. P11.6 (continued)

```
 line := 2;
 WHILE line <= 7 DO
     BEGIN
        frame[line,1] := 1;
        frame[line,7] := 1;
        line := line + 1
     END;
 END; (* ublk *)
PROCEDURE vblk;
 BEGIN
  line := 2;
  WHILE line <= 5 DO
     BEGIN
        frame[line,1] := 1;
        frame[line,7] := 1;
        line := line + 1
     END;
  frame[6,2] := 1;
  frame[7,3] := 1;
  frame[8,4] := 1;
  frame[7,5] := 1;
  frame[6,6] := 1;
 END; (* vblk *)
PROCEDURE wblk;
 BEGIN
  line := 2;
  WHILE line <= 7 DO
     BEGIN
        frame[line,1] := 1;
        frame[line,7] := 1;
        line := line + 1
     END;
  frame[5,4] := 1;
  frame[6,4] := 1;
  frame[7,3] := 1;
  frame[7,5] := 1;
  frame[8,2] := 1;
  frame[8,6] := 1;
 END; (* wblk *)
PROCEDURE xblk;
  BEGIN
   column := 1;
   line := 2;
   WHILE line <= 8 DO
    BEGIN
     frame[line,column] := 1;
     frame[line,8-column] := 1;
     column := column + 1;
     line := line + 1
    END;
END; (* xblk *)
PROCEDURE yblk;
  BEGIN
   frame[2,1] := 1;
   frame[2,7] := 1;
   frame[3,2] := 1;
   frame[3,6] := 1;
   frame[4,3] := 1;
   frame[4,5] := 1;
   line := 5;
   WHILE line <= 8 DO
    BEGIN
       frame[line,4] := 1;
       line := line + 1
    END;
```

(continued)

```
        END; (* yblk *)
PROCEDURE zblk;
  BEGIN
   column := 1;
   WHILE column <=7 DO
     BEGIN
       frame[2,column] := 1;
       frame[8,column] := 1;
       column := column + 1
     END;
   line := 7;
   column := 2;
   WHILE column <= 6 DO
     BEGIN
       frame[line,column] := 1;
       column := column + 1;
       line := line - 1
     END;
END; (* zblk *)

BEGIN (* main body of selectletter *)
 IF (l = 'a') OR (l = 'A')
   THEN ablk
   ELSE IF (l = 'b') OR (l = 'B')
    THEN bblk
    ELSE IF (l='c') OR (l='C')
     THEN cblk
     ELSE IF (l='d') OR (l='D')
      THEN dblk
      ELSE IF (l= 'e') OR (l= 'E')
       THEN  eblk
       ELSE IF (l='f') OR (l='F')
        THEN fblk
        ELSE IF (l='g') OR (l='G')
         THEN gblk
         ELSE IF (l='h') OR (l='H')
          THEN hblk
          ELSE IF (l='i') OR (l='I')
           THEN iblk
           ELSE IF (l='j') OR (l='J')
            THEN jblk
            ELSE IF (l='k') OR (l='K')
             THEN kblk
             ELSE IF (l='l') OR (l='L')
              THEN lblk
              ELSE IF (l='m') OR (l='M')
               THEN mblk
               ELSE IF (l='n') OR (l='N')
                THEN nblk
                ELSE IF (l= 'o') OR (l= 'O')
                 THEN oblk
                 ELSE IF (l='p') OR (l='P')
                  THEN pblk
                  ELSE IF (l='q') OR (l='Q')
                   THEN qblk
                   ELSE If (l='r') OR (l='R')
                    THEN rblk
                    ELSE If (l='s') OR (l='S')
                     THEN sblk
                     ELSE IF (l= 't') OR (l= 'T')
                      THEN tblk
                      ELSE If (l='u') OR (l='U')
                       THEN ublk
```

Fig. P11.6 (continued)

```
                                     ELSE IF (l='v') OR (l='V')
                                      THEN vblk
                                       ELSE IF (l='w') OR (l='W')
                                        THEN wblk
                                         ELSE IF (l='x') OR (l='X')
                                          THEN xblk

                                          ELSE IF (l='y') OR (l='Y')
                                           THEN yblk
                                            ELSE IF (l='z') OR (l='Z')
                                             THEN zblk
                                             ELSE;
    END; (* selectletter *)

PROCEDURE transferletter;
  BEGIN
    line := 1;
    WHILE line <= 9 DO
      BEGIN
        column := 1;
        WHILE column <= 7 DO
          BEGIN
            screen[1+line,p+((p-1)*7)+column]
                    := frame[line,column];
            column := column + 1
          END;
        line := line + 1
      END;
  END;  (*transferletter *)

PROCEDURE displayscreen;
  BEGIN
    line := 1;
    WRITELN(ESC, 'H');    (* Force cursor to upper left corner *)
    WHILE line <= 18 DO
      BEGIN
        column := 2;
        (* column set 2 keeps display width total to 80 *)
        (* throwing away only the left 1-column border strip *)
        (* Can be reset to 1 for wider screen or for paper *)
        WHILE column <= 81 DO
          BEGIN
            IF screen[line,column] = 1
                THEN WRITE('0')
                ELSE WRITE(' ');
            column := column + 1
          END;
        WRITELN;
        line := line + 1
      END;
  END; (* displayscreen *)

 BEGIN (* main body of letterdisplayer *)
   initframe;
   selectletter;
   transferletter;
   displayscreen;
 END; (* letterdisplayer *)

PROCEDURE clearscreen;
  BEGIN
    line := 1;
    WHILE line <= 24 DO
```

(continued)

```
              BEGIN
                column := 1;
                WHILE column <= 81 DO
                  BEGIN
                    screen[line,column] := 0;
                    column := column + 1
                  END;
                line := line + 1
              END;
    END; (* clearscreen *)
PROCEDURE confirmquit;
    BEGIN
       WRITELN('An  @  has been entered.');
       WRITELN('To confirm and quit, type another @');
       WRITELN('To deny and continue, type anything else.');
       READLN; READ(quitsign)
    END; (* confirmquit *)

PROCEDURE displayname;
    BEGIN
       clearscreen;
       position := 1;
       WHILE position <= 10 DO
         BEGIN
           letter := name[position];
           letterdisplayer(letter,position);
           position := position + 1
         END;
       pause
    END; (* displayname *)

PROCEDURE displayreversedname;
    BEGIN
       clearscreen;
       position := 10;
       WHILE position >= 1 DO
         BEGIN
           letter := name[11 - position];
           letterdisplayer(letter,position);
           position := position - 1
         END;
      pause
    END; (* displayreversedname *)

PROCEDURE pause;
    BEGIN
      k := 1;
      WHILE  k < 1000 DO
        BEGIN
          k := k + 1
        END;
    END; (* pause *)

PROCEDURE do3displays;
    BEGIN
       displayname;
       displayreversedname;
       displayname
    END; (* do3displays *)

PROCEDURE solicitname;
    BEGIN
      WRITELN(' What''s your name?');
      WRITELN('If you type it in, I''ll show it to you..');
      WRITELN('Press the RETURN key after each letter you type.');
      WRITELN('Type a period ( . ) to end your name.')
    END; (* solicitname *)
```

Fig. P11.6 (continued)

```
PROCEDURE takename;
   BEGIN
     k := 1;
     WHILE k <= 10 DO
       BEGIN
         name[k] := ' ';
         k := k + 1
       END;
     k := 1;
     nameend := 'N';
     WHILE (k <= 10) and (nameend = 'N') DO
       BEGIN
         READLN; READ(name[k]);
         IF name[k] = '.' THEN nameend := 'Y';
         IF name[k] = '@'
           THEN
             BEGIN
               nameend := 'Y';
               quitsign := '@'
             END;
         k := k + 1
       END;
   END; (* takename *)

BEGIN (* main body of cll *)
   ESC := chr(33B);      (* Loads code for ESCAPE into ESC  *)
   quitsign := ' ';
   WHILE quitsign <> '@' DO
     BEGIN
       solicitname;
       takename;
       IF quitsign = '@'
         THEN confirmquit
         ELSE do3displays
     END;
END. (* program cll *)
```

Fig. P11.6 (continued)

Note the following.

1. The external assignment to deliver the characters to be displayed (1's or 0's in the FPL original) transmits 0's to form the letter and blanks to form the background. (See displayscreen.)

2. The second line in displayscreen is the external assignment to cause screen reuse.

WRITELN(ESC, 'H');

The special message (the contents of ESC plus the letter H) forces the very next item to be displayed in the upper left-hand corner of the screen. The appropriate contents for ESC are assigned in

ESC : = chr(33B);

the first assignment in main line of the program (the tenth line from the END).

This is an example of a command to the screen device, according to manufacturer's specifications. It is peculiar to a particular display terminal. To use this program, you should look up the specification for controlling the next point of display on your terminal and substitute it for the ESC and 'H'. It may require something as complex as this, or they may require something simpler such as the citation of a key word like HOME.

Private Practice Pascal

PP11.11 Create one or more toy programs in your version of Pascal to experiment with controlling your display screen. In particular, discover how to clear the screen, how to direct the display to next begin in the upper left-hand corner of the screen, and how to direct the display to next begin at some specific point other than that upper corner (i.e., line 13, column 8)

PP11.12 Enter the complete program and parametric block from Fig. P11.6 into your computer and run the system.

PP11.13 Use your work on the number display program to produce a Pascal translation of (P11.11).

PP11.14 Use your work on (P11.13) to produce a Pascal program that centers the name displays. Run the result on your computer.

PP11.15 Translate your modified program from (P11.15) into Pascal and run the results on your computer.

PP11.16 Translate your new version (P11.16) of SELECT_LETTER into Pascal, substitute it for the version shown in Fig. P11.6, and run the result on your computer. Insert a counter to demonstrate the number of searches necessary to identify a particular letter.

PP11.17 Using your work on two different sizes of displays (P11.3) and (P11.4), modify your Pascal version of the number display program so that it allows the user to choose one of two sizes for the displayed numbers.

Dividing the Labor– Independent Parametric Blocks

INTRODUCTION

We close our presentation of blocks by introducing the independent parametric block. It is independent in the sense that it declares its own datanames and therefore, apart from parameters, uses storage locations independent of those used by any program that calls it. This has two very significant benefits.

First, software design and construction can be simplified, with the resulting software easier to read. What might otherwise be conceived of as one large program can instead be designed as a much smaller program and one or more independent parametric blocks called by that smaller program. The work of creating, testing, and implementing can then be conveniently divided among two or more programmers without requiring them to communicate endlessly with each other about the details each is developing. Moreover, what they produce is likely to be more comprehensible than the alternative single program could have been.

Second, a block of general utility can be created in a form that makes it callable by any program needing such a utility. For example, had LETTER _DISPLAYER been built as an independent block, it would be callable by any program that wanted to display letters in that fashion. The calling program would need only to know the name LETTER_DISPLAYER and the number and characteristics of the parameters expected.

THE CONTEXT:
ANIMATING THE CHILDREN'S NAME DISPLAY

To illustrate how independent blocks provide these benefits, we will create an animated name display. Its creation will serve the useful secondary purpose of introducing animation.

Like the name displayer in Chapter Eleven, this name animator will solicit and display children's names and will include a means for the supervisor to terminate the activity at will. The screen size (11 × 81), frame size (9 × 7), and representation of letter patterns (1's and 0's) all remain the same. However, instead of doing the triple display (name, reversed name, name), the name will be "marched" across the screen letter by letter until the whole name is on display against the right margin. Figure 12.1 illustrates the 19 displays required to march the name AL. The "marching" effect would be generated by the replacement of one display by the next.

First we must decide how best to divide the work of creating this name animator; afterward we will actually create it.

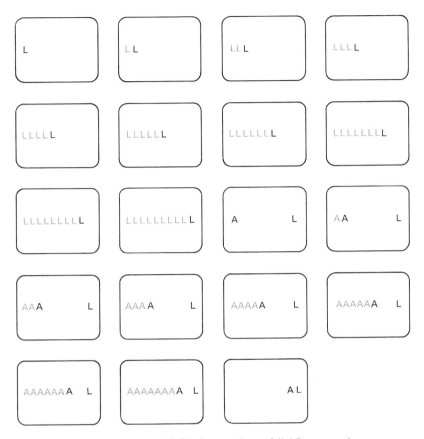

Fig. 12.1 The 19 sequential displays to "march" AL across the screen.

DETERMINING A GOOD DIVISION OF LABOR

An ideal division of labor distributes the work evenly among programmers and assigns each task to the individual or team best suited to carry it out. Such distribution and assignment involves several things to even approximate this ideal.

General Considerations

Experience suggests some simple guidelines for arriving at a suitable division of labor on a software project. A good division should (1) reflect the natural structure of the proposed solution, (2) capitalize upon the availability of programmers, and (3) minimize interunit communication. To use these guidelines, we must answer three questions. What structure will the name animator have? What programming talent will be available to work on the name animator? What information will be shared among its parts?

What is the structure of the name animator? The name display program suggests much of it: soliciting and taking in the name, providing a quit mechanism, and so forth. What that program does not tell us is the structure of the display marching. To make any comprehensive judgment about structure, we must know that as well. Once we do, we can return to the questions of programmer availability and interunit communication. To form a reasonable idea of the structure of the display marching, we must episodically outline it.

Assessing the Unknown: Outlining the Animation Process

Let's consider only the rightmost letter in the name. It must successively occupy each of the ten positions. A first draft of the FPL to do this is shown in Fig. 12.2

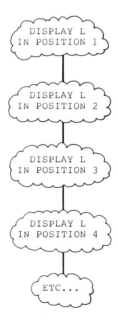

Fig. 12.2 First draft of display marching.

We could refine each episode as in Fig. 12.3. However, repeating the same process would not produce the required second display, even when the position number is changed to 2.

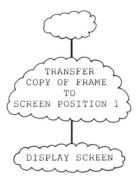

Fig. 12.3 Refinement of first episode.

The screen would instead display

LL∧∧∧∧∧∧∧∧

because the first L loaded would still be in place in the screen array. To produce the required

∧L∧∧∧∧∧∧∧∧

we must *erase* the first L *before* displaying the screen a second time. We need the approach suggested in Fig. 12.4.

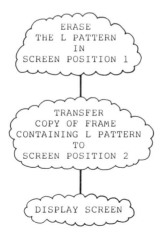

Fig. 12.4 Revised L displayer.

A simple way to erase the previous letter pattern would be to copy all 0's into the frame location where the L pattern is. This could be done by simply copying the equivalent of a frame of all 0's into that location, or by setting up a second frame of all 0's and copying it into the location. Figure 12.5 suggests the process for producing the display of L in the second screen position. It assumes a prior display produced by the process suggested in Fig. 12.3.

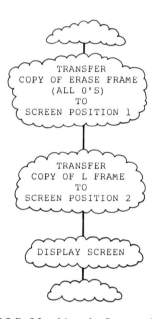

Fig. 12.5 Marching the L to position 2.

To march the L clear across the screen, we need the process represented in Fig. 12.6: display the first L (no prior erasure necessary), then erase and display nine times, incrementing the position each time.

The process for the second letter, A, would be similar. In fact, with slight modification, this process could be used repeatedly to handle an entire name. Modification would be required to avoid marching all letters to the tenth position where each would obliterate its predecessor. (The second letter should be marched only to the ninth position, the third letter to the eighth, and so on.)

From prior experience with blocks like TRANSFER_LETTER and DISPLAY_SCREEN, we can guess how much work the unrefined episodes represent and approximately what will be involved in creating them. Now we can confidently guess the natural structure of the entire name animator and make the division decision.

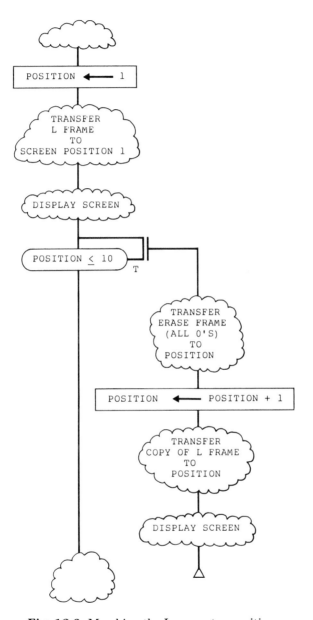

Fig. 12.6 Marching the L across ten positions.

The Division: (1) Main Program
and (2) Independent Parametric Block

From our episodic outline, we see that the overall structure of the animator will be similar to the name displayer from Chapter Eleven. Figure 12.6 suggests that the work to create this animator will be approximately equal to that required for the name displayer. Because the name displayer rather naturally divided into two parts, a two-part division seems natural here too, but let's consider the remaining issues before making the decision final.

Availability of programming talent is a given. Let's arbitrarily assume two able programmers are available for this job. This would be as realistic as any other assumption and would match the two-part division proposed. Let the division be as follows: *Programmer A* creates an independent parametric block to march the letters across the screen; *Programmer B* creates everything else. If this division requires relatively minimal communication between the parts, we'll adopt it; if not, we'll try something else.

This division *does* seem to minimize interunit communication—only the letters and their screen destinations are passed between program and parametric block. Neither needs know anything of the other's datanames or design details. They need only know how the name is to be passed. This settles the division question. Now we can produce the software.

In this particular case of course we began the structural estimation with extended insight about the problem because of our familiarity with the similar name display program. Normally we would have known less initially about the problem and accordingly would have had to do more episodic sketching and rough structural estimation. As it was, we could move rapidly because of our earlier experience with the related display problem. When such relevant prior experience is lacking, more preliminary work is essential.

Private Practice

P12.1   *Without turning back to Chapter Eleven,* sketch out the rest of the program—soliciting the name, handling the quitting, etc. In terms of the work required to implement it, does this appear to be roughly equivalent to the work represented by implementing the details suggested in Fig. 12.6?

P12.2   Consider the survey analysis program and indicate what a good division of labor might be if that project were to be implemented by two programmers.

P 12.3   Given our preliminary estimations and your knowledge of the name displayer software in Chapter Eleven, suggest how you would most effectively deploy *three* programmers to create the name animator software.

THE NAME-ANIMATION SYSTEM

The collection of details needed to animate the name display can appropriately be described as a "system." It is complex enough to require a division of labor and to rely heavily on software work already done for another project (the original name display).

Programmer B's Work: The Main Program

What Programmer B must create is only a variation on the main program we developed in Chapter Eleven. The variant parts are shown in Figs. 12.7 and 12.8.

The differences are minor. Both programs pass the letter to a parametric display block but this one passes the letter's final screen position rather than the letter's only position. This program determines the number of characters in the solicited name and calls the parametric block that number of times (Fig. 12.8); the earlier program always called its parametric display block ten times per cycle regardless of name length.

In this version of TAKE_NAME, two additional assignments appear to record the name's length. Figure 12.8 shows the WHILE structure that uses that length to call LETTER_MARCHER just the right number of times—once for each letter in the name.

The call to the independent block looks no different from a call to an ordinary parametric block; the difference appears in the details. We will see it as we examine Programmer A's work.

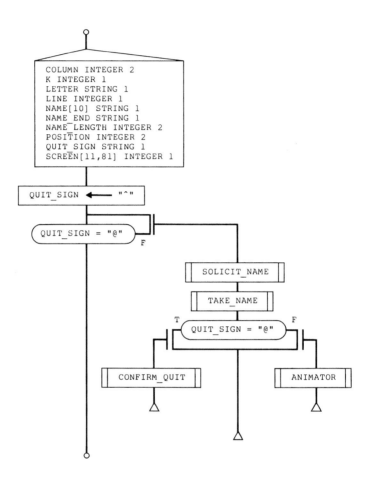

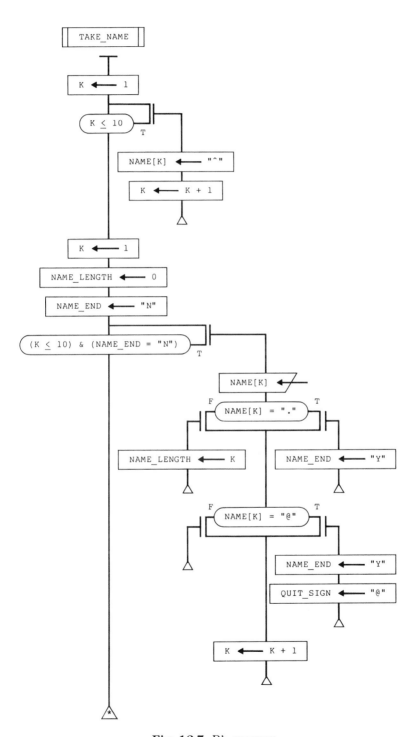

Fig. 12.7 B's program.

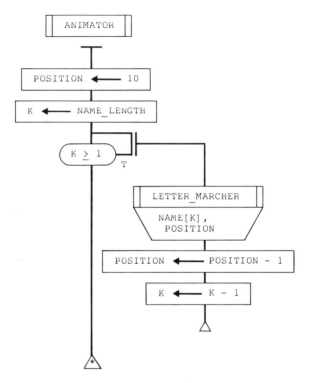

Fig. 12.8 Replacement for DO_3_DISPLAYS.

Programmer A's Work: The Independent Parametric Block

Now assuming the role of Programmer A, let's develop the animating block. Our earlier episodic outlining produced a first draft in Fig. 12.6. Figure 12.9 is a second draft, adding the separate set of declarations that give rise to the parametric block's independence.

We can now refine it further without worrying about inadvertently duplicating datanames from B's program. Because of the declarations, B's datanames refer to distinctly different storage locations. For example, POSITION occurs both in A's independent block and in B's program, yet the computer will not confuse them. The redeclaration in A's block means this second POSITION refers to an entirely different storage location.

This separation of storage is a very powerful benefit. The programmer can select datanames for their aptness rather than whether they have been used by another programmer elsewhere in the system. Thus the entire effort of checking to avoid duplication of datanames is eliminated. This not only increases the descriptiveness of each part of the system but it also frees the programmer to focus on more substantive issues, increasing the likelihood of a better block or program being produced.

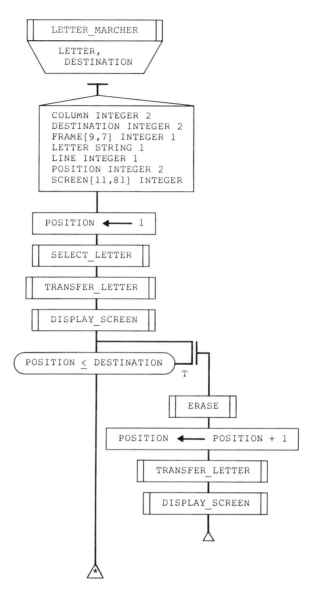

Fig. 12.9 The independent block to march a letter.

The subsidiary blocks are either duplicates or derivatives of blocks developed earlier. Two exact duplicates are not reproduced here: SELECT _LETTER (Fig. 11.6) and DISPLAY_SCREEN (Fig. 11.9). Both TRANSFER _LETTER and ERASE spring from the same source (Fig. 11.9); the first is an exact duplicate of that source, the second, a modification. TRANSFER_ LET-

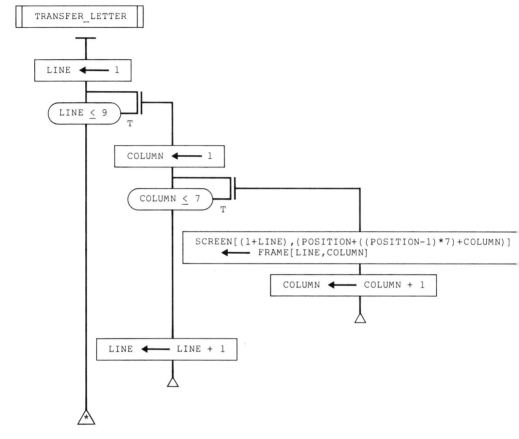

Fig. 12.10 Letter transfer.

TER (Fig. 12.10) copies a 9 × 7 frame to the screen array; ERASE (Fig. 12.11) merely uses the dimensionality (9 × 7) to copy 0's into the screen at the appropriate position. (As implied earlier, ERASE could use a 9 × 7 frame loaded with 0's. Skipping the frame is just more direct.)

Note in Fig. 12.9 that POSITION is incremented *after* the call to ERASE but *before* the call to TRANSFER_LETTER. ERASE is therefore directed at the old position in SCREEN; TRANSFER_LETTER at the new.

Private Practice

P12.4   Develop the modification necessary to "jump" a letter across the screen, skipping every other position (e.g., to end in position 10 the letter begins at 2 and moves through 6 and 8; to end in 9, it begins at 1 and moves through 3, 5, and 7; and so on.

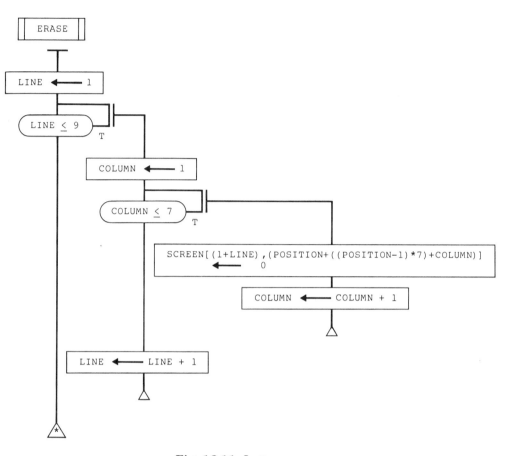

Fig. 12.11 Letter erasure.

P12.5   Develop the modification necessary to display the final name in the center of the screen rather than at its right edge.

P12.6   Develop a scheme by which three programmers could divide work in creating the survey analysis program.

P12.7   Consider the following problem situation and indicate how the work might be equally divided among three programmers charged with developing the system.

A program is needed to harmonize melodies. It must be able to accept a melody up to 2000 symbols long and print out a four-voice harmonization. It must accept a number of special symbols transmitted from a special keyboard for entering music. The symbols it recognizes should include one for each of 50 adjacent semitones and 25 special characters for duration, volume, decay, timbre, and so forth.

IMPROVEMENTS TO THE SYSTEM

No system ever seems to be complete to everyone's satisfaction. Some people always recommend changes that would improve the system from their perspective and, sooner or later, some such recommendations are implemented. Two improvements to the name animation system illustrate.

Smoothing the Motion

LETTER_MARCHER will create a "jerky" march because it steps the image an entire letter's width at one time, taking only ten steps to move a letter across the entire screen. The motion would appear smoother if the distance per move were decreased and the number of moves increased. How wide should the new move size be? half a letter? a quarter letter? (The first would take 20 steps to march the letter across the entire screen; the second, 40.)

We arbitrarily choose the smallest move this screen allows, a single screen column. Figure 12.12 suggests the difference this will make. The L is shown for both stepping alternatives, position and column, for each of the first two locations. The first 20 columns for each alternative are shown, numbered at the top.

Using single-column stepping, the frame is copied into 73 distinct screen locations. For the leftmost, column 1 of FRAME is copied into column 2 of SCREEN (old position 1); for the rightmost, into column 74 (old position 10).

```
                    Step by Position              Step by Column
     Column      00000000011111111112         00000000011111111112
     Number      12345678901234567890         12345678901234567890

                 00000000000000000000         00000000000000000000
                 01000000000000000000         01000000000000000000
                 01000000000000000000         01000000000000000000
     Initial     01000000000000000000         01000000000000000000
     Location    01000000000000000000         01000000000000000000
                 01000000000000000000         01000000000000000000
                 01000000000000000000         01000000000000000000
                 01111111000000000000         01111111000000000000
                 00000000000000000000         00000000000000000000

                 00000000000000000000         00000000000000000000
                 00000000100000000000         00100000000000000000
                 00000000100000000000         00100000000000000000
     One         00000000100000000000         00100000000000000000
     Step        00000000100000000000         00100000000000000000
     Later       00000000100000000000         00100000000000000000
                 00000000100000000000         00100000000000000000
                 00000000111111000000         00111111000000000000
                 00000000000000000000         00000000000000000000
```

Fig. 12.12 Step by position versus by column.

To control motion across such a many-stepped path we need the modifications included in Fig. 12.13. DESTINATION must be converted from a position number to the column number of that position's left edge. EDGE _COLUMN is the SCREEN column with which the left edge of the frame is to coincide.

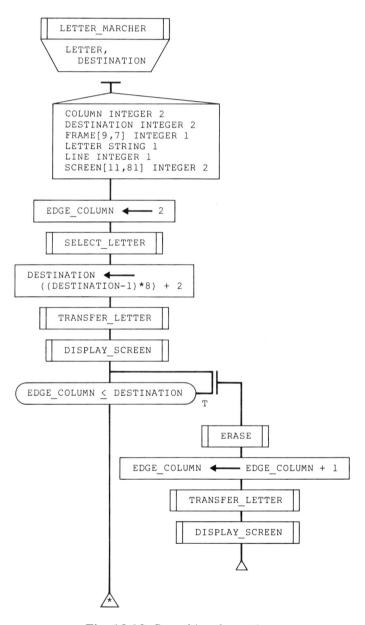

Fig. 12.13 Smoothing the motion.

Assuming the letter passed is L, the two patterns in the right column of Fig. 12.12 would be produced by the block in Fig. 12.13. The first pattern (upper right) would be produced by executing the section prior to the WHILE assertion. The second pattern (lower right) would be produced by executing the digression the first time. For the first, EDGE_COLUMN has the value 2; for the second, 3.

The DESTINATION conversion assumes a position is eight columns wide, seven for the frame, one for the border. The transfer assignment in TRANSFER_FRAME must be modified to the simpler

SCREEN [LINE + 1, COLUMN + (EDGE_COLUMN − 1)]
⟵——— FRAME [LINE, COLUMN]

and in ERASE to

SCREEN [LINE + 1, COLUMN + (EDGE_COLUMN − 1)]⟵——— 0

Private Practice

P12.8   Modify the block so that it first displays each marching letter in columns 10–16 and so that it parks the rightmost letter in columns 50–56.

P12.9   Modify the block so that it works within the margins in (P12.8) but skips every other column as it moves the letter across the screen.

P12.10   Modify the block in Fig. 12.13 so that the letter appears gradually from screen left, beginning in column 1. For example, in the first four displays, L would appear sequentially as

Display 1	Display 2	Display 3	Display 4
0000000000	0000000000	0000000000	0000000000
0000000000	0000000000	0000000000	0000000000
0000000000	0000000000	0000000000	0000000000
0000000000	0000000000	0000000000	0000000000
0000000000	0000000000	0000000000	0000000000
0000000000	0000000000	0000000000	0000000000
0000000000	0000000000	0000000000	0000000000
1000000000	1100000000	1110000000	1111000000
0000000000	0000000000	0000000000	0000000000

Adding a Background

LETTER_MARCHER moves the image across a blank screen. Moving an image across a nonblank background is far more interesting. We will close our discussion of animation by modifying LETTER_MARCHER so it can do this. Several modifications will be required, including a change in parameters passed. Because any figure other than a letter could be the manipulated the same way, in the interest of generality, we will henceforth use the term "image" interchangeably with "letter."

For illustration, let's use a simple striped curtain as background. The FPL to generate it appears in Fig. 12.14. Figure 12.15 (b) represents the data values for the curtain as they would be stored in SCREEN (only a portion of the screen is actually shown). One stripe is stored as 3's in the array; the other as 4's. The values might represent colors or shades, depending on the actual screen in use. One possible display, which appears in Fig. 12.17(c), is labeled "Actual Display." It illustrates the letter L displayed against a striped background formed from #'s and +'s.

LETTER_MARCHER will have to manipulate the background. However, because the *nature* of the background is immaterial to LETTER_MARCHER, that block should not be charged with generating the background. CURTAIN _MAKER must therefore be called from the main program, through the block ANIMATOR. (This is suggested in Fig. 12.14, upper right.) Because the background will be loaded into the screen array *outside* LETTER _MARCHER, the entire array will have to be passed parametrically into the block. Only if it is can LETTER_MARCHER have the access it must have to the background.

Figures 12.15 through 12.17 represent stages of moving the image one step against a background. Two frames are required, one (Copy 2) for combining image and background, and another (Copy 1) for restoring the background before the next step. The FPL to accomplish this appears in Figs. 12.18 through 12.22.

The work represented by Fig. 12.15 through 12.17 is accomplished in that order by one execution of the WHILE digression in Fig. 12.18. All this represents one cycle. This cycle is repeated until the image has been moved to its appropriate parking place.

RESTORE_BACKGROUND (Fig. 12.19) performs the work depicted in Fig. 12.15, to begin the cycle. The frame containing the unaltered background (Copy 1) is copied back into SCREEN, restoring the original background intact.

With only background in SCREEN, COPY_2_FRAMES-_NEXT_BKGD (Fig. 12.20) makes two copies of that portion of the background where the image is slated to go next (Fig. 12.16). Copy 1 is preserved unaltered, to be used later as an eraser; Copy 2 is used immediately to integrate image and background.

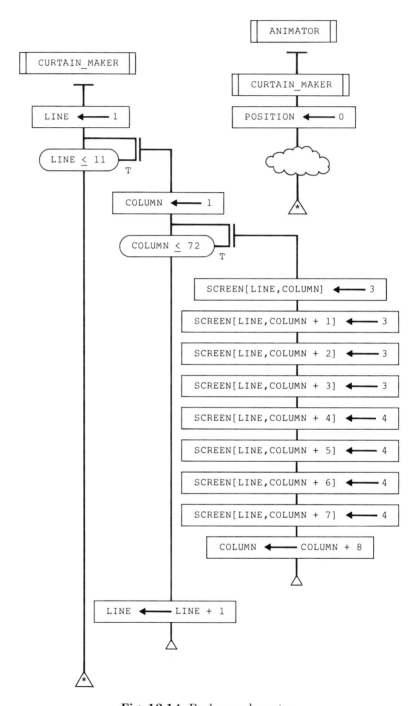

Fig. 12.14 Background creator.

```
3334444    1334444
3334444    1334444
3334444    1334444
3334444    1334444
3334444    1334444
3334444    1334444
3334444    1334444
3334444    1334444
3334444    1111111
Copy 1     Copy 2
```

(a)

```
33334444333334444433333444443333444443
31334444333334444433333444443333444443
31334444333334444433333444443333444443
31334444333334444433333444443333444443
31334444333334444433333444443333444443
31334444333334444433333444443333444443
31334444333334444433333444443333444443
31334444333334444433333444443333444443
31334444333334444433333444443333444443
31111111333334444433333444443333444443
33334444333334444433333444443333444443
            S  C  R  E  E  N
```

```
33334444333334444433333444443333444443
33334444333334444433333444443333444443
33334444333334444433333444443333444443
33334444333334444433333444443333444443
33334444333334444433333444443333444443
33334444333334444433333444443333444443
33334444333334444433333444443333444443
33334444333334444433333444443333444443
33334444333334444433333444443333444443
33334444333334444433333444443333444443
33334444333334444433333444443333444443
```

(b)

```
            S  C  R  E  E  N
```

Fig. 12.15 Restoring the background.

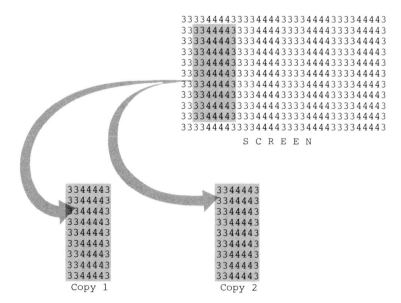

```
33334444333334444433333444443333444443
33334444333334444433333444443333444443
33334444333334444433333444443333444443
33334444333334444433333444443333444443
33334444333334444433333444443333444443
33334444333334444433333444443333444443
33334444333334444433333444443333444443
33334444333334444433333444443333444443
33334444333334444433333444443333444443
33334444333334444433333444443333444443
33334444333334444433333444443333444443
            S  C  R  E  E  N
```

```
3344443    3344443
3344443    3344443
3344443    3344443
3344443    3344443
3344443    3344443
3344443    3344443
3344443    3344443
3344443    3344443
3344443    3344443
Copy 1     Copy  2
```

Fig. 12.16 Copying off the background.

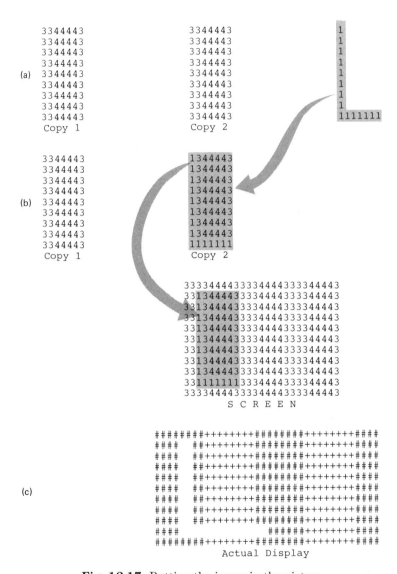

Fig. 12.17 Putting the image in the picture.

COPY_IMAGE_TO_FRAME2 (Fig. 12.21), COPY_FRAME2_TO _SCREEN (Fig. 12.21), and DISPLAY_SCREEN (not reproduced here) successively perform the work depicted in Fig. 12.17 when INSERT_ IMAGE_AND_DISPLAY is called. Copy 2 has the image copied into it, then is itself copied back into SCREEN. The screen is then displayed, producing a picture of the image in place against the screenwide background.

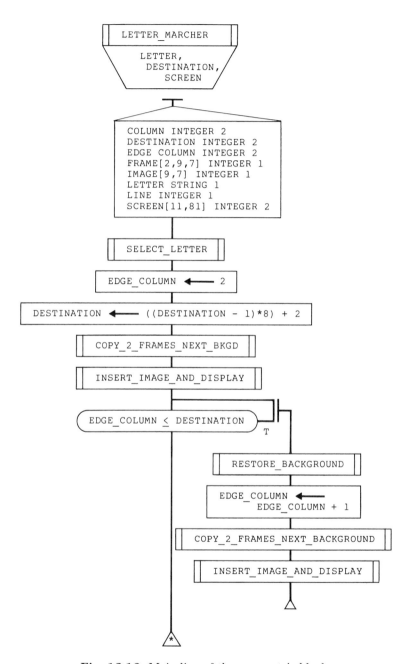

Fig. 12.18 Main line of the parametric block.

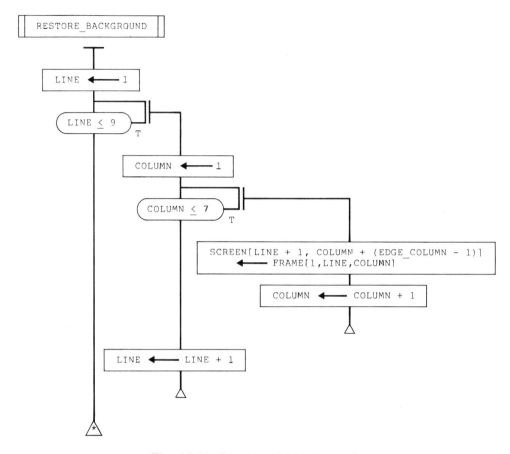

Fig. 12.19   Restoring the background.

The process of selecting the letter is the same as before. However, to simplify things, the pattern selected is loaded into a frame of its own called "IMAGE (Fig. 12.22). IMAGE is loaded with 0's by COPY_ZEROS_TO_IMAGE. Then selected cells are loaded with 1's according to the letter selected. The resulting pattern is used by COPY_IMAGE_TO_FRAME2 to produce the integrated pattern of 1's and background colors (3's and 4's) in FRAME[2, LINE, COLUMN]. All the alphabet blocks within SELECT_LETTER require modification to reflect the introduction of IMAGE. Only one (IBLK) is shown, as an example.

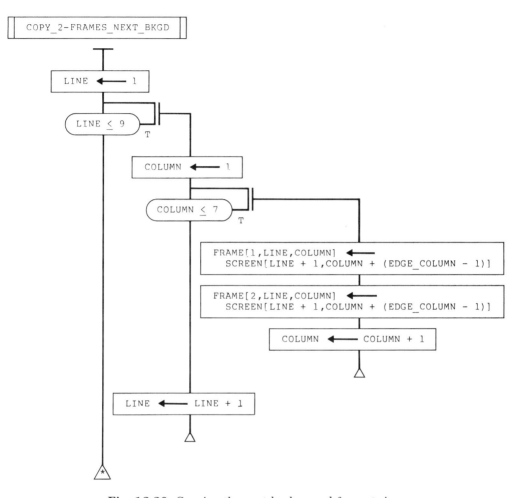

Fig. 12.20 Copying the next background frame twice.

Private Practice

P12.11   Develop a background that includes a box ("color" it 6) in place in front of the curtain, at screen center.

P12.12   Instead of a name, create the image for a solid box ("color" it 7) four columns wide and six lines high. What changes in the LETTER_MARCHER would be needed to move this box across the screen?

P12.13   Create a block similar to LETTER_MARCHER but designed to march the letters from right to left rather than left to right.

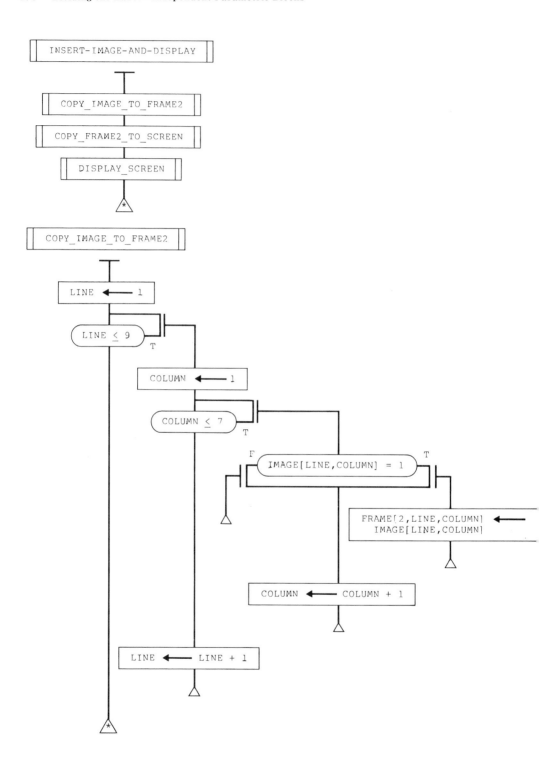

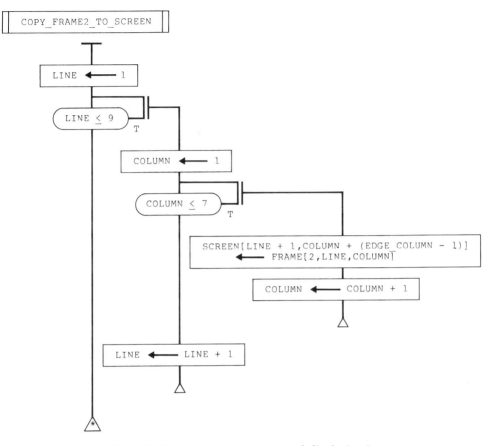

Fig. 12.21 Inserting the image and displaying it.

P 12.14   Create a block that "flies" an airplane instead of a letter of the alphabet across the screen.

P 12.15   Create a program that flies one airplane from left to right and another from right to left simultaneously. Design it so that the plane flying from right to left appears to the viewer to fly between the viewer and the plane flying from left to right.

THE FUNCTION: A VARIATION ON THE PARAMETRIC BLOCK

Many computer languages include the *function,* a variation on the parametric block that differs only in the way it returns results to the referencing program or block. Because the function is important, we must introduce it; because it so closely parallels the parametric block in many respects, our introduction will be brief. If you use a language that supports functions, you will have no difficulty learning how to create and use them.

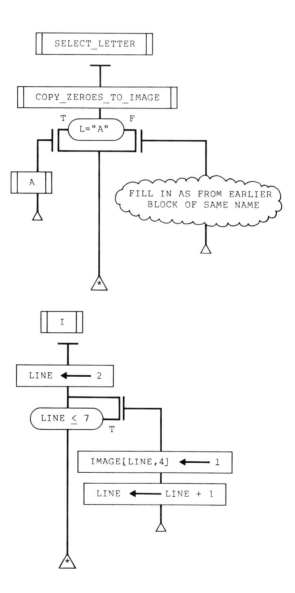

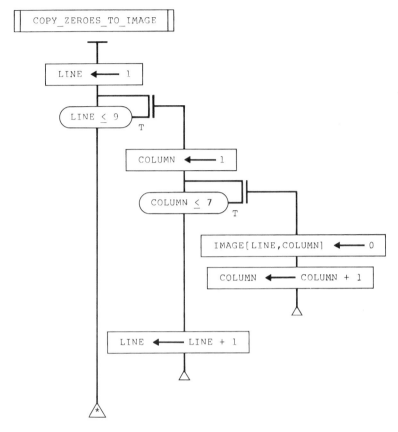

Fig. 12.22 Selecting the letter and loading it.

Like a parametric block, a function has a set of details that is executed when the function is referenced. Furthermore, both reference and details cite the function name and list its parameters. However, the result of executing the function's details is a single value, regardless of how many parameters there may be. That resulting value *replaces* the *function reference* upon completion of the execution of the details, reducing the reference itself to the status of a sort of super parameter. That value is then available just as though the function reference were a dataname. The function reference is therefore typically included within an assignment, and never stands alone like a parametric block reference. The symbol for a function reflects all this: it includes a name box and bin, but the sides of the name box slant like the bin's, reflecting the fact that a parameter-like single value is returned from the details to replace the entire function reference.

Example One: A Date Writer.

Figure 12.23 presents a program portion that references a function. The reference and the function's details are shown, as well as a trace table reflecting the pair's execution. WORD_DATE expects a six-digit numeric version of a date as parameter: two digits for month (01 to 12), two for day (01 to 31), and two for year (00 to 99). The location of this six-digit value is called NUMERIC_DATE in the referencing program; DIGITAL_DATE in the details.

Through details represented only episodically in the figure, the function develops a string version of the date and returns that string value to the point of reference. Note that the function name (WORD_DATE) is declared in both referencing program and details, and that the details include an assignment of the result (in this case, the string version of the date) to the function name. Such assignment is necessary for the result to be returned through the function name to the point of reference.

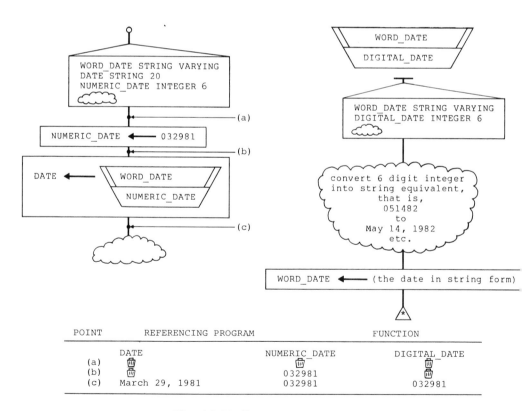

Fig. 12.23 Function with trace table.

Example Two: A Number Selector

Figure 12.24 presents a second function, designed to select the largest value among three numbers passed to it. Note several things. The function reference occurs as part of an external assignment—the last in the program. Inside the function's details, assignment of the value to be returned can be made by either of two assignments (the second EITHER). BIG is declared separately in the details and does not appear outside in the program.

Prewritten Functions

Languages that support the function usually provide a number of prewritten functions. Any function can be used merely by referencing it. For example, LENGTH might be a prewritten function that returns the length (in number of characters) of a string declared STRING VARYING, and SQRT, the square root of a number declared as FIXED 7,2. A full description of how each works and of the parameters each expects would be provided; either could be used without creating any additional details! When a suitable prewritten function does not exist, the programmer may create one by defining an appropriate set of details and referencing the details as in Figs. 12.23 and 12.24.

Private Practice

P12.16   Create the details needed to complete the function shown in Fig. 12.23. Use a trace table to check your details.

P12.17   Label the program and details shown in Fig. 12.24 with execution reference points. Create a trace table by running the program for an X, Y, and Z of 27, 458, and 309.

P12.18   Create a function called MINIMUM_OF_TWO_NUMBERS that determines which of two parameters passed to it is the smaller and returns the smaller value to the referencing program. It should return the common value if both parameters are equal in value.

P12.19   Create a function called LENGTH_OF_STRING that returns the length of a string stored in a 100-celled array. Any string stored in the array always begins in cell 1, so if the string is six characters long, cells 1 through 6 will contain nonblank values; if the string is 21 characters long, cells 1 through 21 will contain nonblank values. Your function should assume that the first blank cell it finds in the array marks the end of the string.

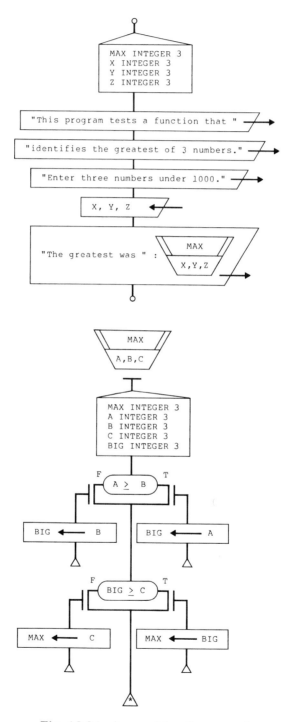

Fig. 12.24. A second function example.

P12.20   A function ZAPZIP is available to convert seven-digit zip codes to the new nine-digit form according the United States Post Office's specifications. Write a program that uses ZAPZIP to create a new version of the file ZIPPER that currently contains 173 frequently used zip codes in the seven-digit format. ZAPZIP expects only one parameter, the seven-digit code; it returns the nine-digit one.

P12.21   Assume the same file (ZIPPER) is to be converted but *you* are required to create ZAPZIP in the form of a parametric block. Create the block name boxes and indicate what parameters would be needed, including the characteristics of each. Modify your solution of (P12.20) so that it references this new block ZAPZIP rather than the old.

BASIC Interpretation of Chapter 12

THE INDEPENDENT PARAMETRIC BLOCK
AND NAME-ANIMATION SYSTEM IN BASIC

Figure B12.1 presents the translation for most of the name-animation program. Much of SELECT LETTER and all the alphabet blocks except ABLK are omitted. The missing details are identical to those in the name display translation (Fig. B11.6) except for the substitution of IMAGE (I5%) for FRAME (F2%) in the alphabet blocks. (See ABLK details.)

```
00100 REM NAME ANIMATION PROGRAM AND PARAMETRIC BLOCK
00110 REM      GRANT WILLIAMS      OCT 1981
00120 REM        MAIN PROGRAM (PROGRAMMER B)
00140 REM C1% : COLUMN INTEGER 2
00160 REM  K% : K INTEGER
00180 REM L1$ : LETTER STRING 1
00200 REM L1% : LINE INTEGER 1
00220 REM N1$(10) : NAME[10] STRING 1
00240 REM N2$ : NAME_END STRING 1
00250 REM N2% : NAME_ LENGTH INTEGER 2
00260 REM P1% : POSITION INTEGER 1
00280 REM Q1$ : QUITSIGN STRING 1
00300 REM S1%(11,81) : SCREEN[11,81] INTEGER 1
00320 REM ------------------------------------------
00340 DIM N1$(10), S1%(11,81)
00420 REM
00460 Q1$ = " "
00480 IF Q1$ = "@" GOTO 660
00500    GOSUB 1000              \ REM SOLICIT NAME
00520    GOSUB 1160              \ REM TAKE NAME
00540    IF Q1$ = "@" GOTO 600
00560       GOSUB 1640           \ REM ANIMATOR
00580       GOTO 640
00600       GOSUB 1780           \ REM CONFIRM QUIT
00620       GOTO 640
00640    GOTO 480
00660 GOTO 2520                  \ REM END OF PROGRAM
00680 REM
00700 REM ------------------------------------------
00980 REM
01000 REM             BLOCK SOLICIT NAME
01010 PRINT "^Z"        \ REM SIGNAL TO DEVICE TO CLEAR SCREEN
01020 PRINT "Hi, what's your name?"
01040 PRINT "If you type it in, I'll show it to you"
01060 PRINT "Press the RETURN key after each letter you type."
01080 PRINT "Type a period and press RETURN when you're finished."
01100 RETURN
01120 REM------------------------------------------
01140 REM
01160 REM             BLOCK TAKE NAME
01180 K% = 1
01200 IF K% > 10 GOTO 1280
01220    N1$(K%) = " "
01230
```

Fig. B12.1 Translating the name animation program.

```
01240    K% = K% + 1
01260    GOTO 1200
01280 K% = 1
01290 N2% = 0
01300 N2$ = "N"
01320 IF (K% > 10) OR (N2$ = "Y") GOTO 1580
01340 INPUT N1$(K%)
01360 IF N1$(K%) = "." GOTO 1400
01370    N2% = K%
01380    GOTO 1440
01400    N2$ = "Y"
01420    GOTO 1440
01440 IF N1$(K%) = "@" GOTO 1480
01460    GOTO 1540
01480    N2$ = "Y"
01500    Q1$ = "@"
01520    GOTO 1540
01540 K% = K% + 1
01560 GOTO 1320
01580 RETURN
01600 REM ----------------------------------------
01620 REM
01640 REM                 BLOCK ANIMATOR
01642 GOSUB 2000               \REM CURTAIN MAKER
01643 P1% = 10
01646 K% = N2%
01649 IF K% < 1 GOTO 1720
01652    CALL LETTERMARCHER(N1$(K%),P1%,S1%(,))
01655    P1% = P1% - 1
01658    K% = K% - 1
01661    GOTO 1649
01720 RETURN
01740 REM----------------------------------------
01760 REM
01780 REM              BLOCK CONFIRM QUIT
01800 PRINT "An @ has been entered."
01820 PRINT "To confirm and terminate, type another @"
01840 PRINT "To deny and continue, type anything else."
01860 INPUT Q1$
01880 RETURN
01900 REM-----------------------------------------------
01920 REM
02000 REM    BLOCK   CURTAIN MAKER
02010 L1% = 1
02020 IF L1% > 11 GOTO 2180
02030    C1% = 1
02040    IF C1% > 72 GOTO 2160
02050       S1%(L1%,C1%) = 3
02060       S1%(L1%,C1%+1) = 3
02070       S1%(L1%,C1%+2) = 3
02080       S1%(L1%,C1%+3) = 3
02090       S1%(L1%,C1%+4) = 4
02100       S1%(L1%,C1%+5) = 4
02110       S1%(L1%,C1%+6) = 4
02120       S1%(L1%,C1%+7) = 4
02130       C1% = C1% + 8
02140       GOTO 2040
02160    L1% = L1% + 1
02170    GOTO 2020
02180 RETURN
02480 REM -----------------------------------------------
02500 REM
02520 END
```

(continued)

```
02540 REM -----        END MAIN PROGRAM        -----------
02580 REM ***                                            ***
02600 REM -----    START PARAMETRIC BLOCK     -----------
02620 REM
02640 SUB LETTERMARCHER(L5$,D5%,S5%(,))
02650 REM    PROGRAMMER A    JUNE 1980
02660 REM C5% : COLUMN INTEGER 2
02665 REM D5% : DESTINATION INTEGER 2
02670 REM E5% : EDGE COLUMN INTEGER 2
02673 REM F5%(9,7) : FRAME[*,9,7] INTEGER 1 (FRAME 1)
02674 REM F6%(9,7) : FRAME[*,9,7] INTEGER 1 (FRAME 2)
02676 REM I5%(9,7) : IMAGE[9,7] INTEGER 1
02680 REM L5$ : LETTER STRING 1
02700 REM L5% : LINE INTEGER 2
02760 REM S5%(11,81) : SCREEN[11,81] INTEGER 1
02780 REM ------------------------------------------------
02785 DIM F5%(9,7), F6%(9,7), I5%(9,7)
02800 REM
02840 GOSUB 3200              \REM SELECT LETTER
02850 E5% = 2
02852 D5% = ((D5%-1)*8) + 2
02855 GOSUB 14000             \REM COPY 2 FRAMES NEXT BKGD
02960 GOSUB 15000             \REM INSERT IMAGE AND DISPLAY
02865 IF E5% > D5% GOTO 2915
02870     GOSUB 13000         \REM RESTORE BACKGROUND
02875     E5% = E5% + 1
02880     GOSUB 14000         \REM COPY 2 FRAMES NEXT BKGD
02885     GOSUB 15000         \REM INSERT IMAGE AND DISPLAY
02890     GOTO 2865
02915 GOTO  42040             \REM END PARAMETRIC BLOCK
02917 REM ------------------------------------------------
02920 REM
02940 REM           BLOCK COPY ZEROS TO IMAGE
02960 L5% = 1
02980 IF L5% > 9 GOTO 3140
03000     C5% = 1
03020     IF C5% > 7 GOTO 3100
03040         I5%(L5%,C5%) = 0
03060         C5% = C5% + 1
03080         GOTO 3020
03100     L5% = L5% + 1
03120     GOTO 2980
03140 RETURN
03160 REM ------------------------------------------------
03180 REM
03200 REM           BLOCK SELECT LETTER
03210 GOSUB 2940              \REM COPY ZEROS TO IMAGE
03220         IF (L5$ <> 'a') AND (L5$ <> 'A') GOTO 4760
03240             GOSUB 5440    \REM ABLK
03260             GOTO 4780
04000     REM          (DETAILS FOR B TO Z CHOICE MISSING)
04760                                         GOTO 4780
04780 RETURN
04840 REM ------------------------------------------------
05120 REM
05440   REM ----   ABLK
05460     L5% = 3
05480     IF L5% > 8 GOTO 5580
05500         I5%(L5%,1) = 1
05520         I5%(L5%,7) = 1
05540         L5% = L5% + 1
05560         GOTO 5480
05580     C5% = 2
```

Fig. B12.1 (continued)

```
05600    IF C5% > 6 GOTO 5700
05620        I5%(2,C5%) = 1
05640        I5%(5,C5%) = 1
05660        C5% = C5% + 1
05680        GOTO 5600
05700    RETURN
06000    REM     (ALPHABET BLOCKS  B TO Z OMITTED)
12020
12030 REM -----------------------------------------
12040 REM
13000 REM             BLOCK RESTORE BACKGROUND
13100 L5% = 1
13120 IF L5% > 9 GOTO 13280
13140    C5% = 1
13160    IF C5% >7 GOTO 13240
13180        S5%(L5%+1, C5% + (E5% - 1)) = F5%(L5%,C5%)
13200        C5% = C5% +1
13220        GOTO 13160
13240      L5% = L5% + 1
13260      GOTO 13120
13280 RETURN
13300 REM -----------------------------------------
14000 REM        BLOCK  COPY 2 FRAMES NEXT BKGD
14010 L5% = 1
14020 IF L5% > 9 GOTO 14110
14030    C5% = 1
14040    IF C5% >7 GOTO 14090
14050        F5%(L5%,C5%) = S5%(L5% + 1, C5% + (E5% - 1))
14060        F6%(L5%,C5%) = S5%(L5% + 1, C5% + (E5% - 1))
14070        C5% = C5% +1
14080        GOTO 14040
14090      L5% = L5% + 1
14100      GOTO 14020
14110 RETURN
14120 REM -----------------------------------------
14130 REM
15000 REM      BLOCK  INSERT IMAGE AND DISPLAY
15050 GOSUB 16000            \REM COPY IMAGE TO FRAME2
15100 GOSUB 17000            \REM COPY FRAME2 TO SCREEN
15150 GOSUB 18000            \REM DISPLAY SCREEN
15300 RETURN
15400 REM -----------------------------------------
16000 REM        BLOCK  COPY IMAGE TO FRAME2
16010 L5% = 1
16020 IF L5% > 9 GOTO 16130
16030    C5% = 1
16040    IF C5% >7 GOTO 16110
16050        IF I5%(L5%,C5%) = 1 GOTO 16070
16060            GOTO 16090
16070            F6%(L5%, C5%) = I5%(L5%,C5%)
16080            GOTO 16090
16090        C5% = C5% +1
16100        GOTO 16040
16110      L5% = L5% + 1
16120      GOTO 16020
16130 RETURN
16140 REM -----------------------------------------
16150 REM
17000 REM            BLOCK COPY FRAME2 TO SCREEN
17010 L5% = 1
17020 IF L5% > 9 GOTO 17100
17030    C5% = 1
17040    IF C5% >7 GOTO 17080
17050        S5%(L5% + 1, C5% + (E5% - 1)) = F6%(L5%,C5%)
```

(continued)

```
17060        C5% = C5% +1
17070        GOTO 17040
17080      L5% = L5% + 1
17090        GOTO 17020
17100 RETURN
17110 REM ------------------------------------------
17120 REM
18000 REM              BLOCK DISPLAY SCREEN
18160 PRINT "^^"
18180 L5% = 1
18200 IF L5% > 11 GOTO 18380
18220    C5% = 2
18240      IF C5% > 81 GOTO 18320
18260        IF S5%(L5%,C5%) = 1 GOTO 18275
18263          IF S5%(L5%,C5%) = 3 GOTO 18266
18264            PRINT "+";
18265            GOTO 18270
18266            PRINT "#";
18267            GOTO 18270
18270          GOTO 18280
18275          PRINT " ";
18278          GOTO 18280
18280        C5% = C5% + 1
18300        GOTO 18240
18320      PRINT
18340      L5% = L5% + 1
18360      GOTO 18200
18380 PRINT
18400 RETURN
18420 REM ------------------------------------------
42040 SUBEND
```

Fig. B12.1 (continued)

Note the following.

1. A manufacturer-supplied specification is used (in SOLICIT NAME)

01010 PRINT "∧Z" \REM SIGNAL TO DEVICE TO CLEAR SCREEN

to clear the screen before soliciting the name, and another is used (DISPLAY SCREEN)

18160 PRINT "∧∧" \REM HOME CURSOR TO UPPER LEFT CRNR

to force each screen display to begin on the top line of the screen rather than where the last display finished.

2. This version of BASIC does not support arrays with more than two dimensions so FRAME[2,9,7] is split into two associated arrays, F5% and F6%

02673 REM F5% (9,7) : FRAME[*,9,7] INTEGER 1 (FRAME 1)

02674 REM F6% (9,7) : FRAME[*,9,7] INTEGER 1 (FRAME 2)

3. The extensive declarations in LETTERMARCHER (as in LETTERDISPLAYER) indicate that all datanames in the parametric block are independent from those in the referencing program.

```
02660 REM  C5% : COLUMN INTEGER 2
02665 REM  D5% : DESTINATION INTEGER 2
02670 REM  E5% : EDGE COLUMN INTEGER 2
02673 REM  F5% (9,7)  :  FRAME[*,9,7] INTEGER 1 (FRAME 1)
02674 REM  F6% (9,7)  :  FRAME[*,9,7] INTEGER 1 (FRAME 2)
02676 REM  I5% (9,7)  :  IMAGE[9,7] INTEGER 1
02680 REM  L5$  : LETTER STRING 1
02700 REM  L5% : LINE INTEGER 2
02760 REM  S5% (11,81)  :  SCREEN[11,81] INTEGER 1
02780 REM  --------------------------------------------------------------------
02785 DIM  F5% (9,7),F6% (9,7), I5% (9,7)
```

As we mentioned in the BASIC interpretation for Chapter Eleven, many versions of BASIC do not support parametric blocks at all (independent or otherwise). This transaction is offered as a model for use with versions that do support them.

If your BASIC does not support parametric blocks, skip to the next section, The Function in BASIC. Otherwise, do the following Private Practice.

Private Practice BASIC

BP 12.1   Enter the program and block in Fig. B12.1 into your computer and run it.

BP 12.2   Add the missing portion of SELECTLETTER to your program and add the missing alphabet blocks (don't forget to substitute I5% for F2% in each), and run the complete version on your computer.

BP 12.3   Translate into BASIC the version of the animation program that included no background (Figs. 12.7 through 12.11) and run it on your computer.

BP 12.4   Modify your translation for (BP12.3) to include the changes developed for (P12.4) and run the result on your computer.

BP 12.5   Translate your solution to (P12.5) into BASIC and run it on your computer.

BP 12.6   Translate your solution to (P12.9) into BASIC, substitute it for the simpler LETTERMARCHER, and run the result on your computer.

BP 12.7   Translate your solution to (P12.10) into BASIC, substitute it for the appropriate portion of LETTERMARCHER, and run the result on your computer.

BP 12.8   Translate your solution to (P12.11) into BASIC and run it on your computer.

BP 12.9   Translate your solution to (P12.12) into BASIC and run it on your computer.

BP 12.10   Translate your solution to (P12.15) into BASIC and run it on your computer.

THE FUNCTION IN BASIC

Most versions of BASIC not only support functions but they also provide a rich variety of prewritten functions. The specifics for creating a function may vary slightly with the version (a few versions support only those functions whose details can be compressed into a single line) but the translation in Fig. B12.2 should be an adequate translation model for most cases.

FPL separates program from function naturally; the BASIC translation cannot. To aid the reader, the BASIC function's details are marked at beginning and end by REMs.

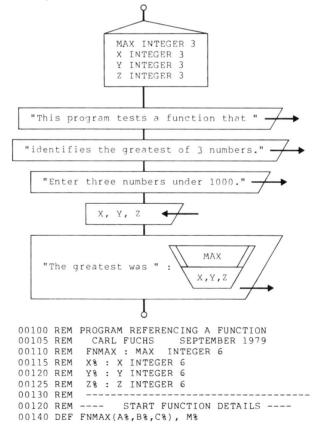

```
00100 REM PROGRAM REFERENCING A FUNCTION
00105 REM    CARL FUCHS      SEPTEMBER 1979
00110 REM    FNMAX : MAX   INTEGER 6
00115 REM    X% : X INTEGER 6
00120 REM    Y% : Y INTEGER 6
00125 REM    Z% : Z INTEGER 6
00130 REM    ----------------------------------
00120 REM    ----    START FUNCTION DETAILS ----
00140 DEF FNMAX(A%,B%,C%), M%
```

```
00142 REM FNMAX : MAX INTEGER 6
00144 REM A% : A INTEGER 6
00146 REM B% : B INTEGER 6
00148 REM C% : C INTEGER 6
00150 REM M% : BIG INTEGER 6
00160 REM ----------------------
00160 IF A% > B% GOTO 220
00180    M% = B%
00200    GOTO 260
00220    M% = A%
00240    GOTO 260
00260 IF M% > C% GOTO 320
00280    FNMAX = C%
00300    GOTO 360
00320    FNMAX = M%
00340    GOTO 360
00360 FNEND
00380 REM ---     END FUNCTION DETAILS ----
00400 REM
00420 REM ----   START MAIN PROGRAM   -----
00440 PRINT "THIS PROGRAM TESTS A FUNCTION THAT "
00460 PRINT "IDENTIFIES THE GREATEST OF 3 NUMBERS."
00480 PRINT "PLEASE ENTER 3 NUMBERS UNDER 1000."
00500 INPUT X%,Y%,Z%
00520 PRINT "THE GREATEST WAS "; FNMAX(X%,Y%,Z%)
00540 END
```

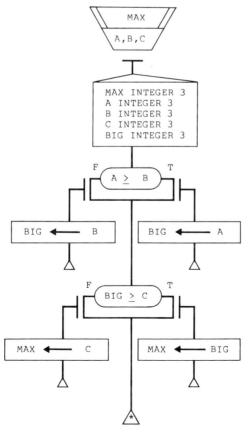

Fig. B12.2 Translating the function (Fig. 12.24).

Note the following.

1. The reference cites the function name and lists the parameters

(00520 PRINT "THE GREATEST WAS "; FNMAX(X,Y,Z)

2. The details begin with an identifying first line that cites the key word DEFFN, names the function, and lists the parameters

00140 DEF FNMAX(A,B,C), M

3. The function's details end with the key word last line

00360 FNEND

4. The variable M (BIG in FPL) is an example of a variable declared especially for use within the function. This declaration is accomplished by listing it *after* the parameters

00140 DEF FNMAX(A%,B%,C%), M%

A dataname used in a BASIC function does not refer to a separate storage location from one identically named in the main program; it refers to a unique location only if the same name is *not* used anywhere in the referencing program. *Hence the function can change values used in the main program in addition to those associated with the parameters!* If a dataname appears in both function and referencing program, and an assignment is made to that variable within the function's details, the new value will be the only one available in the referencing program under that same dataname once the function has been executed. To avoid such inadvertent alteration of values, use unique datanames throughout the function's details.

Private Practice BASIC

BP12.11 Enter the program and function shown (Fig. B12.2) into your computer and run it with various modifications to explore how functions work on your computer.

BP12.12 Experiment with storage use by adding a dataname N% to the main program and trying to PRINT it from inside the function. (Do *not* separately declare N% in the DEF line.) Run the result on your computer.

BP12.13 Modify your solution to (BP12.12) by separately declaring N% in the DEF line of the function's details. Run the result on your computer.

BP 12.14 Translate your solution to (P12.16) into BASIC and run it on your computer.

BP 12.15 Translate your solution to (P12.18) into BASIC and run it on your computer.

BP 12.16 Translate your solution to (P12.19) into BASIC and run it on your computer.

PREWRITTEN FUNCTIONS PROVIDED IN BASIC

Most versions of BASIC provide a number of easy-to-use, prewritten functions. The following Private Practice should be only the beginning of your experimentation with them.

Private Practice BASIC

BP 12.17 Using immediate mode or toy programs, experiment with the functions your version of BASIC provides for manipulating string data.

BP 12.18 Using immediate mode or toy programs, experiment with the functions your version of BASIC provides for manipulating numeric data.

BP 12.19 Using immediate mode or toy programs, experiment with the functions your version of BASIC provides for converting string representations of numeric data to numeric representations and the reverse. ("123" can be glued to "BX3" but it can not be added to 71 unless first converted to 123.)

BP 12.20 Translate your solution to (P12.20) into BASIC, add a fake function to play the role of ZAPZIP, and run the result on your computer. (The fake should be a stub that returns a nine-digit number formed by multiplying the value passed in as a parameter by 100.)

BP 12.21 Translate your solution to (P12.21) into BASIC, add a fake parametric block to play the role of ZAPZIP, and run the result on your computer. Use the same fake specification as for (BP12.20). Compare the program and result with those for (BP12.20).

Pascal Interpretation of Chapter 12

THE INDEPENDENT PARAMETRIC BLOCK
AND THE NAME-ANIMATION SYSTEM IN PASCAL

Figure P12.1 presents the translation for most for the name-animation program. Much of *selectletter* and all the alphabet blocks except *ablk* are omitted. The missing details are identical to those in the name display translation, except that the array *image* is used in place of the array *frame* throughout the alphabet blocks. The details of *ablk* illustrate that substitution.

```
PROGRAM c12(input,output);
  (* Translation of name animation program from Chapter 12 *)
    (* James Kermes        July 1981 *)
  TYPE
    screenarray = ARRAY[1..24,1..81] OF INTEGER;
  VAR
      column, k, line, n, namelength, position : INTEGER;
      letter, nameend, quitsign  : CHAR;
      ESC : CHAR;
      name : ARRAY [1..10] OF CHAR;
      screen : screenarray;

  PROCEDURE lettermarcher(VAR screen:screenarray; l:CHAR;
                              destination:INTEGER);
    VAR
      column, edgecolumn, line, position : INTEGER;
      frame : ARRAY [1..2,1..9,1..7] OF INTEGER;
      image : ARRAY [1..9,1..7] OF INTEGER;
    PROCEDURE copyzeroestoimage;
      BEGIN
      line := 1;
      WHILE line <= 9 DO
          BEGIN
            column := 1;
            WHILE column <= 7 DO
             BEGIN
               image[line,column] := 0;
               column := column + 1
             END;
            line := line + 1
          END;
      END;  (* copyzeroestoimage *)

  PROCEDURE selectletter;

    PROCEDURE ablk;
      BEGIN
        line := 3;
        WHILE line <= 8 DO
         BEGIN
           image[line,1] := 1;
           image[line,7] := 1;
           line := line + 1
         END;
```

Fig. P12.1 Translating the name animation program.

```
                        column := 2;
                        WHILE column <= 6 DO
                          BEGIN
                            image[2,column] := 1;
                            image[5,column] := 1;
                            column := column + 1
                          END;
                      END; (* ablk *)
                                  (* -------------- *)
                            (* bblk to zblk omitted *)
                                  (* -------------- *)
                BEGIN  (* selectletter *)
                 copyzeroestoimage;
                 IF (l = 'a') OR (l = 'A')
                     THEN ablk
                            (* -----------------*)
                      (* choosing b to z omitted *)
                            (* -----------------*)
                                        ELSE;
      END; (* selectletter *)

PROCEDURE restorebackground;
  BEGIN
    line := 1;
    WHILE line <= 9 DO
      BEGIN
        column := 1;
        WHILE column <= 7 DO
          BEGIN
            screen[line + 1, column + (edgecolumn - 1)]
                    := frame[1,line,column];
            column := column + 1
          END;
        line := line + 1
      END;
  END;  (* restorebackground *)

PROCEDURE copy2framesnextbkgd;
  BEGIN
    line := 1;
    WHILE line <= 9 DO
      BEGIN
        column := 1;
        WHILE column <= 7 DO
          BEGIN
            frame[1,line,column]
                := screen[line + 1, column + (edgecolumn - 1)];
            frame[2,line,column]
                := screen[line + 1, column + (edgecolumn - 1)];
            column := column + 1
          END;
        line := line + 1
      END;
  END;  (* copy2framesnextbkgd *)

PROCEDURE insertimageanddisplay;
 PROCEDURE copyimagetoframe2;
  BEGIN
    line := 1;
    WHILE line <= 9 DO
      BEGIN
        column := 1;
        WHILE column <= 7 DO
```

(continued)

```
                    BEGIN
                     IF image[line,column] = 1
                         THEN frame[2,line,column] := 1
                         ELSE;
                      column := column + 1
                    END;
                 line := line + 1
              END;
        END;  (* copyimagetoframe2 *)

     PROCEDURE copyframe2toscreen;
       BEGIN
         line := 1;
         WHILE line <= 9 DO
           BEGIN
             column := 1;
             WHILE column <= 7 DO
           BEGIN
           screen[line + 1, column + (edgecolumn - 1)]
                    := frame[2,line,column];
           column := column + 1
           END;
         line := line + 1
       END;
  END;  (* copyframe2toscreen *)

  PROCEDURE displayscreen;
    BEGIN
      line := 1;
      WRITE(ESC, 'H');  (* Begin display at screen upper left *)
      WHILE line <= 18 DO
         BEGIN
           column := 2;
           (* column set at 2 to keep display width total to 80 *)
           (* only throws  away the lefthand  border strip *)
           (* column := 1 will restore displaying of strip *)
           WHILE column <= 81 DO
              BEGIN
                IF screen[line,column] = 1
                    THEN WRITE(' ')
                    ELSE IF screen[line,column] = 3
                      THEN WRITE('#')
                      ELSE IF screen[line,column] = 4
                        THEN WRITE('@')
                        ELSE WRITE(' ');
                 column := column + 1
              END;
           WRITELN;
           line := line + 1
        END;
  END; (* displayscreen *)

  BEGIN  (* insertimageandidsplay *)
    copyimagetoframe2;
    copyframe2toscreen;
    displayscreen
  END;  (* insertimageanddisplay *)

BEGIN (* main body of lettermarcher *)
  selectletter;
  edgecolumn := 2;
  destination := ((destination - 1) * 8) + 2;
  copy2framesnextbkgd;
  insertimageanddisplay;
  WHILE edgecolumn <= destination DO
```

Fig. P12.1 (continued)

```
      BEGIN
        restorebackground;
        edgecolumn := edgecolumn + 1;
        copy2framesnextbkgd;
        insertimageanddisplay
      END;
 END; (* lettermarcher *)


PROCEDURE confirmquit;
   BEGIN
      WRITELN('An  @  has been entered.');
      WRITELN('To confirm and quit, type another @.');
      WRITELN('To deny and continue, type anything else.');
      READLN; READ(quitsign)
   END; (* confirmquit *)
PROCEDURE animator;
  PROCEDURE curtainmaker;
    BEGIN
      line := 1;
      WHILE line <=11 DO
       BEGIN
         column := 1;
         WHILE column <= 73 DO
           BEGIN
            screen[line,column] := 3;
            screen[line,column + 1] := 3;
            screen[line,column + 2] := 3;
            screen[line,column + 3] := 3;
            screen[line,column + 4] := 4;
            screen[line,column + 5] := 4;
            screen[line,column + 6] := 4;
            screen[line,column + 7] := 4;
            column := column + 8
           END;
         line := line + 1
       END;
    END; (* curtainmaker *)
   BEGIN  (* animator *)
     curtainmaker;
     position := 10;
     n := namelength;
     WHILE n >= 1 DO
      BEGIN
      lettermarcher(screen,name[n],position);
      position := position -1;
      n := n -1
      END;
   END; (* animator *)


PROCEDURE pause;
   BEGIN
     k := 1;
     WHILE  k < 1000 DO
       BEGIN
         k := k + 1
       END;
   END; (* pause *)


PROCEDURE solicitname;
   BEGIN
     WRITE(ESC, 'H');  (* Begin display at screen upper left *)
     WRITE(ESC, 'J');  (* Clear screen device for next display *)
```

(continued)

```
        WRITELN(' What''s your name?');
        WRITELN('If you type it in, I''ll show it to you.');
        WRITELN('Press the RETURN key after each letter you type.');
        WRITELN('Type a period ( . ) to end your name.')
      END; (* solicitname *)
  PROCEDURE takename;
    BEGIN
      k := 1;
      WHILE k <= 10 DO
        BEGIN
          name[k] := ' ';
          k := k + 1
        END;
      k := 1;
      namelength := 0;
      nameend := 'N';
      WHILE (k <= 10) and (nameend = 'N') DO
        BEGIN
          READLN; READ(name[k]);
          IF name[k] = '.' THEN nameend := 'Y'
                           ELSE namelength := k;
          IF name[k] = '@'
            THEN
              BEGIN
                nameend := 'Y';
                quitsign := '@'
              END;
          k := k + 1
        END;
    END; (* takename *)

BEGIN  (* cl2 - main line of program *)
  ESC := chr(33B);   (* Loads  ESC signal for screen device *)
  quitsign := ' ';
  WHILE quitsign <> '@' DO
    BEGIN
      solicitname;
      takename;
      IF quitsign = '@'
        THEN confirmquit
        ELSE animator
    END;
  END. (* cl2 *)
```

Fig. P12.1 (continued)

Note the following.

1. Because both program and block must manipulate the values in *screen,* that array must be passed as a VARiable parameter

> PROCEDURE lettermarcher(*VAR screen:screenarray;* 1:CHAR; destination:INTEGER);

Because the value of *l* and *destination* used in the main program do not in any way depend on changes in either made by the parametric block, they can be passed as regular parameters.

2. The entire screen array must be passed but Pascal does not allow the dimensionality to be included in the parameter list. It requires the dimensions of any entire array being passed to be established indirectly, through a TYPE section, prior to the VAR.

> TYPE
>   screenarray = ARRAY[1 .. 24,1 .. 81] OF INTEGER;

The total size of the array is then passed by citing this TYPEd equivalent in the parameter list

> PROCEDURE lettermarcher(VAR screen:*screenarray;* 1:CHAR; destination:INTEGER);

This indirectness is unnecessary if only a particular element of an array is to be used as a parameter; if the entire array is to be passed, though, its dimensions may not be cited directly in the parameter list and can be established only through use of the TYPE section.

3. A manufacturer-specified device command is used (in SOLICIT NAME)

> WRITE(ESC, 'J'); (* Clear screen device for next display *)

to clear the screen before soliciting the name, and another (in DISPLAY SCREEN).

> WRITE(ESC, 'H'); (* Begin display at screen upper left *)

to force each screen display to begin on the top line of the screen rather than where the last display finished.

Private Practice Pascal

PP12.1   Modify the communication to the screen device to suit your situation (commands may differ from ESC, H, and J), enter the program and block in Fig. P12.1 into your computer, and run it.

PP12.2   To your program, add the missing portion of *selectletter* and the missing alphabet blocks, and run the complete version on your computer. (Don't forget to replace *frame* by *image* wherever it occurs in the alphabet blocks!)

PP12.3   Translate into Pascal the version of the animation program that included no background (Figs. 12.7 through 12.11) and run it on your computer.

PP12.4   Modify your translation for (PP12.3) to include the changes developed for (P12.4) and run the result on your computer.

PP12.5   Translate your solution to (P12.5) into Pascal and run it on your computer.

PP12.6   Translate your solution to (P12.9) into Pascal, substitute it for the simpler *lettermarcher,* and run the result on your computer.

PP12.7   Translate your solution to (P12.10) into Pascal, substitute it for the appropriate portion of *lettermarcher,* and run the result on your computer.

PP12.8   Translate your solution to (P12.11) into Pascal and run it on your computer.

PP12.9   Translate your solution to (P12.12) into Pascal and run it on your computer.

PP12.10   Translate your solution to (P12.15) into Pascal and run it on your computer.

THE FUNCTION IN PASCAL

The various implementations of Pascal support the creation of functions and provide a number of prewritten functions which can be used merely by referencing them. Figure P12.2 provides a model translation of a programmer created function.

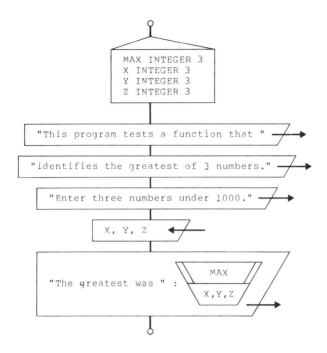

```
PROGRAM maxnum(input,output);
    (* Program to test a number selecting function *)
      (* John Young     October 1980   *)
VAR
 x,y,z : INTEGER;
FUNCTION max(a:INTEGER; b:INTEGER; c:INTEGER):INTEGER;
 VAR
  big : INTEGER;
  BEGIN    (* max *)
    IF a >= b
     THEN big := a
     ELSE big := b;
    IF big >= c
     THEN max := big
     ELSE max := c;
  END; (* max *)
  BEGIN    (* maxnum *)
   WRITELN('This program tests a function that');
   WRITELN('identifies the greatest of 3 numbers.');
   WRITELN('Enter 3 integers under 1000:');
   READLN;READ(x,y,z);
   WRITELN('The greatest was ',max(x,y,z):3);
  END.   (* maxnum *)
```
(continued)

Fig. P12.2 Translating the function (Fig. 12.24).

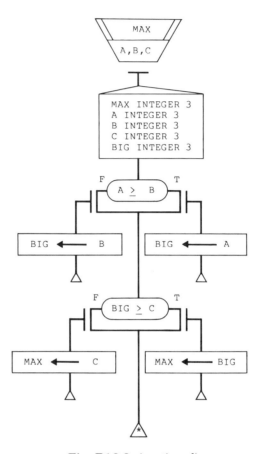

Fig. P12.2 (continued)

Note the following.

1. The reference cites the function name and lists the parameters

WRITELN('The greatest was,' *max(x,y,z)*:3);

2. The details begin with a key word (FUNCTION) first line that names the function,

FUNCTION *max*

lists each parameter and its type,

FUNCTION max(*a:INTEGER; b:INTEGER; c:INTEGER*):INTEGER;

and indicates the TYPE of the value to be returned.

FUNCTION max(a:INTEGER; b:INTEGER; c:INTEGER):*INTEGER;*

3. The function's details end with the key word last line, trailing the name as a comment

END; (* max *)

Any dataname declared in the function's VAR section refers to a storage location different from any known in the referencing program regardless of dataname similarities. Any dataname used in the function but not there declared and not a parameter must refer to a storage location named in the referencing program. *Hence the function can change values used in the main program in addition to those associated with the parameters!* If a dataname appears in both function and referencing program, and an assignment is made to that variable within the function's details, the new value will be the one available in the referencing program under that same dataname after the function has been executed. To avoid such inadvertent alteration of values, declare in the function's VAR section all datanames used in the function's details.

Private Practice Pascal

PP12.11 Enter the Pascal version of the program and function in Fig. P12.2 into your computer and run it with various modifications to explore how functions work on your computer.

PP12.12 Experiment with storage used by declaring

dummy : INTEGER;·

in the main VAR section, assigning it the value 13 in the main program, but WRITEing it from *inside* the function.

PP12.13 Modify your solution to (PP12.12) by separately declaring *dummy* in the function's VAR section as well. Run the result on your computer.

PP12.14 Translate your solution to (P12.16) into Pascal and run it on your computer.

PP12.15 Translate your solution to (P12.18) into Pascal and run it on your computer.

PP12.16 Translate your solution to (P12.19) into Pascal and run it on your computer.

PREWRITTEN FUNCTIONS PROVIDED IN PASCAL

Most versions of Pascal provide a number of easy-to-use, prewritten functions. The following Private Practice should be only the beginning of your experimentation with them.

Private Practice Pascal

PP 12.17 Using toy programs, experiment with the functions your version of Pascal provides for manipulating string data.

PP 12.18 Using toy programs, experiment with the functions your version of Pascal provides for manipulating numeric data.

PP 12.19 Using toy programs, experiment with the functions your version of Pascal provides for converting string representations of numeric data to numeric representations and the reverse. ("123" can be concatenated to "BX3" but it cannot be *added* to 71 unless first converted to 123.)

PP 12.20 Translate your solution to (P12.20) into Pascal, add a stub function to play the role of ZAPZIP, and run the result on your computer. The stub should return a nine-digit number arrived at by multiplying the parametric value received by 100.

PP 12.21 Translate your solution to (P12.21) into Pascal, add a stub parametric block to play the role of ZAPZIP, and run the result on your computer. Use the same stub specification as for (PP12.20). Compare the program and result with those for (PP12.20).

Accumulate   To add together two or more values to arrive at a total.

Algorithm   A procedure, formula, or set of formulas.

Alpha   Data whose value can best be expressed as a string of letters and of symbols such as punctuation marks.

Argument   *See* **Parameter.**

Array   A data structure of two or more elements, all having identical characteristics of type and size. An array has a single name, to which a subscript is appended to identify a specific element (Chapter 5). *See also* **Declaration, Dimension, Square brackets, Subscript.**

Assertion   (FPL) A component of the WHILE and the EITHER that includes at least one data variable in a claim about the value of the variable named, accompanied by appropriate state specification (Chapter 4). *See also* **Claim, EITHER, State specification, WHILE.**

Assignment   *See* **External assignment, Internal assignment.**

Assignment arrow   (FPL) The arrow in any assignment that points to the name of the storage location where a value is to be stored or toward the external world to which a copy of the value is to be transmitted.

BASIC   An old language developed for use from a terminal, widely used in educational circles for problem solving of all types.

Bin   (FPL) The rhombus-shaped enclosure attached beneath the name box of a parametric block or function, in which the parameters must be listed (Chapters 11 and 12). *See also* **Block name box,**

Function, Parameter, Parametric block.

Binary   A two-symbol (0 and 1) system for representing numeric values, widely used within computing because of its parallel to bimodal states in both electrical (on/off) and magnetic (n/s) media.

Block   (FPL) A named segment of code that performs a specific job or jobs (Chapter 10). *See also* **Block details, Block name, Block name box, Block reference, Call, End block triangle.**

Block details   (FPL) The details executed when the block name is cited (Chapter 10).

Block name   (FPL) The name of a block, formed according to the rules for forming datanames (Chapter 10).

Block name box   (FPL) The box-shaped enclosure used to indicate a specific block. It must include the name of a specific block and must occur at least twice in a program (Chapter 10).

Block reference   The citation of a block name, forcing the computer to find and execute the block's details (Chapter 10). *See* **Bin, Block, Block details, Block name box.**

Bubble memory   A relatively new type of computer memory that has been marketed as a substitute for main memory and a substitute for disk storage.

Call   *See* **Block reference.**

Card   *See* **Punched card.**

Card reader   A peripheral device that can "read" the holes punched in standard computer cards and thus serve as a means for entering programs and data into the computer.

Cell   The individual element in any array.

Character   Data that is either alpha or numeric or both but that is not to be manipulated mathematically, even if all numeric.

Claim   In an assertion, the text about data variable values, e.g., AGE ≥ 13, SEX = 'M'. SCORE greater than 120; must be either true or false (Chapter 4).

COBOL   A very old, widely used computer language oriented to business and commercial applications, takes its name from COmmon Business-Oriented Language.

Code   (1) Any segment of a program or its details; (2) the pattern or set of rules used to transform information into a machine-readable form.

Comment   An explanatory note embedded in a program for the edification of human readers, but not initiating any computer action during program execution.

Computer   An electronic machine capable of following instructions in particular forms called computer languages, by translating them into digital electronic codes, and carrying out the instructions on information fed in and similarly translated.

Concatenate   The operation of joining two or more strings end to end to form one composite string.

Constant   An alphabetic or numeric value fixed into a program as part of an assignment or assertion, e.g., 13, "ABC", −2, "The value is".

Construct   Any FPL component. *See also* **Assignment, Block, Declaration, EITHER, Episode, NEXT, Function, Parametric block, WHILE.**

Contents   The current information stored in a specific memory location.

Control   The sequence the computer follows in executing a program, sometimes used as a synonym for execution. *See also* **Control structure, Execution.**

Control structure   Those components of a language that determine the control or flow of execution through a program. *See also* **Block, EITHER, NEXT, WHILE.**

Cursor   The lighted indication of where the next display will begin on a screen device.

Data   A collection of one or more pieces of information that can be used by a computer program.

Dataname   (FPL) The means for establishing which storage location in the computer is to be used to hold a particular set of values. A valid dataname must begin with a capital letter, may include thereafter any combination of capital letters, digits, and the underscore (Chapter 1).

Dataname reference   The citation of any variable by dataname, forcing the computer to look up and use the value of the contents in the

storage location cited (Chapters 1, 3, and 5).

Data stream   (FPL) The collection of data available to a program, the items of which are accessible one by one, in the order they appear in the collection.

Data structure   Any of several collective types of data arrangements. The only two examples discussed in this text are arrays and records.

Data variable   *See* **Variable.**

Debug   To search for, find, and correct the errors in a program or segment of a program.

Declaration   (FPL) The component through which the programmer establishes the characteristics the computer must associate with a particular dataname and the information in its associated storage location (Chapters 2, 3, and 5). *See also* **Array, Declare, Fixed, Integer, Record, String.**

Declare   To state in a declaration the characteristics of type and size and structure for a particular variable (Chapters, 2, 3, and 5). *See also* **Declaration.**

Decrement   To decrease by a fixed amount. In COUNT⟵ COUNT − 1, the value of COUNT is said to be decremented by 1 whenever this assignment is executed.

Details   (FPL) The individual components of a completed segment of a program such as a digression or block.

Device   Any piece of hardware used in connection with computers.

Digression   (FPL) A component of the WHILE and the EITHER, a segment of FPL code to be executed if certain conditions are met, to be skipped otherwise (Chapter 4). *See also* **Assertion, EITHER, WHILE.**

Dimension   The number and also arrangement of cells in an array (Chapters 5 and 6).

Disk   A circular, platter-like storage device upon whose surface information is stored in magnetic patterns; rotated at high speed inside a disk drive. *See* **Disk drive.**

Disk drive   The device that encloses a disk and communicates information between the disk's surface and the computer.

Document   To provide explanation for a program or system, apart from, or in addition to, the code of the program itself.

Documentation   Any graphic or textual explanation of a program or system.

EBCDIC   A standard computer code for representing information. *See also* **Code** (2).

EITHER   (FPL) The construct through which the computer can be forced to choose between two alternatives. It must include one assertion and two digressions (Chapter 8). *See also* **Assertion, Digression.**

End block triangle   (FPL) The symbol used to indicate the end of a block's details, only one may occur for a block, vertically beneath the block name box heading the details. *See also* **Block.**

End digression triangle   (FPL) The empty triangle at the bottom of the last NEXT in the digression, indicating the end of the digression, only one per digression permitted (Chapter 4). *See also* **Digression.**

ENDFILE   (FPL) A special claim complete in itself; true if the data stream is exhausted, false otherwise (Chapter 9).

Episode   (FPL) The cloud-shaped FPL representation of a program or subsection of a program in unrefined state; a rough idea of what must eventually be specified exactly in program details (Chapter 1). *See also* **Refine.**

Evaluate   (1) To determine if a claim is true (Chapter 4). *See also* **Claim.** (2) To determine which cell of an array is intended, by determining the value of any variable(s) or expression(s) used as subscript(s) in the reference (Chapters 5 and 6). *See also* **Dataname reference, Subscript.** (3) To determine the overall value of an expression by looking up all the values referenced by dataname and performing all the operations indicated in the expression. *See also* **Expression.**

Execute   To carry out the instructions represented by the program (Chapter 1).

Execution   The act of executing a program. *See also* **Execute.**

Execution reference point (FPL) A particular point in the program at which the programmer testing the program wishes to know the contents of selected storage location by dataname, must be indicated directly on the program and labeled as such (Chapter 1). *See also* **Execution trace table, Test.**

Execution trace table   A table generated to test a program, recording the contents of selected storage locations as the program executes (Chapter 1).

Expression   Any combination of two or more variables or constants connected by operator(s); e.g., AGE + 6, PAY/.03, "A" : NAME (Chapter 1). *See also* **Operator.**

External assignment   (FPL) The construct for bringing data into or sending it out of the computer. It must include an assignment arrow piercing the slanted end of the assignment box, and may include one or more individual or structure datanames, constants, or label literals, depending on whether it is to send or receive data (Chapter 1). *See also* **Assignment arrow, Constant, Dataname, Literal.**

File   A collection of information in machine-readable form (Chapter 3).

FIXED   (FPL) A numeric data type that includes a decimal portion, whose declaration specifies the number of digits to each side of the decimal point (Chapter 2).

Fixed-length string   (FPL) A data element whose successive values will be strings of the same length (Chapter 2). *See also* **String.**

FLOAT   (FPL) A declared characteristic of numeric data for which only the more significant digits are stored and manipulated, along with exact information on how far to the right or left of the decimal point these digits occur (Chapter 2).

Floating point   *See* **FLOAT.**

Floppy disk   A small, flexible disk used most frequently with microcomputers.

Flowchart   A diagrammatic means for indicating the general structure of a program; widely used as a form of documentation in business and commercial computing applications. *See also* **Documentation.**

FORTRAN   An old, very widely used computer language oriented to mathematical problem solving; takes its name from FORmula TRANslation.

FPL   First Programming Language, the name given the language emphasized in this book because it is meant to be learned first, to serve as a model in learning to program in other computer languages.

Function   A variation on the parametric block. It differs from the parametric block primarily in that a single value is returned *replacing the entire* function reference, (Chapter 12). *See also* **Bin, Function name box, Function reference, Parameter.**

Function details   The details executed whenever the function name is cited (Chapter 12).

Function name box   The rhombus-shaped enclosure used to indicate a specific function. It must include the name of the function and may include a bin beneath for listing the parameters (Chapter 12).

Function reference   The citation of a function name, forcing the computer to find and execute the function's details (Chapter 12). *See also* **Function, Function details, Function name box, Parameter.**

Garbage   (FPL) Meaningless data values.

Glue   *See* **Concatenate.**

Graphics   Information in pictorial form, from simple black and white drawings to complex three-dimensional animation in full color.

IF . . . THEN   A somewhat degenerate IF . . . THEN . . . ELSE, includes a claim between the key words IF and THEN. *See also* **EITHER, IF . . . THEN . . . ELSE.**

IF . . . THEN . . . ELSE   A representation of the EITHER common to a number of computer languages, includes a claim between the key words IF and THEN. *See also* **EITHER.**

Increment   To increase by a fixed amount. In COUNT←— COUNT + 1, the value of COUNT is said to be incremented by 1 whenever this assignment is executed.

Independent block   (FPL) A block whose storage locations, with certain exceptions, are different from those of the program that references it, even for datanames identical to those in the calling program. The exceptions are the locations named as parameters (Chapter 12). *See also* **Parameter.**

Initialization   The process of initializing.

Initialize   To establish a value,

usually of the contents in a particular storage location (Chapter 1).

INTEGER   (FPL) A numeric data type with no decimal portion, whose declaration specifies the maximum number of digits that will be successfully stored (Chapter 2).

Internal assignment   (FPL) The construct for manipulating data inside the computer; must include an assignment arrow pointing to a single dataname, from a dataname, constant, or expression (Chapter 1). *See also* **Assignment arrow, Dataname, Expression.**

Join   *See* **Concatenate.**

Language   *See* **Programming language.**

Light pen   An electronic device similar in appearance to a pen but capable of communicating signals directly to the computer by touching the pen's tip to the surface of a TV-like terminal screen.

Listing   The printed text of a program, generated in any of several situations by the computer.

Literal   A constant string such as "The name was". *See also* **Constant, String.**

Loop   A common name for any of several non-FPL varieties of repetition constructs, usually less comprehensive than the WHILE. *See also* **WHILE.**

Magnetic tape   *See* **Tape.**

Mainline   The part of a program that includes the START and STOP circles.

Matrix   *See* **Array.**

Microcomputer   *See*

Microprocessor.

Microprocessor   A very small computer.

Modify   Alter the details of a program or segment of a program.

Module   A relatively or completely self-contained segment of a program or system of programs.

Multidimensional   The organization of an array whose cells are so arranged that two or more specific subscript values must be provided to specify a cell (Chapter 6). *See also* **Array.**

NEXT   (FPL) A vertical line connecting any two constructs; the construct at the top is executed first, the construct at the bottom, second (Chapter 1).

Numeric   Data whose value can be expressed as a number and that can be manipulated through standard mathematical operations.

One-dimensional   Describing the organization of an array whose cells are so arranged that a single subscript completely identifies a cell (Chapter 5). *See also* **Array.**

Operation   The calculation of a value by carrying out the action specified by the presence of any two items connected by an operator. *See also* **Operator, Expression.**

Operator   (FPL) (1) The symbols (+, -, *, /, :) used to communicate to the computer how it is to combine items in an expression (Chapter 1). *See also* **Expression.** (2) The human being who runs the computer and its peripherals.

Parameter   (FPL) Information needed by a parametric block or

function, included in any citation of the block or function, in a bin beneath the block or function name box, usually in the form of dataname whose storage location contains the information needed (Chapter 11).

Parametric block   (FPL) A block that requires one or more parameters to be included in its citation because it uses the values it associates with the parameters in some sort of computation (Chapter 11). *See also* **Block, Parameter.**

Parametric block details (FPL) The details executed whenever the parametric block name is cited, name box at top of details must include corresponding parameter for each parameter cited in the reference (Chapter 11).

Parametric block name box (FPL) A block name box with a rhombus-shaped bin beneath in which the parameters are listed (Chapter 11).

Parametric block reference (FPL) The citation of a parametric block name and its parameters, forcing the computer to find and execute the block's details (Chapter 11).

Parametric procedure   *See* **Parametric block.**

Parentheses   Standard symbols used to indicate the order in which operations are to be performed in an expression (Chapter 1).

Pascal   A well-structured language originally designed for computer science education, now gaining rapid acceptance in wider circles.

Peripheral   Any electronic or electromechanical device attachable to a computer for purposes such as printing, reading, or storing information used by the computer (for example a printer, terminal, disk drive, card reader, graphics plotter, voice synthesizer, magnetic tape drive).

PL/1   An old, well-established language comprehensive enough to be used in both scientific and business applications and including all the characteristics necessary for writing well-structured programs.

Printer   A peripheral device attached to a computer, capable of printing programs, data, results and other information from the computer; may print at speeds ranging from a few lines per minute to thousands.

Printout   The results of a program's execution as printed on paper at a terminal or printer.

Problem   A situation for which a computer program properly constructed may produce a solution.

Procedure   *See* **Block.**

Program   A complete set of instructions to the computer, the solution to a problem.

Program structure   The overall arrangement of a program.

Programmer   The person who creates a program.

Programming language   The symbols, words, and "grammar" designed to enable human beings to communicate instructions to the computer.

Punched card   A thin card upon which information (data or programs) has been encoded in a series of holes punched through the card.

Rewrite   (1) (A value) To assign a value to a storage location that already has a nongarbage value. (2) (A program) To modify or otherwise alter some or all of the details of an existing program.

Read   Examine the next value or group of values in the incoming data stream and assign the value(s) to the datanamed storage location(s). *See also* **Data stream, External assignment.**

Reader   The person who reads a program. *See also* **Card reader.**

Receive   *See* **Read.**

Record   A data structure that associates several storage locations with a single, record dataname while preserving identity of the individual locations under names of their own; such structural characteristic must be declared (Chapter 3). *See also* **Declaration.**

Reference   *See* **Block reference, Dataname reference,** or **Function reference.**

Reference Point   *See* **Execution reference point.**

Refine   To decide upon and write out the exact details currently represented in episodic form (Chapter 1).

Refinement   The process of refining a segment of code in which some episode or portion of an episode is replaced by actual details.

Repetition   The act of repeatedly

executing a designated segment of code. *See also* **WHILE.**

Root   *See* **Main line.**

Run   Synonymous with execute; also used to refer to one complete execution of a program as in "The run produced the results shown." *See also* **Execute.**

Screen   A TV-like device upon which information sent to or received from the computer may be displayed; may or may not be capable of displaying information of a graphical nature.

Section   Any portion of a program. Because it is not a well-defined construct, the extent of code referred to must be indicated somehow by the context of the word.

Segment   *See* **Section.**

Send   *See* **Transmit.**

Sequential file   A file composed of data arranged in order so that to read in a particular piece from the file, all pieces (records or items) that precede it in the order must be read first (Chapter 3).

Size   (FPL) The component of the declaration of an individual data element that indicates how much storage is required to store the values taken on by that element (Chapter 2).

Solution   The program segment, full program, or group of programs that provides all the information required or requested by a given problem.

Square brackets   (FPL) Standard symbol ([ ]) used (1) in array declaration to enclose the number of dimensions and the number of cells in each dimension, and (2) in array citation outside declarations, to enclose the subscript(s) cited as part of the dataname of any array cell (Chapters 5 and 6).

START circle   (FPL) The circle at the top of the first NEXT in the main part of the program, indicating the beginning of the program (Chapter 1).

State specification   (FPL) The T or F letter in both the WHILE and EITHER indicating the evaluated result that a particular assertion must have if the associated digression is to be executed (Chapters 4 and 8). *See also* **Assertion, EITHER, WHILE.**

STOP circle   A circle at the bottom of the last NEXT in the main part of the program indicating the end of a program (Chapter 1).

Storage   The place within the computer in which data and programs can be stored while the programs are executing, synonymous with memory (Chapter 1).

Storage location   Any of the many individual components of memory, a location is used to store an individual data element within the computer and is addressed by its dataname (Chapter 1).

STRING   (FPL) A character data type whose declaration specifies either (1) how many characters long a string can be and still fit the storage location named or (2) that any length at all will be exactly accommodated (Chapter 2). *See also* **Declaration, Varying.**

Structure   *See* **Data structure, Program structure.**

Structured programming   The kind of programming taught in this book; using analogues to this structure in languages other than FPL.

Subscript   The square bracketed component of an array reference that indicates a specific cell or subset of cells among all those making up the array. Must be either an integer constant or a variable or an expression whose value is an integer (e.g., 3 in AGE [3], ID in NAME[ID]) (Chapter 5). *See also* **Subscript variable.**

Subscript variable   A variable used as a subscript, as AGE in SCORE_AVERAGE [AGE]. The computer must look up the value of the subscript variable to determine the exact cell referred to.

Substring   Any character or collection of adjacent characters from a string, as they appear in the original.

Tape   A magnetic or paper medium used to store programs or data for use by a computer. Information is recorded on magnetic tape through technology similar to that used for audio recordings of music, speech, and so forth; information is recorded on paper tape by punching patterns of holes through it.

Tape drive   The peripheral device on which tape is mounted, including the READ and WRITE heads and the electronics for communicating information between the tape and computer.

Terminal   A peripheral device through which one can send information to or receive information from the computer; usually includes a typewriter-like keyboard, and either a mechanism to print on paper or a TV-like display screen.

Test   Try out a program or segment, particularly to see if there are glaring differences between what it is supposed to do and what it actually does (Chapter 1). *See also* **Execution reference points, Execution trace table, Test data.**

Test data   A collection of data specifically designed to test part or all of a particular program (Chapter 1).

Text   Information in the form of characters, digits, punctuation marks, etc. from cryptic mathematical assertions to long discourses in natural language.

Top-down programming Episodic program development— defining major components first, then subsidiary details.

Trace table   *See* **Execution trace table.**

Transmit   To insert a value in the outgoing data stream, to send information to the world outside the computer.

Two-dimensional   Describing the organization of an array whose cells are so arranged that two subscripts must be specified to identify a cell (Chapter 6). *See also* **Array.**

Type   (FPL) The component of the declaration of an individual data element that indicates what sort of data it is (Chapter 2).

User   The one for whom a program is executed; e.g., a payroll clerk is a user of the payroll system

Value   The human interpretation of a given piece of data or the contents of a storage location; typically what would be printed out by an external assignment citing the dataname of the location.

Variable   A dataname and its associated storage location (Chapter 1).

Variable-length string   (FPL) A data element whose successive values may be strings of different lengths (Chapter 2).

Variable subscripting   Using subscript variables.

VARYING   (FPL) The size component of a string declaration that causes the storage location used to effectively expand or contract to fit the length of any string assigned to it (Chapter 2).

WHILE   (FPL) The construct that can cause repeated execution of a designated segment of code (Chapter 4). *See also* **Assertion, Digression.**

Write   (1) (A program) To set forth the complete details of a program. (2) (A value) To establish a specific value in a storage area. (3) (To an external device). *See* **Transmit.**

index

index